PRAISE FOR
THE JEWISH HIGH SCHOO[
A complete Managemen

UJA FEDERATION
OF GREATER TORONTO
Across the street. Across the globe.

CHIEF RABBI LORD JONATHAN SACKS

"Long ago the Egyptians built pyramids, the Greeks built temples, the Romans built amphitheatres; the Jews built schools. That is why Judaism, alone among the civilizations of the ancient world, has survived. Paul Shaviv is one of the great Jewish educators of our time, and in this new book he has produced an indispensible guide to how to achieve excellence in Jewish education. It is a superb work, emerging from a lifetime of experience and success, and should be read by anyone who cares for the Jewish future. The Jewish world of tomorrow is being built in the Jewish schools of today, and thanks to this fine and practical guide, that future is already looking brighter.

Rabbi Lord Sacks
CHIEF RABBI OF THE UNITED HEBREW CONGREGATIONS OF THE COMMONWEALTH"

RABBI JOSHUA ELKIN
Executive Director,
PEJE – Partners for Excellence in Jewish Educatior

D1289432

"Paul Shaviv's guide represents an invaluable and unprecedented contribution to the field of Jewish high school leadership and excellence. A highly respected and successful Jewish high school visionary and leader, Shaviv has distilled his vast experience and knowledge to create a comprehensive volume filled with vast practical wisdom and insight. I am overwhelmed by the range of topics that he has included in this unique resource. The book is jargon-free, and therefore useful not only to current and prospective high school leaders, but also to board chairs and board members, participants in training courses, and other Jewish communal professionals concerned about and interested in the intricacies of Jewish high schools. Shaviv is right to point out that this guide can help to combat the isolation that a high school leader can feel, given the fact that so many of these schools are the only Jewish high school in their city. I am also struck by his recognition that not everyone is going to agree with everything that he has written. He views this volume as a vehicle to 'open the discussion' about what makes for effective and high quality leadership for our Jewish high schools across the North American continent, and indeed around the world. I believe that he has succeeded magnificently in doing just that."

ALASTAIR FALK
Director of Educational Leadership and former Headteacher
UJIA, London UK

"I loved this book - one of the most interesting and informative books on leading a school I have ever read. It was like being guided through a school by a wise, witty and hugely experienced practitioner, ever alert to organizational and personal dynamics. Packed with intelligent insight and practical advice, it steers a fascinating path between reference guide and inspirational text, helping Principals embed the values that brought them into their work in their approach to the daily issues they face. Rarely have theory and practice been so interwoven, creating a book that is filled with practical solutions and a deep understanding of the Jewish underpinnings of the school as an organization. This is a book worth reading at all stages of a professional's educational journey. It is a genuinely essential read."

Dr. MARC N. KRAMER,
Executive Director, RAVSAK - The Jewish Community Day School Network

"This book breaks new ground. It is a complete, practical guide to running a Jewish high school, and suggests to principals, administrators and board members the methods and philosophies - including the language to use – for dealing with every important issue that a school leader is likely to encounter. This is going to be the standard reference book on Jewish school management from now on. All school leaders - novice or veteran, lay or professional - must have this book on their shelf -- if not on their desk."

RABBI Dr. B. BARRY LEVY
Professor of Bible and Jewish Studies, McGill University
Former Director of McGill's Jewish Teacher Training Program

"A lifetime of experience and practical, education-related wisdom are presented in this up-to-date, thoughtful, thorough, and articulate guide to leading a Jewish high school. Every actual or potential administrator, lay leader, teacher, and parent – at either the elementary or secondary level – should read and periodically reread it. It is a truly outstanding contribution to Jewish education."

Dr. ALEX POMSON
Senior Researcher,
Melton Centre for Jewish Education, Hebrew University of Jerusalem

"Paul Shaviv does everything he promises, and much more. He has crafted with extraordinary attention to detail what should become an essential resource for Jewish school leaders wherever they are in the world. Offering advice that is all the wiser for being forged in the white heat of experience, with writing that is always crisp and unambiguous, and by proving readily accessible scripts, models and examples, he has created an indispensable manual. Shaviv has provided a comprehensive guide to the bewildering challenges of the day-to-day, and at the same time has done something of great profundity; implicitly, he has made a compelling case for the indispensible contribution of intelligent, humane and Jewishly-literate educational leadership to the flourishing of Jewish life."

YOSSI PRAGER
Director, AviChai Foundation

"This is a masterful compilation of issues and considerations facing principals and heads of Jewish schools, written by a long-time head of an outstanding Community day school. 'The Jewish High School' will be a useful guide and reference tool for those interested in the details of day school leadership, especially new and aspiring principals."

leader's success, this book belongs on the shelf of every day school head – and every day school President and every teacher of future day school leaders as well."

STUART ZWEITER

Director, The Lookstein Center
School of Education, Bar Ilan University

"An exceptionally impressive, superb, comprehensive guide, by a true master of the craft. This is a very valuable resource for beginning as well as experienced principals. View this volume as a 'professional colleague, advisor and mentor' that is always available. You will find yourself referring to it often."

THE JEWISH HIGH SCHOOL:

A complete management guide

THE JEWISH HIGH SCHOOL:

A complete management guide

LEADERSHIP, POLICY AND OPERATIONS

FOR PRINCIPALS, ADMINISTRATORS, AND LAY LEADERS

by

Paul J. Shaviv, M.A., M.PHIL.

Director of Education, **'TanenbaumCHAT'**

*-- THE ANNE AND MAX TANENBAUM
COMMUNITY HEBREW ACADEMY OF TORONTO*

RECIPIENT OF THE **MAX M. FISHER PRIZE FOR JEWISH EDUCATION IN THE DIASPORA 2009 / 5769**

THE PRINCIPAL PRESS

THE JEWISH HIGH SCHOOL: A complete management guide
ISBN / EAN: 978-1-449-920586
PUBLISHED BY THEPRINCIPALPRESS VIA CREATESPACE.COM

principalpress@ymail.com

First edition January 2010

Copyright © 2010 by Paul Shaviv / paulshaviv@rogers.com

Available from: www.createspace.com/3413024

PHOTOCOPYING:

You are welcome to make photocopies of material in this book for use in Professional Development
courses, workshops and the like, under the following strict conditions:

- Not more than three pages may be copied
- Not more than twenty-five copies may be made
- Each page must carry the following header or footer:

   "This is an extract from 'THE JEWISH HIGH SCHOOL: A complete management guide"
   by Paul Shaviv / available from http://www.createspace.com/3413024
   ISBN / EAN: 978-1-449-920586 "

For permission to make any more extensive copies or larger quantities, please contact the publisher:
principalpress@ymail.com

Cover design by Lynn Stanley, Graphic Directions / *graphicdirect@tcc.on.ca*
Back cover photo: Frances Kraft, Canadian Jewish News

*A comprehensive 'edit' of this book was done in the summer of 2009 during three wonderful weeks at the perfect
secluded writer's retreat – Apple Cottage, Pibditch Farmhouse, Chiselborough, Somerset, South-west England –
thanks to Susan and Andrew Sutterby.*

Always remembering Judy z'l

5 Kislev 5769

'נשאת חן בעיני כל ראיה '

"She found grace in the eyes of all who beheld her" – Esther 2:15

"KNOW HIM IN ALL HIS WAYS"

- *Proverbs / Mishle 3:6*

"In the post-Holocaust world, every student at a Jewish school
is a precious gift to Jewish history"

- *PJS*

"Civilization hangs suspended, from generation to generation, by the
gossamer strand of memory. If only one cohort of mothers and fathers fails to
convey to its children what it has learned from its parents, then the great chain
of learning and wisdom snaps. If the guardians of human knowledge stumble
only one time, in their fall collapses the whole edifice of knowledge and
understanding." **Our future depends on what we teach our children.**

- *Chief Rabbi Lord Jonathan Sacks, quoting Professor Jacob Neusner*

"The role of the Principal is to lead, motivate and develop the School, so that it
meets the religious, academic, pastoral and social needs of its pupils. The
Principal is responsible to the board of governors for the management of the
School."

-- *Advertisement seeking a Principal for a prominent Catholic School*

"A schoolmaster should have an atmosphere of awe, and walk wonderingly, as
if he was amazed at being himself."

- *Walter Bagehot (1826 – 1877)*

"Do leaders need to be dogged, analytical, and organized, or should
they be empathetic, charismatic, and communicative?
The answer is simple: they need both sets of traits."

- *David Kehoe*

TERMINOLOGY

For convenience and consistency, throughout this book:

- **'Principal'** is used as the title of the senior professional in the school (rather than Head, Head of School, Headteacher, Headmaster, Headmistress, Director of Education, or Rosh Yeshivah). This book focuses on the role of the Principal, but its messages are relevant to all others – professional and lay alike - involved in the operations and policy decisions of the Jewish High School.

- **'Jewish Studies'** for the curriculum Jewish subjects ('Limmudei Kodesh')

- **'General Studies'** for the curriculum general subjects ('Limmudei Chol')

- **'Private School'** is used rather than 'Independent', 'Day' or 'Parochial' school.

- **'Jewish High school'** includes all Jewish schools educating students from Grade 9 through Grade 12 – movement-affiliated Schools, Community Schools, Yeshivot, Seminaries, Ulpanot, Academies etc.

- **'Lay leader'** indicates Board member or other volunteer, non-professional participant in the Governance of the school.

- **'Jewish High'** is used occasionally as a fictional generic term for any Jewish High School.

CONTENTS

Introduction...i

1 THE QUALITY OF THE SCHOOL 1

1.1 Good, excellent and truly great schools 1
1.1.1 Good schools 1
1.1.2 Excellent schools 2
1.1.3 'Truly Great' schools 3
1.2 A note on school size 4
1.2.1 Is there an optimum size for a Jewish High School? 4

2 THE PRINCIPAL 6

2.1 Leadership begins with the Principal...............6
2.1.1 The challenge of vision 7
2.1.2 Creating 'school ethos' 8
2.2 The Principal's overall accountability 8
2.2.1 Principal's responsibilities: Legal 9
2.2.2 Principal's responsibilities: Educational 9
2.2.3 Principal's responsibilities: Administrative / operational........10
2.3 Constituencies 11
2.3.1 Keeping distance 11

3 THE BOARD OF DIRECTORS 12

3.1 The President and the Principal.....................12
3.2 The tasks of the Board 14
3.3 The essential firewall: Policy and Operations.......15
3.4 The Principal's duties to the Board 16
3.5 Board Committees – 'Policy and Oversight'.......18
3.5.1 Education Committee................................20
3.5.2 Personnel Committee................................21
3.5.3 Budget and Finance Committee 23
3.5.4 Building / Plant committee 24
3.5.5 Other committees..................................24
3.5.6 Board and Committee induction processes 25
3.6 And if the Board is crossing boundaries? 26
3.6.1 Occasional crossing of boundaries 26
3.6.2 "By the way, I am a major donor to the school".......28
3.6.3 Confidentiality 29
3.6.4 Constant crossing of boundaries ... .29

4 MANAGEMENT AND STRUCTURE 30

4.1 Leading the team - ONE 'Head of School' 30
4.1.1 Principals' principles 31
4.1.2 Management style and technique 31

4.2 Fair Process 32

4.3 Structuring and delegating operations 33
4.3.1 Designing and leading a management structure 33
4.3.2 Clarity and quality of the team 34
4.3.3 Essential Administration tasks and structure 34
4.3.4 Job Descriptions 36
4.3.5 Job Descriptions – where none exist 38
4.3.6 Meetings, supervision and information flow 39

4.4 Decision making and problem solving 40
4.4.1 Delegated decisions 40
4.4.2 The collaborative / consensual process 41
4.4.3 The Principal as decision-maker or arbiter 43
4.4.4 Overturning decisions made by others 44

4.5 Quality of service 45

4.6 Essential school documents 46
4.6.1 School Constitution 46
4.6.2 'Statement of Philosophy and Purpose' / Mission Statement ... 47
4.6.3 School Handbook 47
4.6.4 Suspension and Expulsion – agreed process 48
4.6.5 Course Calendar 48
4.6.6 Staff Handbook 49
4.6.7 Staff list 50
4.6.8 Application, registration and re-registration documents ... 50
4.6.9 Tuition Assistance request forms 52
4.6.10 Health, safety and emergency documentation 52

4.7 Documenting operations 52
4.7.1 Ongoing correspondence, records of meetings, decisions, agreements and notices. 52
4.7.2 A simple filing system 54
4.7.3 Keeping track of addresses, contacts and diary. 55
4.7.4 Student and other school records. 56
4.7.5 Staff personal files 58
4.7.6 Anonymous letters 59
4.7.7 Financial and accounting information 60
4.7.8 Security and confidentiality 60

4.8 Communications 61
4.8.1 Communicating school values 61
4.8.2 Within the school 61
4.8.3 Conveying difficult decisions to the school community ... 62
4.8.4 Conveying difficult decisions to individuals 62

4.8.5   Rumors 64
4.8.6   The school website 65
4.8.7   The School Magazine – editorial issues 66
4.8.8   Student publications 67
4.8.9   The School Annual report 67
4.8.10 Communications in times of crisis 68

4.9   Consultants and external resources 68
4.9.1   When should the school use an external consultant? 68
4.9.2   Managerial and organizational consultants 68
4.9.3   Consulting on Board Governance and Process ... 70
4.9.4   Legal consultants 70
4.9.5   Curriculum consultants 71
4.9.6   PR / Communications Consultants 74

5   THE INSTRUMENTS OF CHANGE 76
5.1   Challenges 76
5.1.1   Strategic planning 78
5.1.2   Building 'Incremental improvement' 79
5.1.3   School Reviews 80
5.1.4   The importance of data 82

6   THE GENERAL SCHOOL PROGRAM 86
6.1   'Academic excellence' – what does it mean? .. 86
6.2   Options, courses and budgets 88
6.2.1   The basic curriculum 88
6.2.2   Options / electives 88
6.2.3   Special Needs students 89
6.3   Guidance and Counseling 91
6.3.1   Overall functions of Guidance 91
6.3.2   Career guidance 93
6.3.3   Supervision and confidentiality 93
6.3.4   Family issues and child abuse – the duty to disclose 95
6.4   Sports 96
6.4.1   Antisemitism at sports fixtures 96
6.5   Creative Arts 97
6.6   The School library 97
6.7   Computers and computing 98
6.7.1   The changing literacy 100
6.7.2   Plagiarism 101
6.7.3   The digital classroom and the digital teacher 101
6.7.4   Should the school buy computers for teachers? .. 103
6.7.5   Curriculum courses in computer use 103
6.7.6   Should the school mandate students to buy laptops? .. 103
6.7.7   Jewish Studies and the digital age 104
6.8   Extra-curricular activities / Student Activities ... 104

6.9 Visiting Speakers / outside presentations **107**

7 THE JEWISH PROGRAM 111

7.1 'Jewish values', 'Jewish education' and other difficult phrases 111

7.2 Issues unique to the Jewishness of the Jewish school **112**

7.2.1 Psychological 113
7.2.2 Religious 114
7.2.3 Social / financial 116
7.2.4 Educational 116
7.2.5 Operational 116
7.2.6 In times of personal crisis – or celebration 116

7.3 Shaviv's paradox – does "Success = failure"? **118**

7.3.1 The need to supplement formal with 'experiential' in the Jewish program 118
7.3.2 The Jewish Studies classroom – a marketplace of ideas? 119
7.3.3 The lament of a disillusioned student 123
7.3.4 The psychological profile of the Jewish Studies teacher 124

7.4 Professional structuring and staffing of the Jewish Studies Department **125**

7.4.1 The 'School Rabbi /Rav' 125
7.4.2 Director of Jewish Studies 127
7.4.3 Recruiting Jewish Studies teachers 129
7.4.4 Assessing qualifications in Jewish Studies 131
7.4.5 Local Israeli teachers 132

7.5 Employing Shlichim **133**

7.5.1 Shlichim - budgeting 133
7.5.2 Shlichim - recruiting 134
7.5.3 Shlichim – on arrival 136

7.6 Israel **136**

7.6.1 Shaviv's second paradox 136
7.6.2 Israel in the school program 138
7.6.3 Year out in Israel 139
7.6.4 Family disagreement over a 'Year out in Israel' 141
7.6.5 University in Israel 142
7.6.6 "Preparing students for Campus" 142

7.7 Ivrit **144**

7.8 How do you assess outcome? **146**

7.8.1 "Serious Jews" and "non-serious Jews" 146
7.8.2 Graduate surveys 147

7.9 A special plea for Jewish History **148**

8 MANAGING TENSIONS BETWEEN 'GENERAL' AND 'JEWISH' 149

8.1 First rule: one school, not two 149
8.1.1 The basic choice: embrace the world or withdraw from it? 150
8.2 School values for parents, students, teachers – and alumni .. 152
8.2.1 A voluntary association 152
8.2.2 Supporting school ethos and values – parents and students 152
8.2.3 Supporting school values – Board members 155
8.2.4 School values: staff responsibilities 155
8.2.5 Alumni – "L'affaire Noah Feldman" 156
8.3 Classroom and curriculum issues 158
8.3.1 Teachers disagree 158
8.3.2 Debate within the school 160
8.3.3 Traditional problems: Science 161
8.3.4 Traditional problems: Literature 161
8.3.5 Traditional problems: Creative arts 163
8.4 Calendar and other *halachic* problems 164
8.5 Freedom of expression / freedom of thought 164
8.5.1 What are the limits of student expression? 164
8.5.2 The limits of freedom of expression 166
8.5.3 "I don't believe in that" – argument 167
8.5.4 "I don't believe in that" – behavior 168
8.6 Gender issues 169
8.7 Animal rights and food politics 171
8.8 Global issues – universalism and particularism 171
8.9 Israeli and Middle Eastern politics 172
8.10 Sex education 173
8.11 Sports, extra-curricular and 'out of school' 173
8.11.1 Competitions, practices, fixtures 173
8.11.2 School trips 174
8.11.3 "I want to participate on Shabbat and the school is being unfair" 174

9 MANAGING STAFF 177
9.1 Building and leading the team 177
9.2 Terms of employment, contracts and Unions 178
9.2.1 Validating Qualifications 179
9.2.2 Letters of Appointment / Contracts 179
9.2.3 Length of contract 180
9.2.4 The tenure decision 180
9.2.5 Salaries for Jewish Studies teachers 182
9.3 Administrators 183
9.3.1 VP's and Principals 183
9.3.2 Old VP's – new Principal 184

9.3.3   Administrators – recruitment and appointment 186
9.3.4   Induction process 188
9.3.5   Managing and evaluating Administrators 188

9.4   Teachers **190**
9.4.1   The school's core business 190
9.4.2   The Principal and the teacher – basic relationship 190

9.5   Teacher Recruitment **191**
9.5.1   The best teachers...191
9.5.2   Teachers – young, old, retirees...193
9.5.3   Advertising...194
9.5.4   Applications..194
9.5.5   Reading a resume..195
9.5.6   Applicants from other community schools or other local private schools..197
9.5.7   Offers are binding – on both sides 197
9.5.8   Interviewing..198
9.5.9   References (reading and writing) 199
9.5.10   References for staff who wish to move on 201

9.6   Promotions and responsibility **202**
9.6.1   Youth and experience 203

9.7   Staff evaluation and performance appraisal **203**
9.8   The Staff Room **205**
9.9   Protecting teachers **205**
9.10   Professional Development **206**
9.11   When staff leave or retire **207**
9.12   Support staff **207**
9.12.1   Support Staff — recruitment, appointment and management 208
9.12.2   The Principal's secretary 208

10   PROBLEMATIC TEACHERS 209

10.1   The incompetent teacher: the problem is ongoing **209**
10.1.1   The 'support/warning' cycle for ongoing problems............................212
10.1.2   The serious classroom incident 214

10.2   Teachers: six problematic profiles **217**
10.2.1   "I'll only teach this class if ...."..217
10.2.2   'The student's friend' / the 'cool' teacher 218
10.2.3   The 'Pied Piper'..220
10.2.4   The inappropriate teacher – sexual / abusive 223
10.2.5   The staff room agitator 229
10.2.6   The infatuated teacher 230

10.3   "I have a wedding in Israel" **232**
10.3.1   "We want to go to Israel for *Yomtov*, and I'll miss the last days of school"
         233

10.4   Terminating staff **233**
10.4.1   The decision and its implementation...233

10.4.2   Termination for cause 234
10.4.3   Resignation instead of termination 235
10.4.4   Termination –'not for cause' 235
10.4.5   Termination – conditions 236
10.4.6   Termination - Confidentiality and communication 236
10.4.7   Non-renewal of Contract 237
10.4.8   Terminating non-teaching staff 237
10.4.9   Challenge, arbitration and mediation 237

11   MANAGING STUDENTS 239

11.1   How does the school relate to its students?.....................239
11.2   Student Recruitment and admissions............................241
11.2.1   Strategizing basic recruitment....................................241
11.2.2   Feeder Schools..242
11.2.3   Planning a recruitment campaign 243
11.2.4   Application and Admission 245
11.2.5   Who do you admit to the school?................................249
11.2.6   "Which is the best elementary school?"......................250
11.2.7   New arrivals - the Israeli community 252
11.2.8   New arrivals - the Russian community 254
11.3   Special families 254
11.4   Retention and attrition 255
11.5   Graduation and graduates 258
11.5.1   Failure to graduate High School 259
11.5.2   The Graduation ceremony 260
11.6   Keeping the school 'calm, successful and happy' 261
11.6.1   Essential services and facilities 261
11.6.2   Student council and student responsibility 261
11.7   Our students are "Millennials" 263
11.8   The 'Founding Grade' in a new school 264
11.9   The Principal's relationship with students 265

12   DISCIPLINE, RULES, ETC............................... 266

12.1   Who administers discipline?...268
12.2   Fair process in school discipline 269
12.3   The basic areas of discipline 272
12.3.1   THE ESSENTIAL LIST OF POSITIVES...........................272
12.3.2   Attendance 273
12.3.3   Safety and security 273
12.3.4   Honesty and integrity..273
12.3.5   Classroom behavior; respect for the school and staff....273
12.3.6   Drugs 273
12.3.7   Alcohol 275
12.3.8   Sex..275
12.3.9   Bullying and harassment – verbal and electronic 276

12.3.10   Media 276
12.3.11   Computer abuse and harassment 276
12.3.12   Cell phones, cameras, PDA's, Blackberries, iPhones, MP3's and similar 277

12.4   Can the school impose discipline for events that happen out of school hours? 278
12.4.1   Parties 280

12.5   Well-known issues of contention 281
12.5.1   Uniform / dress code..281
12.5.2   Hair 282
12.5.3   Piercings, tattoos etc...283
12.5.4   Grade 12 and Graduation – behavior 283
12.5.5   Cars 285
12.5.6   Right of search / right of privacy / lockers, bags etc. 286

12.6   Consequences 287
12.7   Suspension and expulsion 288
12.7.1   Suspension 288
12.7.2   Expulsion 288
12.7.3   "Zero tolerance"..291

13   MANAGING PARENTS 291
13.1   Parents as partners 291
13.2   Parents and the Board of Directors 294
13.3   Parents and teachers 295
13.4   Meetings with parents 297
13.4.1   Common agendas 298
13.4.2   Preparing for difficult meetings 300
13.4.3   The unexpected 301
13.5   Parents and children in the Principal's office 304
13.6   The school and marital conflicts 308

14   MANAGING COMMUNITY 312
14.1   Rabbis and synagogues 312
14.1.1   Has the school replaced the synagogue? 314
14.1.2   Rabbis as Board members 317
14.2   The Jewish Community 318
14.2.1   The Principal in the local Jewish community 318
14.2.2   The local Jewish press 319
14.2.3   The Federation 319
14.2.4   National and international networks 319
14.3   Wider Community 320
14.3.1   Educational 320
14.3.2   Civic 320
14.3.3   Interfaith and community relations..............................321
14.3.4   Antisemitism..322

14.4   'I'd like to visit the school'......................................**323**

15   MANAGING NON-ACADEMIC ISSUES 327

15.1   Financial management...**327**
15.1.1   Control and authority 328
15.1.2   Accounts and analysis 329
15.1.3   Tuition assistance 329
15.1.4   Annual accounts 330
15.1.5   Statistical data..330

15.2   Budgeting process **331**
15.2.1   The Tuition Fee 333
15.2.2   Privacy in the budget process 334

15.3   Equipment, furniture, plant and maintenance......................**334**
15.3.1   Computers, Projectors, 'SmartBoards' and other digital equipment 335
15.3.2   Photocopiers, fax machines, and phones 335

15.4   Security..**336**
15.4.1   Security Guards and CCTV...338
15.4.2   Computer security and network design......................338

15.5   Emergencies and crises **340**
15.5.1   General guidelines 341
15.5.2   Anticipation and planning 341
15.5.3   The first twenty minutes 342
15.5.4   Authority in time of crisis...343
15.5.5   Communicating in time of crisis 343
15.5.6   Staff and students 346
15.5.7   Back to school 346

15.6   Bereavement...**346**
15.6.1   Suicide...347

15.7   Press and media...**348**
15.7.1   Make the media your partners 348
15.7.2   How to get your material published............................350
15.7.3   Electronic and online media 351

15.8   Health and safety..**351**
15.8.1   Compliance 352
15.8.2   Staff training in First Aid and CPR 352
15.8.3   Student and staff health records 352

15.9   Insurance and liability **352**
15.9.1   Proper reporting of incidents 353

16   FUNDRAISING AND ALUMNI 353

16.1   Fundraising **353**
16.2   Alumni...**355**

17 **Memo To: The Principal** 359

17.1 Your contract with the school 359

17.1.1 Your Job Description 360

17.2 Reviewing your performance 362

17.2.1 Process for Annual performance Review 364

17.2.2 Process for External Review 364

17.3 Personal issues 366

17.4 Family 367

17.4.1 Your children at your school? 368

17.5 Professional enrichment / keeping up to date 369

17.6 Time to move on? 370

17.7 If things go wrong 371

18 **AFTERWORD** 378

Appendix A: Profiles of Jewish School Principals 380

Appendix B: Sample References 382

Appendix C: 'L'affaire Noah Feldman'- a response 384

Introduction

Few readers will start at the beginning of this book and read all the way through. Most will refer to 'stand-alone' sections. For that reason, there are a few themes and comments, relevant to more than one topic that appear in more than one section.

Operating any High School is difficult; operating a private high school can be doubly difficult; operating a private Jewish high school is incredibly difficult, and demands skills and talents way beyond the norm – true for both professional and lay leadership.

Given that in most cases there are no professional counterparts in town, the Jewish High School Principal often works in extreme professional isolation. S/he may also lack formal training for the Principal's position. The lay leaders – the President and Board of Directors – may also find themselves responsible for an institution unlike any that they have encountered in their professional lives and training. Their perspective on the school as a Board member will necessarily be totally different from their perspective as a parent.

The day-to-day responsibility for the operation of the school rests with the Principal. While there are manuals (of varying usefulness) for public School Principals, there are few, if any, for private school Principals and none for Jewish High School Principals. With the massive and rapid expansion of Jewish Day Schools in North America (and elsewhere), now rolling over from Elementary to High School, it is vital that systemic operational standards and processes be established for Jewish High schools. This book is an attempt to open that discussion; intended to help incoming and existing Principals be effective in their tasks, and to be illuminating and helpful to other leaders – professional and volunteer – involved in any way with Jewish High Schools.

Who might benefit from this book?

- **Principals and Administrators in place** should find a comprehensive 'map' of Jewish High School management. I hope that an outside perspective will give some positive ideas. At the very least, they should enjoy reading a colleague's experiences and views, even if only to confirm their own, different views of how to do things.

- **New and prospective Principals,** especially those new to either School administration or to the Jewish school system, should derive real help in understanding the dynamics of the Jewish High School.

- **School Presidents and Board members** (existing and prospective) will find help in understanding their own roles and responsibilities, and those of their Principal and faculty; and in supporting their current Principal, or in recruiting a new one.

- **Faculty and students** in universities, colleges and seminaries will gain a practical view of school management and issues.

- **Participants in PD, training courses, conferences and workshops** should find stimulating 'springboards' for discussion and learning.

- **Jewish Community professionals** in Bureaux of Jewish Education, Federations and Foundations concerned with the quality and process of management in Jewish schools should gain insight and appreciation into the complex issues involved in school operations.

This book concentrates on High Schools, where I have spent most of my professional experience. However, I am sure that some sections will resonate with **all Jewish School Principals**, whatever the level of their school.

The book does not deal with curriculum content, which, although central to the Principal's responsibility, will vary greatly from region to region, and with the ideology of the school. It would be a huge achievement to establish agreed common curricula for the different sectors of Jewish High Schools, so that an exciting Tanakh curriculum of proven quality could be taught in, say, twenty or thirty schools of similar outlook around the world. A parallel curriculum might be developed to serve another twenty or thirty schools of a differing (but also shared) outlook. Such a situation would bring huge advantages to teachers and would provide a shared market for the development of materials. However, it would be difficult to provide a curriculum whose pedagogic (let alone methodological, let alone religious) approach would fit schools across the entire North American continent and beyond. For the same reason, this book does not deal with other educational issues such as student assessment, evaluation and testing, or dealing with Special Needs.

Instead, it deals with the leadership, managerial and operational responsibilities of the Jewish High School, mainly, but by no means exclusively, focusing on the perspective of the Principal.

Although there will always be local differences, many of the challenges of running a Jewish High School are surprisingly similar, wherever the school is situated. Having worked in five Jewish schools on three continents, ranging from Modern Orthodox to Yiddishist-Secular (and currently in a Community School) I have often remarked that the suburban Jewish school has more in common with its counterpart on the other side of the world than with a non-Jewish public or private school along the street. Only the language, or the accents are different. The Jewish parent is very similar – astonishingly similar - all across the world, whether in North America, South America, Europe, Australia or South Africa[1].

I also strongly believe that every Jewish High School Principal faces common operational issues – regardless of the school's position on the religious spectrum. If I may use nautical imagery, my aim is to give Principals, the captains of their ships, a clear, jargon-free chart of their job. This book sets out to provide some navigational beacons that identify the easiest deep-water channels (smooth sailing), the hidden sandbanks (difficulty), or G-d forbid, the rocks under the surface of the water (disaster). As we learn from the tales of the ancient mariners, frequently the sirens and mermaids are perched attractively atop the calmest, but most treacherous waters...

Finally, to some readers this may not seem a very 'Jewish' book, even, perhaps, in the sections that deal solely with the Jewish issues of the Jewish school. It is not a '*sefer*' – it is a book about the theory and practice of running Jewish High schools. Nevertheless, its entire purpose is '*Lehagdil Torah uleha'adirah*'. To a substantial degree, the success and quality of Jewish life in the Diaspora is bound up with its school system. A good Jewish school can transform a Jewish Community. To be effective, it has to be good, and to be good, it has to run properly and professionally. As I comment:

> "*... the good, the excellent and the great Jewish schools are essentially seamless. The overall principles are the same whether the topic under discussion is art or Talmud. For some, that may sound heretical. I don't believe it is, because excellence in education is excellence in education. Transmission of Torah in the school context needs skills and management no less than (and, for a variety of reasons discussed throughout this book, in many ways more than) any other discipline. An excellent school will be excellent in its Torah study as well. If it isn't, it is simply not excellent. Conversely, a school that commands the respect of its students and parents will without saying include respect for the Jewish dimension.*"

****

---

[1] It will be interesting to see how Jewish communities and Jewish schools develop in the rapidly growing communities of central and Eastern Europe.

Thanks and acknowledgements

This book reflects personal and professional experience over more than four decades.

Few readers will recognize the name of an obscure UK Jewish Youth movement of the post-war decades – 'Jewish Youth Study Groups' – and its redoubtable 'Organiser', Harold Levy z'l (1909-1987), a brilliant educator. As a teenager, it was the formative framework of my Jewish experience. Later, during graduate studies at Oxford, it was a rare privilege to be taught by Dr. Isaiah ('Yishai') Shachar z'l (1935–1977). Yishai Shachar was a brilliant, polymathic, versatile scholar who passed away at a tragically early age. Few days go by, even now, when I don't think of him. Rabbi Jeremy Rosen offered me my first full-time teaching post (as Director of Jewish Studies) at the (now defunct) UK Jewish boarding school, Carmel College. During years spent in Israel in the 1980's, I worked for 'Melitz', under the charismatic direction of Avraham Infeld; and then for a number of years as the Director of the B'nai Brith World Centre in Jerusalem, reporting directly to Dr. Daniel Thursz z'l (1929–2000), the Executive Vice-President of B'nai Brith International in Washington DC. From Dan Thursz, who had a passionate vision of Jewish unity and Jewish peoplehood, I learned a great deal about leadership and management of voluntary organizations. Former British Chief Rabbi Lord Jakobovits z'l (1921-1999) brought me back to England in 1990 to be part of the founding team of Immanuel College (Bushey, UK); a brief, interesting spell in Sydney, Australia followed, and then I came to Canada. From 1994-1998 I served as Principal of Bialik High School in Montreal.

I am now in my twelfth year as the very happy, initially Principal, and now Director of Education at TanenbaumCHAT – the Community High School of the Greater Toronto Jewish Community. At the time of writing, TanenbaumCHAT has approximately 1,500 students (G9-G12) on two parallel campuses, and is currently recruiting over 400 new students each year. It is, I believe, the largest Jewish High School in the world, and the largest private High School in Canada (and possibly further afield).

Heading TanenbaumCHAT has been a wonderful, challenging experience. Since 1998, the school enrolment has doubled, and we have established a complete new branch. In partnership with UJA Federation of Greater Toronto, we have carried out over CAN$50m of capital projects. We have close to 200 teaching staff, of whom 65 are teachers of Ivrit/Jewish Studies. Successive Presidents of the school have been valued partners in school growth and management. My colleagues have worked as a close-knit team in running the school and developing the policies, structures and systems needed to ensure that it works effectively. Harriet Israel, my 'solid gold' PA, has kept me organized.

I would particularly like to acknowledge the help and advice given to me over the last decade by Mr. Eric Roher of Borden, Ladner, Gervais - a foremost authority on school law, a wise counsel and an enthusiastic parent in the Toronto Jewish educational system.

The Toronto Jewish school system also greatly benefits from extensive support from the UJA Federation of Greater Toronto, headed by Ted Sokolsky, including the Toronto Centre for Jewish Education, formerly headed by Dr. Seymour Epstein (Epi), whose friendship and company I have greatly appreciated.

While much of this book reflects reality at TanenbaumCHAT, there will be sections here and there where my colleagues (Administrators and teachers, and perhaps even parents and students), will give indulgent smiles and wonder why I don't follow my own advice more closely. Family and friends may do the same. I plead inconsistency and fallibility.

It would be appropriate to note here that all opinions and views expressed in this book are mine alone, and do not represent TanenbaumCHAT. Similarly, the legislation and statutory regulations applicable to schools – including and perhaps especially private schools – vary widely in different jurisdictions. Views, opinions and advice given in this book are non-specific to any particular place, and proposed actions must be carefully checked to ensure that they are compliant with local requirements.

* * * * * * * * * * * * * *

This book is dedicated to the memory of my wife, Judy z'l, who passed away from cancer in December 2008/Kislev 5769. Much of it was written or revised during long hours accompanying her in treatment at Toronto's Mount Sinai Hospital during the six and a half years of her illness. In 2008 we had celebrated 35 years of happy marriage and partnership. Her encouragement and support at every stage of our family travels and adventures were inspirational, and her tremendous good sense was a stalwart influence throughout. In her outstanding career, she managed to superbly organize everyone and everything with which she came into contact – except her husband! She delighted in our children and grandchildren – Miriam and Danny (Eliana and Dalia); Aron and Miriam (Maayan and Gefen); Gidon and Shira (Nitzan). We both enjoyed the deep and devoted friendship of our dear friends in Toronto, Eli and Stella Katz. May we all enjoy many further years of good health.

Paul Shaviv

Toronto, Canada - Fall 2009 / 5770

Leadership, Governance and structure

1 THE QUALITY OF THE SCHOOL
2 THE PRINCIPAL
3 THE BOARD OF DIRECTORS
4 MANAGEMENT AND STRUCTURE
5 THE INSTRUMENTS OF CHANGE

1 THE QUALITY OF THE SCHOOL

1.1 Good, excellent and truly great schools

There is a wide range of Jewish High schools, right across the spectrum of Jewish life, ranging from intensively Orthodox, single-sex schools to far more liberal establishments. Each has its own philosophy. Yet in every category, there can be good schools; excellent schools; and, from time to time, truly great schools. All research indicates that the long-term quality of the school depends on the leadership of the Principal. The ability of the Principal to lead depends on the willingness of the Board to allow professional leadership to be exercised, and on the quality of the relationship between the Principal and the Board.

1.1.1 Good schools

Private schools, especially smaller schools, will often struggle to provide a full range of facilities and resources.

However, a good school will fulfill all or most of the following conditions:

- The school is, overall, a positive experience for its students.

  If a graduate has negative memories of High School, then its educational messages, by association, will also have negative associations. Nothing else you can do will help

- The school deeply respects its students as individuals, and it will be fair and consistent in its dealings with them

  That does not mean that he school abdicates authority, or judgment, or is indulgent of its students (quite the contrary); but it has to respect them, even when they do wrong, and even when it disapproves of them.

- The good school will have a properly constituted governance structure (lay leadership) and a properly run management structure (professional)

- It will clearly communicate its expectations – educational and behavioral - to students, staff and parents

- Communications to all constituencies will be professional, clear and frequent

- It will offer a high 'quality of service' – efficient, responsive and polite – to parents and all others who deal with it

- It will have a coherent, planned curriculum, with clear evaluation and assessment procedures

- Delivery of curriculum will be as required / as promised, and will make allowances, according to the resources available, for differing ability bands of students

- Key resources – library, gym, art, music, and science will be of a reasonable standard

- Staff recruitment will be open, and salaries (whether individually contracted or unionized) will be equitable

- An effective supervisory and review system will be in place for staff and also for non-academic support staff

- Staff will have opportunities for PD

- Students at graduation are well-positioned and well-qualified to have maximum choice of post-High School opportunities

- Students graduate with top qualifications in 'mentschlichkeit'

1.1.2 Excellent schools

Excellent schools will certainly have all of the above, but in addition may have some, most or all of the following:

- An inspirational faculty, carefully chosen and carefully nurtured.

  Encourage the best, but also weed out the teachers who are not reaching the school's standards[1].

- A shared, non-adversarial lay-professional relationship that always has the best interests of the school at heart, and is therefore able to continually advance the facilities and resources of the school

- A reasonable to excellent choice of electives, especially at senior grades

---

[1] A great British school head, John Rae - who passed away in December 2006 - once wrote that what he regretted most during his career were the occasions when he failed to (or was unable to) terminate bad teachers, "leaving them in place to do their damage for years afterwards".

- A reasonable to excellent co-curricular / extra-curricular program at which students can excel

- The ability to give thoughtful and effective support to its weaker-ability students, while giving opportunity and encouragement to its top-performing students to excel and reach for the top opportunities

- A professional and helpful Guidance department

- Enriching programs which 'open windows' spiritually, intellectually and creatively for students

- The school will enjoy the complete confidence of the community

1.1.3 'Truly Great' schools

The handful of truly great schools – very few and far between -- will add most or all of the following qualities:

- Educational leadership at regional, national or international level

- High awareness at every professional level of educational and curricular thinking relevant to their school

- A high level of participation by staff in professional conferences, on-line forums, partnerships with teacher-training programs etc

- A high level of student participation and volunteering in school extra-curricular programs, including local community service

- Recognition that the school truly cares for individual students

- An outstanding 'quality of service' to parents and others who deal with the school

- Constant willingness to introduce students to out-of-school programs and opportunities that widen their horizons

- A curriculum that works; that encourages intellectual and spiritual curiosity, and gives students a robust framework in which to explore and evaluate new ideas.

Readers will no doubt add to the above lists, and perhaps disagree on some of the suggestions. I have not specified the Jewish content separately from the general principles, because, as will be a constant theme in this book, the good, the excellent and the great Jewish schools are essentially seamless. The overall principles are the same whether the topic under discussion is art or Talmud. For some, that may sound heretical. I don't believe it is, because excellence in education is indivisible. Transmission of Torah in the school context needs skills and management no less than (and, for a variety of reasons discussed throughout this book, in many ways more than) any other discipline. An excellent school will be excellent in its Torah study as well; if it isn't, it is simply not excellent. Conversely, a school that commands the respect of its students and parents will without saying include respect for the Jewish dimension.

1.2 A note on school size

'School size' is an often-used comparative metric when planning budgets and determining the appropriate staffing level for a school.

Be careful. School size is not simply a measure of the number of students (although that is an obvious and important factor). For Jewish schools, which run a double curriculum, **the amount of teaching is a much more important figure**. Six hundred students in a school where the typical student is taking five or six courses is a radically different school than the nearby Jewish school, where the same number of students are each taking on average ten or eleven courses. The number of teachers is much larger, and the school day is longer. The budget is different; the timetabling is different; the number of staff is different (at every level) and the space requirement of the school is completely different. The traditionally academic emphasis in Jewish schools also means that the requirement for Guidance Counselors and other pastoral staff is greater.

1.2.1 Is there an optimum size for a Jewish High School?

An entirely different issue is the question of *optimum* size for a school. The school has to have enough students to be viable at High School level. There can be vast differences regarding the notion of 'viability' from community to community. In one place, an intensely-motivated community may be able to satisfy the needs of students and parents with a very small school, whose ideological cohesiveness overcomes social and educational limitations caused by lack of numbers. In another community, a school may need to have a critical mass of students in order to offer the options and other programs that will make it competitive.

Most Jewish schools seek to attract as many students as possible, because maximum enrolment is an ideological aim. However, insofar as it is possible or desirable to plan the size of the school, the following considerations may be considered:

- **Educational** – a small school may offer the chance of "individual attention", and certainly can create a closely-knit 'chevrah'. On the other hand, a larger student body (400-800+ students) enables the school to offer more courses, and more flexible course options, sports and other programs. It also offers a wider social framework for students, the chance of employing a more variegated staff, and altogether offers the opportunity to be a 'real' high school.

- **Economic** – while only one Jewish school I have ever known has actually done this, it is possible to analyze the teaching program of the school and create a mathematical model which will enable the school size to be restricted to an economically optimum number of students. The model may be applied in governing the overall number of students in each grade, in determining which courses are to be offered, and in controlling the number of students allowed in each class. A school functions most economically at certain sizes depending on student-staff ratios, class sizes and numbers of classes. (At its simplest level, one class of twenty-five is cheaper than two classes of thirteen.) While it may not be possible to completely control those figures in a large school (because of electives, required/desired courses, and other necessary variables), it should be possible to significantly reduce school costs by careful management. The downside of such an operation is that you have to restrict student choice and possibly student entry, which may bring its own cost in unhappy students and withdrawal from the school.

- **Social** – It is often assumed – wrongly - that students 'love' small schools. Many teenagers enjoy the relative anonymity of a larger school, and also appreciate the wider choice of friends and the greater range of academic, sporting and extra-curricular options that a larger school is able to provide. (In smaller communities, where there is one Jewish school operating at both Elementary and High school levels, the experience of being with the same, small group of students for twelve years of schooling can be tiresome). From the Jewish programming perspective, it is nevertheless essential to keep the school to manageable proportions – although this is a relative term. While some North American public schools are very large, with several thousand students, few Jewish educators would be comfortable with a school of more than 1,200 - 1,500 on one campus.

- **Professional** – an interesting factor in consideration of school size is the expertise available in the Jewish professional 'pool'. In the continent of North America there are only a handful of Jewish High Schools with over 600 students. This means that there is a severe shortage of Administrators with experience in managing that size of school. There is a parallel shortage of Jewish Studies teachers able to staff large schools – especially non-Orthodox schools. Creating a large school will bring with it challenges of professional leadership and staffing.

- **Impact of widening recruitment** – Successful outreach and recruitment to new constituencies will bring new profiles of students and parents (and teachers) into your school. That will inevitably change the character and atmosphere of the school, and, in some cases, may accelerate changes in the established recruitment patterns. It needs a very strong school, and very skilled leadership, to enlarge a school while maintaining its character[2].

2 THE PRINCIPAL

2.1 Leadership begins with the Principal

The Principal is Head of the School, and CEO (Chief Executive Officer) of the organization. S/he has been employed to lead[3], whether Principal of a school of fifty, five hundred or fifteen hundred. There are many definitions of leadership, and an equal number of leadership styles. A trip to any bookshop, real or online, will lead to many books on the subject. Different styles work for different individuals.

Whatever the style, in Jewish schools leaders should possess the following mix of conceptual and practical skills, able to:

- Organize and administer the school in all dimensions

- Project an inspirational Jewish educational presence

- Reflect, model and lead the values and ideology of the school

- Credibly and positively represent the school in public

- Envision the future of the school

---

[2] Having said that, the Jewish educational community cannot complain that Mr. and Mrs. Average Jewish Parents do not send their children to Jewish schools – but then complain when they do.

[3] It sometimes happens that the Principal has not been employed to lead, but to follow the instructions of the Board and/or the parent body. If, temperamentally, that suits the designate Principal – fine. In that case, quite a lot of this book is not relevant, although I hope that it will nevertheless be a source of enjoyment and of some useful perspectives and tips. But if *both* the Principal *and* the Board wish to run the school, conflict and frustration are on the horizon. (*"We want to run the school, but we want to run the school through you"*, as a lay leader once said to me).

- Conceptualize what needs to be done to get there

- Energize and implement that vision

- Act as the institutional 'ears and eyes' of the school, alert to both challenges and opportunities in every sphere that may affect the school in any way

- Take decisions, including unpopular decisions

- Take responsibility

One of my greatest teachers, Dr. Daniel Thursz[4] z'l, used to define the first duty of a professional in any non-profit organization as the duty to:

- Keep the budget in the black.

If a Principal displays all of the above qualities, the school will be doing very well indeed. Yet, in some way or another, they all have to be present and effectively operating in the school. If there are gaps in the Principal's personal skill-set, it is essential to ensure that individuals who have the missing talents are there in the Administrative team[5].

2.1.1 The challenge of vision

Of all the leadership qualities listed, the cluster most rarely found, and hence the most valuable, are those concerned with vision.

To have a vision of a school is to be able to rise above the complexity of the school as it is, and to be able to see it clearly *as it could be*. A vision has to be credible, and to be credible it has to have support. The most important factor of support is confidence and faith in the visionary leader. All other issues are technical.

The vision of the school may be multi-faceted, or it may be concerned with one aspect of the school only – e.g. the curriculum, facilities, a transformation of the learning atmosphere, or radically increasing enrolment. It may be a large-screen vision; it may be limited. The Principal's vision must be articulated; it must be communicated; and it must have partners.

With vision comes major institutional change.

- **Implementing change is the biggest challenge faced by leadership.**

---

[4] Executive Vice President of B'nai Brith International, 1978 -1988.
[5] In some schools, there will be other leadership tasks as well – for example, serving as a Rosh Yeshivah will have an additional set of expected skills.

2.1.2 Creating 'school ethos'

Ethos: *The characteristic spirit, prevalent tone or sentiment, of a people or a community; the 'genius' of an institution or system.*" (Oxford English Dictionary)

Creating a school ethos is an enormous achievement. The presence of a tangible ethos is characteristic of a highly successful school. Its essential element is a shared sense of integrated values, purpose and identity - the instinctive, unspoken, feeling that "in this school, this is the way things are done".

A positive school ethos is an extremely powerful educational instrument[6], and is in and of itself part of the philosophy and management[7] of the school. How an ethos is established is a more complicated matter, but it must depend on some or all of the following elements:

- A clear vision of school values that is attractive and compelling to the school constituency, and is shared by all involved in school leadership, led by the Principal.

- Consistent statements of principle and operations that reinforce the school values.

- Clear communications that refer to and positively reinforce the school vision and values.

- Opportunities at appropriate intervals for Board and staff to review and discuss the values of the school.

However, none of the other measures will be effective without a last, essential characteristic:

- Students, staff and parents must perceive that the decisions and operations of the school are in accordance with its professed ethos.

2.2 The Principal's overall accountability

The School Principal is ultimately responsible for every aspect of the school's operations, implemented within the agreed policies determined by the Board. Many operational tasks will be appropriately delegated on a day-to-day basis.

---

[6] A *negative* ethos is no less powerful, but totally destructive.

[7] Flying over the Atlantic, I watched an in-flight interview with Peter Brabeck-Letmathe, the Chairperson of the huge international conglomerate Nestle S.A. Asked how he preserves consistency in the three thousand companies that are part of the whole, he replied: "It is only the strong central culture which allows you to be so generous in decentralizing decision-making."

The Principal may consider himself/herself accountable to Heaven. There are (also) three human, earthly groups to whom the school as an institution, and therefore its Principal, owe primary responsibility:

- The school community – Board, students[8], staff and parents, as a group and as individuals

- The 'sponsoring' community – in this case, the Jewish community

- The wider community – educating for citizenship

The Principal also has a series of formal responsibilities[9], hopefully mirroring the skills brought to the post (or subsequently developed).

2.2.1 Principal's responsibilities[10]: Legal

SEE SECTION 15

- Ensuring a safe school environment, and taking care of the health, safety and security of all staff, students and visitors to your school site

- Ensuring that all aspects of school operation are in compliance with educational, employment, human rights and other statutory regulations and legislation affecting your school

- Keeping order in the school and keeping accurate attendance and other records

2.2.2 Principal's responsibilities: Educational

- Ensuring that the school is at all times a seamless learning environment in both general and Jewish dimensions, following a coherent philosophy that furthers the aims of the school and the interests of every individual student

- Ensuring the delivery of the agreed curriculum in a professional and effective manner, consistent with the educational ethos and values of the school

- Ensuring that the Jewish dimension of the school – formal and informal – is inspirationally taught in a manner that enhances

---

[8] While technically the Principal reports to the Board, the students are the first responsibility of everyone and anyone connected with a school.

[9] They should be described in your own Job Description, which should be part of your contract. See Section 17.1

[10] Local legislation may mandate these or other specific duties of a School Principal

the Jewish experience, knowledge and motivation of the students

- Ensuring access to guidance and counseling for students

- Ensuring the design and operation of consistent and fair evaluation and testing procedures

- Overseeing the sports and extra-curricular (co-curricular) activities of the school

- Designing and implementing appropriate professional development for staff

- Ensuring appropriate mechanisms of communication with parents

2.2.3 Principal's responsibilities: Administrative / operational

- Acting as the CEO / Chief Executive Officer of the school

- Ensuring the operation of the school on a daily basis

- Ensuring 'quality of service'

- Reporting to and working with your Board

- Overseeing the preparation of budget, and subsequently monitoring expenditure and the financial administration of the school

- Maintaining student (academic) and personnel records

- Producing and administering the School Calendar, the school timetable / schedule, the class lists, student and teacher schedules, and all necessary documentation and process for the operation of the school

- Recruiting, managing, supervising, evaluating and reviewing staff

- Designing and implementing recruitment and retention strategies for students

- Supporting the Development / fundraising / alumni relations program of your school

- Representing the school to the community

In short, the Principal's responsibility is to envision, establish and apply the educational, spiritual, moral and behavioral ethos of the school.

2.3 Constituencies

As a function of leadership, the Principal has to relate to a number of different constituencies, internal and external, and balance them all. The major constituencies are discussed at length in this book.

Many Principals are seen as relating to one (or more) better than to others - they may be a 'Teachers' Principal', or a 'Students' Principal', or a 'Parents' Principal'; in a private school they may also be a 'Board Principal', and in a Jewish school a 'Community Principal' – or combinations of two or even three of them. A rare Principal is versatile enough to be completely at ease with more.

The constituency with whom the Principal is most effective and most identified may change in the course of a career for all sorts of reasons – age and career progression is an obvious one; the size of the school is another. A Principal at age forty will relate very differently to students than when close to retirement. The Principal of a school of eighty students will have far more time to relate to teachers than the Principal of a school of eight hundred. There comes a time in the career of many Principals when they suddenly notice that the new parents (who used to be part of their social circle) look terribly young.

One way or another, every group within the school ambit has to feel that they have a sympathetic 'address' within the school Administration, whether from the Principal or one of the VP's, and a skilful Principal will build their team accordingly.

A successful Principal, like a successful politician, must try and nurture all the constituencies, and should know by instinct or experience the different approaches needed for each. However, closeness is not always possible, nor always desirable (see below), and the result will be inevitable complaints that the Principal is 'distant' or 'cold'. The complaints come with the job.

2.3.1 Keeping distance

One of the most difficult self-disciplines that the Principal has to learn is social distance. It is difficult, because the adults with whom s/he has professional relationships – Administrators, teachers, Board members and parents – are often wonderful and interesting people, with whom the Principal (and spouse) would in other circumstances choose to develop natural and close friendships. However, the Principal has to be impartial, and has to be seen to be impartial. Personal relationships must not influence his/her decision-making, and they must not be suspected of doing so.

It is a sad fact that others will notice very quickly who the Principal's personal friends are, and, for example, whether certain teachers or Board members are regular guests at the Principal's Shabbat table. All must be invited, with equal regularity – or none. The Principal's social circle may have to be distinct from his/her professional circle. It can be difficult to maintain simultaneous professional and personal relationships without complications ensuing (for both the Principal and his/her colleagues).

The position requires appropriate distance from those with whom, paradoxically, the Principal may work the closest and like the most. Difficult as it may be – it is essential.

3 THE BOARD OF DIRECTORS

While not a comprehensive guide to school governance, this section discusses some aspects of the structure and functioning of the Board of Directors as it impacts on the running of the school. Material on the principles of school governance is available from many sources – local associations of private schools, Independent School Management (ISM) and Partners for Excellence in Jewish Education (PEJE) are good places to start.

3.1 The President and the Principal

The relationship between the President of the Board and the Principal is critical for the school

Both have to work hard to build and nurture that relationship. A good beginning is for the Principal to invite a new President for a personal 'induction', which might include a tour of the school (seen through the Principal's eyes), a briefing about challenges on the horizon, and perhaps an invitation to sit in on an Administration meeting. It is essential that the President have a good understanding of the realities of how the school is run[11].

The President – Principal relationship has to be one of mutual respect, mutual confidence and mutual trust. A Principal who does not have the trust of the President will find it exceptionally difficult to command the confidence of the Board[12].

---

[11] The President and other senior leadership should also be involved in organizations like PEJE, and should be recipients of ISM mailings (if the school is a member).

[12] The only exception to this is where for some reason the President and the Board are at loggerheads. In that situation, political trouble is on the horizon, and the Principal may end up as the sacrifice in the middle. Involvement here means vulnerability. Advice to the Principal in

Without that, the Principal's position is untenable. Equally, the Principal must be able to feel that the Board – and especially the President of the Board – are persons of integrity, whose governance of the school is appropriate, fair and sensible.

As in every relationship, communication is key. The Principal should take care to keep the President informed of what is going on in the school. They must be in frequent contact by phone or email. A message must quickly get to the President (and other senior lay leaders) if any emergency or crisis happens at the school. "No surprises" is a very sound operating procedure. The two leaders should meet every week or so.

The nature of the relationship must be correct. The President should not give instructions, nor should the Principal be asking for them. The English constitutionalist[13], Walter Bagehot (1827 – 1877), in another context, pithily described what should also be the reciprocal relationship of President and Principal: the duty of each is "to counsel, to warn and to encourage" the other.

Both positions can be lonely.

The President may not have any background in leading a voluntary organization, let alone a school Board, and may sometimes be ill-prepared for public leadership. The Principal will have few colleagues or peers with which s/he can share their most private dilemmas or information.

The school President should be a confidante and sounding board for the Principal, able to bring a lay perspective on school issues – including perspectives from their own business or professional lives. The President can also perform an invaluable service to the Principal by being an objective source of parental and community 'buzz' – not always to be taken at face value, but an important source of the perceived 'image' of the school.

The Principal should, in return, be able to give a view on Board proceedings (including, occasionally, a discreet view on candidates for school lay office) from a school operational perspective.

In a well-run school, there can be many items of information to which the Board and even the Executive are not party. These can include, for example, confidential information about personal or medical problems affecting students or staff, or professional conversations Administration has held with staff members. A Principal may advise the President, in confidence, of a conversation or incident that has the potential to be problematic[14], and about which the Principal feels that someone else

---

such a case is to be careful, and think about whether or not you might best be served moving on.

[13] ... and founder of *The Economist*.
[14] Examples would be apparently illegal or inappropriate approaches to the school or a member of staff.

ought to know. Except in really confidential circumstances, the President should be the one person (and it has to be the *one* person – a President must be able to keep confidences) with whom the Principal should feel able to share information, ask for a view, or test instincts, on a non-judgmental basis.

Whatever passes between the President and the Principal – and they will, on occasion, disagree – in public they must be completely supportive of each other.

It has to be said that this relationship, too, can have its complexities. As with staff and parents, both have to learn how to calibrate both the appearance and the actuality of that relationship so that it remains appropriately close without being personal.

3.2 The tasks of the Board

Boards of Jewish schools vary widely in their make-up, constitutions and – especially – behavior. There are 'best-practice' standards to which private schools – certainly including Jewish schools - should aspire.

The Board of a school has a series of responsibilities, including, but not limited to:

- Setting policy for the operations of the School, and setting structures to oversee and receive reports on school operations

- Setting the budget and the Tuition fee

- Ensuring the long-term fiscal security of the school

- Appointing and dealing with the employment contract of the Principal.

The Board should have a Constitution, and should hold regular elections. The nomination and election process will be specified in the Constitution, but should be one that ensures accessibility to the Board, and ensures a regular flow of new leadership. No person or group should have unlimited tenure[15] as members of the Board. Models of governance vary according to many factors, including school size and local private school culture. In recent years, there has been a greater emphasis on encouraging correct Governance in Jewish schools, and rightly so.

---

[15] Many Jewish schools (and other institutions) are over-hasty in appointing 'Life Members' of their Boards, and live to regret it. The status and privileges of Life Members should be carefully considered. The position, if it exists at all, should be honorary, and should not carry voting rights.

Nothing can be more destructive to a school than an irresponsible or capricious Board[16].

As schools have grown, as tuition has risen, and as more 'consumer conscious' parents have entered the system, they have become more vocal and more demanding. Nor have the revolutions in corporate governance escaped the Jewish community – service, transparency, communication and accountability are the buzzwords. Given the financial investment that many parents are making in their child's education (after the mortgage, probably the single largest family expense for many families), that is not surprising. Equally, the budgets of schools – both operating and capital - may now be very considerable, running into millions, and occasionally tens of millions, of dollars. The responsibility of the Board is serious.

An important part of Governance is instituting safeguards against questionable practice and the appearance of questionable practice. The minimum acceptable provision must be that no member of the Board or any of its committees may participate in discussions or votes regarding any matter in which they have a direct or indirect financial interest, or in which they are involved[17] as parents or relatives of students or staff.

3.3 The essential firewall: Policy and Operations

> *To run a successful, professional and effective school, one principle needs to be enshrined as an impermeable firewall in the structure – the separation of* **policy** *(the task of the Board) and* **operations** *(the task of the professional staff).*
>
> - The Board determines policy and budget; employs the Principal; and exercises oversight.
>
> - The Principal and professional staff run the operations of the school.

Neither the Board collectively, not Board members individually, should be involved in day-to-day operational decisions ("micro-managing").

For example, the Board cannot be involved with decisions regarding the allocation of teachers to duties or classes; or of the way that Yom Ha'atzmaut is to be

---

[16] A school can survive a disastrous Principal (assuming that the Board exercises its control and deals with the situation); it cannot survive for long with a disastrous Board.

[17] Many schools do not permit spouses, parents or children of teachers (or other school employees) to be members of the Board.

celebrated[18]; or what desk or computer is to be purchased in the school office. They cannot be involved in disputes between students and teachers, or parents and teachers. They cannot decide whether the basketball team is going to play in the tournament in another city (except if it is school policy that such trips need Board approval), or which staff are to accompany the team. All of these are operational decisions. Board members must not micro-manage. A school where the Board micro-manages cannot ever progress.

Jewish schools frequently have their origin in lay initiatives. Lay leaders may have been deeply involved in the early days of setting up the school, and there may be a strong residual 'tradition' of Board management. Reference to any of the local or national associations of private schools will show that **separation of policy and operations is the recognized norm of good school governance** - and for good reason.

A President and Board are entitled to full information regarding what is happening in the school (appropriately hierarchied in detail and confidentiality); they may – in fact they should - advise, counsel, encourage or warn. It is a very foolish Principal who constantly disregards that input, and it is an equally foolish Principal who does not 'bounce ideas' off his senior lay leadership.

However, lay leaders cannot run the school on a day-to-day basis, and operational decisions have to be those of the professionals.

3.4 The Principal's duties to the Board

The Board probably meets between six and ten times each year, depending on the size of the school and local structures[19].

The Principal, with his/her Administrators and/or Heads of Department, should give a written report[20] to each meeting. The report should include a short review of major events and issues in the school since the last meeting; plus a short listing record of school activities, achievements etc. It can be 2-4 pages long. Difficult issues should

---

[18] But it does have the policy say of whether the school will or will not celebrate Yom Haatzmaut....

[19] More than ten times a year (i.e. once a month from September to June) may mean that the Board is too involved in running the school. The Board has to give its staff 'breathing space'. Less than six meetings per year would probably be unusual for a Jewish school. Years ago I was friendly with the Principal of a major non-Jewish boys' private High School of international reputation, with several hundred students. His Board of Governors met twice a year, "and they complain strongly if my report is more than a page and a half long".

[20] The Executive Committee report may be at a higher level of confidentiality than the full Board report.

be reported appropriately, without revealing confidential information. These reports give the Board confidence that they know what is happening in the school.

These can be supplemented by short weekly email updates/advisories, especially useful when some incident or crisis happens in school that has set the parking-lot rumor mill into action. Parents will start calling the Board. The Principal should pre-empt the calls with a clear, accurate summary of the facts, including a short summary of how Administration would like to see the issue presented, and an invitation to call for further info. The Board should be co-opted as part of the positive communication network to parents – not left "defensive-because-uninformed" in the face of parental enquiry. The school, in transmitting information, should not speculate on motives or variables – just give accurate facts, even if they are unpleasant. The school may not be able to disclose how it is dealing with an issue (and in many cases should not); but it should allow Board members to be able to say, with confidence, that they know that the Administration is taking action.

As appropriate, more focused reporting is made to Committees of the Board.

The Principal and senior Administration should attend Board meetings[21]; whether others than the Principal should attend Executive meetings depends on the size of the school, and, occasionally, the agenda.

At Board meetings, the Principal, sitting at the right side of the President (or Board Chair, if the functions are separated), may occasionally murmur guidance *("Time to move on"; "This discussion is off subject"; "Should the board really be discussing this?").*

The duties of the Principal to the Board and Executive Committee are:

- Ensuring that the Board/Executive are accurately informed of the on-going operations of the school.

- Ensuring that the Board/Executive have accurate and full information on which to make decisions regarding school policy, and on which to exercise their fiscal responsibilities.

- Ensuring that the Board are informed of anything that may affect the school's legal liability, or which may expose the school to legal action.

- Informing the Board of any situation in the school that may affect the safety or security of the students or staff.

- Giving considered, professional advice to the Board, and its officers and committees, with the sole purpose of enabling them

---

[21] ....sitting round the table, and NOT to one side.

to act in the best interests of the school and its students. (The Board has a reciprocal duty to ensure that the Principal is properly advised of events or other information that affects the school or the exercise of his/her responsibilities).

The Principal (and other Administrators) should be a key participant in Board discussions, in an appropriate fashion. One task of the Principal is to ensure that the privacy of staff, students and parents is properly protected at meetings. A Board should never discuss or name individual classes, teachers or students. (The Principal's 'Board Report' may, of course, report positive news about named students and staff.) If the Principal has to report a specific incident to the Board, or is asked a question about a specific incident, the answer should under all but the most exceptional circumstances be phrased in general terms.

The only exceptions – and they will be very rare exceptions – may be at Executive meetings where the school as an institution is faced with legal, safety or security issues.

The Board does have full prerogative, however, to deal with the matters that are its direct responsibility – school policies, financial and asset management and fund-raising, strategic issues and community relations, and, hopefully not too often, the Principal's contract.

The School Executive committee will normally meet in between Board meetings to review the business arising at the Board, to make recommendation to the Board, and, if necessary, to act on behalf of the school at short notice, subject to subsequent accountability to the Board.

3.5 Board Committees – 'Policy and Oversight'

The number, nature and 'Terms of Reference' of Board Committees should be part of the School Constitution. All Committee Chairs report to the Board, and the Board may discuss the content of their reports. It should not second-guess them or do their work for them a second time.

All sub-groups operating in the name of the school, or on behalf of the school – including the Parents' Association, the Alumni Association and the various fund-raising groups – should be accountable to the Board, have their Constitutions and Terms of Reference set by the Board, and may be represented on the Board. The functioning and administration of the committees is the responsibility of the President.

The Principal should attend every Board and Executive meeting as a non-voting member, and should be an ex-officio member of other major committees. Other Administrators should be (non-voting) members of the Board and other appropriate committees. The Board and Executive (but only very rarely other Committees) may meet 'in closed session' to discuss highly confidential issues[22], either asking all professional staff to withdraw, or asking the Principal alone to remain. That is their prerogative. A much less satisfactory alternative to the 'closed session' is the clandestine meeting held in someone's basement, outside the normal process of the Board....

With certain well-defined exceptions, Committees should not be involved in managing school operations. Their task is to provide policy decisions and oversight of school activities – ensuring on behalf of the parent body that the school is being run according to the policies of the Board. It is very much in the interests of the Administration to be full partners in this process:

- Lay leadership may give valuable input and productive ideas to school operations in a mutually respectful spirit, and offer an opportunity to Administration to utilize the range of expertise (often formidable) in the community

- A good committee provides a valuable 'sounding board' and 'reality check' for Administration

- A good committee is a more reliable and responsible indication of opinion in the parent body than 'parental phone calls' or the 'parking lot network'

- A Committee's exercise of oversight provides the Administration (and the Board) with a degree of protection against random criticism, and demonstrates that the processes, programs and activities of the school are regularly under objective review, and that the school is properly a collaborative enterprise

Dear Mr. and Mrs. X,

Thank you for your letter regarding the school's Math / Tanakh / Art / Rabbinics curriculum, which I note was also copied to the local Jewish newspaper.

This department and its curriculum were thoroughly reviewed by the Board's Education Committee earlier this year, as part of its ongoing program of oversight of the school's academic program. A comprehensive report was submitted to the committee by the Department Head, which indicated awareness of some of the

---

[22] These may include matters relating to school financial or legal decisions; crises involving the school or persons involved with the school; the Principal's contract; or matters involving another Administrator. The Principal, with the agreement of the relevant Committee chair, may ask for an 'in camera' session to discuss, for example, matters concerning one of the Administrators, or other highly confidential school matters.

challenges facing the Department. Valuable comments and suggestions were made in the course of the subsequent discussion.

However, the Committee noted that "this Department is functioning excellently overall, and is in compliance with school standards and expectations." Let me address some of your specific queries.

- is a much better position than a "you say … we say" argument.

3.5.1 Education Committee

The Education committee is one of the most important committees of the Board. There are many Jewish schools where the Education Committee is heavily involved in decision-making regarding practical operations of the school – deciding curriculum, allocating teachers (and even students) to courses, employing teachers, and a host of other matters. I was once at a conference where an enthusiastic lay leader of a new school related that the Education Committee was called to an "emergency meeting" to discuss whether the new tables to be bought for a classroom should be square or oblong…. In worse cases, Education Committee members will call teachers directly to reprimand or pseudo-supervise them in some other way.

As is unambiguously clear throughout this book, I do not believe that any of this should be happening. A good formulation of the Education Committee's mandate could read:

'The Education Committee, in collaboration with the Administration and senior staff, should review, recommend and report to the Board the status of the curricula, both secular and Judaic and any other matters that may be referred to them for consideration by the Administration.'

Note that the Committee cannot decide or give instructions; nor does it deal with personnel issues. A wise Administration will listen very carefully indeed to what is said at Education Committee, but it should not be a threatening or professionally confrontational setting, because the Education Committee can only "review, recommend and report". It is a collaborative, collegial setting which gives professional freedom – *but also professional responsibility* – to the Administration. It provides a sounding board that a skilful Administration will use to build partnerships.

There are different ways of managing an Education Committee, and it is the prerogative of the Chair to decide how the committee will operate. If the Committee wishes to exercise 'rolling oversight' over the school's program, it may schedule a series of departmental presentations at its regular meetings, where Department Heads give an overview of their departments – programs, recent developments, and a critical appreciation of issues to be faced by the department in the foreseeable future. (This does not include lobbying for departmental budgets over the heads of Administration). This process may be extended to cross-departmental topics or issues relevant to the delivery of the school educational program. Special topics[23] or broad educational issues may be considered, usually backed by a briefing paper, position paper or report from the Administration.

Such reports may be a setting for open collaborative discussion between professional and lay leaders. Over time, the lay members of the Education Committee gain a wide-ranging, fairly comprehensive and deep understanding of the delivery of the curriculum, and a realistic understanding of the challenges faced by the school. They are carrying out their mandate of oversight on behalf of the Board of Directors.

> *Notwithstanding the above, the institution of the 'Education Committee' is by no means universal in private schools, and seems to be a cultural feature of governance especially prominent in Jewish schools. I know one large Jewish (elementary) school that has abolished its Education Committee, determining that all educational issues are solely the prerogative of the professional educational faculty.*

3.5.2 Personnel Committee

The Personnel Committee has a different status than other committees, because to do its work properly it must operate with the highest possible degree of permanent confidentiality.

The Personnel Committee should include Board members and other appointees – perhaps external -- with experience in labor relations and labor law, especially in schools. In conjunction with the Principal, the CFO and Administration, it oversees and advises on personnel issues and policies in the school, with the exception of the Principal's own contract. While it certainly may be involved with policy and process for specific appointments, and should be represented on Search Committees for senior (Administrative) appointments, it does not directly recruit, select or appoint staff. Teachers will normally be interviewed and appointed directly by the Principal and/or Administration; Administrators will be normally be interviewed by a Search Committee and appointed by the Principal   SEE SECTION 9.3.3

The Personnel Committee may typically deal with the following issues:

- If the school has a unionized workforce, a primary duty of the Personnel Committee is to negotiate the Collective Agreement with the Union. The school will retain the services of experienced Labor lawyers, who will direct the process in accordance with the local practice.

- Drafting and approval of other Personnel policies, benefit packages, and general policies and codes of conduct and

---

[23] Examples might include, for example, 'Technology in the school', 'University/College counseling', 'Teacher recruitment', 'Our Counseling service', 'Special needs'.

employment for academic and non-academic staff. The Principal will work with the Personnel Committee on establishing the salary ranges and terms of employment of Administrators, the CFO, the Director of Development and other individually contracted employees.

- Administration will normally bring to the Personnel Committee proposals for the creation of new posts or allowances within the staff. At Personnel, the need is explained; and the budget approval is then sought 'with the approval of the Personnel Committee'. If appropriate, the proposal may have already been discussed at another committee (e.g. Education)[24].

- An important function of the Personnel Committee is to act as a consultative Committee to the Administration, and particularly to the Principal, on all personnel issues – for example, disciplinary issues, disputes, or unusual requests for leaves of absence. Some of these include decisions that may involve the school in legal action, and therefore must be considered by a lay body; others may be important as – like all staff decisions – they establish precedents.

- In a school that grants tenure, recommendations by the Administration for the granting of tenure to probationary teachers should have the approval of the Personnel Committee before being presented to the Board. A report to the Committee will include a brief assessment of the probationary teacher's performance, as properly documented by class observations and visits, with an Administrative recommendation. Approval by the Committee in confidential session should mean that recommendations regarding individual staff members are passed at the Board without discussion. Should the Administration recommend against tenure, the report to the Board will only say that 'Tenure was not granted to [one] teacher[s]'. (The document may 'leak' and compromise the position of the teacher concerned.)

A very fine line of judgment governs the degree of disclosure made even to the Personnel Committee. As in every instance, the lay leadership has to trust the Principal. A Principal may make statements to the Committee referring to "an incident" or "an individual", without identification or detail. The Committee will give views or advice without knowing who is being discussed. There may be instances

---

[24] The Budget and Finance Committee should never be involved in a discussion of the merits of whether the Head of Maths needs to go to a professional conference or not. They can assess the financial – but not the educational – issue.

where discussions may take place, not necessarily with the whole committee, in conditions of the highest confidentiality, and there may be occasions where the only discussions that take place will be with the legal advisers of the school and the Chair of the Committee. This degree of confidentiality is not always found (although certainly not unknown) in parochial schools. Yet it is exactly this level of principled operations that allows staff to rely on the knowledge that their dealings with Administration are confidential, and totally professional, and are insulated from any possible repercussions arising from the low mark they gave a Board member's child in class the previous week. It also means that teachers (or their 'supporters') cannot lobby Committee members; and they, too, can exercise their responsibilities objectively.

Quality of process in governance can only contribute positively to the running of the school.

3.5.3 Budget and Finance Committee

The Budget and Finance Committee (or its equivalent, however named) is a third key committee of the Board/Executive.

In a larger school, an accounting-oriented CFO/Executive Director will work closely with the School treasurer, who will normally chair this committee. While the Principal is always a member of the Committee, s/he does not necessarily have to attend every meeting.

As in every organization, if the finances are not right, the organization cannot ever flourish. The tasks of the budget committee include:

- Overseeing the financial management of the school in all of its aspects on behalf of the Board of Directors.

- Ensuring compliance with accounting and legal requirements.

- Establishing the annual budget well in advance of the school year, and presenting it to the Board for approval, together with a recommendation for a Tuition Fee.

- Establishing and implementing mechanisms for accounting and control of income and expenditure in the school.

- Ensuring that accurate financial accounts are prepared for each financial year of the school operation, and presented to the Board.

- Making appropriate arrangements, compliant with local practice, for the independent auditing of the school accounts. There may be a separate 'arms length' Audit Committee of the Board to supervise the Audit. SEE SECTION 15.1 / 15.2

3.5.4 Building / Plant committee

The physical state of the school is an important indicator of school standards.

Common areas under the purview of the Building Committee include:

- Building maintenance and repair

- Cleaning and custodial services

- Utilities

- Leases and rental agreements

- New construction, including additions and extensions

- Maintenance of the sports field

The Committee will normally include lay leaders who are experienced and knowledgeable in buildings and construction. It is essential that the Principal and the CFO/Executive Director be members of this committee, because any and every decision regarding building and plant affects the running of the school. How the committee functions will depend on the state of the building and plant, but also on how far the CFO/Executive Director (or another member of staff) is comfortable and reliable in dealing with building maintenance. In many smaller schools the lay committee directly undertakes these tasks.

Protecting the school from conflicts of interest can sometimes be a problem. Building maintenance, repairs and construction often involve major expenditures, and there can be complications arising out of good motives ("*I can save the school a lot of money*") and the opposite (seeing an opportunity to "*put business someone's way*"). No member of the committee should be directly involved, or have any interest, in work done in the school. If a generous supporter of the school wants to be helpful in providing goods or services, they should not be on the building committee. The problem with goodwill is that it is exceptionally difficult to make it accountable. All work involving expenditure above a Board-determined limit should be put to tender[25].

As with so many other areas of school activity, concentrate on value and quality rather than cost. In all issues involving flooring or finishes, choose long-term low maintenance. Your school deserves to look its best.

3.5.5 Other committees

The Board may establish other committees from time to time to meet different needs, according to the Constitutional procedures, which must include:

- Clear terms of reference

---

[25] This also applies to many other items purchased by the school.

- Clear directions regarding size and membership

If the committee is being convened to address a specific problem, it should have a clear reporting deadline, and its terms of reference should provide for it's disbanding once its job has been done[26]. Is the committee being convened to report, to recommend or to decide? The President should work with the Principal on the formation of new committees, including a discussion of appropriate professional representation.

School committees should be positive contributors to the Governance of the school, offering valuable – and real - opportunities for participation to volunteers and professionals alike.

3.5.6 Board and Committee induction processes

New Board members or Committee members should be invited to an 'Induction briefing' – perhaps an hour or so before their first meeting. The President / Committee Chair, and the Principal (or other appropriate Administrator) should make a 35 – 40 minute joint presentation covering the following:

- Current facts and figures about the school, including data relevant to the area of Board / Committee concern

- Explanation of school lay and professional management structure

- Terms of reference, Governance principles, responsibilities and process of the Board / Committee

- Responsibilities of individual Board/ Committee members, including confidentiality, impartiality and their role as ambassadors for the school

- Guidance on how to respond if approached by other parents

- Briefing on major issues likely to be dealt with during their term of office

- Contact information for school lay and professional personnel

Depending on the legal / constitutional status of the Board, induction may include briefing and information on the legal responsibilities of a Board member, and possibly signatures of non-disclosure/confidentiality agreements and other documents. It is a good idea for this information to be presented as a PowerPoint, and for the new

---

[26] Nothing wastes more time than Committees who have no usefulness, but are being kept alive for some artificial reason.

volunteer / committee member to be given a 'Board folder' containing printouts of the information displayed, plus any other relevant information. The Administration should invite the new members for a tour of the school.

3.6 And if the Board is crossing boundaries?

3.6.1 Occasional crossing of boundaries

Every school, from time to time, may face issues of inappropriate Board behavior – either collectively or by individual Board members. There are infinite possibilities, but typical problems might include:

- Interference in school operations / micro-management

- Using a Board position to intimidate teachers ("Before we discuss my daughter, I just want you to know I am a member of the Board.")

- Inappropriate discussion at meetings

- Personal 'lobbying' on admissions or disciplinary issues

- "You know that I am just canvassing the X family for a major gift to the school – can you just make sure that their son gets on the basketball team?"

- "My friend is very upset that he didn't get a refund ......"

- Indiscretion by a Board member in discussing school matters in the community.

These issues need great diplomacy. The best way to deal with them is to try and make sure that they never happen, by creating a healthy and responsible Board culture.

In many cases, if the incident is relatively innocent – an uncharacteristic lapse by a Board member – it is easier if the Principal deals with it directly rather than embarrass the Board member by asking the President to deal with it. A tactful conversation with the person concerned will usually do the trick, and it is always useful to refer to the 'Guidelines for Board members', or the President's remarks at the 'Induction Briefing' for reference. In such a conversation the following points might feature:

- If this concerns a matter that has been reported to you by a third party - check the facts:

Mrs. X, I need to raise a sensitive issue with you. I don't know exactly what happened, which is why I am calling you directly. A teacher has complained to me that at a recent community wedding you reportedly said something like 'I only got on the Board so that I could get [that teacher] fired'. Can you tell me if that is in fact what was said?" …. I am sure you understand that the comment was unfortunately out of place, even if it wasn't as explicit as reported. You will recall the President's request to Board members at the beginning of the year about discretion and confidentiality. Our staff must be confident that the Board deals with school matters fairly and responsibly. Administration does have some concerns about [the teacher's] performance, and we are addressing them through the professional means open to us. Suggestions that the teacher is being 'targeted' by a Board member will only make it more difficult for us to deal with the real problem.

- Depending on the issue, point out that the school has to treat all students / parents / staff fairly, and that although you appreciate the sensitivities of everyone, the school's reputation for fairness has to be preserved:

Mr., I know that the student's parents are very upset at what happened, and that they are close friends of yours. For reasons of privacy, which as a Board member I know you will respect, I cannot discuss the details of what happened with you. I can assure you that the Administration investigated this incident very thoroughly, and the punishment was very carefully considered. You may appreciate that the parents may not have disclosed all the details to you. Our School Handbook is very clear on the issue, and what the consequences will be. I cannot treat this student differently because of her family's position in the community. We have to relate to all students fairly, impartially and confidentially – and every student, parent and teacher has to know that.

- Inappropriate pressure on a staff member makes it more difficult for Administration to do their job.

Mr. L, telling the teacher that you are a member of the Board and that you will be taking the matter up at the highest levels was not helpful, because that has made it more difficult for the school to deal with the incident. The teacher is now claiming loudly in the staff room that she is being 'persecuted' because Sally's father is a member of the Board. As the President stressed at the beginning of the year, Board members must separate their function as parents from their function as Board members. There is definitely an issue of concern here, but it is being appropriately handled by the Administration. Please allow us to do our job. We are very concerned with the situation, and we are urgently addressing the problem.

If one member of the Board is a constant offender, you have to ask the President to intervene. Board members are on their team.

3.6.2 "By the way, I am a major donor to the school"

The pressure around donors[27] or prospective donors is more difficult to deal with. No Principal wishes to offend or alienate a benefactor to the school, whether their contribution is in time, dollars or influence. There is also a valid issue of 'hakarat hatov' (expressing legitimate recognition of someone who has done you a good turn). Nevertheless, the guidelines are clear.

The school -

- Cannot under any circumstances alter marks, grades, or change disciplinary consequences because the family of the student are donors. If it does, it will have irrevocably compromised its integrity and its good name. Such favoritism is remembered for years afterwards. ("Old D was a good Principal, but he always favored the children of the rich families")

- Cannot give the child or grandchild of a benefactor any privilege which they have not legitimately earned – for example, giving them a leadership position, a place on a team or in a play, or a place a particular class - all of which will always be at the expense of someone else

- Can try and be helpful if the request is not outlandish, and it is a request which you would try and accommodate from any other parent, regardless of who they were

- Can definitely put in an extra phone call to the donor/parents to explain a situation personally, if this is helpful. You should be prepared to do this for anyone, but if the family are giving generously to the school – in whatever way – it would not be unreasonable or unusual for the Principal to be a little more pro-active in making the call.

On everything else, that does not compromise the integrity of the school programs – front seats at school events, special updates on school progress, recognition in every dignified and appropriate manner – give every courtesy and thanks to your supporters.

---

[27] In my experience, donors often appreciate that their generosity to the school does not entitle their children to special treatment. The trouble is often with a more nebulous category – the 'potential donors'!

3.6.3 Confidentiality

Unfortunately, breaches of confidentiality are a common problem in many organizations, and community organizations are certainly not immune. The temptations to share information are magnified in situations where the possessors and the seekers may be related to each other, may be business partners, may be close friends, may sit next to each other in synagogue – and at the same time share strong involvements in local institutions. The late Oxford philosopher, Sir Isaiah Berlin[28], once said that "In Oxford, a secret is something that is only told to one person at a time". That is enough!

What the Board member's brother-in-law knows, his children will overhear. Both staff and lay leaders have the right to know that they may discharge their responsibilities without being the subject of 'leaked' information, and without their judgment and even motivations being the subject of speculation and gossip.

Protecting confidentiality extends to being careful about documents, voice messages and emails. Spare Board minutes and suchlike should be gathered and shredded after every meeting, and not left in a waste bin or recycling bin to be retrieved the following morning by curious students or staff. Board members should be careful, too, that such documents are not left around in their houses or cars. Emails can be very dangerous, and confidential information should never be circulated by email unless the security at the receiving end is known to be reliable. Board members – especially Executive members - who receive school email at home must be asked to provide an email address that is not accessible by other members of their family.

3.6.4 Constant crossing of boundaries …

If the Board as a whole is constantly crossing boundaries, the school has a serious problem. The school Principal has influence, but no authority over the Board. Change in the Board must come from the Board itself, and it is very difficult, very dangerous, and very foolhardy, for the Principal to set out to challenge the Board.

In this case, it is difficult and perhaps misleading to give suggestions of alternative courses of action to the Principal. The key, and only, strategy here is influence. If the school has a relationship with, or is affiliated to, a wider network of schools, advice may be sought from there. If the President is interested in school governance (but recognizes that s/he needs some help), then attendance at a conference or course may help. There is also widely available printed material on School Governance. An external consultant may be invited to speak to the Board, or lead a Board retreat. But at the end of the day the push to change their ways must come from within the Board, or – sometimes – from the parent body. Where there is no end in sight to the Board's interference in school operations, and inappropriate

---

[28] 1909-1997. Sir Isaiah, who came from a distinguished rabbinic family once personally told me that he, the [7th] Lubavitcher Rebbe and the world-famous violinist Yehudi Menuhin were "equal cousins to each other". One can only imagine the talents of their common ancestor!

behavior appears to be irrevocably ingrained in school process, the Principal may want to consider his or her own position[29].

4 MANAGEMENT AND STRUCTURE

4.1 Leading the team - ONE 'Head of School'

Whether the post is termed Principal, Headmaster/Headmistress, Head of School, Rosh Yeshivah or Director of Education, there should only be ONE senior professional in the school, able to lead in exercising ONE vision and ONE school philosophy. All staff and Administrators[30] report to the Principal, who, in turn, reports to the Board. That senior leadership position must be clear and contractually defined to all parties.

The reason for this is that otherwise there will be two schools under one roof, and the school will never progress beyond a certain point. Regrettable variations of this – excellent recipes for school dysfunction - include:

- the 'Jewish Studies' school and the 'General Studies' school, in theory operating under the same name, but in fact subtly[31] antagonistic entities

- the 'Professional School', run by Administration, and the 'Lay School', run underneath it by the Board, who are directly (or covertly) giving operational instructions and undermining the management of the school

- the 'Academic school' - run by Administration, and the 'Business school', run by a CFO who reports directly to the Board, and who uses financial control to influence (or block) educational decisions. A variation of this is the 'Fund-raising school', where

---

[29] But didn't you know about the Board when you accepted the appointment?

[30] In North America, the term 'Administrator' in a school context has a specific meaning. An Administrator (Principals, Vice-Principal etc) is part of school management, distinct from the teaching faculty. An Administrator (generally) hires, may discipline, evaluate, supervise, determine the duties of, and terminate a teacher. In the UK, South Africa and Australia the structure is somewhat different. The distinction between Principals (or Heads), Vice-Principals (or Deputy Heads) and teaching faculty can be far less sharp, and there are certainly cases where senior teachers will exercise responsibilities that in North America would be the prerogative of Administration.

[31] Sometimes not even subtly……

the Director of Development may enjoy inappropriate influence over, for example, setting school priorities.

4.1.1 Principals' principles

After robust and healthy Governance, the school's next essential is effective organization and management. The Principal must again be the leader.

Much of what follows may be summarized in seven[32] 'Principal's principles':

- **DELEGATE** – trust and empower colleagues, leaving time to deal with the 'big picture' issues

- **DOCUMENT** – ensure that policy, decisions[33], process and records are scrupulously documented

- **'NO SURPRISES'** – do not deliver surprises to others, and make it clear that you do not expect others to deliver surprises to you

- **BE REASONABLE** - take an objective view; be careful not to take decisions that are unreasonable or extreme. Your job is to act in the school's best interest

- **ENSURE FAIR PROCESS** - in all interactions with students, staff and parents, follow fair process and allow every point of view to be heard with respect and dignity

- **EMBED A QUALITY OF SERVICE** – ensure that at every single level of the school, at every 'access point', school business is conducted politely, efficiently, responsively, respectfully and with a smile

- **ALWAYS CHECK THE FACTS** – before you jump to action.

4.1.2 Management style and technique

'Management style' is infinitely variable. There is no single technique suited to everyone, or to every institution. A Principal must develop an interest in management. Even a scanty reading of the popular business literature will suggest some universal patterns that help, and some obvious ones to avoid. Much can be learned from books, magazines and online resources on management techniques, or from the 'pop-management' short courses or seminars available to businessmen and

---

[32] Some readers may have heard me claim now and again that in fact there are six principles:"Delegate, delegate, delegate; document, document, document." I have revised the list for this book ....

[33] Especially disciplinary decisions regarding students or staff... When a crisis occurs, your paper trail will be essential. Resist the temptation to deliver only a verbal warning.

organizational managers in most large cities. The Board should be delighted that the Principal is interested in attending such courses, and if they are not, it may be a danger signal.

4.2 Fair Process

Implementation of 'fair process' is the essential underpinning in operating a school, whether it involves students, staff, or parents. It establishes the credibility and equity of the school Administration. In a school, trust is largely built on fairness. If staff, students and parents believe that the school is always fair and reasonable (*"Tough but fair"* is a good reputation to have), there will be far less contention and controversy. Ensuring fair process also provides a measure of protection against legal challenges to disciplinary rulings[34].

A teacher, parent or student[35] has to leave the Principal's office believing that the school has been fair, responsible and respectful – whatever the subject of the meeting.

'Fair process' is a subjective term (ultimately subject to legal assessment), but it includes the following elements:

- Clear, published expectations of behavior and conduct

- Equal, fair treatment for all parties, without discrimination, bias or pre-judging

- Equal access to Administration for all parties who feel aggrieved

- Thorough and impartial investigation of problematic incidents, suspicions or allegations

- Opportunity always given, without exception, for every party to voice their concerns and/or their version of events

- Timely, swift and open process

- Reasonable, fair decisions and consequences

- Documentation of the process and the decision

- Right of appeal in serious cases (expulsion or dismissal)

---

[34] Should you ever get to Court, the concepts of 'fair process' and 'reasonableness' will figure prominently in the proceedings.
[35] See Section 12.2

Schools, including private schools, are now functioning in social and legal contexts which stress the rights of the individual, of 'consumer rights' and 'consumer protection', and which have expectations of accountability and transparency. The aware school leadership will conduct itself accordingly. It is a common fallacy that 'religious' institutions are 'exempt' from legal challenges.

4.3 Structuring and delegating operations

The school is an organization; some schools are large and complex organizations. There has to be a planned management dimension to the school's operation. While management training is reasonably common in large public school systems, it is less common in the private school sector, and perhaps even less common in the Jewish school system. What follows are very tentative and basic comments, but investment in thinking about the school in purely organizational terms will pay excellent dividends.

4.3.1 Designing and leading a management structure

Given this, a critical part of the Principal's job is to institute and operate an effective management structure that is appropriate for the size of the school. The Principal needs to possess or acquire the following management/leadership qualities:

- The ability to conceptualize the school in structural and organizational terms

- The ability and authority to delegate without interfering (i.e. the ability to trust colleagues)

- Team-building, negotiation and diplomatic skills

- A sense of effective process and communication

- The personal qualities and 'affect' appropriate to the position.

The Principal must give the team overall direction and inspiration, making sure that they are all working to a set of shared values and aspirations, and, most subtly, ensuring that their different talents are complementing each other in a way that produces a harmonious whole. A good Principal will recruit and promote with that in mind. If, for example, one member of the team is intense and – accurately or not - perceived as unsympathetic, then their tandem partner may be deliberately recruited for 'warm and fuzzy' qualities; or if one is a brilliant educator, but bad at following through, a counterpart may be especially thorough. A Principal's responsibility in team-building often includes non-academic staff, who should be seen as integral parts of the team 'map'. (A disorganized Administrator – and I speak from personal experience – needs a highly organized secretary!).

Performing in harmony also means having the collegial largeness of vision to support others in their own performance tasks. How the leadership team functions – whether it is small or large – makes a critical difference in the overall quality of the school.

4.3.2 Clarity and quality of the team

The management effectiveness of the school – whatever its size – depends on several factors:

- **Clarity of structure** – every member of the team should have a logical area of responsibility clearly understood by themselves and by the school 'constituencies'

- **Clarity of function** – the specific responsibilities of each team member should be defined

- Collegial decision-making and collegial functioning – the team has to work as a team

- **Shared values** – the school leadership must all share and promote the school ethos

- **Sharing and flow of information** – the flow of information must be free and relevant.

The collegial culture is extremely positive. 'Turf wars' of every description are highly toxic, and will counter every quality of good management.

4.3.3 Essential Administration tasks and structure

Conventionally, in Jewish schools, administration and supervision of the Jewish Studies curriculum and the General Studies ('Secular Studies') curriculum are split, with a Vice-Principal (or equivalent) in charge of each. In a smaller school, the Principal may fill the role of one or the other. In addition to VP's, in larger schools each academic department, if its size warrants, will also have a Head of Department.

The school will also have financial / accounting staff. In a small school, the school (lay) treasurer sometimes directly oversees these functions; a larger school will have a CFO (Chief Financial Officer)/Executive Director, and may have a substantial accounting department. Some schools may have a full-time Development Officer / fundraiser -- SEE SECTION 16

A typical school professional structure may look like this:

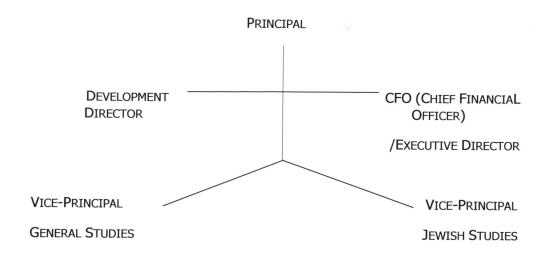

PRINCIPAL

DEVELOPMENT
DIRECTOR

CFO (CHIEF FINANCIAL
OFFICER)

/EXECUTIVE DIRECTOR

VICE-PRINCIPAL

GENERAL STUDIES

VICE-PRINCIPAL

JEWISH STUDIES

In schools that have more than one component part (either several campuses or several levels – K, Elementary, High) – the structure may have a level of Campus Principals or 'Level' Principals, probably with their own self-standing Administrations.

There should still be one overall Principal[36].

- **The Principal** SEE SECTION 2 is the senior professional in the school, and should be dealing with the 'big picture' items – school vision, school values, policy, direction, standards, ideology and ideas, overall operational supervision (including close supervision of Administrators[37]) and major decisions. He/she should be dealing with the Board, and representing the school in the community. There may be a small group of 'oxygen functions' portfolios that the Principal deals with 'hands on' – for example, student and staff recruitment.

  Operationally, the paradox – perhaps part of the attraction - of the Principal's position is that he/she has to be master of the overall and master of the detail at the same time. On the one hand, s/he has to be able to see the school in its very widest context – including the broadest contexts of social, religious and cultural trends that way transcend the institution ("What is happening to culture?" "What is

---

[36] In a multi-level or multi-campus school probably designated 'Director of Education' or 'Head of School'.
[37] Conventional management wisdom states that no one person can directly supervise more than seven others.

happening to Judaism?"). At the same time, the Principal must be interested in every single detail of what happens in the school, whether it is how the Grade 11 Tanakh test was set and marked, or whether the hinge on the door in the washroom was correctly fixed.

- **The Vice-Principals** should be responsible for ongoing, day-to-day school operations, ensuring the smooth and consistent running of the school. In a large school, VP's are also often assigned to timetabling/scheduling.

- **The CFO/Executive Director** is responsible for budgeting, accounting, fiscal control and reporting; the collection of Tuition Fees; school building maintenance; and other non-academic operations of the school. He /she should also supervise the non-academic staff.

- **The Development Director** is responsible for raising funds to support the school's activities, operations and programs, normally in close cooperation with volunteers.

4.3.4 Job Descriptions

An essential element of effective management is a set of comprehensive Job Descriptions for everyone involved in the school.

Those for Administrators will be individual; for others they may be more generic. Job Descriptions can take a long time to formulate, but they are essential.

A clear Job Description:

- Gives clarity to every member of staff regarding their own responsibilities and duties.

- Avoids staff either claiming authority over areas for which they are not responsible or disclaiming responsibility for areas for which they are.

- Avoids destructive 'turf wars' between colleagues.

- Allows fair supervision and performance evaluation.

- Allows other colleagues to know the division of responsibilities within the school.

- Gives the Board comfort that the school is properly supervised and the operations of the school are satisfactorily organized.

- Should be used as part of the Staff Recruitment process, and sent to every applicant.

Common headings in a Job Description – obviously, flexible according to circumstances - may include:

Title:	*Exact title of position*
Directly reports to:	*Name direct supervisor*
Evaluation:	*How often, and by who*
Salary:	*Annual salary (is in contract, and may be omitted if the Job Description is circulated)*
Administrative / non-Administrative:	*Management status*
Length of Contract:	*How long is the contract for this post?*
Essential Qualifications:	*What are the essential qualifications and experience needed for this post?*
Overall responsibilities:	*A list of the general areas of responsibility pertaining to this position*
Direct supervision of:	*Who does this person directly supervise?*
Reporting responsibility – general:	*In addition to their direct supervisor, to which lay and professional persons or committees does this post report?*
Budget / fiscal responsibility:	*What responsibility does this person have for submitting and administering a budget line or lines?*
Educational responsibility:	*What is the direct, detailed list of tasks for which this person is responsible?*
Community relationships:	*Is this person responsible for liaison, contact or maintaining relationships with bodies outside the school?*

A Job Description should be sent to every applicant for a post at the school, so that all prospective employees know exactly the responsibilities and duties of the post to which they are applying. It then forms part of the contract or letter of appointment. Every Job Description should contain a clause that allows the Principal or the school to allocate "*other duties as specified from time to time by the Principal in accordance with the needs of the school.*" This clause allows the school to vary an Administrator's duties if circumstances – of the person or of the school – change.

There should be a central file of Job Descriptions for every post in the school, held by the Principal and/or the CFO.

4.3.5 Job Descriptions – where none exist …

A much more difficult situation exists where a school has never had formal Job Descriptions. This may be because the school has been small, or new (or both) and somehow there has been an assumed or agreed division of responsibilities.

Tasks will be assigned because "*X likes that sort of thing*", "*X has always done that*" or "*X is always good at it*". It is an axiom of good management that the person follows the task, not the task the person. Where anomalous responsibilities (and therefore authority) exist, there is a long-term problem. When staff member X is doing something that really should be in the area of responsibility of staff member Y, then Y's ability to comprehensively plan and implement their job is inevitably compromised; and X is by definition spending time on something that is taking time away from whatever X is meant to be doing.

It is never easy to deal with these situations, because they are frequently 'sweetheart deals', whose origins are in special relationships or friendships between (often veteran) members of staff. More problematic is when a staff member is being 'protected' by a Board member. ("*Rabbi X has always dealt with this, and he's very good at it*"). If, as Principal, these have been instituted or tolerated by your predecessor, then you will face additional complications when you try and regularize the situation ("*The new Principal is upsetting everyone*"). It may take years[38], and may have to wait until individuals retire or leave, but the Principal should not let pass opportunities that may be a diplomatic moment to regularize the situation.

Where no Job Descriptions exist, the Principal has to initiate a process. It may begin in different ways; for example, a discussion at the Board, resulting in a mandate to the Board Personnel Committee. Alternatively, the Administrative team may decide to undertake the drafting. At individual level, you may have to deal with contractual issues that will have to be resolved before you can make a Job Description binding on a particular individual. The Principal as CEO has to be the leader in deciding how to navigate the issue. It may be advantageous or necessary (or both) to have the help of an outside consultant, or of a committee (with some independent members) specially convened for the purpose.

---

[38] Unless, of course, the Principal straightens things out in the first month.

The process may include the following stages:

- Discussing the idea with key individuals, and ensuring that you have supportive voices before introducing the proposal.

- Introducing the idea at school level – "This year, I'd like our team to look at school organization, which will include drawing up an organizational 'map' of the school, and then drawing up Job Descriptions for each of us."

- Initiating an agreed general process, perhaps using an existing template. The process should include a timetable and deadlines for the drafting of documents, review, consultation and adoption. It is important that the Principal lead this process. Delegating to others may unwittingly open the door to political manipulation.

- Discussing the individual Job Descriptions, as they are drafted, with the individuals to whom they will apply. Ensure that there is agreement in principle, even though you may not get agreement on every detail.

- Determining the process by which the Job Descriptions will be adopted, whether by contract or by agreement.

- Provide for a review and assessment after a reasonable period of time

Your Job Descriptions are the foundation for a school operations plan.

4.3.6 Meetings, supervision and information flow

Whatever the size of the school, senior Administration should meet as a group at least once a week. Some schools begin each day with a short meeting. If the agendas are very thin, meetings may occasionally be cancelled[39], but it is a mistake to cancel more than one consecutive meeting – there is an intangible value in just having the team sitting round a table.

An agenda should be set, and a timeframe established.

Meetings are information exchanges and decision-making forums regarding developments in the school, and issues that are appearing on the horizon. These can be general school issues, or issues involving a particular student, family or teacher.

---

[39] Alternatively, if your meeting participants are scattered, the agenda is thin, and travel time is precious, use a conference call or another online meeting technology.

The Principal should be continually disseminating information to colleagues that will help them understand dynamics happening in the school and in the community. A flow of information – via meetings, emails, staff newsletters or just 'networking' helps everyone make balanced decisions.

In general, the Principal should be speaking very frequently in person, by phone or by email with individual colleagues. According to style, all sorts of technologies for sharing information, or for having online meetings are now available, and are continually getting more and more advanced.

4.4 Decision making and problem solving

- The best staff will bring you solutions, not problems.

Decision-making in schools, large and small, should be collaborative/consensual in almost every case. However, as Principal, major and serious decisions may be referred to you directly; occasionally you will be called on to resolve an undecided issue; and occasionally you will either reserve the right of decision on a particular issue or, in very rare cases, overrule a decision that someone else has taken.

4.4.1 Delegated decisions

> *A Principal who was responsible for running several campuses once boasted to me that "none of my Administrators take any decision, big or small, without phoning me". I could neither admire him, nor envy them. To have a healthy school, you must choose the very best; promote them, trust them, allow them to exercise their skills -- and occasionally make mistakes (as you do).*

The Principal should not be deeply involved in day-to day decisions.

Principals of larger schools – 800+ students – should not normally be involved *at all* in day-to-day decisions. These should be delegated to Vice-Principals and others. Their decision-making has to be within the policies and ethos of the school. There may be decisions that they are required to check first with the Principal; but their authority must be trusted, and supported.

A Principal who doesn't delegate runs the risk of being totally preoccupied with routine operational issues, easily within the trustworthy discretion of others, which eternally prevent the Principal from spending time on the larger issues for which s/he is employed. (This may be consciously or unconsciously deliberate...[40])

---

[40] Or it may be symptomatic of a 'control freak' personality profile. 'Control freaks' are very rarely liked, and others do not enjoy working for them.

In some cases, decisions will be delegated to a team, rather than an individual. Choose Chairs of teams / committees carefully.

4.4.2 The collaborative / consensual process

Decision making in the school can take place in several forums – the Board, the Administration and the staff. As outlined earlier, *policy* should be the province of the Board (although as Principal you, and your colleagues, should certainly have input); *operations* should be the province of the professional educators.

As part of management, every manager and every leader develops the decision-making process within their own team, and there is a rich literature that will introduce you to a whole range of different mechanisms. In a well-run and cohesive team decisions should flow easily, because the team should have common goals, a common understanding of the context in which the decision has to be taken and, more importantly, its practical consequences when implemented.

Email is a quick and easy way of gathering opinions if a decision is needed in a hurry. Rather than have decisions made on an ad-hoc basis, the weekly Administrative Team meeting should be the forum where ongoing or arising issues of school operations are efficiently considered and decided. Many decisions will be taken at Administrative team meetings almost without anyone being aware of it.

Simple techniques can ensure that no colleague's view or input is overlooked – for example, going around the table, by name, and inviting any further comment – *"Syd, do you have any further comments on this?"; "Naomi, anything more that you would like to add on this issue, before we close it?"* Note when colleagues are not contributing to a discussion, and check that their non-participation is from comfort, not from unspoken or unarticulated annoyance (*[THINKS:] "How dare this be brought to the table – I'm responsible for this, and no-one else should be involved!"*). When a decision is taken, it should be verbally confirmed, recorded, and communicated to whoever needs to know it.

Occasionally things get stuck. The team may differ about how to deal with a student (or staff) disciplinary issue. When they do, some of the following questions may be useful:

- Is the real problem being correctly identified?

- Is the necessary decision being correctly identified?

- Are the correct criteria being applied? (No decision should be taken that does not, broadly, serve the school's interests.)

- Is all of the data available?

- Has everyone's voice been heard?

- How far can the consequences of the decision be assessed or predicted?

- What do the school values and beliefs have to say about the issue?

Try and agree a framework and a timetable for resolution (*"We should not spend more than another fifteen minutes on this issue, and if possible I'd like us to be in a position to decide by 11:30."*)

Most problems can wait for (and sometimes benefit from) overnight or longer consideration. If a problem is complex, one of the team may be asked to write a short 'position paper'. A simple, two-column " + / - " list, where the pro's and con's of a particular course of action are listed, is often quick and illuminating; alternatively, there are numerous 'SWOT[41]' analysis templates available. The Principal may also need to speak to the team one-on-one, to clarify exactly 'where they are coming from'. Issues may surface that the colleague, rightly or wrongly, has not wanted to put on the table. They can be the most important.

If the issue is really stuck, and it is important that the decision be consensual, then the Principal has to switch to negotiating mode. Everyone has to be prepared to move their own position in order to reach a decision that everyone can support. The conversation may then include some classic negotiating gambits:

- "What has to be done here to create a situation that you could live with, or, better, support?"

- "What do you think we are missing in our suggested solution to this problem?"

- "If Esther agrees not to insist on x, will you agree not to insist on y?"

- "If we agree to meet you in your request for x to be incorporated in the decision, will you quietly forego insistence on y?"

- "Suggest a way in which we can reach the same result here, but framing it in a different way?"

- "Is there a way we can phrase this that would make you more comfortable?"

Team members must feel free to voice their opinions, and if necessary their disagreement. They have to be allowed to exercise the skills and judgment for which they have been promoted or appointed.

---

[41] 'Strengths, Weaknesses, Opportunities, Threats'

A leader who brooks no disagreement or dissent is not a leader.

Whatever the process, when all leave the room, everyone supports the decision. Principal and Administration must function in a mode of collective professional responsibility. No colleague may go into the staff room and undermine the group's decision. An even worse breach of professionalism is for any of the group to undermine a decision to Board members, parents – or students.

4.4.3 The Principal as decision-maker or arbiter

The quality – and the process – of the decision-making in any organization is a determining factor in establishing confidence in leadership.

In some circumstances, the Principal will be the person making a decision. If the Principal wishes to reserve the right to make the final decision in a team process (for example, in a staff appointment, or on an expulsion issue), others involved must be told at the beginning of the process that their role, while very valuable, will formally be consultative:

> *I'd like everyone to be clear on the process – although I want a full and frank discussion, on this issue I have to reserve the right to take the final decision.*

When a decision has been made, the Administrators – if not part of the decision-making group - should be told of the outcome, in confidence, and if appropriate, the reasons behind the decision. They should not learn the outcome at the same time as, or worse, after, everyone else.

Difficult decisions may be discussed[42] – in confidence - with others, including local Rabbis, the school President, other School Principals, or others with appropriate experience and expertise whose confidentiality can be trusted.

---

[42] Two difficult decisions on which I consulted widely were, first, an incident where a girl who was the Student President-elect was part of a group who had to take a public exam under very difficult, unsuitable, squashed conditions while away at a camp retreat. (The exam had to be taken on a particular day). She had done nothing while aware that another girl was copying from her answer paper. The conditions almost guaranteed that this would happen. She would have had to tell on the other girl to stop the copying. Should she be disqualified from her leadership position? It was not a clear-cut case, and those whom I asked were completely divided. I decided that the conditions brought the incident into the category of 'Lifnei iveir...- *setting up a situation that would tempt the inevitable',* allowed her to take up her position, and set her a community-service assignment as a consequence. On reflection, I think I made the right decision. The second involved a young man suspected of calling in a bomb threat to the school. His message had been recorded. It was quite clearly his voice, although a forensic report was equivocal. However, a member of staff had let slip information that allowed him to 'arrange' an alibi. We had overwhelming suspicion, but no actual proof. Again, opinion was divided. I gave him the benefit of the doubt, and took no action. On reflection, I think I was wrong.

Not every school decision will be correct. Most of them should be. All decisions should be considered, and should be moral. Some of the most difficult decisions will be unpopular.

For a Principal or Administrator, a reputation for being "indecisive", or "unable to take decisions" or "swayed by the last person who went to the office" – are all worse than a reputation arising out of occasional decisions that others (usually without full knowledge of the facts) may feel are wrong.

4.4.4 Overturning decisions made by others

This should only be necessary – if ever - on very rare occasions. Times when the Principal must overturn a colleague's decision include:

- When a decision results in a clear, indisputable injustice

- When a decision would permit an unsafe activity or situation to take place

- Where the situation has either come about as a result of, or creates the possibility of, the law being broken or dishonesty taking place.

- Where a decision has been taken that is clearly against the standards, practices and ethos of the school (to the extent that it cannot be allowed to take place)

- Where the budgetary implications of the decision have not been authorized, and are likely to be exorbitant.

The need to overturn a decision is an indication of a failure of management and leadership. Somewhere along the line, the school has failed to communicate the standards on which the school should be running, and someone has been able, in comfort, to take a very wrong decision. That may turn out to be a failure of process; it may be a failure of judgment; or it may have been good-intentioned, but misinformed. Occasionally, the Principal should be prepared to help the teacher, and take personal responsibility for cancelling an event.

If a situation arises where the Principal feels that a decision taken in the school must be reversed, careful thought is necessary:

> *If the consequences of the decision are undesirable, it is better to ask the person responsible to amend the decision rather than cancel it. "John – I don't want to cancel this and spoil everyone's preparations, but for it to go ahead, we need to work together and make some changes." It is extremely demoralizing for someone who has been entrusted with a decision to have it overturned completely, especially if that*

becomes obvious and public. If at all possible, treat it as a "This time we'll let it pass, but it cannot happen again."

Proper process would then require an evaluation with the staff concerned, which if no damage has been done can be informal. If, however, legal or safety issues or other serious questions have been raised, then the follow up with staff may be more serious, and may result in a letter placed in the file of the person responsible.

There is also a hard calculation to be made of what is ultimately in the school's best interests. If the decision made is problematic, but not especially harmful, it may be better to let it stand (perhaps with some changes) rather than allow the issue to become not the original decision itself, but the school's action in canceling it.

If there are regular instances where the Principal overrules others, Administration (and staff) will become very reluctant to take responsibility; and the Principal should carefully question whether vision and standards are clearly being communicated within the school.[43]

4.5 Quality of service

A second essential, after 'Fair Process', is 'Quality of Service'. The latter precedes the former in daily life, although not perhaps in fundamental importance.

- How does the school present to those who deal with it? Is it considered 'a pleasure' or 'a pain' to deal with the school? How is the telephone answered? How quickly and how tactfully are calls and messages returned? Are communications clear and helpful? Are staff always professional in their communications? Is the school efficient? Is it perceived in the community as 'user-friendly'? Is information accessible? Is it a pleasant experience to deal with the school – or is it wearying and frustrating? Does the school 'deliver' when it makes promises? Does the school give the impression that it is happy to deal with parents and prospective parents – or the opposite?

'Quality of Service' is a very familiar, and recognized, concept in the commercial world. It is less often considered in the non-profit environment. Yet how the school "interfaces" with individuals and organizations largely pre-determines how they interact with the school.

---

[43] Of course, if the decisions which frequently need review all come from one source, then you have a different situation to deal with ....

This is again a question of ethos and school culture. Staff training and staff supervision can make a huge difference – including every person who works for the school, in any capacity.

As noted, parental (and other) expectations have risen considerably in recent years. There are some areas where that is problematic for the school – for example, there is no 'entitlement' to marks or grades, as some parents seem to believe. But a modern organization cannot operate and expect the cooperation and loyalty of its constituencies unless it provides a perceived high level of service.

Fortunately, of all the possible problems affecting a school, this is one of the easiest to tackle. If the school thinks that its level of service needs to be improved, tackle the issue at a PD day or a staff meeting. You can invite an external speaker to talk about the issue (there are many available). Set up a staff committee (possibly a joint staff-parent committee) to examine the problem, come up with a list of suggestions, and, importantly, a list of targets. Review after a year or so. The difference should be striking.

4.6 Essential school documents

A well-managed school will generate a series of documents that set out the policies and processes that govern the conduct of the school. These may take several years to fully develop, but the process of developing them is in itself a valuable way of clarifying and discussing important school principles.

They are a function of good management, fair process and clear communications. Relevant documents should be widely available to the applicable constituencies. Those concerning parents and students should be circulated, every year, to all parents and all students, and should be part of your recruitment literature. The expectations, standards and processes of the school are 'transparent' and clear to everyone. You have communicated how your school runs – what it promises to students, parents and staff, and, reciprocally, what it expects from them. No surprises, more clarity and consistency, no guesswork, easier accountability and far fewer arguments.

Essential school documents – separate or integrated – may comprise the following:

4.6.1 School Constitution

The School Constitution has to be professionally drafted for the Board, and is the legal statement of school governance. It defines the legal status of the school, and the composition, duties and processes of the Board of Directors.

4.6.2 'Statement of Philosophy and Purpose' / Mission Statement

Like the School Constitution, this document is a document of the Board of Directors (or, if your school is so structured, the trustees). A Principal should certainly have input into drafting or revising such a document, but it is the prerogative of the Board to set the school's aims, ideology and principles. The Administration operates the school within those principles. The 'Statement of Philosophy and Purpose (SPP)', which may incorporate a short 'Mission statement', must be very carefully written; should be confined to principles and values (not practical details) and should be short. The SPP should not need revision more than once every decade or so, if then. A well-drafted SPP is invaluable.

4.6.3 School Handbook

The School Handbook is the responsibility of Administration, although parents and Board members should have input. Depending on the size and culture of the school, and the breadth of its program, the School handbook can be a complex document.

The purpose of the Handbook is to set out the standards of behavior required of all students, and the procedures and expectations that are followed in the operation of the school. It should be comprehensive. There may be additional, parent-oriented information relating to the school.

Topics covered in the Handbook should include, but are not limited to:

- The school's "Statement of Philosophy and Purpose'.

- Safety and security of the school buildings and personnel.

- The School Safety and Behavior Code, and policy regarding consequences for infractions.

- The school's agreed policy regarding Jewish observance and Jewish practice.

- Sexual harassment and bullying code.

- Attendance requirements, and procedures for reporting absence, 'signing out' etc.

- Classroom expectations and standards.

- Test and exam protocols.

- Rules relating to student lockers and personal property.

- Rules relating to student parking and use of cars

- 'Acceptable Use' policies for computers, emails, internet and all other electronic recording, photographic and communication devices – SEE SECTIONS 12.3.10, 12.3.11, 12.3.12

- All other details of required school procedures and processes.

The Handbook should be updated each year, and circulated to all students, parents and staff. Good practice is to indicate annual changes and additions, which may be printed in a different color. The provisions of the School Handbook should include the duty to read it! There will be few who do so, but they ignore it at their peril.

Clear drafting of a School Handbook is a definite skill, and the task should be entrusted to someone who is good at it.

4.6.4 Suspension and Expulsion – agreed process

In the life of every school, students have to be suspended and occasionally expelled. SEE SECTION 12.7 .

In private schools, including Jewish schools, expulsion has historically (one might almost say traditionally) been exercised 'on the spot' and somewhat arbitrarily. However, expulsion from school (and to a lesser degree suspension) is a grave matter for a student and his/her family, and increasingly results in legal action.

If the School Handbook is clear on the applicable consequences for specified disciplinary offenses (*"Students found in possession of an offensive weapon in school, or at a school-sponsored activity, will be expelled"*), then the legal challenge will focus on the process by which the expulsion was implemented. Was 'fair process' followed? Were the rights of the student respected and protected? Did the student and/or his parents know the process being followed by the school?

A school should have a clear, published 'Agreed process' which - allowing for inevitable variations in circumstances -- sets down what steps the school will take when considering suspension or expulsion of a student. This document need not be in general circulation, but it should be clear in the School Handbook that it exists and is available on request. Its existence should be brought to the attention of the student's parents when expulsion may be contemplated.

4.6.5 Course Calendar

Each year a school should publish a full listing of courses it will be offering (or will offer subject to demand) in the following year, giving course codes, prerequisites, and a description of the course curriculum. The Course Calendar is usually published in Spring, giving students a basis on which to select the following year's courses. The 'Course Calendar' normally also contains other useful information and advice regarding course choices, academic planning, study skills etc.

4.6.6 Staff Handbook

The Staff Handbook is the comprehensive professional resource document and guide for your teachers, which describes in detail their professional duties, their rights as employees, the school's expectations of them as professional teachers, and the operational processes of the school as they may affect teachers. Like the School Handbook (which should be an integral part of the Staff Handbook), it should deal with both school policy and process.

A Staff Handbook might contain:

- Relevant basic School Documents (e.g. Statement of Philosophy and Purpose, School Handbook)

- An explanation of the Jewish dimension of the school.

- An outline of the responsibilities of the School Administration

- An applicable 'Teachers' Code of Professional Practice'

- Staff dress code

- Detailed policies regarding classroom practice, including evaluation and assessment policies and procedures to be applied consistently in the school.

- Instructions regarding the administration of the school's absence / late procedures for students.

- Instructions regarding teacher's duties outside the classroom, including health, safety and security issues, procedures and policies for student supervision during extra-curricular activities

- Procedures for organizing and running school trips, Field Trips, Shabbatonim / retreats, sports matches, and other school events, including sample 'Permission / consent' forms

- Other school procedures and information which teachers need to know

- Information regarding teachers' legal rights and responsibilities, including a sexual harassment policy

- A comprehensive school calendar, including dates of all Staff meetings, PD days etc.

- A full staff list, with addresses, email contacts and phone numbers.

Not all of the above will be relevant to every school, and every school will be able to add headings not included. The Staff Handbook should be printed in a loose-leaf binder, of which sections can be updated yearly.

4.6.7 Staff list

Part of the school documentation (it can be part of the Handbook) should be a annually updated full staff list of Administration, teaching staff, and support staff, giving their correct names, titles, degrees, and subjects taught. If it is your school policy, include contact information for teachers (email addresses or phone extensions/mailboxes).

SEE ALSO: 9.2.1 – VALIDATING QUALIFICATIONS

4.6.8 Application, registration and re-registration documents

Application Forms for new students and re-registration forms for existing students should be comprehensive and thorough. They are important parts of school documentation. The Application Form may be several pages long. Again, the local requirements for every school will vary, but the Application Form for new students should incorporate requests for the following information (to be listed or attached):

- Full biographical information about the student, including place of birth, and identifying photograph

- All relevant information concerning names, addresses, telephone and email contacts for the student and his/her responsible parents/guardians.

- Brief family profile, including details of siblings

- If the parents are separated or divorced, this information must be fully given for both natural parents and current family, and supporting legal documentation should be supplied describing custody agreements

- Contact information for friends or relatives to be contacted in an emergency if parents are not available.

- If necessary, immigration/visa/citizenship status of the student.

- A complete record of all schools attended by the student, including dates entered and dates left.

- Recent Report Cards.

- Copies of results of any educational testing, psych-ed / special needs assessments or similar processes undergone by the student, with professional notes of any diagnosed learning difficulties or special needs.

- Full disclosure of any medical or emotional diagnoses of which the school needs to be aware for any reason (many schools require a pediatrician's certificate).

- Disclosure of any family circumstances (e.g. medical, social, emotional, financial) of which the school should be aware, and which may impact on the student's school life.

- Details of synagogue membership and family Jewish involvement.

The Application Form should also provide for a short essay, in the student's own handwriting, explaining why they wish to come to your school. Eventually, the documentation will include notes on the admissions interview and other entrance information.

The Application Form (or a separate form) should (if permissible) incorporate a waiver giving the school permission to speak to the student's previous school(s).

Both the Application Form and the annual Re-registration form should require the signatures of both student and parents. It is useful to include a short series of waivers and undertakings above the signatures – for example, that by applying

'*Parents and students accept that*':

- They will abide by the provisions of the School Handbook and other instructions issued by Administration from time to time.

- They recognize the right of the school to (e.g.) determine student placement, and add or cancel courses.

- They recognize the right of the school to decline registration/re-registration on academic, disciplinary, or unsatisfactory attendance grounds.

- They grant the school the right to contact current and previous schools for further educational information on the applicant

- [In some jurisdictions] They give the school the right to use digital images of the students or their work for purpose of school publicity.

The operating principle here is to consolidate as many permissions, agreements and waivers as possible in one place, at the time of registration; save time and energy during the school year in chasing parental signatures; and give the school a good measure of protection on several important counts.

4.6.9 Tuition Assistance request forms

Documentation required will vary from community to community.

In many places, comprehensive financial documentation will be required, including copies of tax returns, bank statements, mortgage documentation, salary details, accountants' declaration and other income/expenditure details. The Tuition Assistance Committee will determine the information needed. For many families this is a very painful and embarrassing process; the utmost tact at every stage of the tuition assistance process is absolutely necessary, and the confidentiality has to be absolutely watertight. Rather than have parents request assistance forms, some schools automatically send the application form to every parent.

4.6.10   Health, safety and emergency documentation

See Sections 15.4.2 and 15.8

These may be mandated by local statutory regulations, and would normally include:

- Emergency evacuation procedures

- Procedures for dealing with emergency and crisis

- Easily accessible records of students with medical or other needs (including allergies)

- Records of equipment, addresses of emergency maintenance personnel and utilities

- Plans of the school building

4.7 Documenting operations

Properly documenting process – meetings, decisions, policy, events – is essentially building your school memory. A school is responsible for young people; it is an employer; it carries fiscal responsibility, and in all of these it carries legal responsibility. As a school functions, it has to have an accessible memory. Without it, you are organizationally and even legally vulnerable. With a comprehensive base of school documentation, you are immensely strengthened. 'Document' (verb imperative) is the second commandment of school management.

Documentation should cover most school activities and operations.

4.7.1 Ongoing correspondence, records of meetings, decisions, agreements and notices.

Apart from the official school records of students, the personnel files of staff, and, of course the school accounts – all of which need meticulous organization, upkeep and eventual archiving – every school generates a large volume of ongoing correspondence and other communications.

Typically, these records may now be nightmarishly scattered between paper files, computer files, email files (incoming and outgoing) and messages received and sent on PDA's. Even telephone calls – once only conducted sitting at a desk, in an office environment – may now be made or received in any place, at any time, in any circumstances. It is increasingly difficult to keep control over the organization and documenting of what may be very important texts and messages. Diaries are increasingly ephemeral documents. However, correspondence that may have consequences or that represent important exchanges must be kept. Emails and text messages that are important should be copied to yourself or to your secretary 'For file'. Use the 'Save as' or 'labeling' options to keep messages and other communications in the relevant file. That is easier than searching through thousands of emails months later to find a key message, when you have only a vague memory of when it was received or sent, the sender used an eccentric address, you cannot remember the subject line ... and your email service provider may have archived or, worse, automatically deleted it anyway. Alternatively, just print it out and file it as hard copy (see below). Whatever your system, make sure that you have as few 'file repositories' as possible. Make sure that work you do at home, or on your laptop, is 'synched' with your school computer – it is particularly annoying when different versions of the same document exist on different computers. If you work from several different computers, consider using 'Google docs' or some similar online central filing system.

Meeting records should be filed and kept, including notes of decisions taken for implementation, 'follow-up', and report-back.

Ideally, important telephone conversations – incoming and outgoing – should be logged, and notes made of important content[44].

Organize and systematize your paper and digital filing in a way with which you are comfortable, and which enables you and others if necessary to locate records and files. Realistically, you may be running both a paper file (in a filing cabinet) and a digital file (on your or your secretary's computer – or both)[45]. At the very least, the filing system should be common (see below), so that when you are searching for the

---

[44] It is very difficult to be disciplined enough to record a call received on a cell-phone in your local supermarket on a Friday afternoon, however important it may be.

[45] For example, your secretary may have typed the document for you – it will be on her computer. You may have edited the document and emailed it to colleagues for review and comment, and then distributed it by email yourself; it will be on your computer. You may have responded to an incoming email; it will be on your email archive. You may have received an email, downloaded it at home after school, and replied to it from home; depending on how it was sent (email or attachment) it may be on your email archive or on the hard drive of your home computer..... Or the whole correspondence may be on your Blackberry. Three years later the correspondence is needed for, say, a hearing concerning a labour dispute.

copy of a memo or a letter to a parent, you know that it will be similarly filed in each of the two or three places where it may be recorded.

- Back up every computer memory regularly. If you do not know how to do this, get your computer technician to set up automatic, regular back-ups for you.

- Increasingly, the digital record is the only record – just as you have a lock on your office and your filing cabinets, ensure that your computer(s) are appropriately secure and password-protected.

4.7.2 A simple filing system

For many years, in different places, I have used an easy and reliable system that leaves little to chance (*"Should this be filed under the teacher's name, the parent's name, 'Chemistry Department' or 'Safety'?' "*). My office runs a series of numbered files, parallel for physical files and computer files. Every file has a number (and a name), and they run in roughly classified series. Under each file number, every document has a unique serial number.

- All files concerning the School Board of Directors, Board Committees, Governance, and my personal files have a serial 100 prefix (101, 102, 103…)

- All files concerning the internal running of the school have a serial 200 prefix

- All files concerning Jewish Community organizations with which the school works have serial 300 prefixes

- All files concerning outside organizations have a serial 400 prefix

- When we ran a very large new building operation, we assigned a serial 500 prefix to all of the related files, including the fund-raising files relevant to the project

Clearly, the list of file-names must be common to both the main user (the Principal) and his/her office, and every time a new file is created, both must be updated.

- Within every file, every document is given a unique number and title, and suffixed with the month/year in which it was written or revised.

Thus, for example, the school's Education Committee may be allocated the '105' file number. A memo written by you to the Chair of the committee about Math in Grade 12 may be the twenty-seventh document in the file, written October 2007. It will appear in your computer as:

105-27 G12 Math memo 10-07.doc

Your directory structure will look (in part) like this:

MAIN DIRECTORY	Sub-directory	Sub-directory
C:/.../SCHOOL DOCS/		
	/100	
		/101 Board /
		/102 Executive /
		/103 Finance Cttee /
		/104 Personnel Cttee /
		/105 Education Cttee/
		▶ /105-1 Mandate 09-06.doc
		▶ /105-2 Ivrit policy 10-06.doc
		....
		▶ /105-27 G12 Math 10-07.doc
		▶ /105-28 Chair response to 105-27 11-07
	/200/	....
	/300/	....
	/...../	....

Incoming documents, when read, and if they need to be filed, are marked with the file number and then placed in the appropriate file. Incoming emails, if they need to be kept, are 'Saved as' in the appropriate 'Word' or 'Excel' file, and given a number - see 105-28 above.

You may create additional 'series' or sub-folders according to need and preference. It is very easy to do on Microsoft 'Word'. If you are comfortable with it, you can cut out one stage of the process and have you and your secretary keep a common, web-accessible file on Google docs.

4.7.3 Keeping track of addresses, contacts and diary.

There are now several frameworks for doing this – online and offline, using desktops, laptops, PDA's, Blackberries or, increasingly, devices that merge and synchronize all of these functions. Addresses and contacts are hugely important, and utilizing the ability of these programs to classify and label your addresses can give you access to a large and very important bank of contacts and names. Never lose a chance to record a name, address, phone number and email, 'tagged' with a short reminder of who your contact is, what they do and why or how you met them – you never know when it will be useful.

Have an updated school student/parent list, with phone numbers, on your PDA.

Using password-accessible online diaries (for example, the facility offered by Google) allows your secretary to manage your diary and meetings, and can also allow your colleagues to see when you are free.

I have not found a really good diary program that combines the Gregorian and the Jewish calendar without affecting the data transmission abilities of 'Outlook'. There are several Jewish calendar programs available (I use 'Kaluach') which you can run simultaneously on your desktop.

4.7.4 Student and other school records.

Your school should be using one of the specialist software programs available in your district for keeping student records[46]. These are increasingly flexible, and, properly used, can be extremely powerful support systems for school Administration. Private schools frequently do not utilize these systems to their full advantage, and smaller schools tend not to use them at all. They offer many features that increase the effectiveness, communication and hence credibility of your school, as well as automating many assessment, scheduling and Report Card functions.

Care has to be taken regarding the confidentiality, access and updating of school records.

Every student in the school should have an individual (physical) file[47]. Setting up the student file should be an automatic part of the admissions procedure. Student files must be conscientiously updated, organized and handled with care. In some places there may be applicable legislation that has to be taken into account, and there is usually student or parental rights of access to school files. A student file must be a record of the student's progress through the school. Its contents must be accurate, and its contents must be fair to the student.

A student file (or a combination of the digital and the physical file) must contain:

- The student's original Application Form for the school. There may also be material from the student's previous school.

- Details of the student's academic record and copies of Report Cards.

- Results of educational testing / psycho-educational testing

---

[46] In some jurisdictions – e.g. Canada – where all schools have a duty to report statistics to the Provincial Education Ministry, only an approved list of programs can be used. Elsewhere, every area has programs tailored to local curriculum systems.

[47] This discussion refers to a formal student file. Portfolios of student work etc. are a different issue. They may be an appreciated part of the school record, but they do not have the same Administrative/legal importance as the student's main file.

- Records of student and parent correspondence with the school relevant to the student's progress and welfare.

- Notes of meetings held with the student and/or parents that are concerned with the student's progress.

- Memos and records from staff, where significant.

- Records of disciplinary incidents involving the student (these may, by agreement, be withdrawn from the file after a reasonable period of time has passed without further disciplinary problems).

- Records of the student's major achievements and distinctions in school.

- Details of medical or other information.

- Other information relevant to the student's welfare and progress.

The file should *not* contain unsubstantiated material that is adverse to the student's name or reputation, or material to which the student has not had a chance to respond. (Examples would be a note from a teacher or another parent stating that they "suspect" the student is in possession of drugs, or a note from a teacher recording that the student was 'suspected' of cheating on an assignment). Some material may be periodically 'weeded' or removed, at the discretion of Administration or at the request of the student or parents. Minor misdemeanors committed in Grade 9 should not still be in a student's file in grade 12. On the other hand, a serious misdemeanor in Grade 9 or Grade 10, or a perceptive comment by a teacher, may be very useful and informative in assessing a situation involving a student in Grade 12.

Student files are consulted for a variety of reasons, which may include:

- Teachers wishing to learn 'background' on a particular student

- Administration referring to a student file in assessing a new situation involving a student, or in responding to a parental concern

- Writing a reference for a student for another school, a University or College application, a prize or scholarship, or a job.

When a student leaves, files should be reviewed and material that is no longer useful or appropriate should be shredded.

Files of graduates should be kept on school premises for a year or so, and should then be securely stored, with reasonable possibility of access. Some schools store for a period of time (7 years); but student files should be stored permanently. There are legal standards in some jurisdictions.

4.7.5 Staff personal files

Correct practice is that all employees – including non-teaching staff – should have a personal (sometimes called 'personnel') file. These, too, must be kept safely and in complete privacy, and there are almost certainly legislative requirements regarding employee files with which the school must comply. If you are uncertain about the legal requirements, a local Human Relations professional or a labor lawyer will advise you. A file should be opened as soon as employment is agreed. Files may be kept in the Principal's office or in the office of the Vice-Principal who has direct supervisory responsibility for that member of staff. The Principal keeps the personal files of Administrators, and the CFO/Executive Director of non-academic staff. The School President should hold the official 'Personal file' of the Principal.

Staff personal files represent a record of employment and performance on which someone's livelihood may depend. It is absolutely in the interests both of the school and the teacher that the personal file be comprehensive. In most jurisdictions, a teacher (or any employee) has the right to examine his/her file, usually on giving reasonable notice to the employer and at a reasonable time and place.

Normally, a teacher is informed when a copy of a document is being placed in their file, and, if necessary, is given an opportunity to comment or respond to that document. The response should be filed with the original.

Personal files may include the following documentation:

- The teacher's resume, including copies of certificates and other relevant personal and professional documentation.

- Documents relating to the application and employment of the teacher, including references, a Letter of Appointment and, if applicable, Job description.

- Copies of all Performance reviews / Professional Evaluations, together with the teacher's comments.

- Records of courses and Professional Development attended by the teacher.

- Records of outstanding service by the teacher – for example, in sports coaching, supervising extra-curricular activities, arranging a celebration or activity in connection with a Jewish Festival, for outstanding work on a staff committee, or in connection with an individual student.

- Correspondence, notes and memos between the teacher and the school, including both letters of commendation and disciplinary communications.

- Copies or originals of letters of compliment or reasonable complaints received by the school about the teacher. Letters of complaint must not be filed unless they have been discussed with the teacher and the teacher has been given the right of response – a record of which should be attached to the original letter in the file.

- Any other material relevant to the teacher's employment and performance as a member of staff.

The teacher may request that copies of positive documents be placed in his or her file, which the school should be glad to do. Conversely, teachers must always be given the opportunity to respond to negative letters, notes or emails. It is then the Administration's judgment as to whether or not such communications – with the response - should be placed in the teacher's file. Staff files are consulted in a variety of benign circumstances – when considering promotion, or when writing a reference for a teacher who wishes to move on.

However, if you ever wish to terminate a teacher's employment SEE SECTION 10.3 the file will become critical. Except where the proposed termination is clearly and indisputably 'For cause', if your school is unionized you will almost certainly face a grievance. If it is not, you will almost certainly face the threat, if not the actuality, of legal action. Under these circumstances, the teacher's personal file, and the 'paper trail' that you have accumulated may well be the decisive factor in substantiating the case for dismissal. If the file is well maintained, the record is there, and you can be seen to have followed 'fair process' (advice, warning, 'progressive discipline') – you are on much stronger ground. If there is no record, or a skimpy record – the issue becomes one of "He said /she said". The file may be equally critical to establish the positive record of a teacher if that teacher is facing aberrational or unjustified criticism. In all cases, the paper trail is crucial, and must be properly maintained.

Finally, a personal file is a valuable tool in discussing performance with a teacher. Everyone has a tendency to highlight the good in their own memory, and suppress the bad. Sitting with a teacher and pointing out that over a period of years certain patterns of behavior have recurred, as documented, provides an objective record with which it is hard to argue.

4.7.6 Anonymous letters

Anonymous letters, emails or phone messages – whomever or whatever they concern - must be treated very carefully. In most cases, they should be ignored and/or immediately shredded / deleted. They must not be given credence.

Nevertheless, there is some information, even if anonymous, which the Principal cannot ignore. An allegation that a member of staff is having improper relationships with a student, or that a student is in physical or moral danger, cannot be ignored and must be appropriately investigated. No direct allegations should be made based on anonymous information that is not separately, and properly, corroborated, but explanations may be requested.

> *Jack – this may be an uncomfortable conversation. I have to let you know that the school received an anonymous message yesterday, alleging [X..Y..Z]. Is there anything you wish to share with me – either about the alleged incident or the circumstances of the message?*

Legal advice on how to proceed may be needed.

Anonymous letters must never be placed in a teacher's file, unless the allegations have been fully and independently substantiated (in which case the full record of the investigation, and the credible substantiating material, will be included).

4.7.7 Financial and accounting information

SEE SECTION 15.1   Financial and accounting records of the school should be maintained in accordance with the applicable professional and legal standards, as overseen by the school treasurer, the Budget and Finance Committee and the school Auditors.

4.7.8 Security and confidentiality

School files – both physical and digital – must be securely protected. Do not keep physical files in an open office or anywhere else where unauthorized personnel (or students...) may access them. File cabinets should be lockable and secure. Encourage staff to shred anything remotely confidential that is otherwise going to be thrown away. Be warned that unauthorized access to confidential school documents will cause havoc.

Get expert advice on how to protect Administration computers, from 'hacking' (at which teenagers are expert). If you have a student-accessible network (in a computer lab or the school library, or if your school is wired or wi-fied) – ensure that there is a complete separation (physical and electronic) between student and staff computers.

Make sure – doubly sure – that your data is frequently BACKED UP[48].

---

[48] No apologies for repeating this particular piece of advice!

4.8 Communications

4.8.1 Communicating school values

The overall image that the school projects to the school 'family', to prospective parents and to the outside community is extremely important. It predisposes the way that everyone acts towards the school. That image is transmitted by every expression of the school – in print, in the deportment of the Administration and staff, by the appearance and activity in the school building itself, and by the credibility of the communications of the school.

Communications – whether in print, email or any other medium – should be clear, accurate and short. They should reflect the dignity of the school. It is worth investing in graphic artists and similar professionals – the difference in appearance and quality in even the smallest print item is striking. Text must be free of spelling and grammatical mistakes.

The positive qualities of the school should be consistently projected. That does not mean that the school should seek to project an inaccurate or untrue image. That will quickly be perceived, and will give the school an undesirable reputation for professing to be one thing, but in practice not living up to its image. But there is nothing wrong, and a great deal right, in effectively building a positive school image, allowing everyone connected with the school to be proud of the school, its values and its achievements – especially the achievements of the students, both individually and collectively. It will help when the school has to make occasional difficult decisions.

4.8.2 Within the school

Communications and sharing of information are essential to a healthy organization. Apart from its obvious benefit of people being updated on what they could, or should, be doing, there is a reassuring quality when there is a flow of useful information and news. In a professional sense[49], a flow of information is also stimulating.

There should be a short weekly newsletter to staff – by paper or email. In some schools there is a weekly short meeting in the staff room during recess (incentive in the form of 'Danish' usually increases attendance!). Let teachers know what is happening in and around the school – decisions taken by the Board that will affect them, interesting activities and achievements. Incorporate thoughts, teachings, thanks, congratulations, tips, aphorisms, links to interesting websites – according to inclination and choice. Copy the weekly newsletter by email to Board members.

From time to time, there are issues of substance and/or controversy to communicate to staff. Such communications should be quick, clear and succinct. If communicated

---

[49] Management guru Henry Mintzberg once stated that "Management is the art of disseminating the right information to the right people", on another occasion ('Managing', 2009, p. 55) succinctly stating: "Like bees: managers cross-pollinate".

verbally, follow it with a notice or memo in writing. Give the facts, and the reasons behind decisions (if applicable). Invite staff to come and discuss the issue with the Principal personally, if they wish. Do not let news or decisions 'trickle out'; decide who needs to know, and take care in planning the announcement. Do not allow rumor or speculation to flourish.

Most important – the school must always, always be honest. If the background to certain news cannot be divulged, simply say so:

> *Staff, parents and Board will be aware of an incident at the school on Monday last. Consequently, a student has left the school. The school has conducted a thorough investigation into the events which lead up to this incident, and we are satisfied that it may now be regarded as closed. For reasons of the confidentiality of some of those involved, we regret that we cannot divulge any further details. Parents who have concerns are invited to call the Principal at the school office.*

Trust is one of the school's most important assets. Don't squander it.

4.8.3 Conveying difficult decisions to the school community

From time to time, the Principal will have to announce difficult decisions – perhaps personnel decisions, or budget-driven decisions, or simply school operational decisions that are going to be unpopular.

There is no easy way of doing this. Begin by warning the audience – in speech or in writing – that you have a difficult message to convey. Give the message plainly, simply, and truthfully. Do not over-elaborate; express appropriate emotions without exaggeration. If you cannot give full details, say so. Don't be humorous. Offer concerned individuals a chance to discuss the issue with you privately.

If the decision, or news, is likely to be really difficult, controversial or traumatic – consider taking the advice of a PR Consultant – SEE SECTION 4.9.6

4.8.4 Conveying difficult decisions to individuals

Communicating difficult decisions to individuals is often more stressful[50] than communicating to a larger group. The most difficult are:

- Terminating employees

- Expelling students

- Declining students who are seeking places at your school

None of these decisions can ever be easy, and they need to be conveyed clearly, but with great care and sensitivity. Remember always that the decision being conveyed

---

[50] The Principal should always have a box of tissues strategically positioned on the opposite side of his/her desk.

may have huge consequences on the lives of the people most affected, and on their families. It is never easy, and if a Principal does ever find it easy, s/he should be worried.

Some guidelines for the Principal include:

- Never hold these meetings[51] by yourself. Ask a senior colleague (or if appropriate a senior Board member) to participate in the meeting with you. Your colleague should take notes. If the colleague is part of the meeting, ask a third party to take notes, which when typed up may be shared with all present. (The only exception to this would be necessary 'one-on-one' conversations with senior and close colleagues.)

- Prepare the meeting well in advance. If documentation is needed, have it ready, in the necessary number of copies.

- Carefully prepare what has to be said, and how you are going to say it. If an employee is to be terminated, consult the school's labor lawyer before the meeting. If some sort of settlement is to be offered, make sure you have the details available at the meeting. Make sure you have information regarding the rights of the person with whom you are meeting, and that you advise them carefully of their rights; and of where they can turn for help and advice.

- Consider the time and place of the meeting. If possible, avoid giving traumatic news at times that will impinge especially badly on family or personal life. Give thought to what is going to happen immediately after the meeting. If you have to give serious, possibly traumatic news to an individual or a family, will they be able to travel home? Will they have to walk out through a crowded office or crowded school corridors? In some circumstances, people may need to be escorted from the premises.

- Speak directly, quietly, and allow the recipients of your decision time to 'vent'. State the decision, and try not to get into rationalization or explanation. If pressed, simply restate the decision quietly and state that the decision is unfortunately not open to review.

- Keep control of the meeting.

---

[51] Or, for that matter any meeting that is sensitive, and likely to become a point of contention, challenge or possible legal action.

- If needed, afterwards confirm or summarize the content of the meeting in writing, including any decisions taken.

4.8.5 Rumors

Schools are the subject of rumors; private schools more so, and schools that are part of close-knit communities particularly so. Rumors, even if absurd, can be poisonous and destructive to individuals, to families and even to the school as an institution.

The parent parking lot, the local synagogues, and the local supermarkets are fertile ground for rumors. Given contemporary technology, rumors can spread throughout the school community in minutes. You cannot stop rumors, but you can try and minimize their occurrence and their effect by doing the following:

- At Parents' meetings (including – especially – meetings of prospective parents) and Board meetings the Principal should make it clear that s/he and the Administration are always happy to answer questions about the school – however minor they may sound. If any parent, at any time, hears rumors about the school that concern them – ask them to please call and find out the facts.

- Board members, who are ambassadors for the school, must take care never to even appear to be confirming rumors. If asked a question to which they do not know the answer they should clearly say that they do not know – and not reply "Well, I haven't heard that ….", or agree because they do not wish to appear to be uninformed. Then they should both encourage the questioner to call the school; and call the school themselves.

- If reports of dangerous rumors reach the Principal ("The school is closing three classes …. Last week they found drugs and hushed it up …. They have no applications for next year ….. One of the teachers has been arrested … One of the students was trafficking drugs in the school canteen..") – try and track a source. The Principal should call the person/people in whose name the rumor is being repeated, respectfully but firmly put them right – and ask them to personally correct the information with anyone to whom they remember repeating the rumor. Put a notice in the staff room. Send an email to your Board:

"Some Board members may have heard a rumor currently circulating among parents that ……….. The facts are as follows: …………. Please counter the rumor firmly if you hear it repeated. Please don't hesitate to call any of the Administrators if you require further clarification, and please tell other parents that they can do so as well."

- If the rumor is persistent – consider putting a short notice on the school website (take it down after a week), or even writing to or emailing parents.

- If students are spreading the rumor ("I was doing car pool this morning, and I heard one of the students in the back saying that ….") speak to them directly. If they are spreading rumors by email – they are contravening a school rule.

- Occasionally, you may find that a member of staff is spreading rumors. An employee has a professional and legal duty to be an 'employee in good faith'. They may disagree with school decisions or policies, appropriately and within school professional forums; but they do not have the freedom to undermine the school to students, parents, or others outside the school, or to defame or make disparaging remarks about the school or any of its employees or lay leaders. A teacher may not discuss his or her dissatisfaction with school policies with either students or parents. If they do so, they are in clear breach of professional behavior, and should be called in and, if necessary, disciplined.

As in all communications, the school's credibility in denying rumors depends on its general credibility and reputation for honesty.

It always pays to be factual and open to all of your constituencies. Unfortunately, the school is at an immediate disadvantage to rumor-mongers, as they are free and unaccountable to say whatever they want. The school is accountable for every word.

- Do not succumb to the temptation to explain the rumor and its background if it means breaking confidentiality or professional/ethical standards.

The sad, exasperating reality is that rumors, like conspiracy theories, have an irrational life of their own. Many otherwise sensible parents, students, staff and community members will prefer to believe a rumor than the truth; and many will instinctively stand in 'solidarity' with their peer(s) who are being 'persecuted' by the school Administration. Whatever means the school takes to counter the rumor will inevitably give it further credence in some quarters. While many parents will find any explanation from the school reassuring, others will find the communication problematic. SEE ALSO SECTION 15.5.5

4.8.6 The school website

School websites vary greatly in scope and complexity. They need careful design, and they need constant updating. The larger the website – the more it needs keeping up to date. In general, it is probably better to have the website current than to have it look stunning, but outdated.

There are two varieties of school websites.

- The first is the public 'shop window', there to give information to prospective parents and community. When commissioning a new website, have the decision-making group look at as many websites of other local (or competitor, or similar) schools as possible, and decide in general terms what you want to incorporate on yours. Draw up an outline specification, and ask four or five web-designers to give presentations to your committee of work that they have done, and their general ideas of what they could do for you. Make sure that the website can be edited, updated and added to by the school, so that a teacher, or secretary, can always post news and images on the website. You should not have to call your web designers (and pay) for routine changes and updates. Do not ever allow students to have access codes.

- The second website – effectively an 'intranet' -- is interactive, and can be a powerful tool in the school's communication between staff, students and parents. Information is hierarchied and protected. Commonly, students, staff and parents are assigned unique passwords which control their access. These programs and services are usually remotely hosted[52], and the school pays a yearly fee. They offer the possibility to post and access assignments, marks, news and much other information, allowing teachers to send and receive email to all of their classes, coaches to send information to sports teams, and the school office to email many different groups within the school. These are very popular programs, which greatly facilitate communication (and, properly used, can save a school a lot of money in printing and postage). The biggest problem in introducing these programs is staff training.

4.8.7 The School Magazine – editorial issues

Every school publishes a school magazine for parents, alumni and other 'friends of the school'. These range from photocopied occasional newssheets to highly professional, full-color productions. In the main, they are 'shop-window' publications, designed to publicize life and times in the school, calendar occasions, and news of students, parents, staff and alumni. In some cases, there is a strong fund-raising content.

---

[52] Increasingly their features are found integrated into comprehensive school management/administration programs, together with fund-raising and a range of financial management modules.

The school magazine can be a powerful vehicle of 'feel-good' public relations – holding the school community together and engendering ongoing school spirit. In many cases, dedicated volunteers will manage the editorial and production of the publication – occasionally there may be a professional editor, internal (on staff) or external (contracted). School magazines and newsletters typically appear between two and four times per year.

> *"But even the apparently innocuous school magazine, filled with pictures of happy students, teachers, parents and Alumni, can generate problems"* - SEE SECTION 8.2.5

4.8.8 Student publications

- **Just make sure that there is a sensible, alert staff member who is there to supervise....**

In some ways, student publications are part of the system of 'safety valves' in a school. Allow controversy *as long as it is expressed appropriately and respectfully.* Do not, under any circumstances, allow student publications to undermine teachers. (Students who have issues with a teacher should have other avenues to express concerns.) Occasionally, student publications will go over the limits. Take each case individually. Unless the content is really outrageous, tend towards tolerance.

Student Yearbooks need special supervision. Ensure that nothing is published which is hurtful to students or staff. Keep a close eye on content, including advertisements. Discourage excess that makes the book more expensive (*"Last year they had eight color pages – we'll have sixteen!"*).

4.8.9 The School Annual report

Every Board should issue an Annual Report to parents and community. Usually, these are issued in the Fall following the year under review, timed either to coincide with School opening, with Rosh Hashanah, or with the Annual General Meeting of the school.

As a minimum, the Report should contain:

- Report of the President

- Report of the Principal

- Summaries of the work of each Board Committee

- A summary of the Financial Report and accounts

- Recognition of donors and supporters of the school

Other material can be added without limit, including an annual record of school achievements and activities.

However, an Annual Report should first and foremost reflect a sense of accountability by the Board to the parent body.

4.8.10   Communications in times of crisis

SEE SECTION 15.5.5

4.9 Consultants and external resources

4.9.1 When should the school use an external consultant?

> *An external consultant should bring uninvolved, objective, short-term professional expertise to the school, to the Board, or to the Principal as leader and manager. Only think of engaging an outside consultant when you are sure that they are providing expertise that you cannot access or develop from within the school.*

Carefully chosen and carefully used – the keys to a successful exercise - consultants and external resources can be very useful. Commonly used consultants include Personnel/Human Resources consultants, Governance consultants, Management/Organizational consultants, and Curriculum Consultants. Strategic Planning Consultants are discussed in SECTION 5.1.1.

External consultants are brought in to address academic and non-academic issues. If the school seems to be in overall difficulties, the Board may invite a wide-ranging 'School Review' – see SECTION 5.1.3 .

It is possible to spend a lot of money on a Consultant and end up with a frustrating experience. Do not commit to a long-term contract without thoroughly testing the services first, and insist on 'let out' clauses in any agreement.

4.9.2 Managerial and organizational consultants

External management or organizational consultants may be considered in situations where:

- Areas of school organization are not functioning, and it is not clear why.

- There are symptoms of organizational dysfunction that cannot be explained (e.g. high staff absenteeism, high rates of seemingly minor parental complaints).

- The Administrative 'team' has broken down

- There is ongoing tension between the Administration (including the Principal) and the Board

- Where major change or transition is to take place, which is likely to be controversial, and/or which is going to affect key staff.

- Where individual senior colleagues are having difficulties[53] that are impeding their performance (for example, anger issues, or inability to negotiate with colleagues or parents) and which you have been unable to deal with.

There are many individual managerial and organizational consultants available, coming from very different backgrounds (e.g. financial, psychological, organizational, business), and, it has to be said, of very varied expertise. They have to be researched very carefully, and full references taken from others who have used them[54]. To be avoided are the 'jack-of-all-trades' "Consultants", who are basically motivational speakers. They will assure you that they can deal with any problems you present.

The expertise sought by the school is that which enables the team to become better leaders and managers, and it has to judge when and how these resources may be used or invited into the school. Utilizing such expertise properly is a sign of managerial maturity, not a sign of weakness. The Board should recognize it as such, and provide the budget where necessary[55].

A consultant may be employed to work with an individual or a group within the school. Sometimes, an hour or so of one-on-one conversation will give enough insight and ideas to enable a situation to be viewed completely differently, and give direction of how to go forward. It will not be at the same level of sophistication as if the professional was working longer-term in the school – but it has the very great advantage that it is incrementally, and irreversibly, adding to the 'bank' of the school's 'managerial intelligence'. A new Principal, or a Principal facing a particularly

---

[53] If a staff member – whoever they are – have emotional, mental health, medical or substance abuse problems (including alcoholism) consult as soon as possible with the Personnel Committee and labour lawyer for strategic advice. The school's first duty is to its students.

[54] Some problems can be solved by sending school leaders (professional and lay) on short two-three day management courses, covering issues like 'Team Building', 'Decision Making', 'Strategic Planning', 'Emotional intelligence in the workplace' and similar topics. They are not magic, they are short, and they are normally aimed at middle management; but school Administrators have often never been exposed to management thinking, and they can be very useful in allowing school leaders exposure to different ways of organising themselves and their work. The insights are always valuable. There are also much more complex MBA (or similar) courses offered by business schools which are long and very expensive. Some advocate their usefulness.

[55] Depending on circumstances, there may be parents or former parents who are, for example, organisational consultants, and who are willing to volunteer a reasonable amount of time to the school. My experience is that parents are delighted that the school thinks of utilising their expertise (which both legitimises them, and also signals forward and professional thinking on the part of the school). As professionals, they can usually be trusted to separate their parental and professional roles.

difficult period in the school, may consult an 'Executive Coach' (in another guise, a professional mentor) for a period of time[56].

4.9.3 Consulting on Board Governance and Process

While outside the purview of this book, many school Boards engage organizational consultants who specialize in 'Not-for-profit' consulting, normally to help them clarify their role in the correct Governance of their organizations. Such exercises may lead to revision of the Constitution and restructuring of the Board – hopefully in a way that makes them a more effective Board, leading a better school.

4.9.4 Legal consultants

Given our litigious age, and the increasing vulnerability of schools to legal challenge on several different fronts, access to expert legal advice is essential to a School Principal. A small school may not need to access such advice more than once a year; in a large school it may be much more frequent.

Nowadays, the complexity of legal issues surrounding schools is intense. Specialist knowledge is needed[57]. The list of efficient, authoritative and sympathetic lawyers should be kept easily accessible.

Legal issues in schools generally revolve around the following areas:

- Property issues – the school premises

- Labor law – employees, contracts, and, unfortunately, issues of harassment and discrimination.

- Family law – issues with family conflicts, divorce, custody, access and child care

- Education law – the school's legal duties to its students; admissions and re-registration; school discipline, including suspensions and expulsions; students and the State / Federal law.

---

[56] If the Board suggests this, the Principal should overcome the defensive urge to reject the suggestion, and accept it. It means that the Board wish to strengthen his/her performance. Caution has to be exercised, and the Principal has to have confidence in the nominated Consultant. The terms of reference under which the Consultant has been engaged also have to be clear; what is their mandate, to whom do they report, and is any report going back to the Board? If the Principal is to confide in the consultant, interactions must be completely – but completely – confidential.

[57] The traditional response when a school needed a lawyer used to be *"Call Morry – he's a lawyer"*. When for the last thirty years, Morry's practice has been exclusively focused on Florida real-estate transactions, 'Morry' - who might otherwise be a wonderful *mentsch* - is no longer sufficient.

Use a lawyer to preview sensitive correspondence or important school documents. Consulting with a lawyer before difficult meetings with parents or staff, and employing the tactics suggested, can raise the school's perceived level of authority and responsibility – and avoid a great deal of trouble. It also ensures that you are dealing with all of your constituencies in a fair and responsible manner.

4.9.5 Curriculum consultants

A school may decide that curriculum consultants are needed to rewrite sections of the school curriculum, to adapt an existing curriculum to the particular needs of your school, or to ensure compliance with accreditation (or other external) requirements.

Curriculum Consultants - General Studies

Curriculum development for General Studies is a long and carefully managed process (whether sponsored commercially or by a School Board or other government body), lasting years, involving teams of teachers and extensive classroom testing. Material may go through numerous drafts. The final scheme may include provision for extensive teacher training. Budgets, especially for 'core subjects', may run into millions of dollars.

In practice, General Studies teachers in a Jewish High School will already be working to established curricula, or will have a choice of commercially available teaching schemes to adopt. It may happen that, for whatever reason, the school is unhappy with the teaching in a particular subject, and will invite an external review – examining the teaching and the curriculum as it is being taught in the school. In some Jewish schools, the time available may be restricted because of the Jewish Studies program, and there is be a need to restructure the teaching to fit the time available. However, it is extremely unlikely that a General Studies review will result in a commission to design a complete, new subject curriculum. That would be a very extreme and expensive decision.

If the subject(s) under review are in General Studies, and for some reason a school-specific 'fine tuning' is needed, there is normally ample local expertise available. It should not take more than a few telephone calls to locate it. Frequently, your own staff will be able to suggest someone from their knowledge of the local teachers' 'network'. It remains only to specify the task needed and to negotiate a price.

Jewish Studies

See SECTION 7.2 – Designing the program – Shaviv's paradox.

A far different situation exists in all areas of Jewish Studies and Ivrit. For all the reasons discussed at length in this book, and impacting on almost every chapter, the Jewish dimension of the school – the *raison d'être* of our system – is also the most difficult to manage. This is no less true in the area of curriculum development and curriculum consultants.

Here there are few, if any, available templates[58], and the external resources are thin on the ground. Except in the very largest communities, they are rarely local, often overseas or on the other side of the continent, and usually very expensive in relation to a single school's budget. It is always tempting for a Board to look to the outside for salvation, coupled with the seductive idea that if it is expensive – and curriculum development can carry six-figure costs – it must be something that will solve the problem.

There are few Jewish organizations able to invest in development at that scale, and there is no apparent commercial market for High School Jewish Studies materials. Even if a system of Jewish schools agrees on a curriculum (rare, in my experience, because of the denominational differences), there can be significant resistance at local level.

> Rabbi X has been teaching the same Chumash class for forty years, and won't change. In fact, he has support on the Board from members whom he taught, and whose children he is now teaching.

Attempts to really grapple with the issues and teach classic texts in innovative ways may be met in some circles with fear of changing 'the traditional way of teaching Torah'[59]. Finally, the notions of 'Curriculum', 'teaching materials' and – especially – assessment and evaluation are increasingly specialized. It is a rare personality or team who can combine the requisite depth of subject knowledge with the up to date pedagogic expertise, and who can produce materials that will be consonant with the best that students are used to having in general Studies.

Until, and unless, someone creates a 'North American Centre for Jewish High School Education', choices for a school seeking Curriculum consultants for Jewish Studies are limited. At the time of writing, they are the following:

OPTION 'A": **The Israeli option** – Several Israeli universities have faculties or linked institutes (the Melton Centre at the HU, the Lookstein Institute at Bar-Ilan) that will undertake contract curriculum work. In addition, several other equally

---

[58] While there have been some interesting isolated initiatives (for example, in Talmud teaching), at the time of writing, the only really comprehensive curriculum initiative relevant to the High School is the NETA program. NETA is attempting to develop a generic curriculum for High School Ivrit. While its content and methodology have their supporters and detractors, the initiative must be admired. A similar comment applies to the Elementary school Tel-Am program.

[59] This was apparently the fate of one of the truly excellent curriculum ventures – the 'Tanakh Sheli' course pioneered and authored by Rabbi Professor Dr. Barry Levy of McGill University in the late 1990's. The material taught skills, not content. It was brilliant (in my view) but could not get past the question of 'How many perakim do the students cover?'. A similar reaction met my own efforts, much more modest and less accomplished, in introducing innovative methodology in teaching beginners' Talmud in London, earlier in the decade. The classic case of resistance to methodological innovation was/is the reaction in some circles to the Steinsaltz Talmud.

reputable institutions (for example, The Hartman Institute, Oranim, and the Jewish Agency) will work with schools or groups of schools. The advantages of working with any Israeli institution is that their personnel are usually outstanding, and frequently themselves former education professionals who have made *aliyyah*.

Disadvantages of the 'Israeli option' include:

- These contracts can be enormously expensive (distance alone adds greatly to the cost) – usually more than a single school can justify

- The writers of the material are not on site in your school, and simply may not be able to 'meet the students where they are' – in any sense

- It is sometimes difficult to get a cultural, methodological or ideological 'fit' with the local community or local classroom.

- The material meets with resistance from local teachers, who may not have (= probably do not have) the same pedagogical training, background and approach as the authors of the material. Training your teachers is expensive and often impractical (few teachers can go to month-long summer schools in Israel for two or three years running; and new teachers will need fresh induction training in the material)

- The time demanded to teach the materials 'properly' may be way ahead of the teaching time available[60]

- Especially in Tanakh and Rabbinics, the (enviable) level of expertise of Israeli-trained teachers and students simply does not exist in the Diaspora.

- In some communities (the UK and Canada, for example), where courses are externally accredited, the material has to conform to local educational method, and allow for assessment and evaluation that is uniform to local pedagogy.

---

[60] Many years ago, at a school where I was Director of Jewish Studies, a well-known Israeli/American educational personality presented a teaching scheme for teaching the Jewish calendar, in which several hundreds of thousands of dollars had been invested. The first few units dealt with the mathematics of the calendar, and would have taken twenty or thirty classroom hours to teach, even if the average teacher was able to teach the math involved. The booklet contained some forty more chapters, each of which would take several hours teaching, totalling some two hundred hours. It was a wonderfully thorough treatment of that important subject – but it took no account of the constraints of the school. The time allocated to the subject in the existing school curriculum (for better or worse) was – three hours.

OPTION 'B" – The local option: Sometimes a school will contract with a local resource – a retired Administrator, a local Rabbi, a local University professor or even a Graduate student – to write curriculum. For all the reasons detailed in the introduction to this section, in Option 'A', and more, it rarely works. The results are often abandoned after a short time.

* * * * *

Is there an answer? However imperfect, there is a realistic option which is relatively low budget and which can work if the school and the Administration persevere. This has the advantage of probably 'fitting' the school very well; its disadvantage is the same, which is that the final product is unlikely to be useable in other schools. Yet reality demands that the school needs a curriculum. This is Option 'C'.

OPTION 'C' -School-developed curriculum, incrementally improved – there are two possible models.

Model #1: A large school, or one that has a highly experienced staff, may simply devise a curriculum development program using its own staff, with a team leader (key to the success of the project) and appropriate technical support. For this to be successful, it should probably be a project scheduled for vacations, and involve separate payments for the writers and authors of the project. Year by year, staff may comment and give feedback on the curriculum in the light of experience having actually taught it. Digital technology makes it relatively easy to produce and update material, teachers' guides and other supporting material. The result will not be as lavish as the curriculum and teaching materials for Physics or Eng Lit, but it will be the best you can do under the circumstances, and your teachers should be enthusiastic participants in the project.

Model #2: Not every school will have the expertise to mount that sort of internally directed project. A good alternative is to hire a local curriculum development specialist – who need not be Jewish, and who need not know anything about Judaism or Hebrew, but must know local curriculum standards – and have that specialist work with your Jewish Studies teachers. All members of the team should be paid for their work. (Curriculum development, when done properly, unless specified in a Job Description, is beyond normal teaching duties). The specialist supplies skills, structure, procedure and methodology; the teachers supply content. For most teachers, this will be an enriching experience, and will immeasurably improve their teaching and professional expertise. There will be a pride in school achievement. There will be a steady incremental improvement in the JS curriculum materials as a result.

4.9.6 PR / Communications Consultants

Most schools will use professional advice in their ongoing recruitment advertising, in constructing the school website and perhaps in 'feeding' news and photos of school events and activities to local news media. There are occasions when the advice needed is of a different nature, and goes beyond any of the above categories. These are when the school suddenly finds itself under intense public or community scrutiny – for good reason or bad.

Typical issues that trigger that sort of situation may include:

- **Crisis:** A major incident occurs at the school. See also SECTION 15.5.5

- **Problems with neighbors:** the school announces major redevelopment plans, or announces purchase of a new campus, and neighbors object.

- **Scandal:** involving students, teachers (or students and teachers) or prominent school Board members or contributors.

- **Scare:** a security or other safety/health-related incident occurs at the school.

- **Rumor:** a particularly damaging rumor or 'everyone knows' discussion about the school spreads in your community, and won't go away.

- **Change:** a major transition is imminent in the life of the school (e.g. a major Administrative appointment, or the departure of a 'stalwart' teacher).

- **Competition / threat:** the opening of a new, competing school (Jewish or non-Jewish).

- **Enrolment:** a whole group of students leave the school, and provoke a crisis of confidence.

In times of stress, where the school's credibility and perhaps integrity is on the line, a wrong phrase used by someone to the local TV news reporter can haunt the school for years to come. If the parent body feels the school 'tried to cover up the whole incident' you will suffer in the future from the loss of trust. If the image persists that 'the school can't even get its best students into good colleges' – then some parents will hesitate before sending their children, or will pull them out after Grade 10.

There may be times when the school is clearly losing ground, and you need serious market research to understand how your school is perceived among its present and potential parents, in order to plan a different recruitment campaign.

In all of these situations, you need to engage high-level communications consultants, who can give guidance on the messages that the school should be sending, right down to giving you the best phraseology to use, and the right media and images needed to get that message across. This is not 'spin', and it is not trying to hide the truth. It is using the experience of others to identify what you want to say, and what you *need* to say, and then ensuring that it gets across without ill-chosen communication making the situation even worse, and creating secondary problems.

It may take a few phone calls, but locating the consultants used by corporations, public bodies (and even politicians) will be exceptionally helpful in getting through difficult times.

- The best times to locate (and get to know) such professionals are the calm, uneventful times BEFORE any event has taken place, or 'news' has broken! 'Pro-active' is much easier than 'damage control'.

5 THE INSTRUMENTS OF CHANGE

5.1 Challenges

During the life of the school it will move through several different phases. An alert institution will position itself in each stage to be ready to meet the needs of its students and their families. That is much better than having to 'catch up' in a panic because the school has fallen behind. Schools do not fare well in panic mode. The ability of the school to continually morph depends on:

- Quality of vision – educational and ideological

- Ability to recognize challenges

- Quality of planning, data, and research

- Ability to adapt and change

In all of these, the role of the Principal is critical.

The social, technological, cultural and moral changes in general society that have taken place during the memories of every reader of this book are huge. Equivalent changes and challenges have taken place in the Jewish community worldwide[61], and continue to develop. (The exceptionally serious rise in anti-Semitism, fuelled by militant Islam, is likely to be the largest item on the Jewish community agenda for decades to come.)

Schools, as educational institutions dealing with young people, cannot ignore those challenges – if they do, they will quickly become irrelevant. A school must recognize

---

[61] For example, who, twenty or thirty years ago, would have predicted that the issue of same-sex marriage would constitute a serious classroom topic in Jewish day schools? Whether your school chooses to oppose or endorse the idea – it is there in your classroom.

and deal with change – or it will decline. That does not mean – it definitely does not mean – that schools must embrace or approve of *every* change. But they must recognize challenges and deal with them. Some current major challenges affecting Jewish schools include:

- Cultural and educational change brought about by digital technology

- The changing nature of the suburban Jewish family

- The decline of the synagogue and the rise in importance of the Jewish day school

- Rising costs of Tuition fees in a context of economic crisis

- Trends towards religious polarization, and the subsequent fragmentation of the Jewish school system

- Competition from the non-Jewish private school sector

- Increasing parental demands for special needs and other services in Jewish schools.

- Changing demographics in the Jewish world – locally and globally.

- Increasing pressure on 'Ivy league' College entrance as a measure of school success.

- Polarization in Israeli society and its effect on Diaspora-Israel links.

- The necessity of bringing North America's large ex-FSU and Israeli-born Jewish populations into the Jewish educational system.

- Security and safety concerns, linked to rising anti-Semitism.

- Problems of teacher supply, especially in Jewish Studies

Whatever the issue, it means change in your school.

Schools are notoriously conservative institutions, to a degree insulated[62] from some of the pressures of the 'real' world. But *'If it isn't broken, don't fix it*[63] is a deadly

---

[62] There may be merit in the suggestion that some school personnel gravitate to education for precisely that reason.

[63] The full, and depressing speech goes something like: "We've never done it that way. We don't need it. No one wants it. It won't work. I'm not doing it." Whether vocal or silent,

mantra, because by the time 'it' breaks, you may have lost the ability or opportunity for repair, and your rivals – other schools, Jewish or non-Jewish – will have pulled ahead. And you will have failed your students.

There are many books written about organizational change. They are in the same section of the bookshop as the books on leadership, management and marketing[64]. There are some overall principles - the notions of preparation, 'buy-in' and 'ownership' are crucial for success. The ability to lead and effect change is a major quality of leadership.

Change involves planning. A school may enter into a **Strategic Planning process;** it may institute a conscious process of **Incremental Improvement;** as a precursor to either of these two, or without connection, it may commission an external **School Review.** Each of these mechanisms, with their differences, advantages and disadvantages, is discussed following.

5.1.1 Strategic planning

Some schools formulate 'Strategic Plans', with the help of (often expensive) outside consultants. It needs very careful consideration to avoid the common result of many such exercises, which is to generate a document that is expensively printed, immediately irrelevant, and is never implemented.

Two crucial considerations are always:

- Do your consultants have a proven track record of effectiveness with similar institutions and constituencies to your own; and do they have the capacity to really understand your school?

- Is your school ready for such a plan, and does it have the means and the will to implement it?

Strategic Plans are good ways of focusing the thinking of a wide range of 'stakeholders' of the school onto its future challenges, and the way in which the school needs to 'position itself' to meet them effectively. There is a great value in the exercise, because without strategic thinking the school will always be lurching from crisis to crisis, and will always find itself either reacting to trends and events - 'putting out fires' the whole time. This is stressful and often wasteful. In theory, a strategic plan gives the school a three, five or seven-year plan for its operations.

---

every organisation – including every staff room - has a constituency of passive-aggressive 'spoilers'. The theory of group dynamics, especially the theory devised by Wilfred Bion ([1897-1979]) suggests that every 'group' (two or more people) invariably include a number of common 'role players', who, consciously or not, fulfil recognizable dynamic influences, positive and negative.

[64] A good Principal will know that section very well.

The phrase 'strategic planning' has a certain seductive quality. However, there can be major practical problems with strategic planning, which may include:

- Changing variables - a school President may change; the Principal may move on; an unforeseen capital expenditure may mean that the budget doesn't balance, forcing retrenchment. All are unpredictable, so that what looks like smart planning in Year#1 for Year #5 may be irrelevant or inapplicable by Year #3. Smaller schools are particularly vulnerable to small variables that can totally upset the strategic plan.

- A voluntary organization cannot enforce a plan. Next year's Board may not have been involved at all in the Strategic Planning process. (It probably started three or four years previously). They may decide that they are not going to approve the budget for the new music room or the new Vice-Principal mandated by the Strategic Plan They want to spend the money on a computer lab or a Bet Midrash instead (or not spend it at all).

- The plan itself may call for budget expenditure that the school does not have. Few Strategic Plans come to the conclusion that the school should continue exactly as it is. They tend to suggest appointments, programs, buildings or other (probably very desirable) changes in the school.

- Sometimes a Board will take a Strategic Plan after it is presented and then cut it down, rendering it useless.

So while the focus on the school is useful; the end document may not be quite as practical. But if your school has the human, organizational and financial capacity to go through the Strategic Planning exercise *and then see it through* – it can be an outstanding experience.

5.1.2 Building 'Incremental improvement'

An alternative model is incremental improvement; the continual, deliberate monitoring and fine-tuning of school operations.

In this model, there is an annual review of priorities, involving both professional and lay school leadership. The process should have a gentle, 'rolling forward' perspective of perhaps one, two or three years. This should lead to identifying two or three areas that can be addressed each year.

The Administration should then determine process, which might include a steering committee coordinating a program whose implementation might stretch over more than one year. Additional advantages are that the decisions are more closely tuned to changing circumstances – and, perhaps more importantly, to current resources, financial and human. The effect on the school will be quickly felt. Under the best of circumstances, school culture will naturally adopt a culture of "how can we continually improve?".

It is a less grandiose, but perhaps more effective model that 'Strategic Planning'.

* * * * * *

There are pitfalls in both of these approaches, and as with everything, the golden mean is the desirable position. Diagnosing whether something is 'broken' (i.e. not working, or in need of attention), and the degree of fixing needed, is to a degree subjective. Some areas of school performance, however, are easily measurable – recruitment / retention is an obvious one. It is far better to identify the weak areas *before* urgent attention is needed. If the school don't want change or improvement, band-aid solutions are always attractive, but you end up with a system held together by band-aids. On the other hand, change for the sake of change is extremely foolhardy, and the school community – teachers, students and parents – will not only soon tire of it, but will become frustrated, confused and angry.

Slow, steady, small steps are – most of the time – the natural and good pace. There will be times when radical and far-reaching change will be needed.

5.1.3 School Reviews

The Board may invite an external 'School Review', which examines and assesses the functioning of the school[65]. It is not a strategic plan – it is an evaluative and diagnostic process, sometimes seen as a diagnostic preliminary to the 'Strategic Planning' exercise. The circumstances that can generate this move are varied, including the healthy desire to have an external audit of the school, providing a professional measure of school performance for the benefit of school leadership. Similar reviews may be undertaken as part of an accreditation process.

In some private schools – although rarely in Jewish Schools – external reviews are mandated to take place at regular intervals (usually between five and seven years). This removes the automatic identification of a Review with a real or imagined crisis, and provides a regular, objective, 'audit' of school performance. It can be a valuable check to the tendency of private schools to be somewhat isolated and even inward looking.

Another time when reviews are commissioned is if major change is on the horizon – for example, the retirement or departure of a long-serving Principal. The Board is seeking an answer to the question of what 'profile' it should search for to replace the retiring Principal, who has served the school excellently over many years. Can it be

---

[65] The Principal's 'Performance Review' (see Section 17.2.2) examines and assesses the performance of the Principal. In theory, these should be two separate processes, although in the nature of things they are often inextricably linked.

sure that the structures, policies and leadership that have been in place for so many years are in fact the 'set' that will take the school forward into the next phase of its life? An external review may provide the answers.

- If the review is because the Principal is leaving or retiring, the Principal should keep distant and uninvolved, except when specifically asked. The ability to retire or leave gracefully is a valuable asset. The Principal has the right to move on – and so has the school.

An external review can also be a signal of unease with the present or future leadership of the school, and/or because the school is perceived to be failing. In these circumstances, it can be a very political move, often adversely aimed at the Principal.

It is the Board's prerogative to invite a 'School Review', and a good Principal should not fight it. These reviews are usually commissioned from independent educational consultants, often from one of the school accrediting organizations, or other well-established bodies. Many of the organizations specializing in private schools know and understand Jewish schools well.

Those implementing the review must be completely uninvolved in the school, and preferably from out of town. A review should give the Board of the school an objectively assessed picture of the strengths and weaknesses of the school, and of its Administration. They can be extremely perceptive; they can be wide of the mark, depending in part on the expertise of the Review team. If the review has a political context, groups within the Board, the parent body or the staff room will attempt to use the Review for their own agendas, and will be the first and the loudest in making their views known. A good review team will recognize this phenomenon.

The incumbent Principal may even initiate the Review, and suggest it to the Board. If not, the Principal should be part of the process from the very beginning, and should not be surprised by the proposal to review the school. 'Surprise' in these circumstances is a clear sign of adversarial process. Whatever the circumstances, the Principal should act completely professionally, and give the review team whatever information, access and support they request – plus whatever information and data are essential to understanding the school and the Principal's performance.

The review will very likely involve canvassing Board, Administration, staff and parents (and possibly even students) for their views on the school and its leadership. It is common to also canvass community and other school leadership. That can be an upsetting process for a Principal, and it will generate a flurry of gossip and rumors. The President and Board leadership have an important part to play in making it clear to staff and parents that the purpose of the review is to enable the professional and lay leadership to take the opportunity of an objective, authoritative look at the school so that they can, together, take the school forward.

The Principal should see a draft of any report, correct any errors, and, appropriately, comment on the contents. A school Board's attitude to the completed review may range from simply shelving it (the review's recommendations may not be judged to be practical or desirable) to uncritically recommending adoption of all of its suggestions. Usually, the result is somewhere in between, often generating an added stimulus for the Board and Administration to do some original thinking of their own.

Reviews may not always be so constructive. If the Review took place in an adversarial context, there may be a recommendation regarding the Principal – either a change of Job Description or a recommendation for termination and replacement[66]. In such circumstance, the Board should conduct itself discreetly, generously, and with regard to the dignity of the Principal.

The question that lingers here is whether a School Review should be necessary altogether if school leadership are doing their jobs well.

It is a Principal's full-time job to worry about the school, and it is the Board's job to exercise oversight. If the Math, or English, or Ivrit, or Tanakh department(s) are not functioning well – the Principal and/or the Education Committee should know that well before any external reviewer. If the local community does not have confidence in the school's University entrance record, or the level of preparation of its graduates for Israel study programs – the Principal and/or the Education Committee should know that before any reviewer. If the General Studies in the Middle School and the Jewish Studies in the Senior School 'lack direction' (a favorite phrase often used in such contexts) – the Principal and/or the Education Committee should know that before any reviewer. *Together, they should have already expressed concern to the Board, together with a realistic estimate of what it would take to put those things right.*

5.1.4 The importance of data[67]

As guidance and background to any of the above, there are enormous benefits to keeping sets of data on school operations and programs. Data is a far more desirable commodity than rumor, speculation or 'impressions'[68].

---

[66] For a discussion of how a Principal should react in these circumstances, see SECTION 17.7 – 'If things go wrong ....'

[67] This section could belong in different sections – but ultimately, the Principal should be the driver in ensuring that the school constantly has reasonably accurate data about its operations.

[68] In a community school, minor events or decisions can be quickly, and falsely, magnified. For example, one or two students in a grade may decide to move to another school. This may be statistically average – each year the school may expect similar attrition. Yet if the students, or their parents, are 'high profile', the parking-lot network may very quickly relay this into "This year everyone is leaving". It is good to be able to show that the pattern is no different than it has been for the last five years.

Clearly, and distinctly, financial analyses are indispensable in controlling expenditure and planning budgets – that essential, but specialized area is discussed in SECTION 15.1.5.

But there are several other sets of simple data that are easy to gather, easy to tabulate, and which can be very useful indeed in tracking what is attracting students and parents to your school, what is keeping them there, who they are, and how they evaluate their experience. A different set of data relates to staff.

Online and standard computer programs now make simple surveys easy to implement and easy to tabulate. Any spreadsheet can be used to record and graph data. Versatile and user-friendly survey programs such as www.surveymonkey.com easily enable online surveys, with the ability to analyze and filter results. They also allow for simple entry of data gathered on paper questionnaires. Focus groups can be extremely informative, but should be professionally facilitated for maximum reliability.

Every school will determine its own questions. Surveys and data that are particularly useful include:

- Recruitment and re-registration statistics, tracked month by month, and compared over a period of years

- Year by year, where do your new students come from? Who are they? What percentage of students from the graduating classes of your feeder schools is continuing on to your school? What are the retention statistics for each grade, compared year by year? Is your demographic changing? How many registration enquiries do you get each year, and how many – and who – translate into actual registrations? Why do the others choose other schools? When do they send in registrations? Do particular sets of parents always register late? Information from the registration/Application form itself may form part of this data.

- Intake survey of new parents

  This survey may be given to new parents when they come with their children for interview, as a five-minute paper questionnaire. It can be exceptionally helpful in targeting / designing your recruitment campaign. For example, at TanenbaumCHAT we found that '*The school as a safe environment*' scored unexpectedly highly on the list of parental reasons for choosing the school. We immediately featured it prominently in our advertising and marketing. 'Filtering' showed us that among former-Israeli parents it rated higher than among others – so we stressed it even more in our Ivrit advertising.

Where did they hear about your school? Which advertising reached them? Who or what was influential in their decision to register? What features of the school do they find most important? Did they find the school application process easy? Are they themselves school Alumni? Is this their first child at the school? Did they consider applying to other schools – if so, which?

- Parent survey

Many schools will survey parents at regular intervals. Are they satisfied with the school? Does the school communicate usefully and effectively? Is the school responsive quickly and effectively to parental concerns? Is the Parent Association offering interesting programs? Are they prepared to volunteer for the school?

- Student destinations

Particularly in a larger school – and depending on the details of University application in any particular area - it may be difficult to know exactly where students are headed on graduation, and what they intend to study. At graduation (*"You only get your Grad gown in exchange for a completed questionnaire"*), ask your G12 students to list where they are going... what they intend studying ... whether they are going on an Israel (or other) year program before University... what scholarships they may have been offered. The range of courses selected is always interesting, and can be a pointer to strengths and weaknesses in the school program.

- Graduate / Alumni survey

More complex than some of the others – see Section 7.8.2

Operations – educational

6 THE GENERAL SCHOOL PROGRAM

7 THE JEWISH PROGRAM

8 MANAGING TENSIONS BETWEEN 'GENERAL' AND 'JEWISH'

6 THE GENERAL SCHOOL PROGRAM

6.1 'Academic excellence' – what does it mean?

Every private school – including every Jewish school - declares its commitment to 'academic excellence'.

For a school of integrity, true academic excellence is a *relative* term -- meaning that the school succeeds in bringing every student as close as possible to the top limits of their individual potential.

For some students this will mean academic brilliance, and stellar careers in University, Yeshivah or professions. But for others – *equally precious to the educator* – it will mean leaving school with the basic tools to live independent lives of satisfaction and dignity.

There is undeniably a strong academic aspiration and a strong academic tradition among Jews[69].

In the Jewish High School, 'excellent' academic standards should be seamless right across the program. Skills and knowledge should be reinforcing each other from classroom to classroom, and in the extra-curricular program as well. There are some universal principles:

- Employ the very best teachers, and supervise them professionally and well.

- Make your school a gateway for student access to the world of ideas and culture.

- Ensure that the school ethos engenders a high regard for academic achievement and effort.

- Encourage an atmosphere of intellectual curiosity, enquiry and rigor.

---

[69] On vacation, deep, deep in the rural English countryside, I got into conversation with the local Anglican Vicar and his wife. She remarked that her academic success was due to having to compete with the intensely academically motivated Jewish girls with whom she had been to High School in London. "When the teacher asked a question, a forest of hands went up immediately. When we moved away", she commented, "no-one in my class at my new school could be bothered to answer a single question in class." The same academic motivation exists among other ethnic minority groups in different societies.

- Ensure that your students are trained to read, write, think and analyze to standards way beyond the required minimum.

- Institute and maintain credible evaluation and assessment of student work.

Real academic excellence distinguishes between marks and education. *Grades and marks are earned by the student, not given by the school.* In a current world of grade inflation and 'soft' marking, it is extremely difficult to maintain consistent standards of integrity. Publish clear guidelines about how assignments and tests are marked; what allowances are made for different circumstances; and what the appeal procedure is for contested marks. All of this should be clearly stated in your School Handbook. Marks have different importance in different jurisdictions; they are especially difficult when High School transcripts figure in University entrance procedures[70].

However, educational excellence is not about marks, although marks are an inescapable *accoutrement* of High school. The quality of teaching in the classroom is the decisive factor. Educational excellence has to be grounded in some basics, which in the Jewish school include the following:

- Literacy in Hebrew[71] and English – there is no education without the ability to speak, read and write clearly and articulately

- Analytical and comprehension skills – the ability to read, hear or see a narrative and to analyze it objectively

- Critical thinking skills – the ability to distinguish between sound and unsound data and arguments

- Intellectual curiosity – encouragement of the desire to know more, to understand and to appreciate

- Numeracy - the ability to understand numbers, and to calculate and compute reasonable scenarios without a calculator ....

---

[70] Where this is the case – Canada is the prime example in North America – the school is in a 'no-win' situation. The Grade [12] transcript has to be consistent with the standards of marking current in the 'marketplace', or your students will be in the unenviable position of having uninflated marks of high integrity, but will be unable to get into University .... There is an extensive, if depressing, on-line literature on 'Grade Inflation'.

[71] It is astonishing how many students get through Day Schools and Yeshivot without basic Hebrew skills. While the problem is not by any means limited to the Yeshivah sector, it is particularly shocking to meet students who have been in yeshivah-type elementary and high schools for years but who cannot read Hebrew properly (let alone have any knowledge of the most elementary Hebrew grammar). Despite the fact that their curricula are almost entirely text-study based, they frequently have report cards that give no hint of their weak (to non-existent) skills, which is, in turn, a comment on the Administration of the schools ....

- Digital literacy – an essential contemporary skill

- Aesthetic appreciation – the ability to appreciate the lasting and the valuable in art, literature and music

- Religious sensitivity – an awareness of the spiritual and the inspiring, and a sense of the 'still small voice'

None of the above has any meaning or effect without the indispensable moral component of education:

- A simple sense of right and wrong.

The above are the principles. The curriculum content through which they are taught will vary.

6.2 Options, courses and budgets

Both in Jewish and General Studies, the range of courses and electives offered by the school is very important.

6.2.1 The basic curriculum

In some places, governmental or non-governmental accreditation requirements may determine the list of 'core courses'[72]. Otherwise, the design of your general curriculum will follow local standards, but may also be determined by the character (religious or cultural) of your school. The Jewish Studies curriculum needs careful planning. If it is not planned – completely – it will forever be a cause of problems.

See SECTION 4.9.5 for some notes on Curriculum Consultants.

6.2.2 Options / electives

Course choice is an extremely important factor in a school's popularity. Students and parents like choice – and it makes sound educational sense. Offering choices indicates that the school recognizes and legitimizes individuality among the student body. Conversely, lack of choice is

---

[72] All such systems generally allow varying degrees of flexibility regarding what is taught in the classroom, as long as the overall parameters are kept. In locations where High School credits operate, there may be opportunities to receive accreditation for 'locally developed courses' – usually for Jewish Studies. Wherever this is possible, it is highly desirable. Although the tradition of '*Torah lishmah*' - learning Torah for its own sake, without ulterior motive or benefit – is deeply embedded in Jewish tradition, the practical reality is that having your Jewish Studies courses accredited will immensely improve their status in the school, provide incentives for students, and also supply an external benchmark for teachers to satisfy.

a major focus of dissatisfaction in some schools. A standard range of compulsory courses can never appeal equally to all students. Choices also provide faculty with a chance to vary their teaching assignments, and to teach more specialized topics.

Schools do not always offer choices in Jewish Studies.

The school must determine the minimum number of students who need to be registered before they will run a course. This decision is a function of the Budget Committee[73]. Appropriate procedures and deadlines for registration (and for withdrawal) must be put in place. The policy decision should take into account:

- the cost of providing the teacher (and all associated overheads)

- the academic viability of the class

- the fact that some students who register will either change their choices or will be 'no-shows' – so that if, for example, twelve is the determined minimum class size, the school may require fifteen students to register before running the class in September

Sometimes, exceptions should be made. There may be courses that a small number of students need for College entrance, or which are 'flagship' or 'magnet' courses that parents expect a good school to provide. A school may initiate a new or experimental course that it is keen to promote, with an initial small class. These are all simple judgment calls, where the factors have to be weighed against each other. Options and electives may be desirable, but they can be expensive, and need to be carefully monitored.

Principals may sometimes find it difficult to deal with staff who have a 'great idea' for a new course, option or elective. They are convinced that it 'is just what the school needs' and that 'all the students want it[74]'. Administration must stand firm where the proposal simply cannot be fitted in to that year's budget, requires too great an investment in equipment or materials, or where the Administration is not convinced that it fits in to the school needs or philosophy.

6.2.3 Special Needs students

Recent years have seen a huge increase in the willingness of schools to deal with students who have special educational needs.

---

[73] The function of the budget Committee is only to determine the economically viable minimum number of students per class – not to decide which classes should be run, and which not. That should be an Administrative decision.

[74] Staff will occasionally pressure students to register for a new course they want to introduce.

The development of 'Special Ed' facilities in the general school system has been paralleled (albeit with a time lag) in the Jewish system. A properly coordinated support program can help students succeed in the Jewish school system, which can be particularly challenging for students with learning difficulties or other problems. Every student deserves access to the Jewish High school experience. Jewish schools have tended to imagine that every Jewish student is highly academic. That is clearly not[75] the case.

Whether the issue is learning difficulty, or physical disadvantage, it is a moral obligation on every school to make the maximum accommodation possible in program or physical plant. Since these provisions are often costly, outside funding (from your local Federation or other sources) may be sought.

While the details are outside the scope of this book, every school should acquire 'Special Ed' / Special needs expertise on their staff. For a small school, part time help may be sufficient. Larger schools will develop full-time departments. Special Ed provision relies on the 'buy-in' of other teachers (and may require training), and for this reason the Special Ed staff need particular diplomatic and negotiating skills. They also need to be realistic about the real needs of students, and realistic about the ability of the school or of any individual teacher to provide support, assistance and accommodation. In a typical class of, say, twenty students, three or four[76] may have psycho-educational assessments, with perhaps four different professionals prescribing four different strategies for the already beleaguered class teacher to implement. It is somewhat unlikely to happen in practice, and that is why a skilled Special Ed coordinator is needed to translate that into a practical and realistic set of protocols.

Parents, too, need to understand that there are limits to what the school can provide; and that accommodations are exactly that – they may ease pressure on a child, but they do not automatically solve the student's problems and transform them into stellar achievers.

In all schools, including those schools where it is not possible to provide Special Education, a 'Remediation Studies' programme can be very helpful. In Remediation, students may be withdrawn from regular classes for small group (or 1-on-1)

---

[75] Some years ago I tried very hard to establish a non-academic, vocational stream in our school, providing courses and training for students who would enter the workforce directly from school. It is still a cause of intense personal regret that I was unable to raise the necessary funding at the time.

[76] This figure may be exceeded – sometimes drastically so – in private, and, it has to be said, Jewish schools. The school faces a dilemma. Students present with psych-ed assessments, and request – in some jurisdictions may be legally entitled to – 'extra time' or other accommodation. At the time of writing, I was visited by a voluble and upset mini-delegation of parents who claimed that their non-assessed, regular children were disadvantaged by the number of other students receiving extra time. Since in extending accommodation to students with professionally diagnosed learning difficulties, the school was fulfilling a legal obligation, I found it difficult to deal with their complaint....

instruction. This may be short-term duration (the student missed school and needs to catch up; or did not understand a particular unit) or long term (a student who finds difficulties with High school needs continual, long-term support). Schools have to decide whether to charge extra for these facilities.

6.3 Guidance and Counseling

6.3.1 Overall functions of Guidance

Guidance Counselors[77] are an essential part of the Jewish High School, not least because the intensive nature of the double curriculum and the academic pressure on students in Jewish schools. Larger schools will have full-time Guidance Counselor(s); smaller schools may have part-time appointments. Depending on the school structure, and other support and advice frameworks available to students, the ration of Guidance Counselors to students may range from 1:150 – 1:250 or even more. The Guidance Office must be a place where every student knows that they will find a sympathetic, confidential, supportive and non-judgmental ear (subject to the exceptions noted below). A good Guidance Department will be a valuable part of the school structure, contributing significantly to a 'calm, happy, successful school'.

Guidance normally provides pastoral and academic guidance to students, and College Counseling services. Counselors may come from different backgrounds – educational counseling, social work or even clinical psychology. It can be an advantage to deliberately recruit for that mixture.

Their functions may include:

- **Advocating for students** – students who are in conflict with the school or with a particular teacher may turn to Guidance for help and mediation. If, for example, assignments are overdue in several courses, or if the student needs some special consideration, the Guidance counselor will intercede with colleagues on a professional basis, and work with the student and the teacher(s) to resolve the crisis. If the student feels that a particular teacher is not listening to them, or if they are in conflict with a teacher, they may approach guidance for help and advice.

Clearly, part of the Guidance Counselor's role is to assess the student's responsibility for the situation, and advise and guide accordingly. Skills come into play. A Guidance counselor who regards students as always blameless will quickly lose the confidence of the teaching staff, and the effectiveness of the Guidance program will

---

[77] The Guidance Counselor seems to be more or less unique to North America. In the UK, Australia and South Africa, the functions of the Guidance Counselor tend to be split among several teachers, usually as a relatively small part of their duties. The North American model seems to me to have a great deal to recommend it.

suffer as a result. A counselor who never gives the students' complaints credibility will eventually not have many students coming for help.

Guidance also offers general academic counseling, and may arrange for peer tutoring or other 'extra help'.

- **Advising students on courses and electives** – helping students to construct their timetables and choose their courses in a way that best serves their ambitions and talents.

- **Pastoral advice and support** – counseling students who have personal, family or social issues. In some cases, Guidance may refer students (and/or their parents) to outside professional help. Counselors will also deal with students at times of illness, bereavement, family breakup or other family difficulties. If a student has to miss a lot of school for medical or other reasons, the Guidance Counselor will stay in contact, deal with school work, and also make necessary practical arrangements for the student's return to school.

- **College counseling** – advising on options for post-High School study, and disseminating information and advice on colleges, Universities, scholarships etc. In some schools, knowledgeable Guidance Counselors also advise on post-High School Israel programs.

- **Running special school programs** – Guidance normally organize programs for different grades on personal issues affecting teenagers – e.g. substance abuse, relationships, bullying. In some schools sex education is organized by Guidance, often in cooperation with Jewish Studies and/or other departments.

- **Courses for teachers and parents** – advice and suggestions on how to deal with different teen phenomena for staff, or courses on different aspects of parent problems with teenagers. (The parents who conscientiously attend such evenings are usually those that need them least.)

- Counselors who have no sympathy for young people will not get far in the profession, and their office will be empty much of the time. Those who have unlimited sympathy, and believe that young people can do no wrong, may well get far, but they are dangerous to their students and to the school. They will be manipulated by students, and disliked and distrusted by the teachers and Administration. Somewhere in the middle are the providers of sensitive and sensible advice, who help students through periods of real difficulty, encouraging them to get over both their real and imagined difficulties.

6.3.2 Career guidance

Career Guidance can be a weak link in Jewish schools. Alumni sometimes complain that they were never made aware of a wide enough range of career options when at High School, and that they were steered into 'traditional' choices when they might well have chosen something else. (A particular blind spot of Jewish schools is manufacturing industry and engineering.)

There is a range of options of how a school can provide career information. The traditional model is a corner of the Guidance office or the school library that houses a shelf of usually dusty pamphlets or out-of-date videos.

More effectively, Guidance may run a 'Careers Day' or 'Career Week', where graduates of the school, or parents, who work in a variety of careers are invited to come to the school and talk about what they do and how they came to do it. Bring the unconventional as well as the doctors, lawyers and businessmen – everyone will enjoy it. 'Work Shadowing' days can give students a practical glimpse of the workplace. The school can direct students to one or several of hundreds of useful websites. Guidance or other careers staff may have one-on-one interviews with students to discuss career choices.

Many schools incorporate a short curriculum course on careers in grade 10 (prior to G11/G12 subject choices), which may also incorporate popular personality/aptitude tests.

Whatever the means used, it is serious part of the school's educational responsibility to start students thinking about careers. It is a commonplace to point out that the workplace is changing. There are many new, and different, careers opening, many as a direct or indirect result of technological change. The old certainties of pursuing a fixed career for decades may no longer be there. The perception of how well the school prepared its students for the "real world[78]" is a factor in formulating the retrospective image of the school held by its graduates.

6.3.3 Supervision and confidentiality

Student consultation with Guidance is a confidential process. The exceptions are where a Guidance Counselor learns of illegal activity, where the Guidance Counselor believes that a student or students are in danger, or may be a danger to themselves or to others, or where the Guidance Counselor learns of information relating to third parties which s/he has a legal duty to disclose. In these cases, the Counselor must

---

[78] Another function of the 'real world' that is probably under-represented in the classroom is the management of personal finances. How many students graduate our schools without any notion of mortgages and pensions? And how many really understand what it means to run up a balance on a credit card?

report to Administration, and possibly to other agencies as well. It is a good idea to display a notice in the Guidance office that spells this out[79]. Under the strictest conditions of personal confidentiality, the school Principal may also be advised of other information concerning students or their families which may have importance for the school or the student(s). This may be information on which the Principal cannot act, or may not need to act, *but there cannot be secrets from the Principal*[80], who is legally responsible for the safety and security of the school – and who is at the top of the school's 'confidentiality pyramid'.

Examples of other issues needing careful management are:

- Students may come to Guidance with problems centering on behavior that contradicts the school ethos. The Guidance Counselor must use sensible judgment. The student's welfare must be – unequivocally - the paramount consideration. A Guidance Counselor cannot condone or indefinitely conceal illicit behavior that takes place in school, or which affects the school or its students. If the student is talking about behavior that takes place out of school, or is strictly personal, the situation may be different. A Guidance Counselor who enjoys a good and trusting relationship with a sensible Principal may share the case, in confidence, perhaps without identifying the student. Depending on the issue, there may come a point where the Counselor will tell the student that they cannot continue the counseling without breaking their own professional boundary, and suggest that the student takes further advice from a non-school source.

- Cases where the student's counseling needs are beyond the capacity of the Counselor, or beyond the proper function of the school. A Guidance Counselor, giving advice to a student, may become aware of deep psychological or emotional issues, requiring expert therapy or other treatment. The urge to take the case on in school must be resisted. Schools cannot provide therapeutic services, nor are they equipped to do so. In consultation with the Principal, who may call in outside professional advice, the student should be referred to a third-party qualified professional.

- Families who ask the Guidance Counselor for therapy. Up to a point, a Guidance Counselor may provide advice on parenting. However, a school Guidance Counselor cannot undertake family

---

[79] "Everything said in this office is confidential, except information about illegalities, and information that may suggest that you or others are in danger."
[80] …. anywhere in the school – professional or lay.

or marital therapy of any description to school families, and must refer the family to an outside professional.

6.3.4 Family issues and child abuse – the duty to disclose

There are now legal requirements to report children believed to be 'at risk' to child protection agencies, social service agencies, or police. Within the school, often Guidance Counselors have the first knowledge. Information may come from a student first-hand; from a teacher; or from another concerned student.

The Principal's first responsibility is to understand the applicable law, the reporting responsibility and the reporting procedure. Staff must be informed of their responsibilities. In most jurisdictions, failure to report is itself an offense.

In some cases, there is no doubt that a child is suffering. In others, there may be legitimate concern regarding how evidence is to be interpreted, and whether there is actually cause to report. In a Jewish school, where there may be close community relationships between staff and parents, reporting suspected abuse to an outside agency can have an incendiary effect. In some schools, there may be resistance to acknowledging the phenomenon altogether.

The Principal must act with prudence, but must not under any circumstances suppress information, or agree to acquiesce in seeking non-intrusive solutions (*"Let the local rabbi deal with it"*) or, worse, no solution at all (*"We know the family, and nothing like that could be happening"*).

A close reading of most legislation shows discretion at various stages of the process. It is in your interests to establish a relationship with your local Child Protection Agency (which may be a Jewish community agency) before any situation occurs. You may also consult with a lawyer specializing in family law (or in child protection law), both generally or in specific cases. If a report is made, you should advise your school President, without disclosing names, as an 'outraged' parent will frequently react by calling the Board.

> *I need to advise you that following some information that became known to a teacher, the school has contacted Jewish Family Services regarding our concern for the welfare of a student in the school. We are satisfied that there is a situation that needs enquiry, and a quick check with the school lawyer confirmed that we have a legal duty to make a report. I am sure you understand that I can't disclose names. If you get a call, please tell the family that the school has acted responsibly and in accordance with its legal duties. You might refer any calls to the school lawyer or to back to me. This is a very difficult situation, and we are acting very carefully. I will update you on progress.*

Key to the process is confidentiality.

The first responsibility is to the child; but the school also has a responsibility towards the family and its privacy. The very last thing that should happen is that allegations or the fact of reporting become common knowledge in the local community. It is the responsibility of the social service agency (or the police) to investigate. No one can presume to know what is going on in a home when the front door is closed. Yet at the same time, great caution has to be exercised. Allegations of 'abuse' may be used as weapons by unhappy children, by children needing to draw attention to themselves, by estranged spouses, or by others wishing to cause harm to family members. Once public in any way, such allegations can follow an individual for years afterwards.

6.4 Sports

A frequent perception of Jewish schools is that they do not have good sports programs. Sport – like student activities, creative arts and music – is an essential component of a healthy school, especially when the overall program is highly pressured.

For both girls and boys, the sports program should go beyond the ubiquitous basketball. The program will depend on the facilities – gym and field – to which the school has access. If the school is embarking on capital improvement, lobby for sports facilities as part of the package. Sports and gym programs are not difficult to formulate, and sports staff are not difficult to recruit.

An extensive sports program will only enhance the school. A Jewish High School will deal with a number of special issues, including different tensions between the sports program and the Jewish character of the school - see SECTION 8.11 for a detailed discussion.

6.4.1 Antisemitism at sports fixtures

Every Jewish school, unfortunately, experiences antisemitism from other schools at sports fixtures. It can be genuinely malicious, or it can be a superficial attempt to rile your players and put them off their game. Either is inexcusable, and should not be ignored under any circumstances. Students must be encouraged to report incidents and comments to their coach (or other supervising teacher). The coach / teacher must not brush off or ignore the reports. The coach, together with the school Principal, must make a series of judgments regarding the level of response, which may be:

- Coach-to-coach at the match.

- Coach to referee

- School Principal to School Principal after the game. If the offending players are identifiable, then an appropriate reaction is to tell the other School Principal that those players are not welcome again at your school.

- School to league. If no satisfactory response has been forthcoming from the Principal of the offending school, then a complaint to the sponsoring / organizing league may be the necessary next step.

In really difficult cases, your response should be crafted in conjunction with local Jewish community organizations.

6.5 Creative Arts

Parents looking at Jewish schools often enquire about the creative arts programs available - art, drama and music. There is a hierarchy in the Jewish world of what is easier and more problematic depending on the Orthodoxy of the school – visual arts are less contentious than music[81], and music is less contentious than drama. Many Jewish schools will be happy to provide all three.

A lively Creative Arts program will immensely enhance the quality of the school, and the quality of the educational experience available to the students.

There will be students for whom the Creative Arts program will be a life-saver, and who will find opportunities for self-expression that are simply not available to them in other parts of the school program. These students will haunt the art room, the drama studio, or the music room at every available spare moment. A wise Principal will be grateful for the built-in 'safety-valve' thus provided, and will leave well alone.

- See SECTION 8.3.5 for a detailed discussion on how to approach tensions between Creative Arts programs and school values.

6.6 The School library

The school library should be the academic heart of the school, for students and staff alike. The key to a good library is a good librarian and a good library will be an educational experience in and of itself to individual students. Libraries are rapidly changing, and few institutions have yet caught up with the full implications of the digital revolution - SEE SECTION 6.7

---

[81] In intensively Orthodox schools, visual arts may be provided, but with restricted opportunities for student expression. In some cases, the program will be crafts rather than art.

The library's first duty is to serve the research needs of the school, based on the curriculum. Yet a library whose resources stop there will be impoverished. The library should be a place of intellectual discovery and enrichment, offering the student both the incentive and the facilities to explore the frontiers of knowledge and the marketplace of ideas.

In some schools, there may be a debate regarding the accessions policy of the library. A school that restricts the knowledge available in the school library to materials that do not challenge the school's ethos will encourage the curious student to seek elsewhere. Once 'elsewhere' meant the local public library, which generated a certain romantic literature of the teenager secreted in the stacks seeking truth, art, or enlightenment. Nowadays it probably means the internet café. Either way, it is better that the student is able to satisfy their curiosity in the school, rather than outside. The presence of a New Testament, or a controversial work of Jewish thought, in a Jewish school library does not mean that the school believes in it or approves of it; it means that the school recognizes it as an important part of world culture and knowledge, and as such worthy of a place in a good library.

Even if the school chooses to restrict students' exposure to general society and its culture, the library should be fully representative of all ideas within the school's self-imposed parameters.

The Librarian should be literate in both general and Jewish information needs. If a suitably qualified individual cannot be found, then a 'Library Advisor' may be appointed to advise on library policy in the complementary area. It is crucial that the librarian(s) are able to exercise judgment in acquiring and referencing materials — especially in the area of Judaic Studies.

A school library is budget-hungry, but, unlike other departments, rarely has a staff complement of more than one or two[82]. Libraries need 'champions', especially at budget time; and being the champion of the library is one of the pleasanter duties of the Principal.

6.7 Computers and computing

- Computer-based School Administration and record-keeping programs are discussed in SECTION 4.7.4

- Intranet websites for Teacher-student-parent communication and contact are discussed in SECTION 4.8.6

---

[82] Sometimes not even that.

- Disciplinary issues around computers and digital devices – cell phones, PDA's, Blackberries, iPhones etc – are discussed in SECTION 12.3.12 and preceding sections.

We are currently living in a cultural revolution no less far-reaching than that generated by the invention of printing.

The digital age is profoundly – and permanently – changing our culture, and changing education. There is no question about adapting to the digital age (no longer even the 'computer age') – every school has to. With caution, I would suggest that a Principal has to take into account the following:

- Your school must embrace the digital age. Your students already have.

- To be an effective school leader, you must have good digital literacy

- Understand that the pace of innovation is extremely fast

- Just as forty years ago no school had a budget line for photocopying, so your school should now expect to be spending significant sums per year on computers and associated technology

One of the biggest problems in this area – possibly the largest – is staff training. Digital technology is an intensely age-biased culture, and the bias is towards the young. Students may be producing projects and assignments that the teacher cannot evaluate, and in some cases in formats or media that the teacher cannot even access.

Some of the changes discussed below may be "bad"; some may be "good". The judgment is academic, because they are "here".

Computers and the Orthodox school: Orthodox schools, particularly of the Haredi (intensively Orthodox) sector, face particular sensitivities around computers and internet use. The policy of the school will depend on its Board and the local Rabbinic leadership. Each school must find its *modus vivendi*. No school can assume that its students will not have access to computers or the internet outside school, at home or elsewhere. "Banning" the internet is both unrealistic and impractical. Paradoxically, the Orthodox – even *haredi* – presence on the internet is huge. The spread of other digital devices means that the penetration of popular culture into even *haredi* circles must be assumed – the internet is accessible through the simplest cell-phones. It is better to deal with it than try and ignore its reality.

6.7.1 The changing literacy

The notion of literacy itself is being radically redefined by technology. The process is nowhere near completed, and for that reason is very unnerving and perplexing to educators. Some of the effects seem to be irreversible. They include, but are not limited to:

- Handwriting as a skill will disappear. People will be able to write their signature, but will never need or want to write more than a few lines by hand[83]. Biometric identification may eventually make the signature obsolete as well. In the interim, functions like note taking in class will become increasingly problematic for some students.

- Paper books may be replaced as educational resources, although not (yet) as recreational or religious resources.

- The search engine has changed forever the process of researching information. The effect on school libraries is already visible, as book and journal space shrinks to allow more space for computers.

- The skill of evaluating information will become (is already) critical, because every student has digital access to undreamed-of quantities of undifferentiated material.

- Composition of original prose, with its attendant skills of argument, logic and style, is endangered because of the ease of plagiarism (see following).

- Visual information[84] of all types, whether from life or as composed graphics, will become much more important in education and communication as images become easier and easier to reproduce and manipulate.

- The perceived ease of access to information will make memorizing another fading skill.

The school is a foremost platform for all of these changes, positive and negative. The School Principal is in the exciting, if challenging, position of having to cope with them.

---

[83] Not a single word of this book was written by hand, other than a few marginal scribbles and notes on print-outs.

[84] If you, the reader, wish to be really ahead of the team in this field, investigate the work of Edward Tufte (b. 1942). Incidentally, if you think that use of 'PowerPoint' presentations represents sophistication or progress in the field of information presentation, read Tufte on the subject.

6.7.2 Plagiarism

"Plagiarism: *the attempt to pass off the ideas, research, theories, or words of others as one's own"*

Plagiarism is, unfortunately, endemic in the use of computers and is one of the accompanying phenomena of 'The changing literacy'. Whether it is simply cut-and-paste or downloading (sometimes purchasing) complete assignments, it is easier than ever to do, hard to detect, and, as noted above, itself getting more difficult to define. In the humanities, schools should subscribe to some of the mega-programs[85] available that will check the content of any assignment against a huge database of known work. Ultimately the only recourse is to the common sense of the student –

What are you learning when you simply copy someone else's work?

A strict policy on citation of sources can be a deterrent to plagiarism. This can be incorporated in a school 'style book', compliance with which is mandatory in all courses.

Students caught plagiarizing get a zero on the assignment. Depending on the circumstances, the school can then decide whether or not to give the student a chance to re-submit.

6.7.3 The digital classroom and the digital teacher

The key to the successful use of computers in the classroom is bringing teachers on board from the very beginning.

A fully wired classroom, with an imaginative and computer-literate teacher can be an extremely exciting place. The school has two areas of responsibility:

- Ensuring that the school is technically equipped for computer use, with reasonably up to date equipment. Parents and students will expect that the school give every encouragement and facility for computer use. All public areas of the school should be wireless-accessible for internet use, which is now cheaper and easier than hard-wire connections. 'Wi-fi'ing individual classrooms is a different decision

- Ensuring that your school is up to date with what is happening in the educational technology field – both hardware and software. Be proactive in ensuring that teachers are trained and receptive to the possibilities of the digital classroom. Send selected teachers on courses and conferences. Invite suppliers in to demonstrate new products.

---

[85] www.turnitin.com is one of the most widely-used.

There is an easily accessible literature on the use of computers and other rapidly developing digital technologies in the classroom. 'SmartBoard' technology is particularly attractive, and can transform teaching when used by talented teachers. Other technologies are on the way. The school's should encourage and facilitate good practice.

- Allow teachers time at staff meetings to show how they are using computers or other digital technology in their own lessons. These can be relatively short 'show and tell' sessions. Take other appropriate opportunities to showcase good use of technology in the school.

- As suggested above, encourage teachers to go on courses and conferences that demonstrate and train for digital tech use in their disciplines.

- It is now a completely reasonable professional expectation that all teachers are computer literate. If not they should be prepared to undertake necessary training (in their own time). Make provision for basic training in computer use for any teachers who are still computer-illiterate, or computer-uncomfortable.

- Ensure that computers are easily available in staff rooms/staff workrooms.

If the size of the school allows it, appoint a member of staff who shows special aptitude for using technology to mentor and train other teachers[86]. Have a cross-departmental technology committee that acts as a catalyst and clearinghouse for the spread of technology in the school. Make sure that it has credible leadership.

You may set targets for staff to achieve in computer use. In jurisdictions where curriculum and assessment standards are externally set, it is now almost universal that demonstrated use of IT is a required part of student coursework.

Teachers must also expect that within the near future most, if not all, lesson planning, resources, and student record keeping will be computer-based. There are both 'stand-alone' and integrated School Administration programs that include sophisticated modules for teacher organization and planning. Using email to maintain communication with students is already commonplace, and extensive online teacher-student communication – posting of course outlines, assignments, resources, notes –

---

[86] This post – which can be designated 'Head of Educational Computing' – is distinct from the Head of Computer Studies. Computer Studies teaches students how to use computers. The post described trains and encourages teachers to use computers and computing in teaching their own subject.

is not far behind. Many Universities, and some schools, record lessons and make them available online.

6.7.4 Should the school buy computers for teachers?

Some schools offer staff loans or grants to buy their own computers. The home computer is now becoming a commodity and a standard family appliance. The costs are much less than they used to be, although still significant. In early days there was an advantage in encouraging standard hardware and software in use among staff. That is no longer relevant, as there are now very few examples of incompatibility[87] between programs, especially as web-based programs spread. There is a relatively inexpensive PR advantage to giving laptop grants/loans, which also encourages classroom use by staff. If the school offers such a scheme, ensure that there is an agreed document which both parties sign, outlining the terms.[88]

6.7.5 Curriculum courses in computer use

Students should have had some computer training at Elementary School. A surprising number of students may arrive at High School only able to use computers in a very limited way. The school should certainly offer a Grade 9 course – curricular or extra-curricular - in basic computer use, including simple keyboard use[89]. Students will eventually thank you for training them in ten-finger typing. A student who is not reasonably computer literate is now at a major disadvantage at High School and probably cannot function at post-High School level.

Most schools will also offer more advanced options in programming and specialist applications - e.g. graphics, robotics, integrated media etc.

6.7.6 Should the school mandate students to buy laptops?

Some schools offer students opportunities to buy computers – similar considerations apply to those discussed above in relation to staff. If the school wants to mandate students to have laptops or notebooks in school, obviously there is an advantage to uniformity, and probably a price advantage in bulk purchasing. Mandating students to have laptops can only be done as part of a planned, comprehensive school policy about how that technology is going to become an integral part of the school program.

---

[87] At the time of writing, the school may still have to make a decision between the two competing platforms (PC and Mac) – although Macs will run Windows if necessary, and there is compatibility for Microsoft Office applications. This book started life on a succession of PC laptops, but will finish it on a Macbook. Late in life, and after some twenty-five years of working on Windows, I am a Mac convert. It is – forgive me – a superior machine in every respect. But it is still a minority choice, although less and less so in educational environments.

[88] Is the grant/loan a taxable benefit? If a grant, is it written off over a period of service? A condition must be that the machine is used primarily by the teacher for professional purposes. It may not be passed on to another family member for use.

[89] Or, alternatively, send them a keyboarding self-tutor DVD with their 'Acceptance Letter', and tell them to learn it....

6.7.7 Jewish Studies and the digital age

The internet has brought immense opportunities to the Jewish Studies classroom, because the needs of the Jewish community – a thinly spread, highly computer-literate group – are very well suited to the www.

There is a huge Jewish 'presence' on the net, encompassing every section of the community. There is also an enormous reservoir of easily accessible information covering every area of Jewish Studies, from the most obscure to the most popular – far more than any school or community library could provide. Add to this the information available on CD-rom / DVD technology, and it may be seen that the potential exists to really expand the horizons of the Jewish classroom. There are comprehensive databases of texts[90] (in both Hebrew, Aramaic and English); major databases of Jewish history; lively forums on Jewish thought and Jewish issues; and many images covering every aspect of Jewish life, and virtually every community in history. There are rapidly expanding databases of music, art, artifacts, archaeology, film and video, both historic and contemporary.

Many readers will be familiar with the online discussion and information-sharing forums for Jewish educators. It is easy to locate and purchase online all types of educational resources, books (including books from Israel), Jewish ritual objects and services.

All of these may serve as resources for the teacher and for the curriculum, and as research resources for students. Like much else on the www, they are of varied reliability and accuracy, and some are highly partisan. There are also some very promising experiments in getting classes to compose web-based joint projects of rapidly increasing sophistication.

However, we still await a single, educationally oriented comprehensive web presence, serving as one central resource for all Jewish High Schools.

6.8 Extra-curricular activities / Student Activities

The extra-curricular[91] program is an integral and valuable part of the High School experience, and a powerful educational setting for many lessons that cannot be communicated in the classroom. Whatever the character of the school, a healthy program can:

- Offer students opportunities for leadership and responsibility, and be a setting for many non-academic 'life lessons'

---

[90] Including many digital images of early manuscripts of primary texts.
[91] Alternatively called 'co-curricular', 'informal education', or Student Activities program.

- Enable them to get involved in all sorts of activities which otherwise they could never experience

- Allow students with talents to 'shine' outside the classroom

- Give opportunities for the school to be involved in the local community

- Provide irreplaceable 'school spirit' occasions

- Be a powerful attraction for student recruitment

--- and, not least,

- allow students an opportunity to have a lot of fun within the framework of the school.

Whether it is school newspaper, drama, volunteering, camping, fundraising, origami, Jewish learning, music, films ... (and the list is endless), almost every student can find some constructive role in a school club or society. Apart from the 'stars', there are students who get involved in tech support, or logistics, or being the treasurer, or some other role that gives them a chance to be part of the team without being front and centre. Their experience in extra-curricular can be formative both in their own development, and also in defining the student's school experience. An extensive extra-curricular program is a powerful recruitment asset.

Students and staff will generate a wide range of extra-curricular initiatives. That does not mean that 'anything goes'. It takes skill and judgment to build a healthy program, and it needs to be carefully supervised, advised and guided. Like all parts of the school's program, it must be seen as an educational activity, with educational goals.

Individual teachers will help with specific programs[92], but one teacher should be given overall responsibility of coordinating student activities – preferably, someone who is sympathetic but firm, is very sensible, is practical, and who has experience of working with students in informal education. In a large school this may be a substantial part-time post, although the staff member concerned should retain some partial teaching load – retaining contact with the school routine, and retaining credibility in the staff room.

There has to be structure and supervision to the program, including:

- Structure / process for starting a new activity.

---

[92] The wise Principal will understand that the areas of extra-curricular activities and sports coaching require a careful eye to ensure that all staff-student relationships remain within appropriate boundaries.

- Supervision regarding the content and program, including provision for safety and security of all activities, especially if activities are taking place out of hours and/or out of town.

- Supervision of budget and finance[93], including clear rules about collecting, handling, spending and accounting for money, and rules for student fundraising

- Provision for appropriate leadership functions, and democratic /accountable structure, including checks and balances, for each activity

- A staff member who acts as the 'sponsor' or supervisor of each activity. Note that it is highly problematic to have outside adults (parents or others) who are not staff members (and therefore not responsible to the school) in charge of extra-curricular programs. Even where the school agrees to have a volunteer involved, there must be a teacher assigned to supervise, to whom the students are responsible.

- Occasionally, limits on the amount of time a student can spend on Student Activities.

- Clear rules about under what circumstances, and with whose permission, Student Activities can impinge on school teaching time.

- Appropriate parental consents.

The student activity program is tied to the work of Student Council – see SECTION 11.6.2

Student Activities cover both general and Jewish dimensions of the school, and may include significant school events. Student-generated celebrations and presentations such as (but certainly not limited to) Yom Ha'atzmaut, Purim, Sukkot, and, in a different tone, Yom HaShoah and Yom Hazikaron can provide powerful educational and community experiences. Current technology – of which students are masters - can provide awesomely powerful content.

- Other opportunities for informal education in the school's Jewish program – staff-led and student-led - are discussed in SECTION 7.3.1

---

[93] Potential complications in this area are huge. The first rule is that all accounts must be held and administered by the school accounts office; no independent bank accounts, and certainly no credit cards. Budget and proper accounts / records must be kept. Expenditures must be approved. Your CFO or school treasurer should oversee the arrangements.

6.9 Visiting Speakers / outside presentations

Visiting speakers, or other presentations from external sources, are very common in Jewish schools.

These can be inspiring, interesting, and enriching occasions. A good school will certainly offer opportunities to encounter and experience unusual or otherwise interesting personalities, relevant both the Jewish and General Studies dimensions of the curriculum.

However good the programs, they are usually an interruption to normal lessons, and from that consideration alone should be carefully limited.

These occasions can also be embarrassments[94]. You cannot know what a speaker is going to say, or how they are going to say it, until they are already speaking. By that time it is too late to do much about it.

- Ensure that the microphone (and any other equipment) is tested and prepared before the speaker arrives and begins. If a visual presentation (video, digital projector, SmartBoard) is being given, check that the screen is visible to all areas of the room, and that it is sufficiently bright. If the speaker misuses the microphone, do not hesitate to adjust it or advise him/her. If the speaker says that they 'prefer not to use the mike', but you know it is essential – insist on it. If the speaker is simply boring, there is not a great deal that you can do, except to make a mental note about the speaker and the reliability of whoever recommended them.

- If a speaker makes a clearly offensive or inappropriate remark, you can deal with it in a variety of ways. In such circumstances, you will find yourself thinking on your feet. If the remark is really offensive – you may wish to correct it as soon as the speaker finishes:

  Just before we have questions, I would like to clarify to the school that our guest's remark about people who hold different views than he does about Israel is his opinion, and I am sure that he will welcome questions on it. The point of view he referred to is, of course, one that is held by a major political party in Israel, elected by Israeli citizens.

---

[94] Among the worst are when the speaker simply doesn't show (or the video/powerpoint won't work) which leaves you with a room of annoyed students and teachers ...

- If the speaker is less radically offensive – he or she is a guest in the school, and most of the time should not be challenged publicly (except by the questions). Afterwards, you should make it clear to staff and students, either verbally or even in writing, that you share their discomfort and disapproval. However, if the speaker has attempted a joke[95] that misfires, or with obvious good intentions simply misjudges a comment – let it go.

Even on occasions when 'someone' has heard the speaker before, knows them, or knew them twenty years ago, every school has experienced the occasional disaster. If you subject the students to a series of boring speakers, they will automatically 'turn off' for all that follow – including the worthwhile ones.

There are occasions when you or another member of staff learn that a good speaker (or a good band, or a good theatre group) is going to be in town, and you take the initiative in extending an invitation. The only thing to then consider is the format of the presentation (see below).

Sometimes, Principals may find themselves under pressure to invite "X" to "talk to the whole school", or show the "whole school" a "fantastic video". In a large community, if every such offer were accepted, students might spend some weeks doing little else than being pulled out of class to listen to speakers.

Other recognizable scenarios (apart from a 'cold call' directly to you) include:

- A local organization is bringing in a speaker for its annual dinner/for a parlor meeting, and is looking for ways to fill the speaker's day. Someone has the bright idea of 'sending them to speak at the Jewish school'.

- A major donor to the school is also a major supporter of another institution or cause somewhere else, and wants their 'other' institution to gain exposure in the community.

- A parent gets a bee in their bonnet about a particular (worthy) cause, and insists that the school students "must" hear the speaker who is on a national speaking tour (normally for fundraising).

- Institutions trying to recruit students for post-High School programs try and press the idea of their traveling recruiter speaking to the 'whole grade'.

---

[95] A returning school alumnus, addressing the school as a 'keynote' on a certain occasion, made a joke about the subject she least enjoyed at school. The rest of the speech was marvelous. A deputation of staff from that department tried to insist that I write her a letter and ask for an apology. I wouldn't.

- A visitor to the city on behalf of some organization wants to report that they 'spoke at the local Jewish high School'.

There will be occasions when some of these offers represent excellent opportunities, and the school will be happy to take advantage of them. However, you may also want to avoid them at all costs.

There are several ways to bring these situations under control:

- Have clear criteria for evaluating programs on offer. The school's duty is to its students. Students are interested in hearing about issues and experiences, not organizations. Does the speaker have something interesting to say? Will the students really gain enough from this presentation to justify missing a class? (Remember that every time a class is cancelled, it sends a silent message to the student body.) Will they be interested in the proposed topic? Is the person a good speaker? What is their level of English (or what is the student audience's level of Ivrit?)? At certain times of the year (exam periods, or when there have been several recent interruptions to school routine and neither Administration nor staff want another one) there are no visiting speakers. Period.

- Don't be afraid of turning down suggestions[96]; explain why, tactfully but firmly, and refer to the school's criteria. Alternative formats for a visit (see below) may be more appropriate.

- Devise a standard sheet of 'Information for visiting speakers' in English and Ivrit, which should include a few lines about the school, the nature of the student body, and guidance as to how long is available to the speaker.

  It will take approximately ten minutes for the students to arrive in the hall. This leaves not more than 45 minutes for your presentation, including time for questions and discussion. At the end of the lesson, the bell will ring and the students will then have to go their next lesson. The session cannot be extended. Our students are most interested when you get directly to the point of your talk.

Email this sheet to the speaker well before the date. If that is not possible, ask the speaker to take a moment to read the info sheet before they begin.

---

[96] I have declined aggressive presentations of gender issues which I felt went beyond community consensus; presentations by visiting speakers advocating refusal to serve in the IDF; and would not allow visiting speakers who advocated views I considered racist in any context.

- Make it clear that the school cannot entertain last-minute requests for speakers to visit, and needs reasonable notice to rearrange the school program. In a large High School this may be very complicated, perhaps requiring rescheduling of classes, schedules, tests etc. 'Reasonable notice' can be a week or so.

- Set limits on how often the school is prepared to interrupt learning for any class during the year/semester, and keep to them.

  Sorry, Mr. X – but Grade 9 have already had three guest speakers recently, and I am afraid that we can't interrupt classes again at this time. Next year, we will be happy to consider the opportunity again, but you must let us know well in advance when Rabbi/Professor/Mrs. W. will be in town.

However, consider alternatives to offer speakers:

- If not for the whole school, would the speaker be appropriate and interesting to a grade? To a particular class?

- Sometimes visitors are more interested in meeting students than speaking to them. A very good way to accommodate this, which also avoids interrupting lessons, is to invite the guest to meet with a small group of students at lunch break. Offer a dozen or fifteen students a free lunch (falafel, pita / pizza, salads is fine) in a convenient room. The pupils will appreciate the privilege of the invitation, and the guest will have a chance to really speak to them. The discussion is over lunch. It can be fascinating, and is often more productive than the speaker trying to get the attention of a large group, a proportion of whom will not be attentive.

- Allocate a regular spot (Friday lunchtimes is always good) for outside speakers, and make attendance voluntary. The market will decide attendance.

7 THE JEWISH PROGRAM

7.1 'Jewish values', 'Jewish education' and other difficult phrases

The *raison d'être* of the Diaspora Jewish school system[97] - that which justifies its separate existence -- is the transmission of 'Judaism', 'Jewish values' and 'Jewish identity', via 'Jewish education'.

This is by far the most difficult area of the school to manage, to plan, and to lead, for the following reasons:

- There is not even a remote consensus in the Jewish community as to the meaning of any of the above concepts

- Because they involve emotionally laden and faith-laden ideas, feelings run high

- Parental feelings and emotions regarding how the school, its Principal or any individual teacher approaches any Jewishly-connected subject are often completely irrational, and often have their source in family or out-of-school related incidents over which the school has no control (and no responsibility)

From an Administrative point of view, there are challenges connected to Jewish Studies teaching and teachers:

- There are no nationally-available, professionally produced textbooks, curricula or other teaching schemes designed for teaching High School Jewish Studies[98].

- The opportunities for full-time teacher-training for High School Jewish Studies teachers are very few, very restricted, and still need a great deal of development.

---

[97] One of the paradoxes and tragedies of Jewish life is that that the Israeli *Mamlachti* school system hardly, if at all, sees its mission as having anything to do with any of these categories.
[98] A teacher wishing to teach any subject in High school – ranging from Math to Ecology to Ancient Greek – may buy complete off-the-shelf teaching schemes of textbooks, videos/DVD's/ teachers' guides/ ready-designed assignments etc. For popular subjects there may be an embarrassment of choices. The *chagim* are taught in every single Jewish school in the world. I do not know of a single textbook available for teaching Chagei Yisrael (the Jewish festivals) at any level, in any way, at High School level – let alone a complete teaching scheme.

- In all Jewish schools a very large proportion of JS teachers come from the Orthodox community[99]. For the last forty years, the trend in the Orthodox community has been to discourage men (less so women[100]) from entering any sort of professional training, including teacher training; and from going to university. The result is a chronic shortage of properly trained[101] and qualified personnel; and very varied profiles of those who do want to come into teaching – even though Orthodox candidates are the majority of candidates for teaching positions.

- The General Studies teacher often becomes a teacher because he/she is devoted to teaching. The Jewish Studies teacher often becomes a teacher because he/she is devoted to 'Yiddishkeit'.

- JS teachers tend to come from a variety of backgrounds, enter the profession at different times in their career, and often do not have the same classroom / pedagogic skills as their General Studies counterparts.

The Principal, as champion of school vision and school values, has to have a vision of the Jewish standards of the school, be credible in talking about them and be a forceful proponent of them. A Principal may well have a vision that is individual and somewhat independent. However, it has to be consistent, and it has to be an *educating* and *educational* model.

7.2 Issues unique to the Jewishness of the Jewish school

Unlike issues surrounding the Math curriculum, or the Science Fair, or the lockers, issues special to the Jewishness of the Jewish school do not have the mediating and

---

[99] This is true whatever the orientation of the school. There are very few non-orthodox Jewish Studies teachers at High School level, and the lack of training schemes probably reflects the relatively small number of non-Orthodox High Schools. The demand for non-Orthodox pulpit rabbis is also high, and schools cannot compete with congregational salaries (especially for young and inexperienced candidates).

[100] Until very recently, Jewish single-sex girls' schools – in their nature Orthodox – tended to be much more professional and much better run than their male counterparts, especially when run solely by women. I believe the reason for this was that Orthodox women, including the most talented, had few other professional opportunities, and therefore the quality of leadership in these schools was frequently exceptional. In recent years, talented Orthodox women have seen many other professions open to them, and therefore fewer enter education.

[101] This situation seems to be improving, very slowly, although I cannot quantify it.

reassuring property of 'This is how all schools work'. They do carry with them some, all, or most of the joys, complexities and *angst* of "being Jewish". The very uncertainty of that definition is a destabilizing factor in the lives of many Jews.

An abbreviated summary of some significant sensitivities affecting Jewish schools might include:

7.2.1 Psychological

Contemporary Jewish life exists in the shadow of a series of profoundly powerful realities, all of which – in different ways – affect the psyche of every Jew, whether they are near or far from Judaism, Jewish life or the Jewish community. Emotions generated by these issues are never far from the surface, and are intensified and aroused around Jewish institutions, particularly schools.

- The Shoah (the Nazi Holocaust) is a huge underlying factor in many Jewish families. Many of our parents, teachers and students are from families who were, and still are, deeply and directly affected by the Shoah. It shows itself in many ways – in sensitivity and protectiveness towards children (and towards parents), to insecurities of different sorts, and of (in some cases) highly ambivalent feelings towards Jewish identity and Jewish religious belief. ("Being Jewish is the most important thing in my life, but it is also what made me a victim'). Learning about the Shoah can be traumatic for teenagers. Paradoxically, the very high importance put on the Shoah in Jewish life may make it difficult for them to acknowledge that trauma.

- Ongoing anti-Semitism – an increasing feature of contemporary life – is equally a disturbing phenomenon to every Jew, and especially to adolescents. Recent trends and growth in worldwide anti-Semitism have seen revivals of the crudest and psychologically most irrational targeting of Jews and Judaism. Being a student at a Jewish school, however comforting that may be in other ways, is an act of identifying that opens the student to certain vulnerabilities.

- A new (or renewed) factor, tied to both of the above, is concern regarding school safety and security. Many School Principals will have encountered students and parents who are terrified regarding potential threats to the school – even to the extent of withdrawing students, or not sending them in the first place. It is irresponsible to disregard those threats, or those fears. We should not live in daily fear, but we should certainly live in daily awareness. That, too, is a psychological pressure.

Similarly powerful conflicts arise surrounding Israel. The life and ideals of every Jewish school are closely bound up with Israel, whatever its ideological affiliation. A whole gamut of emotions may come into play around this issue as well – ranging from the effect on the school of tragedies or loss of life in Israel, to feelings and conflicts over Israeli political issues, to feelings and conflicts among the student (and parent) body over media reporting. A common demand in High Schools is that the schools should 'prepare' students for anti-Israel and antisemitic environments on campus. SEE SECTION 7.6.6 . Feelings run high. The Administrator's task is to manage them.

7.2.2 Religious

No less easy than psychological currents in the school are religious issues. Few groups in the contemporary Jewish community – of whatever stream - have clear ideologies, accepted practices or accepted, authoritative leadership at local, national or even international scale. Recent decades have seen a move towards intensification of Jewish traditional or neo-traditional observance, of which the huge growth in the Jewish school movement itself may be a sign.

Fragmented authority + move to more observance = trouble!

No sector is free from the resultant twin pressures, and, without assigning any judgment to the phenomenon, every school, from the most liberal to the most Orthodox, has experienced 'right-wing drift' in recent years.

Common manifestations of religious issues in school management are:

- Parents feel 'the school is not religious enough', which usually means that their own children are not displaying the attitudes, conformity or beliefs that the parents want (even though other children in the same school may well be). This frequently also translates into 'Not enough time is being spent on Jewish Studies'.

- Parents feel that the school is 'too religious' – the signs of which are pretty much identical to the first category, except that the accompanying complaint is that 'Too much time is being spent on Jewish Studies'!

- The curriculum is wrong.

- The students are not learning 'enough'.

- 'When my kid is in shul, she/he doesn't want to daven'.

- The other students are a bad influence on my son/daughter.

- 'Religious parents' no longer want to send their children to the school; another school is opening up, which will be a "real" Jewish school.

- A textbook at the school is problematic from a religious point of view – too lax, or too extreme.

- A student comes back and reports a teacher's remark in the classroom – resulting in a "Is this what the students are being taught?" phone call – in the best of circumstances, initially to the Principal rather than first to all the Board members

- "When the students are out of school, they do x, y, or z."

- The students cannot reconcile the instruction and inspiration they receive at school with their parents' own Jewishness as they observe it in the privacy of the family, or in their community.

The full list, it may be said, is as long as the Exile, and just as wearying. While sometimes the complaint may have some merit, and needs some action, in many cases it reflects discomfort of the parent(s), rather than educational shortcomings of the school, and only very rarely discomfort of the student. Every Principal has also experienced the phenomenon of parents who reach a certain level of Jewish observance where their enthusiasm is still ahead of their knowledge, and who are persuaded by some third party to pull their children out of the school, without regard to the child's interests or needs[102].

No school can answer the needs of every single student or every single family. A family who feels that for socio-religious reasons they wish to leave the school will do so. Little that you can do or say will stop them.

Another religious pressure is from outside the school. *"The school should..."* (or, perhaps more frequently, *"The school shouldn't...")* - begins advice emanating from Rabbis or community members who would never send their own children to your school (and this is true wherever you are on the religious spectrum).

There are two ironclad principles:

- The school can only be run for the benefit of the students who come to it. It cannot be run according to the standards of students who don't.

- You must run an honest school – without hypocrisy.

If a parent wishes to enroll a student – they are part of the school, and the school should do whatever it reasonably can to ensure that that student will feel comfortable

---

[102] Very often leading to disaster.

in the school[103]. Those who do not have, and will never have, children at the school cannot try and dictate the school's religious or other standards.

7.2.3 Social / financial

It is a hard fact of life that being an involved Jew today is a very expensive commitment, of which Jewish school tuition fees are a major part. That creates a series of tensions, many of them hidden, but many featuring as painful memories of school days when Alumni gather to talk. Students from homes of more modest means (which can include homes with relatively good incomes) may find life at school difficult.

7.2.4 Educational

Every Jewish school is highly academic, in part for sociological reasons, but in part simply because of the Jewish Studies component of the timetable. A fellow-Principal[104] once coined the expression 'JDSD – Jewish Day School Disabled' to describe the perfectly wonderful, normal children of our community who are effectively disenfranchised by the Jewish community because they cannot cope with the abnormal academic workload of the Jewish school system. While Special Education /Special Needs schools and facilities have rapidly developed in the Jewish school system, we are not providing for the students *who are simply average students.*

As well as the workload, elements of the curriculum may also be particularly difficult for some students – Ivrit, for students who struggle with languages; and Talmud in Orthodox boys' schools.

7.2.5 Operational

The two greatest operational problems in the Jewish dimension of the Jewish school are the shortage of trained teachers, and the lack of suitable teaching materials.

Period.

7.2.6 In times of personal crisis – or celebration

A unique feature of Jewish schools is the support offered to students, staff and their families in times of personal crisis. SEE SECTION 15.6 The Jewish quality of *chessed* has to be real in the school community, or the credibility of its value system may legitimately be called into question.

---

[103] This applies as well if a student becomes more religiously observant while they are at the school. TanenbaumCHAT has arranged 'glatt kosher' meals for a single student on a school Israel trip, delivered to all sorts of places as the group toured Israel. It was a pleasure to do so.

[104] Dr. Shimshon Hammerman, of the Solomon Schechter Day School in Montreal.

The willingness of the school community to rally around in times of crisis should need little organization or encouragement. Staff – obviously including Judaic Studies staff and Guidance Counselors – should be proactive in ensuring that hospital visits, *shivah* calls, phone calls and other support initiatives are reasonably coordinated, and, particularly, that there is follow-up in the weeks and months that follow an immediate crisis. Counseling may form a large part of the school's support. At the very least, appropriate letters of support and condolence from the school should always be sent to students and staff members who have suffered bereavements[105].

Students may feel deeply affected – one way or another – by the help and sympathy they receive from school. Many of our students – more than we might assume -- live with excruciating family circumstances that they never 'bring to school'. But when crisis occurs, the school should never assume that "X can manage". Failure to express sympathy – especially if the student is not one of the 'cool' or popular students – can leave deep feelings of hurt. A particular, and unfortunately common, insensitivity is the teacher who demands 'work as usual' from a student who is undergoing, or recovering from, trauma.

A school should establish policy regarding the practicalities and mechanics of expressions of pastoral care, concern, and condolence. When, and for whom, does the school publish a condolence notice in the local Jewish newspaper? If there is a policy, a Board member cannot feel personally wronged when the school fails to publish an ad expressing condolences to his/her spouse on the sad loss of their brother-in-law in a community hundreds or even thousands of miles away. Similarly, there should be a careful and dispassionate policy governing when commemorative events (such as school assemblies) should be held, or under what circumstances school should be cancelled to enable school members to participate in happy or, unfortunately, sad events. There can always be exceptions, but it is easier to have recourse to a policy than to enter into argument, especially at times of heightened emotions.

A school should have a sense of appropriate response to community, national and international incidents and disasters. Responsible school leadership will take a similarly dispassionate and reasonable decision about the scale and extent of response. A fine line has to be drawn between appropriate expression of sympathy, and judgment of the correct time to return the school to normal routine[106].

---

[105] Particularly in a large school, the Principal must make sure that s/he is advised about all family illnesses and bereavements. It is easy for staff to assume that 'everyone' knows.
[106] Usually best sooner rather than later.

7.3 Shaviv's paradox – does "Success = failure"?

7.3.1 The need to supplement formal with 'experiential' in the Jewish program

In its Jewish dimension, the Jewish school embodies a fundamental paradox:

"The more successful it is, the less successful it is"

To be successful, the Jewish Studies program has to be structured in a way that fits a school, and that the students recognize as a school model. The JS lessons have to be taught according to a planned curriculum, and have to have assignments, homework, tests, exams and marks. Even a 'Bet Midrash' has to have a school structure. Experience shows that students cannot cope with moving from first lesson Eng Lit to second lesson Civics to third lesson Hassidic *'farbreng'* ("happening") and then back to fourth lesson Chemistry. Generally, the more organized and structured the JS curriculum, the more it is regarded as successful.

- *The problem here is that the more JS is made into a classroom subject, the further away it becomes from the affective, spiritual world that we wish to transmit.*

Most of us would agree that many of our most formative feelings about our own Judaism are related to moments of high experience[107]. For this reason, it is essential that a good Jewish school balance its program with an experiential component.

This has to be more than just the occasional event. The experiential components might include:

- Shabbatonim

- Retreats

- Camps

- Celebrations

- Exhibitions

- Visits

- 'Encounters'

- Israel trips

---

[107] The late Emil Fackenheim ztz'l once referred to the concept of "orienting experiences" – those single moments after which you are never quite the same again. Most Jewish experiences in this category are emotional/affective, rather than rational/cognitive.

- Lunchtime concerts ... etc.

It has to be a designed and resourced part of the school program, with clearly allocated staff and budget resources. It should not be left to ad-hoc serendipity, although that certainly has its (unprogrammable) place.

The experiential component of the program has to 'balance' – not replace. There is no substitute for hard learning and for knowledge.

Without the classroom component, the experiential is often ephemeral. Without the experiential, the classroom is only theoretical. The Jewish program has to give students rich opportunities to explore and access a range of Jewish experiences that have their base in the classroom *but go far beyond that*.

Skillfully done, this effectively transforms the Jewish school into a 'living experience', where values are learned and lived. That is a much more difficult institution to lead and manage. It also creates an institution that has no well-defined place in the conventional school–family–synagogue structure, although I predict it will become a powerful model for the future. This can only contribute to the complexity of the Principal's task............

7.3.2 The Jewish Studies classroom – a marketplace of ideas?

The Jewish Studies classroom determines the central messages of the Jewish school. The school cannot succeed if the experience of the student at classroom level contradicts the school's professed values.

Whatever the curriculum, the competitive school will ensure that its Jewish Studies classroom is engaging, challenging, interesting – and inspirational. The classroom does not have to promise 'fireworks' in every lesson (such an approach carries significant dangers), but it does have to be a consistently high-level educational experience for the students. Each course has to be planned and structured. The overall curriculum must be spiral, with a perceptibly more complex and mature content as the student moves through the school.[108]

In the best of circumstances, the school itself, led by the individual teachers in the classroom, is in dialogue with the students – not only *educating*, but being *educated*. Education in Jewish Studies should not be dogmatic. The school is in a marketplace of ideas, and – like every other institution of Jewish life - wherever it is situated and

---

[108] I once visited a K-12 school in a certain city, and was being shown around. The first classroom we visited was a Grade 4 class, where a teacher was teaching the lesson of Abraham's hospitality from the beginning of *Parashat Vayera*. At the end of the tour – an hour or so later – we happened on the same teacher teaching Grade 11. His lesson was word for word identical. The students, who had probably heard the same lesson every year for their entire school careers to date, were totally tuned out. Would the teacher – as a parent - have accepted the identical history lesson, or the identical science lesson, being taught to his own child in both Grade 4 and grade 11?

whatever its community it is competing for the life-long allegiance of the student. Since Emancipation, being Jewish has been voluntary[109]. The students can choose. I believe it is illusory to act as if that were not so.

In some schools, only one interpretation of Torah – in its widest sense - will be given at any level. Teachers will have been recruited in great part because they conform to the 'authorized version' in thought, speech and dress[110].

Yet every student is an individual. A good Principal will encourage a variety of views and styles among the faculty, and will deliberately recruit for that diversity. This allows different types of students to be exposed to different approaches and to have different opportunities for personal/spiritual resonance. For every topic studied, each teacher should offer students a range of views and interpretations. **The parameters of that range will depend on the school and on the teacher**; but for it to be education, there must be a genuine choice, and the student must be challenged to understand and critically examine each point of view. The teacher must teach viewpoints that are not the teacher's own, and with which the teacher does not agree, and may even disapprove. It is always helpful if education reflects reality.

> *In today's Jewish community, you will meet a range of different attitudes towards the laws of kashrut. You may well have relatives or friends whose practice is different from your own. Briefly, these are the different views ..... Our school community, which as you know tends to look to Rabbi X's philosophy and teachings as a model, usually supports the third point of view. You will make up your own mind....*

That does not mean that the teacher cannot express their own views – on the contrary, they must.

> *On this topic, I've given you three different views, two of them held by respected thinkers; and a third that is considered by many to be outside acceptable interpretation. As it happens, I don't agree with any of them; I'd like to give you my view.*

Students are looking to what the teacher actually believes, and the teacher must articulate and explain his/her own beliefs and opinions, provided that:

- Within reasonable parameters, those beliefs and opinions are compatible with the school's philosophy and ethos.

- The teacher identifies the views as his/her own.

---

[109] For Jews; not, tragically, for antisemites.
[110] Conformity is not the exclusive preserve of the intensively Orthodox ...

- Within agreed school policy (which may vary greatly according to the ideology of the school), respectful space is given for other viewpoints – introduced either by the teacher or by the students.

The teacher should be a guide but also a partner in exploring Judaism with the students, open to new insights, to new knowledge, and to continuing learning. A teacher whose knowledge is static will quickly bore his/her students; true in the Jewish Studies classroom more than any other.

It is particularly important that the relationship to the students in the Jewish Studies lessons exemplify the school's overall philosophy. The conditions that allow the 'educating and educated' model to thrive in the classroom include, but are not limited to:

- RESPECTING THE STUDENT AND THEIR INDIVIDUALITY

- Meeting the student at a realistic 'place', and acknowledging the reality of their lives[111]

- Allowing for dissent and questioning

- Allowing for informed and polite discussion of controversial issues

- Providing a range of role models in the Faculty

- Allowing the students to have outlets for expression and energy

- Within the parameters of school philosophy, actively promoting and encouraging a range of legitimate Jewish views

- Teaching and modeling tolerance and the ability to respectfully 'agree to disagree'

- Building on and nurturing the positive in every student's Jewishness, and not stressing the negative.

- Not making huge issues out of fundamentally unimportant or adolescent affectations

- Encouraging students' individual growth and interests

A school that sees its task as enforcing conformity is not educational, and is engaged instead on the thankless task of battling the teenage psyche.

---

[111] The tale of Nachman of Breslov and the King's Son who thought he was a turkey is highly relevant here.

In the classroom, other views and opinions must be treated with respect. Even where disagreement exists, no other student, teacher, group or individual should be delegitimized or denigrated. The arguments may be given; the reasoning explained; but never, ever, should another person be belittled. A teacher may say clearly that s/he does not agree with, or does not believe in, the approach of others, but has to do so in a spirit of respect.

> *The book is excellently written, and the author makes a very strong case. The argument against it was put very strongly by XXXX in his online review. I'll print it out for you and maybe we'll read it in class next week. But you have to read the book first!*

> *Did Rabbi K. really tell you that? That's interesting. I respect Rabbi K. very much, and you can learn a great deal from him. He always has interesting things to say. We agree on many issues, but actually I don't agree with him on that point. I hold differently.*

- are a great deal better than:

> *That book! It should be burnt!*

> *Rabbi K. said that! Students, you should know that Rabbi K. often says unacceptable things that shouldn't be taught in this school. I'm going to discuss this with the Principal right after the lesson. Meanwhile, take no notice of what he's teaching you.*

The last necessary sensitivity in the Jewish Studies class is to the (unknown) family circumstances of the students. Because the teacher rarely knows the complete extended family background of all the students in the class, let alone what is going on inside their heads, ill-considered statements such as :

> *"If you don't believe that, you're not Jewish"*

> *"XXX denomination is not really Jewish"*

> *"Someone whose family has a relative who is an XXXX should be ashamed of themselves"*

-- can all do lasting damage.

A school that respects – will in turn win respect, loyalty and affection. A school that tries to brainwash its students with a single, unchallengeable point of view will quickly lose its brightest students (spiritually or actually). For the others, the glow of enjoying the school's approval because s/he is conforming will wear off as soon as the student achieves maturity and independence.

7.3.3 The lament of a disillusioned student

Some time ago, a 'blogger' who ran one of the many 'blogs' where wandering and wondering Jews create web-based public platforms to air their issues and invite comment and dialogue from anyone and everyone, posted the following[112]:

> *"Leaving it behind:*
>
> *Looking back on my own journey of transition, I can clearly identify a variety of factors that were instrumental in the weakening of my allegiance and devotion to a committed torah life (in no particular order):*
>
> - *Frustration that I was not allowed to pursue activities and experiences that were enjoyable and meaningful to me. And the opposite:*
>
> - *Being forced to constantly engage in activities that I found boring, meaningless, and even painful (and even being taught that I must be devoted to it and enjoy it!).*
>
> - *Engaging in innocuous activities, but because they have been characterized as unkosher, feeling guilty about it and reinforcing the self-image of a transgressor.*
>
> - *Witnessing hypocrisy, lies and injustice perpetrated in the name of Torah, halacha, and Yiddishkeit.*
>
> - *Being made to feel second-class.*
>
> - *Not being allowed to freely express my true feelings and views about many issues.*
>
> - *The constant and endless harping about so many trivial and irrelevant halachos and issues as if they were the most important issues of life.*
>
> - *Discovering that certain basic tenets of Jewish life and thought might not really be as true as I was led to believe; that facts, history, and even torah were being distorted to further an agenda.*
>
> - *Realizing that those charged with my upbringing (family members, rabbis, teachers) made decisions which were far from*

---

[112] Reproduced with the permission of the (anonymous) blogger. The original was posted at http://daashedyot.blogspot.com/2005/02/leaving-it-behind.html. The phenomenon of the 'blogosphere' and of its Jewish corners is truly fascinating, and gives a very sharp picture of what many young Jews are actually thinking and feeling.

being in my best interests because they felt that a proper frum upbringing demanded that such a path be taken.

- When I realized that the trust I had in the torah system may be a bit unfounded.

- When I came to the conclusion that I was just not going to be happy living a typically frum, torah lifestyle.

These are all general categories, each of which has myriad examples, some trivial, others more significant. All of which probably contributed in some way to my loyalty to frumkeit *being reduced to a mere echo of it's previous commitment."*

This writer was describing an awful experience in an apparently Orthodox school. However, his (? perhaps 'her') experience *in principle* could have been in many Jewish schools, of very different types, with adjustments for a different set of expectations. The lessons are clear, and do not need further comment.

7.3.4 The psychological profile of the Jewish Studies teacher

A friend of mine once commented that "In the Jewish Studies classroom every student has their entire family invisibly sitting with them". Both the motivations and the pressures on the Jewish Studies teacher are significantly different from the pressures and motivations of most General Studies teachers.

Teaching Torah is a *mitzvah*. The conscientious Jewish Studies teacher has an emotional investment in the school and in the students that is connected to his/her most personal religious and community commitments. A commonly found challenge is balancing the metaphysical and spiritual sense of purpose with the mundane demands of structure and management.

As noted above, most general studies teachers enter teaching because they are interested in teaching. Most Jewish Studies teachers enter the teaching profession because they are interested in 'Yiddishkeit'. This difference can occasionally manifest itself in several recognizable characteristics of Jewish Studies staff:

- They take their teaching and the students' reaction to it very personally, with both positive and negative consequences. Their dedication to students can be impressive; their reactions to students failure to accept their teaching can be deeply personal

- An occasional disdain for the essential administrative routines of the school ("This school is more concerned about whether the marks are in on time than with the neshamas [= souls] of the students")

- An occasional lack of sympathy for the necessary balancing act(s) of the Administration. ("If this was really a Jewish school, the Administration would cancel the sports and arrange extra learning")

- Occasional preparedness to ignore the curriculum in favor of what the teacher thinks the students should know, or to deal in an ad-hoc manner with current issues

- Demands for mid-term leave to attend family 'smachot' (= celebrations), or requests to take time off to travel before festivals – understandable in terms of Jewish community culture, but very difficult to accommodate in a professional environment SEE SECTION 10.3

Some of these can be symptomatic of ambivalence towards the school as an institution – regarding it as a utilitarian platform for 'chinuch' or 'kiruv' but without intrinsic value, and not deserving respect in and of itself. To overcome these somewhat immature expressions of religious /cultural "attitude", the school must assert its own identity as an institution. Being a member of staff entails a professional and responsible commitment to the routines necessary to run the school.

The effective school must work to be one seamless school, where every member of staff shares common values and a common professional ethos. The Jewish Studies teacher must take ownership – even if from a distance – in the Art and Drama program, and the Art teacher must take ownership – even from a distance – in the Tanakh program. Because JS teachers tend to come from a variety of professional and educational backgrounds, the school may have to work hard on providing PD to the Jewish Studies staff, or persuade the local BJE to do so on a community basis.

Either way, every teacher must share in the common responsibility of implementing the essential processes of the school.

7.4 Professional structuring and staffing of the Jewish Studies Department

For issues around the engagement, recruitment and management of shlichim – teachers on contract from Israel -- SEE SECTION 7.4.5

7.4.1 The 'School Rabbi /Rav'

In addition to Rabbis who are on the teaching faculty, many schools will want to appoint a 'School Rabbi', whose function – broadly – is to provide leadership and organization for ritual and spiritual areas of school activity. Where the school is associated with a particular stream within the Jewish community, the School Rabbi will also have a role as keeper and symbol of the values and ideology of the denomination, and, in most cases, will be the 'Rabbinic authority' or *Posek* for the school.

The School Rabbi may be on staff, or may be a local Rabbi who occupies an honorary position.

An effective 'School Rabbi" on staff – wise, knowledgeable, understanding, inspiring – can be a huge influence in a school, and can be part of the irreplaceable positive memories of the school held by students, staff, and parents alike. Preferably, a school Rabbi should have some teaching load; effective classroom presence will increase credibility with professional peers, understanding of school life and school routine, and will afford an opportunity to build relationships with students.

There are occasionally tensions between a School Rabbi and a Principal, particularly if the Principal (Jewish or non-Jewish) is perceived as a 'Secular' Principal. The Rabbi may feel that the Principal is not sensitive to the Jewish dimension of the school, or not giving enough importance to Jewish themes or calendar occasions. Calendar clashes are a fertile ground for disagreement, because they have implications about public priorities and thus have symbolic importance[113].

If the Principal is a Rabbi, the Principal may exercise the function of 'School Rabbi', or be able to establish authority over an appointed School Rabbi. Non-rabbi Principals may have a problem with the appointment of a School Rabbi. If this is a staff appointment, it has to be clear that the Rabbi is not, and cannot be, autonomous, and should work with the Principal under a clear Job Description, agreed by both before employment commences. (No staff member – whatever their function – can undermine the Principal's decisions or leadership[114]).

Alternatively, the post of 'School Rabbi' and 'School Posek' ('Rabbinic authority') may be separated, and the 'School Posek' may be external.

Whether internal or external, **only the Principal may seek a Rabbinic ruling on behalf of the school**. The rabbi must also recognize and respect the Principal's prerogative.

> *It is unacceptable to have groups or individuals (teachers, parents or even students) bypassing the Principal, obtaining a "ruling" on some issue and then presenting the Principal with a fait accompli.*

The pluses and minuses of having an external rabbinic authority include:

- An external authority is more objective, and can give decisions without pressure from peers in the staff room. (Sometimes, this

---

[113] "Should the Debating Team be allowed to compete in a local competition on a minor fast day?".

[114] Argue with, appropriately – yes; disagree with, appropriately – certainly. Undermine – no.

can be a relief to the 'School Rabbi', who may not want the responsibility).

- The Head of School may be able to confidentially share a fuller picture of any given issue with a Rabbi who is not a member of staff.

- A community Rabbi may be able to apply a broader perspective of Community concern to any issue.

However, the opposites of all of the above are also true:

- An external authority may not appreciate the school context, or understand the way a school works.

- You may not always be able to share the full background of an issue with someone outside the school.

- The 'community perspective' may not work in the interests of the school.

All of the above considerations also apply to the issue of 'internal' (Faculty) School Rabbi vs. 'external' (Community) School Rabbi. Whatever the local arrangement, it is essential that the post have written, agreed, terms of reference, which appropriately respect the authority and the responsibilities of both parties.

7.4.2 Director of Jewish Studies

In some schools, the Principal functions as the Head of Jewish Studies. Otherwise, many Jewish schools have a designated 'Director of Jewish Studies[115]' as their senior educational professional, responsible for the design and implementation of the Jewish Studies curriculum, and reporting directly to the Principal. In some schools, the responsibility of the DJS may be wider.

The post of DJS can be the most difficult in the school, for the reasons discussed at length in this book, including:

- Lack of definition of an agreed JS curriculum.

- Severe difficulties in both recruitment and supervision of staff.

- Conflicting criteria for measuring success in Jewish Studies.

- Internal and external pressure around the Jewish identity and aims of the school.

---

[115] Alternative designations include 'Head of Limmudei Kodesh', 'Vice-Principal, Jewish Studies' etc.

- Conflicts in some schools surrounding the relative importance of 'Jewish' and 'General' studies.

- Student emotions regarding their own identities and beliefs.

The duties of a Director of Jewish Studies may be wide-ranging (up to overall responsibility for the entire Jewish program of the school), but will at least include:

- Determining and coordinating the delivery of curriculum

- The preparation of materials

- The setting and maintenance of standards

- JS timetabling and course allocations for staff and students

- The supervision of staff.

Duties may also include:

- Recruitment of staff.

- Supervision of the extra-curricular Jewish dimension of the school.

- General responsibility for the Jewish ethos of the school.

The post requires individuals of uncommon skills – equal, in many cases, to those of a Principal. The Director of Jewish Studies, however, is not necessarily the inspirational or spiritual head of the school, but, if you will, the senior manager of the Jewish dimension of the school. The task of the DJS may not necessarily be to define the Jewish dimension of the school (although every management decision certainly has a values implication) – but to ensure that it works

The DJS has to possess a formidable list of talents. They include:

- Excellent organizational, planning and administrative skills.

- A knowledge and appreciation of curriculum planning and design, and of good pedagogy.

- A profound Jewish knowledge and sensitivity.

- A wide-ranging understanding of different areas of Jewish Studies.

- A good eye for talented teachers.

- Ability to understand the Jewish concerns of parents and students.

The DJS has to enjoy an excellent working relationship with the Principal, who must be able to trust the DJS to an exceptionally high degree. Equally, the DJS has to enjoy the confidence of the Board of Directors.

The function of the DJS is not necessarily the same as that of a School Rabbi. The managerial function of the DJS is essential to the organizational and educational framework of the school - the ability to operate the Jewish classroom, with all of its complexity. Without that skill as part of the management team, the school will lack the means of translating inspiration into education.

An essential part of the skills necessary for the Director of Jewish Studies is sympathy for the Jewish struggles of students. Teenagers are unlikely to navigate their High School years without questions, the occasional rebellion and a tendency to 'test' their parents and their teachers. The DJS will frequently be in a mediating position.

7.4.3 Recruiting Jewish Studies teachers

Recruiting and managing the Jewish Studies teaching staff is a major key to the success of the school. Principals find themselves with little choice when seeking to fill Jewish Studies teaching posts, when at the same time faced with many applicants for General Studies vacancies.

Most aspects of the Jewish Studies teacher shortage are beyond the control of the Principal. Nevertheless, the Principal has to do the maximum possible to try and ensure that the school has the best teachers. There are, unfortunately, no secret or magic strategies, and the process is doubly complicated because candidates will often make their choices on grounds that have nothing to do with the post being offered *("We're going to x because that's where my spouse's family live")*.

No stone should be left unturned in the search for staff. There are direct and indirect channels of recruitment. They include:

- Local advertising (in larger communities)

- Online forums and Jewish job-seeking bulletin boards

- Liaison with teacher-training institutions and placement agencies

- Local networking with rabbis, Judaic Studies departments at Universities, and with other Jewish institutions

- Keeping an eye out for "accompanying spouses" arriving in your area with partners who are coming for research, work or study at local corporations, hospitals and universities

You may partially staff the school with shlichim SEE SECTION 7.5. However, there must be a majority of 'local' staff who share a similar background and language with the students.

Plan your recruitment strategy. Questions to ask include the following:

- What type of teacher(s) do you want?

- What subjects do they have to teach?

- What are the most likely sources for recruitment – geographically and institutionally? Where are your target constituencies likely to see advertisements?

- What are the contractual conditions offered?

- How much flexibility do you have in offering incentives (if any)?

- What can you do to present the opportunity of teaching at your school in the best light – for example, what community facilities (synagogues, 'chevrah', schools) are available to teachers if they come to join your school? If, realistically, the answer is "few", then you have to frame an appeal to the "pioneering spirit" of candidates.

- Are you projecting a professional image of the school?

- How can teaching at your school advance the personal / professional status or experience of the teachers?

Networking is also a valuable means of hearing 'who is around'. Networking should be used with caution, as the Principal has to reserve the right to be the judge of who are the best teachers for the school. Often a (well-meaning) parent, Board member or local Rabbi will call, offering a candidate for consideration as a teacher. This can be fruitful; but sometimes they are promoting an individual's employment at the school as a solution to another community problem. The Principal has to be uncompromising in putting the school's interests above all other considerations.

Care has to be taken in approaching potential teachers on the recommendation of others; the recipient of a phone call may interpret that as an offer of a job. A better course of action is to insist to the intermediary that the candidate must call the Principal. When they do, ask for a resume and covering letter, and ensure that the contacts are kept on a professional basis. Make it clear that "this is an exploratory conversation, without commitment on either side". Make sure that every application is acknowledged, politely thanked, and given clear indications of the status of their application.

Jewish Studies staff will present with very diverse qualifications and experience.

Assessment of a potential teacher comprises several areas – personal and professional SEE SECTION 7.4.4, below. The school will want to satisfy itself that the candidate is personable, has integrity, and is an educational personality – and either has, or can acquire, the qualities and skills of a successful teacher. It is essential that the teacher feels comfortable with the values and ethos of the school.

Some candidates will assure you that they can "of course" teach Jewish History SEE SECTION 7.9, as though that is a field that requires neither training nor knowledge. Check them out – carefully[116].

Every credible candidate should be interviewed, and it is important to check references. References from previous posts may be reflecting settings very different from those in which the potential teacher will be required to perform. The vagaries of the Jewish community being what they are, occasionally the traditional warning signs of past record (a series of posts in quick succession being the most common) may not be that significant, although they should always be carefully investigated.

Often you may not be assessing past performance, but future potential.

> *With good supervision, and consistent guidance and professional development, will this person become a good teacher?*

While standard procedure for all potential teachers, it is especially important that potential Jewish Studies teachers give a sample lesson or two. Ask a senior teacher to relinquish their class for a lesson, and provide an outline of what they would be teaching. Give your candidate plenty of notice, and whatever material he or she needs, and send them into the classroom. If possible, it is a courtesy to the candidate to allow them to sit in on one or two classes before they have to give their own sample lesson. A senior Administrator should observe the lesson(s). You will learn a great deal from the questions that the candidate asks beforehand, and of course you will learn a great deal from observing the class, making every allowance for the fact that the teacher will not be familiar with the students. Casual feedback from the students after the lesson is always very valuable.

Follow up soon after the interview. If you are rejecting them, be polite. If you are offering a post, give a written offer and ask for a return of a signed copy of your letter by a given date, signifying acceptance. From that point on, both parties are committed to the agreement[117].

7.4.4 Assessing qualifications in Jewish Studies

A particular difficulty in recruiting Jewish Studies staff is the lack of uniformity in qualifications. Unless candidates are graduates of one of the recognized Jewish University or Seminary training programs, or have rabbinic ordination from a well-established institution, the school may have difficulty in evaluating qualifications.

---

[116] The number of teachers actually qualified to teach Jewish History is miniscule, which is a great pity, as properly taught Jewish History can be one of the most effective programs in any Jewish school. Horror stories abound of what some schools teach under the rubric of 'Jewish History'.

[117] SEE SECTION 9.5.7 – 'Offers are binding – on both sides'

Sometimes yeshivot and seminary qualifications include academic degrees, which also need validation – SEE SECTION 9.2.1

Candidates may present Yeshivah or Seminary[118] qualifications from totally unregulated institutions. Can your candidate really teach text? Does he or she really know enough to teach Tanakh? Or Mishnah – let alone Gemara? Will their knowledge of "Jewish Philosophy" (whatever that means) really stand up to the questions of bright, inquisitive, Grade 12 students, who may bring all sorts of knowledge to their classroom? Will your candidate *teach* – or *preach*? Is your teacher interested in *'kiruv'* – or in education?

There are similar problems in evaluating graduates of University programs in Judaic Studies, which vary wildly in their content and standards.

One recent proliferation seems to be programs which encourage students to go straight from undergraduate degrees to Masters' programs in either "Jewish Education' or 'Administration' – without ever having set foot in a classroom. Graduates of these programs, with little or no classroom experience, apply for senior posts in schools. Avoid them.

7.4.5 Local Israeli teachers

Teachers from Israel currently living in the school's community (i.e. not *Shlichim}* sometimes need a different set of questions. Written references from Israeli schools tend to be formulaic and relatively uninformative. An Ivrit speaker is not necessarily a good Ivrit teacher, and Israeli Tanakh (from both the religious and non-religious systems) is very different than Tanakh taught in most Diaspora schools (greater emphasis on text, lesser emphasis on message).

Often, the first thing to establish is the teaching credentials of the teacher. Tour Guides, informal educators, Community Center workers etc. have many skills, but none of these are teaching qualifications – especially for a Diaspora classroom. In a small community, you may not have much choice, but in that case the teacher needs careful supervision. Teachers of 'Civics' *("Ezrachut"*) or 'Israel Studies' *("Moledet")* do not have relevant experience for teaching Jewish Studies in a Jewish High school. On the other hand, Israeli teachers of other subjects who have a personal background of religious education – especially if they have taken courses of study at post-High School level – may make excellent Jewish Studies teachers.

A qualified teacher from Israel should have a printout from the Israeli Ministry of Education *("tadpis")* that shows their qualifications and experience, the subjects they are qualified to teach, and at what level.

If the post is for teaching Ivrit, you will want to know:

---

[118] Seminary qualifications tend to be more reliable / rigorous.

- Does the teacher have, or is the teacher willing to acquire, any training in language teaching?

- Does the teacher understand correct 'nikkud' and grammar?

Finally, does the teacher understand the Jewish aims of your school?

7.5 Employing Shlichim

The role, or potential role of *shlichim*[119] in Diaspora Jewish High Schools is much debated.

If skillfully recruited, used correctly, and properly managed with preparation and planning, *shlichim* can add a huge, positive, extra dimension to a school[120] and to its community - both in the classroom and in extra-curricular life. But just bringing over a *shaliach* and sending them into a classroom with the instruction 'do something' is a recipe for disaster, and a guarantee of frustration, failure and crisis for the *shaliach* and his (or her) family.

Successful use of *shlichim* depends on planning. What is the *shaliach* going to teach? Ivrit? Tanakh? Talmud? Are they to have a formal role in the extra-curricular program? Do you have an Ivrit b'Ivrit program, or is it necessary that the *shaliach* /*shlichah* be fluent in English? In the post you are designating, how important is it that the teacher is able to deal with issues that demand a thorough knowledge of the nature of the local community?

7.5.1 Shlichim - budgeting

Work out a thorough budget for employing the *shaliach*. Properly arranged, a *shaliach* can be a relatively expensive[121] proposition, costing perhaps a third as much again as employing a regular full-time teacher.

---

[119] *Shaliach* (m), *shlichah* (f), *shlichim* (pl) – Israeli teachers brought over on three-year contracts to teach in the school, frequently through the good offices of the Jewish Agency/WZO Education Department in Jerusalem.

[120] At the time of writing, at TanenbaumCHAT in Toronto we have (I am told) the largest group of *shlichim* at any school in the Diaspora – fifteen in all (seven couples and one single), of a total Jewish Studies and Ivrit staff of over sixty. They are an integral, successful and immensely important part of our school. Having between a quarter and a third of JS staff as *shlichim* seems to be a comfortable and workable proportion.

[121] At one time, *shlichim* used to be subsidised – if not paid for – by the WZO/Jewish Agency. The WZO/JA no longer subsidises *shlichim* in North America, or other affluent countries. However, as will be explained, there are advantages to working with and through the WZO/JA. From the *shaliach*'s point of view, status as a *shaliach* of the Jewish Agency/WZO gives them certain protected rights under Israeli law, including the right to return to their previous place of work within three years.

Your costs may include:

- Advertising costs

- Interviewing / recruiting costs

- Legal costs

- Family travel and shipping costs (outward and return)

- Relocation allowance

- Housing subsidy (if applicable)

- Salary and benefits

- Childrens' school/education costs

- 'Home leave' tickets (once during *shlichut*)

When you have the budget, make sure your Board approves it.

7.5.2 Shlichim - recruiting

Begin by consulting a local Immigration lawyer who should advise you of the legal applications necessary to bring over a teacher from overseas for a defined—limit contract. Act accordingly. Do not employ *shlichim* (or anyone else) in contravention of local legislation. In some jurisdictions, there are long-standing bi-lateral agreements regarding *shlichim*; the Jewish Agency should be able to advise you if these operate in your area.

In most cases, *shlichim* may be located via the Jewish agency in Jerusalem. The recruiting 'season' generally lasts from January through May.

Finding good shlichim is as difficult as finding good JS teachers. To even be candidates, the shlichim have to fulfill the following conditions:

- As noted below, both[122] partners have to be experienced teachers, or at least have some credible educational background

- They have to be prepared at the time of the opportunity to work in the Diaspora for three or more years

- Their family situation – age and number of children – must permit this

---

[122] Unless your budget allows for one non-salaried partner. Occasionally, communities can put together 'packages' that enable this. In some cases, a partner may be in receipt of a pension, or is involved in some net-based profession that allows them to be completely mobile.

- They must have relevant qualifications and knowledge to teach in the Diaspora, and be prepared to work in a very different Jewish environment

- They must be flexible personalities in order to cope with the challenges of shlichut, able to adjust to the different realities of Jewish life in the Diaspora, and to the mentality of students in your community; ready to accept a challenge, and ready to learn and adapt

- They have to be very stable and sensible individuals

As will be appreciated, each condition substantially narrows the field of eligible candidates.

While the 'Sochnut' (the Ivrit term for the Jewish Agency) generally provides an excellent service, it pays to invest a little more in order to ensure that the shlichim are the best for your school. All of these arrangements may be coordinated with the Jewish Agency. The school may retain a recruiter in Israel, who will independently locate and pre-interview shlichim, and observe candidates in the classroom in Israel. At the very least, either the school Principal or someone who knows your school well (a former teacher or Administrator living in Israel, or a former shaliach) should interview candidates.

All candidates should be provided with a full 'Information Pack' about the school, including a summary in Ivrit, and should be encouraged to independently research the school and the community. Practical information regarding living costs, insurance, etc. should also be available in Ivrit. If you have shlichim in place, give the prospective shlichim their phone numbers. Different profiles of shlichim will succeed in different situations, but in every case:

- Candidates must be qualified, experienced High School teachers. It is difficult enough inducting and training shlichim. You do not have the time or the resources to simultaneously teach them how to be teachers. Do not accept non-teachers, or inexperienced teachers, even as 'accompanying spouses'.

- Engaging (young) singles is far more risky than engaging couples, for obvious reasons. A single, young man or woman far away from home has the potential for finding themselves (and the school) in inappropriate situations.

- Your expectations must be clear, and carefully laid out in a contract, of which a summary should be available in Ivrit, explaining the terms and conditions of employment. For what will the school be responsible, and for what will the shaliach be responsible?

- Arrangements for the shaliach's children must be carefully considered. Shlichim arriving with large families (more than three or four children) may find it very difficult to manage their children, and to give of their best to the school at the same time.

- Well before their summer of arrival, ship them copies of teaching materials and curriculum relevant to their projected teaching.

7.5.3 Shlichim – on arrival

It is best to have the *shlichim* arrive at least two or three weeks before the beginning of school. Meet incoming *shlichim* and their families at the airport. Don't forget to bring drinks and snacks for the children. Make sure that they have food and necessary supplies for the first two or three days. Assign a teacher or a veteran *shaliach* to see them through steps such as opening a bank account, buying a car, getting insurance etc. The local synagogue will often arrange for initial hospitality, and the sight of a local community member appearing with hot pizza on the first evening will create instant goodwill.

In the first few days, arrange a tour of the city and of the community. Well before school begins, brief the *shlichim* clearly about the school, the students, the parent body, the school procedures, and the classes they are to teach. At the opening staff meeting, introduce them to staff. Again, assign a mentor who will be available to answer all questions, large and small.

For the first few weeks, carefully support and advise your new *shlichim*. Meet with them frequently. However experienced they are, the ethos and atmosphere of a Diaspora Jewish High School are very different from what they are used to in Israel. In many cases – especially if your recruitment has been skillful – the *shlichim* will be excellent teachers who will quickly adapt. However, the school, too, has to learn how to use *shlichim* most effectively; understand the areas where they will have most challenges, and ensure that quick and sympathetic support is available.

7.6 Israel

7.6.1 Shaviv's second paradox

Every attempt to relate to Israel in a Diaspora school has to grapple with 'Shaviv's second paradox':

**At one and the same time, Israel is the most Jewish place on earth –
and the least Jewish place on earth**

It is the most Jewish place on earth for a series of obvious reasons – theology, geography, history, language, national culture and so forth. But it is the least Jewish place on earth because many of the characteristics that powerfully define Jewishness in the Diaspora are completely absent in Israel, either by circumstance or design. Examples include, but are certainly not limited to:

- Jewish minority status, with all of its accoutrements

- A sense of Jewish community

- Relationship to religious Jewishness as an integral feature of Jewish identity

- Jewishness as nostalgia

- Concern for particularistic 'Jewish survival' in a societal/sociological perspective, and recognition and willingness to invest in personal, family and community Jewish identity and lifestyle

Israeli society, on the other hand, exercises a different set of characteristics and responsibilities, including (but, again, certainly not limited to):

- Jewishness as a majority status, with significant issues of relating to minorities within Israel

- Jewishness as a national culture, with minimal conscious effort required to 'live' Jewishly

- Identity as a predominantly national issue

- Concerns regarding the responsibility of political and military power

- Religious-secular animosity, which in the Diaspora is not present to anywhere near the same degree

- Frequent lack of interest, lack of concern, and certainly lack of information about the Diaspora – 'al achat kamah v'chamah' (= even more so) about the contemporary Jewish Diaspora

- A universalism and self-perception of 'Israelis as citizens of the world'

I am sure that every reader will be able to augment both lists.

To make it even more difficult, our schools are totally products of the Diaspora world-view.

The answer to the paradox can only be in education, understanding, dialogue, and flexibility.

7.6.2 Israel in the school program

Israel, in all its dimensions, has to be central to the ethos of every Jewish school. Different schools will position and highlight that centrality in different ways.

High Schools will reflect the complexities of contemporary Israel-Diaspora relations, often in more direct ways than the public stance of central Jewish community organizations. Imaginative and honest educational programs offer the opportunity to create deep engagement with Israel that will continue for a lifetime.

From a school management perspective, the school's responsibility – as opposed to the responsibility of other agencies – is to educate as well as to celebrate. \Knowledge – real knowledge - of Israel comes from school. It is the school's responsibility to lay the foundations of an informed relationship based on something more than falafel – *important as that emotional attachment is*.

The Israel dimension of the school should not be left as an ad-hoc 'add-on'. Do not take for granted that students who may have been born in the mid-1990's or later know any basic facts about Israel. The list of basics includes knowledge of the following:

- Basic geography and historical geography of Israel (every classroom should have a large-size laminated map[123] of Israel of display)

- An understanding of 'Kedushat Eretz Yisrael' (the holiness of the Land of Israel) in Jewish text, belief and practice

- a serious Ivrit program

- History of the Yishuv with at least a survey course from the time of the Tanakh to modern times

- An appreciation of the historical context and main ideas (in their diversity) of the modern Zionist[124] movement, and the history of the Yishuv from the nineteenth century up to 1948

- The history of the State of Israel from 1948 to the present day

- A familiarity with the sociology and reality of contemporary Israel

While this list sounds daunting, films, videos and internet can provide lively resources that can quickly and effectively provide much of this information, especially the last

---

[123] See also the excellent interactive map of Israel at http://www.eyeonisrael.com

[124] I am writing this within a few days of the passing of Rabbi Arthur Hertzberg z'l, whose book "The Zionist Idea" remains a brilliant and comprehensive anthology and survey of classic Zionism.

two items.   A serious school will allocate substantial teaching time to a planned curriculum for much of the rest.

The pitfalls of teaching about Israel include the temptation to allow teachers to deal with "current events" without giving any background, and often from a personal or individual viewpoint. That serves a purpose, but it is not educational.

The school must also recognize the diversity of identity and outlook (including political outlook) in contemporary Israel. It may not feel it wishes to teach that diversity (although I would argue that it should), but failing to recognize it means that you are effectively teaching about a society that does not exist – a Diaspora vision of 'what we think Israel ought to be', rather than what it actually is.

To make the Israel program effective, it has to incorporate an active, affective component. The single most effective program is a school Israel Trip.   There is great flexibility and choice, and local community agencies (and the WZO) can be very helpful and supportive.

Every school knows that there is also a huge range of other resources (visitors, twinning schemes) available to enrich the Israel content of the school program. Celebrations of Yom Hazikaron and Yom Ha'atzmaut can be transformational.   The internet and video conferencing have opened up new possibilities of school-to-school contact.

7.6.3   Year out in Israel

A 'year out' in Israel is a great conclusion to Jewish High school.

Through the 'MASA" initiative, the Jewish Agency/WZO are currently putting considerable resources into promoting the appeal of the 'year out' by widening the programs on offer. Programs are emerging which offer all sorts of combinations of volunteering, archaeology, sports, and environmental projects, often with touring and study built in.   In many cases, programs may offer University credits valid in American Universities[125].   Every school will be familiar with the various Yeshivah/Seminary programs, energetically marketed every year, and the overseas programs of the major Israeli Universities.

These are all, unfortunately, still expensive options.   The year out schemes await their 'birthright'-style philanthropists and visionaries.

Schools should act as information channels, and good schools will put only minimum restrictions on the programs advertised through the school. If your school has a particular denominational or ideological commitment, by the time the students graduate you should have convinced them to go to a sympathetic Israel program. If

---

[125]   Students should check carefully before the program begins that the credit offered is acceptable to the proposed destination University/program, and should – if possible – get that assurance in writing.

you have – alternative institutions should not tempt them. But if you haven't, then as a school you have a responsibility to serve the needs of those students as well. The choices that students make after school (whether in Israel programs or otherwise) can be revealing, and often surprise teachers and Administrators (not to mention parents, grandparents and rabbis). As happens occasionally with University/College choices, whether the surprise is pleasant, the opposite, or simply puzzling, sometimes you realize that you have not understood at all what has been going on inside a particular student's head as they have progressed through the school. Under those circumstances, it is better to have the student remember the school respectfully and gratefully for opening a window of opportunity than to resent the fact that the school only offered a narrow choice.

Larger schools will establish relationships with different institutions, which will help with student applications to competitive programs. Often the personal relationships between Administrators and admissions faculty are decisive in deciding between competing applicants from different schools. That is a diplomatic way of saying that lobbying by the school (phone calls, emails, and I regret to say, pressure from well-placed rabbis, donors and persons of real or supposed influence) can be important in securing places. It is in the school's interest to be honest:

> *The student is one of the very, very best we have seen in the school for several years. S/he is excellently suited to the style and content of your program. I unhesitatingly recommend – on a 1 – 10 scale s/he is a 9.5. You 'must' offer a place. You know that I rarely make these calls!*

> *I'm happy to place a call on behalf of 'M'. S/he is a very good student indeed – conscientious, bright and motivated. S/he would flourish in your program, and would contribute well to the 'ruach'. I think she is a little shy, and her personality may not have come across fully at interview. if you can give her a place – it would be excellent for the student, good for you, and I'd be very grateful.*

> *'G''s parents asked me to place this call. I know that 'G' has applied to the program, and his/her parents are very concerned that s/he should be accepted. In confidence – this is a borderline case. We have had many concerns about 'G' over the past year, and I'm not sure that a year in Israel at this stage is a good idea. The Report Card indicates some areas of concern. On the other hand – being away may be a maturing influence, and perhaps s/he will flourish being at a distance from his/her parents!*

> *Please call me regarding 'T'. I need to check that the application fully discloses certain issues.*

The senior Administrator coordinating Israel programs should be able to visit Israel every year or so to personally visit the institutions and programs to which your students are applying.

Ask returning graduates of year-in-Israel program to visit the school and speak to G11 students (well before they begin applying, before 'recruiters' appear in the school, and while they have a chance to think carefully about choices).

- Finally, be sure to note – in writing - somewhere along the line that the school cannot take responsibility for recommending any program or institution, and that it is the ultimate duty of parents and students to check carefully whether or not the program is well-organized, properly supervised, suitable for the particular student, and educationally responsible and sound.

7.6.4 Family disagreement over a 'Year out in Israel'

Occasionally, students will either acquiesce in parental pressure to apply to Israel programs when they really don't want to go; flatly refuse to consider the option for reasons that are unclear; or desperately want to go to Israel against parental wishes. In all of these cases, quiet, discreet, sympathetic 'talking the issue through' can normally either resolve the issue or reach a compromise.

Parents may oppose their child's wish to spend a year in Israel. It tends to be a very emotional opposition, based on religious, educational, security or financial grounds. In the first three, what parents fear the most include:

- Parental alienation based on religious transformation – their child will no longer relate to them ("We will lose our child")

- Relinquishing of educational (i.e University) opportunity

- "Unhealthy influence" of "someone" who has "persuaded" their child to take this course

- The perception that it is physically dangerous to be in Israel at any time

Assuming the school judges the student's judgment to be reasonably mature – whether it is being exercised in one direction or the other - it has to be gently pointed out to the parents that the student is entering adulthood, and deserves respect for their independent decisions. For parents who believe their children are in physical danger in Israel – it is often helpful to have other parents talk to them.

The student, too, must be aware that if funds are not available (from whatever sources) then they cannot impose a cost on their parents that they, the parents, simply cannot afford. In many such cases, students go to University, work in vacations, look for funding opportunities, and are able to have their year in Israel either during or following their student years.

In most cases, whether the parents object or the student doesn't want to go, common compromises include undertakings by one or both parties that:

- The student can go on a program that is not pure 'learning', but includes recreational, volunteer or other varied elements

- The student gives an absolute undertaking that they will return after one year (frequently combined with:)

- The student gives an absolute undertaking that they will not give up their University place

- The parents agree that if the student is not happy, s/he may return at Chanukah (with some agreement of what the student would then do...)

- The student promises they will not change their program, or volunteer for military service, without parental permission.

7.6.5 University in Israel

Going to University in Israel can be an attractive option. Programs and opportunities change, but can normally be checked through the 'Friends' organizations that exist in most Jewish communities or the relevant website. Within different frameworks, substantial funding can be available to overseas students at regular programs in Israeli universities.

A growing phenomenon seems to be a 'College Year abroad' option – taking the second or third year (or a semester) at an Israeli University as part of a regular University program. There is often University financing available.

7.6.6 "Preparing students for Campus"

There is a constant expectation that the Jewish school system will "prepare" their students to deal with anti-Israel and antisemitic activity on university and college campuses. This expectation is voiced by community organizations and occasionally by parents.

- A clear distinction has to be made between the school's ability and duty to educate its students and its ability to 'prepare them for Campus'

- **A school cannot 'train' high school students to be political activists on University campuses. It is not fair, practical or realistic to expect them to be able to do so**

The students have not yet left school, and almost by definition live in relatively sheltered social environments. They cannot understand the university campus until they experience it, and for the most part have never set foot on a campus. It is facile, unrealistic and misleading to think that providing students with "answers" will in any way enable them to deal with the battle on campus.

High school students cannot even begin to imagine the politicized hostility they may encounter on the contemporary campus. The Jewish community itself does not encourage Jews to be politicized[126]. Experience suggests, too, that students in their last year of high school simply do not see such preparation as a priority – they are too busy with all the other preoccupations of G12 students. In Grade 11 they are too young.

- Attempts to 'make high school students aware' – including the dramatic programs brought by outside agencies ("We'll shock them!") – are totally counter-productive. The students are traumatized, and take the view that they want to stay as far away as possible from Jewish activity on campus, if it will involve such vulnerability and attack.

The school faculty cannot provide 'activist' training. The alternative – of bringing in outside agencies or personnel to provide seminars and courses is not a substitute, and, while it certainly has some value, can only provide very surface orientation.

What a school should try and do – at the most profound and at the deepest conceivable level – is to give each student the will to face whatever challenges they encounter, from an informed, inspired, embedded sense of Jewish self and Jewish community. An effective education should give knowledge, values and most important – if most intangible – motivation.

Other agencies, foremost among them Hillel, must add the skills of campus advocacy and representation.

At a practical level, *in addition to the curriculum provisions discussed above*, the school should ensure that:

- At 'college counseling' level, students are made fully aware of Hillel and other Jewish community facilities on different campuses; and the websites and other resources where they can locate that information themselves

- Students may be presented on graduation[127] with books such as Dershowitz' 'The Case for Israel'

- School Principals and/or Board Presidents should make their voices heard to University Chancellors where the rights of Jewish students are threatened, expressing concern about the safety and the status of their school graduates

---

[126] Whether they should be, given the current nature and depth of antisemitism in academic, political and cultural life is a different question.   But until and unless the Jewish community itself is much more aggressively and urgently political, it is unfair to expect its teenagers to be.
[127] I have often thought about producing a 'Jewish Survival Guide' for High school graduates, in similar size and format to the Student Agenda book, which would include a variety of 'Essential Information' sections – including, sadly but necessarily, a section outlining their comprehensive legal and civil rights as Jews on university campuses.

- Express public support for school grads who take leadership positions on Jewish campus life, and invite them back to school to talk about their own experiences.

7.7 Ivrit

From both an educational and management perspective, Ivrit is often the most difficult department or program within Jewish Studies. There are a substantial number of Jewish schools in North America (and worldwide) who have effectively given up teaching Ivrit in any systematic or serious manner; and even those who on principle do not wish to teach Ivrit as a modern language do not teach classical Hebrew either. The results are disastrous[128].

No person can be a serious Jew without a skill in Hebrew, and a school that does not tackle the teaching of Hebrew – as a language, or a textual necessity, or both – is failing its students. A Jew who does not have a reasonable knowledge of Hebrew is Jewishly illiterate.

In a book for Jewish High School lay and professional leaders, it should not be necessary to defend or explain the necessity of teaching Hebrew. In fairness, the reasons for the virtual abandonment of Hebrew are largely (but not completely) pragmatic. They include:

- As in other Jewish Studies areas, the lack of materials and trained teachers – especially since teaching Ivrit requires expertise in language acquisition. As far as I know, the Brandeis M.A. program is the only specialist training scheme for teachers of Ivrit in North America

- The ascendancy of English as a global language has lead to an overall decline in second-language teaching in the Anglophone world, in turn causing decreased prestige and interest in second-language teaching in schools

- Changes in overall school curriculum at Elementary levels mean that many students reach High School without any appreciation or understanding of grammar, grammatical concepts or

---

[128] On the day of writing this passage, I interviewed a student who had been in Haredi Day Schools and Yeshivot for over ten years. He could not read a Hebrew text (Pirkei Avot) except with difficulty and with many mistakes; could not translate an unseen pasuk of chumash; and could not recognise masculine/feminine, singular or plural in Hebrew. His report cards from his various educational institutions recorded marks from 60's to 80's in Chumash, Mishna, Navi, Gemara etc.

grammatical terminology, even in English. A student who does not have a grasp of grammar will not be able to learn Ivrit.

To these reasons must be added two ideological biases that exist in some more Orthodox circles – a bias against teaching Ivrit as representative of 'secular' Israel, and a different, but equally pervasive bias against systematically teaching even classical Hebrew grammar as supposedly representing 'Enlightenment' or 'non-traditional' educational methodology.

Schools are entitled to their views. But the overall effect is highly destructive. Whether the school wishes to teach Ivrit or Classical Hebrew, or both, it needs a strong policy of encouragement from the top of the school, and in current circumstances it needs a disproportionate investment of time and budget.

Every school can take a series of practical moves:

- Make it clear that Hebrew is a 'non-negotiable' part of the curriculum.

- The Faculty and the Education Committee, backed by the Board, should devise a plan to strengthen Hebrew in the school. Find partners. Be slow, but totally determined.

- Spare no effort to recruit and retain strong staff who are passionate and knowledgeable about Hebrew. If you are teaching Ivrit, insist that your teachers either have or acquire training in language teaching. Do not rely on local Ivrit-speakers who are not language teachers.

- Formal instruction in Hebrew must be a constant part of the curriculum throughout the school.

- Arrange PD for staff whose Hebrew is weak

- Aspire to have 'Ivrit b'Ivrit' instruction

- Institute testing and evaluation in Hebrew, and make attainment in Hebrew a prerequisite for promotion. Institute compulsory Summer School and make-up tests for students who fail at the end of the year.

While you will meet resistance from many quarters (all of them non-expert in Hebrew), the qualitative improvement in your school as the knowledge and expertise in Hebrew grows will be astounding.

There is a place to begin. And that is to check that ALL of your students can actually **read** Hebrew. If you have never done it, run a simple reading test, according to the level you assume of your students. You will be shocked at the results. Then do a 'crash course' blitz. A high school student can normally be taught accurate Hebrew reading and writing in a few hours.

7.8 How do you assess outcome?

7.8.1 "Serious Jews" and "non-serious Jews"

It is very difficult to assess outcome for the Jewish program of the Jewish school.

'Outcome' is clearly not simply academic – few, if any, readers of this book would regard the school as successful if a student obtained high 90's in every Judaic subject in Grade 12, but from the day they graduated never again had any involvement with anything Jewish.

In this, the Jewish dimension of the school is, again, very different from many other disciplines. If a student taking French never uses the language again after graduation, the French teacher may be sorry, but will probably not take it personally. If a student totally rejects Jewish practice, a Jewish Studies teacher may well regard it as personal failure.

It may not be possible to assess the impact of the Jewish High school experience until graduates are themselves parents. The definitive 'metric' at the point of graduation is elusive. Does the student keep kosher on June 30 in his/her year of graduation? S/he may not be by June 30 of the following year. (The reverse may also be true.) Does the student "love" Israel? That love has not yet withstood the tests of the wide world.   Has the student registered with Hillel? They may never go. If a student is not involved in any campus Jewish life, but out of profound sense of *chessed* is a leader in campus aid to local homeless – is that success for his/her Jewish education?

Although there is no obvious way of measuring it, the yardstick suggested by Rabbi Harold Kushner[129] is useful.   I found the following extract from one of his books, quoted in a Yom Kippur address by a California Rabbi:

> "... *if you have learned something about Reform, Conservative, and Orthodox Judaism, let me share with you ...that all these labels and divisions are meaningless and obsolete. There are only two kinds of Jews—serious Jews and non-serious Jews. Serious Jews try to do what Jews have always done... to pattern their lives on the insights of Judaism, whether in a Reform, Conservative, or Orthodox idiom, while to the non-serious Jew, it doesn't matter what style of synagogue*

---

[129] Rabbi Kushner is the well-known author of "When Bad Things Happen To Good People".

service he stays home from or which definition of mitzvah he ignores....

.... The question is whether you are interested in doing what Jews have always done, recapturing the feeling of standing at Sinai, bringing holiness into your life by sanctifying even its ordinary moments --- especially its ordinary moments". [130]

In Rabbi Kushner's comments, two things stand out: the distinction between "serious" and "non-serious" Jews, and the observation that the denominational "labels and divisions" are "meaningless and obsolete".

His words resonate strongly.

7.8.2 Graduate surveys

A more practical strategy for assessing outcome is to survey your graduates. I would caution against 'exit surveys' that seek your students' views of the school as they graduate in G12. It is the wrong time to ask. More valuable is the wider-cast net – surveying all of your graduates, from the beginning until those who have been out of school for a year or so. Take professional advice from a market-research company, who will be skilled in framing the questions, once the school has indicated the areas in which it is interested. For the survey to be useful, both the size of the group and the size of the response must be statistically valid. If you have email addresses for your alumni, investigate on-line survey programs are quick and cheap to utilize. A larger school will want to use a more sophisticated program.

This sort of survey can only be done every few years. Both the single results and the cumulative results of successive surveys can be fascinating, and invaluable sources of data for all sorts of school purposes.

Obvious areas to explore include:

- Demographic data – where do your alumni now live?

- Where do they work, and what are their professional profiles?

- What educational and professional qualifications did they obtain after leaving school?

- What are the Jewish profiles of their lives?

---

[130] "To Life!" by Rabbi Harold Kushner, Little Brown and Company, 1993. I believe that I first heard reference to the expression "Serious and non-serious Jews" from Mr. Chaim Klein.

- How do they view – in retrospect – different aspects of their High School experience?

The overall results should give a picture of how well the school is doing its job, or how well it used to do its job. Comparisons between recent and more veteran graduates should show how the school is educating successive generations. Interpreting the data, even in a superficial manner, needs skill. Those who were at the school in the 1960's will have been coming from very different families than those attending in the 1990's. Is there a changing pattern of satisfaction with the school? Why is that? Would your graduates send their own children to the school? Did your students feel well prepared for life after high school? How do the various indices of Jewish living of your alumni compare to other groups? Do they give *tzedakah*? Are they involved in Israel? Are they members of a synagogue? Is it the same synagogue to which their parents belonged? Do they feel that they live more, or less, active Jewish lives than their parents?

All of these questions – and more – will be illuminating, and will give data-driven guidance for future planning and programming.

7.9 A special plea for Jewish History

It is a tragedy that very few Jewish schools teach Jewish history[131] seriously or systematically, let alone critically. It is an orphaned subject in many Jewish schools.

High School students respond enthusiastically and appreciatively to serious Jewish history, taught by historians. It gives them a sense of who they are and where they have come from, as well as a realistic understanding and picture of how Jews and Judaism have developed over the centuries[132]. It helps them make sense of the 'map' of contemporary Jewish life and attitudes, and it makes them deeper, more serious Jews.

The operative word, however, is "serious". Hagiography – idealized portraits of individuals – is not history, *nor can serious Jewish history be taught without reference to the general historical context in which it took place.* It has to be honest, and describe the problematic events as well as the phenomena and movements of which the teacher "approves".

---

[131] ... and that schools generally have drastically weakened the teaching of history, period.

[132] At TanenbaumCHAT in Toronto, Jewish History is a major subject. The JH course covers four years (x 3 hrs. per week). G9 deals with the history of Jewish settlement in N. America, and the Toronto Jewish community; then in the second half of the year students study the Second Temple era up to and including the rise of Christianity. G10 covers the Medieval period; G11 Emancipation, the emergence of modern Jewish movements and the nineteenth century; and G12 the twentieth century. I believe it is one of the most valuable and effective parts of our curriculum.

A major problem is the dearth of teachers. Knowledgeable personnel are truly rare. A common – far too common – fallacy is that "anyone" can teach Jewish history. "Anyone" can't – but a talented and knowledgeable history teacher can make the subject sparkle.

8 MANAGING TENSIONS BETWEEN 'GENERAL' AND 'JEWISH'

8.1 First rule: one school, not two....

> "...ONE school philosophy... otherwise there will be two schools under one roof, and the school will never progress beyond a certain point. Regrettable variations of this – excellent recipes for school dysfunction – include...the 'Jewish Studies' school and the 'General Studies' school, in theory operating under the same name, but in fact subtly antagonistic entities (sometimes – not so subtly) "

--- SECTION 4.1 – "Leading the team"

In some form or another, every Jewish educational institution faces tension between the Jewish ethos of the school, and the society in which we live. It finds many different manifestations, from the obvious - we don't celebrate Christmas - to the more subtle –"Should Harry Potter books be in the library?". The tension may be philosophical, theological, political, or cultural; it is very often practical. The setting may be the classroom, the staffroom, the phys ed program, the parents' meeting, the Science lab... anywhere. It can be an openly confrontational situation; it can be as ephemeral as an eloquent, but silent, raised eyebrow at a certain moment.

The Principal is the 'keeper' of cultural and religious balance in the school.

S/he must ensure that the delivery of program throughout the school is consistent with policy. The school policies and practices should be clearly communicated to all members of staff (Jewish and General Studies), and must form part of the orientation or induction to new teachers. There will be huge variations in the practice of different schools. As usual, the operational principles are common.

The school should be conceived and run as a coherent, seamless entity. The worst of all situations – referred to above - is where there are effectively two schools operating under one roof – a Jewish Studies school and a General Studies school, each trying to undermine and/or de-legitimize the other. Such situations are not unknown. The students are likely to end up saying 'a plague on both of your houses'; the school will be rent with controversy and acrimony; the staff room will be divided and simmering; and, worst of all, no education will be taking place[133].

8.1.1 The basic choice: embrace the world or withdraw from it?

The school has to determine its basic philosophy of Jewish life. There are two competing strategies for the survival of Judaism in the open society. History suggests that neither is perfect, and the choice is particularly acute in educational environments. Nevertheless, the choice[134] has to be made. It will completely govern the school's attitude, in theory and in practice, to all of these issues.

- **The first strategy** is to 'embrace the world', and accept that in an Emancipated, open society, Judaism has to be in the marketplace of ideas. Within reasonable limits, modern Jewish life will be a synthesis of Judaism and modernity. It may take our community in unexpected and perhaps even radical directions, but knowledge is knowledge, and it cannot be denied. Judaism has to take a deep breath, and deal with it.

The advantages of this approach are:

- o   *Students should emerge better prepared to cope with many of the challenges of the wide world*

- o   *They should not be surprised or unnerved at views or ideas they encounter*

- o   *They will approach their Judaism from a more sophisticated and cosmopolitan viewpoint, understanding better the relationships – positive and negative – between Jews, Judaism and general society.*

The pragmatic disadvantage is that the complexity of the broader view may have been achieved at the loss of personal intensity and intensive personal commitment. The student has been taught multiple – not necessarily equal – loyalties.

---

[133] Although grades will continue to be given, exams will continue to be set, and graduates will continue to get into programs of their choice.

[134] The dilemma of the Jewish response to the opportunities and challenges of Emancipation and modernity is the basis of all Jewish history since the end of the Middle Ages. In writing the history of that fascinating time, the late Jewish historian Prof. Jacob Katz z'l, (1904-1998) is unsurpassed. Moses Mendelssohn (1729-1786) on the one hand, and the brilliant rabbinic personality Rabbi Moses Sofer (the 'Hatam Sofer') (1762-1839) on the other, formulated the theoretical underpinnings of the two competing philosophies. Mendelssohn urged Jews to enter European society and embark on a great adventure; Sofer urged cultural self-isolation as a survival strategy.   Both are insufficiently studied.   Knowingly or unknowingly, every contemporary Jewish movement, from 'Jewish Renewal' to the Satmar Hasidim in Williamsburg owes its identity to one of these two figures. As the school of S.R. Hirsch (1808-1888) demonstrates, neither is it a simplistic Orthodox/non-orthodox split.

- **The second strategy** is to deliberately restrict the worldview of your students with the aim of insulating them from an external society that is perceived as inimical to Jewish values. One of the freedoms of the open society is the freedom not to take part in it[135].

The advantages of the second philosophy are:

o *It does what it sets out to do – it shields students from the hostile world. Moreover, it educates them to regard the outside world as hostile.*

o *It creates powerful loyalties, and works well as long as the student – while at school or after – is content to live in a self-isolating or compartmentalized world.*

Its disadvantage is that the student is actually made more vulnerable to the influences from which the school seeks to protect him/her – whether religious, cultural, intellectual or political. They get no chance to develop critical faculties, and so when or if they encounter the culture of the outside world – they are defenseless. In facing challenges or unexpected realities, the student may feel anger at the school for not giving adequate education. It sometimes generates extreme reactions:

"If they didn't tell me the whole story about X, can I trust anything else they taught me?"

My own sympathies, by instinct and training, clearly lie with the first, more open option.

Yet other educators, whom I deeply respect, will choose the second. If you choose the second, only parts of the rest of this section will apply.

The school 'Statement of Philosophy and Purpose' should give unambiguous guidelines regarding the school's orientation and outlook. The Principal has the task of managing practical implementation. Whatever the circumstances, however, no Jewish school (and only the most avant-garde of other schools, few in number) will allow unlimited freedom of expression, and nor should they. Setting limits is a function of leadership.

---

[135] The supremely astute, early, insight of the Hatam Sofer.

8.2 School values for parents, students, teachers – and alumni

8.2.1 A voluntary association

It is important to understand the status of the school. It is a private, voluntary community of people with a shared value system. To attend the school, to be a parent at the school, to work at the school, or to be part of the governance of the school involves acceptance of the 'Statement of Philosophy and Purpose':

> Acceptance of a place at the school signifies acceptance by students and parents of school values and ethos, as specified in the 'Statement of Philosophy and Purpose', and of school policies and procedures as set out in the School Handbook, and as amended by Administration from time to time.

> Acceptance of employment at the school signifies understanding of its values and ethos, as specified in the 'Statement of Philosophy an Purpose', and of the duty of all staff to support the school's mission.

> A member of the Board of the school accepts and supports the values and ethos of the school as specified in the 'Statement of Philosophy and Purpose', and of school policies and procedures as set out in the School Handbook, as amended by Administration from time to time.

Occasionally (and sometimes uncomfortably), a parent, student or staff member may reach the conclusion that their participation in the school is no longer compatible with their beliefs. This can be coming from either side of the school's perceived or actual position.

> This is not a really Jewish school – I want a school that doesn't compromise!

> I need a place where I can ask whatever questions I want.

> Too much Jewish stuff.

8.2.2 Supporting school ethos and values – parents and students

The Jewish school system has succeeded in attracting a far broader range of families (especially at High School level) than most people would have thought possible thirty or forty years ago. With the broader range of families comes the broader range of problems.

With the broadening of our constituency and with the continuing changes in the social values of the Jewish community the demands and expectations of parents and students of the Jewish school also change. Parents do not automatically stand in awe of the school, or of the Administration. At broader-based schools, a constituency of parents and students – relatively small – will take the view that they are paying sizeable school fees and expect 'service' from the school to their specifications, regardless of the school's values and priorities.

- A wise Principal will act with latitude and discretion in situations where parents and, more so, students, dissent from the school consensus.

Some of those situations are discussed below. We try and teach our students to be independent, critical thinkers, and therefore shouldn't really complain when they are. A paradoxical element may be involved. (See following SECTION 8.2.5 for an Alumnus' perspective on that issue). A cool head, unhysterical treatment, skilful diplomacy and a lot of tolerance will leave the student feeling validated (as opposed to victimized) and prevent a furore.

There have to be limits. Tolerance, mutual respect and the ability to 'agree to disagree' have to be reciprocal. Both students and parents have to be supportive members of the school's general ethos. They cannot 'wage war' on the school for an unlimited length of time, or sustain fundamental objections to the nature of the institution, and continue to be part of the 'family'.

Occasionally, the school may have to suggest to a parent or student, or, if necessary, a staff member (see below) that they should not continue in the school unless they are comfortable within the school's ideological (or operational) 'umbrella'.

> *Mrs. Q: I understand your view that the school should not allow the girls' basketball team to play in the gym in front of boys or in front of the fathers. Ruthie is still sitting out of her English lessons with the alternative assignment while the class are studying 'Romeo and Juliet'. We also agreed to transfer Dovid's Tanakh class so that he would have an acceptably Orthodox teacher. But I think the time has come for a different discussion. I know how much you appreciate the general level of education at our school – but we are a community school, and parents and students have to feel comfortable with our Jewish ethos. Are you sure that this is still the right school for your family? Would you and the children not be happier in an environment more in tune with the family 'hashkafah'?*

> *Mr. G: This is the third time that teachers have reported to me that your daughter has either not handed in assignments, or done them in a very perfunctory manner, and each time declared 'My dad told me not to bother with the Jewish subjects as they aren't important'. This school regards every subject as equally important. We run a seamless curriculum, and the School Handbook clearly states that students are required to be 'assiduous in their studies' in every course. The Jewish dimension of our school is integral to what we are. It is simply not acceptable for a student to choose to disregard a section of the curriculum, especially the JS. I am sorry that you seem to be advising her to do so. Unless there is a clear change in her attitude, and unless she begins to approach all of her subjects with equal care, I think you should explore a different school for next year. If her JS marks at the end of the year reflect a continuing negative attitude, then I should advise you that her re-registration will come under review.*

> *Mrs. G: The founders of our yeshivah were very clear. Our mission is to teach a Torah way of life and exclude areas that we find problematic. Chaim persists in asking difficult questions in Tanakh and Gemara that the other students find upsetting*

and the teacher finds disruptive. They are questions that introduce ideas that we do not wish to deal with in our Yeshivah. I am worried about Chaim, and I am also concerned about his influence on some of the other boys. Perhaps he would be better suited in another school, where his views won't be so unusual? By the way, I want to remind you again that he must come to school properly dressed according to our rules.

Mr. T: I understand that Zev is an outstandingly talented swimmer, and may reach national standard. As you know, the school has made significant accommodations in his program to allow him time to go for training. However, I cannot agree to your request that he be exempt from two JS courses to further lighten his workload. JS is at the core of the school's values. It may be that you sent him to Jewish High 'for social reasons'; but the school's policies apply to all students, and Jewish Studies are a non-negotiable part of our program. I have asked the Vice Principal to meet with Zev and look at his schedule again, to see whether we can find another way to help him. But if there isn't, and his swimming training is a priority, you may have to look at a school with a much shorter working day.

Mrs. D: I understand your enthusiasm for the musical 'Jesus Christ Superstar', and appreciate that you have very successfully produced this in several other schools. I'm afraid that I cannot agree with you that it would be a 'wonderful multi-cultural gesture' for Jewish High to present it. I am concerned at the publicity your suggestion has received, even before the school has had a chance to properly respond to your communication. If, indeed, you feel that the school's decision shows 'prejudice and small-mindedness', and that 'this was not the school I thought I was sending my children to', then I am afraid we may have to agree to disagree. I noticed that the re-registration forms for Jenny and Michael have not yet been returned. Please decide as soon as possible what your intention is for next year.

And finally – politics:

Mr. and Mrs. J: Thank you for your letter regarding the school's charity campaigns for this year.

Version 'A': Of the six campaigns run by students this year, two were for Israeli causes, one for a local Jewish cause, two for famine relief, and one for medical research. I should point out that the students choose which causes to support, with some staff advice. Of the total funds raised, one Israeli cause and one famine relief cause easily raised the most. I am not unhappy with that balance. The support of the school for Israel and local Jewish causes is indisputable. We also believe it is part of our educational task to make our students aware of the suffering of all peoples, and encourage them to have a global humanitarian concern as part of their Jewish education, and as part of Jewish values. I cannot agree with your demand that henceforth student fundraising should only be for Jewish or Israeli causes. May I also observe that your personal attacks on staff members are unwarranted, and unacceptable. Whatever their personal views and beliefs, our staff act professionally in school. It is part of our educational experience that students will meet teachers of different views, approaches and opinions as they progress through the school. There are no grounds for you to demand that the three teachers you specify should not teach your children. As specified *on our Application Form, the school reserves the right to allocate students to classes as it sees fit. I do not accept your comparisons between our school and another school in the city, but of course you are entitled to your view.*

Version 'B': *Of the six campaigns run by students this year, two were for Israeli causes, one for a local Jewish cause, two for famine relief, and one for medical research. I should point out that the students choose which causes to support, with some staff advice. Of the total funds raised, one Israeli cause and one famine relief cause easily raised the most. I am not unhappy with that balance. Our school raison d'être is its Jewish commitment. Our 'Statement of Philosophy and Purpose', which is part of the school's constitution, and which parents and students agree to support on application to the school, clearly states that the school 'supports the State of Israel' and the 'Zionist movement'. All charity fundraising is exactly that – for humanitarian and charitable purposes only, without political bias. I am concerned by the implications of your demand that the school no longer raise money for any Israeli cause 'until Israel stops persecuting the Palestinians'. I am not going to comment on your political views, to which you are fully entitled, but I do not believe that your suggestion would have any significant support at all in the school. Further, it would constitute a radical rewriting of our school's character. Individual members of our school 'family' are fully entitled to their political views, respectfully expressed; but the school's support for the local Jewish community and for Israel – whatever the government in power – is not, and is not going to be, in question All constituencies in our school are part of that commitment.*

8.2.3 Supporting school values – Board members

Board members have an absolute duty to support school values in public and in private. Fundamental opposition to school values is incompatible with continuing Board membership. A Board member elected in parental capacity who withdraws children from the school because of disapproval with the school's values (as opposed to say, because of some individual educational or other valid reason) should resign.

8.2.4 School values: staff responsibilities

Teachers must distinguish (if necessary) between their private views and their professional responsibility. All staff – Jewish or non-Jewish, General Studies or Jewish Studies - have a professional and legal fiduciary responsibility to be good-faith employees, supporting the school, and upholding school values.

John: When you joined our staff, the school 'Statement of Philosophy and Purpose' was part of the Staff Handbook, and was, separately, part of the literature about the school which you received when you enquired about the post. Our school, part of the Jewish community, strongly supports of the State of Israel, and our community values and education reflect that. Your beliefs are your private affair, but in your professional capacity you have a duty to be a good-faith employee, supporting or at the very least not contradicting the values of the school. This is now the third time we have discussed complaints from parents and students that you have made offensive remarks in class about the Israeli government, and I now have two complaints from parents that you told students that they should 'arrange to have a cold' on the upcoming Israel Independence Day celebrations in school. Please tell me exactly what you said? ... Under the circumstances, I will be writing to you after this meeting giving you notice that further remarks or actions that contradict and undermine the values of the school will bring your employment under review.

Rabbi T: I appreciate your personal views that the school is not strict enough on matters of tzniut ('modesty'). But the duty of the students is to observe the dress code – not more. You cannot force the girls and boys in your classes to observe a stricter code than that specified by the school. I also have a problem with your reported comments about the school Administration being 'Ignoramuses' and 'Destroyers of Yiddishkeit'. What, in fact, did you say to the class yesterday?

Joan: As you know, this is a Jewish community school. I am concerned that Mrs. G. has complained that you told her daughter 'not to bother about that Shabbat nonsense' and 'get on with your project – it's more important'.

Ms.V: I appreciate that as a Chabadnik you hold a certain view of the origins of the Universe. But you cannot instruct students to 'take no notice' of their science teacher, just as other staff may not undermine your lessons. If it arises in class, I have no problem with you explaining your beliefs, as long as you adhere to our guidelines – you have to clearly identify your beliefs as your own, and you have to leave respectful space for other views. You may, if asked, politely indicate that you respect the view of the science teacher, but don't agree with it. You cannot negate his views. The students will hear different points of view, and make up their own minds.

8.2.5 Alumni – "L'affaire Noah Feldman"

The clash of values has a particular, and difficult variant where Alumni are concerned. These are former students at the school, legitimate 'life members' of the school family – but they may have made life choices that are not resonant with the school culture. You cannot suggest to an 'Alum' that they retroactively graduate from another school ...

Even the apparently innocuous school magazine, normally filled with pictures of happy students, teachers, parents and Alumni, can generate problems.

In July 2007 the 'New York Times' published an essay by Noah Feldman, a regular contributor and a distinguished graduate of a Boston Jewish school. Professor Feldman lamented that pictures of he and his non-Jewish then-girlfriend-later-wife had been deliberately airbrushed out of a published picture of an alumni reunion[136]. There was subsequently some argument about whether this had been deliberate or not. The same magazine had ignored the 'Mazal tov' announcements that he had sent in when he got married, and when his children were born.

---

[136] As far as I am aware, all associated with the school in question – both professional and lay – maintained a complete silence throughout the controversy. I think this was a very good, and dignified, strategy. The circumstances of how the photo was changed remain unknown.

"What remains of the old technique of excommunication is simply non-recognition in the school's formal publications, where my classmates' growing families and considerable accomplishments are joyfully celebrated."

The article continued to reflect on his continuing personal commitment to live in two worlds, as originally encouraged (sometimes awkwardly) by his *alma mater,* despite his conspicuously dissonant life-choice. The tone of the article is, in my reading, affectionate, if hurting.

Noah Feldman's article is archetypical of boundary issues in a changing Jewish community.

Does marrying a non-Jewish partner still mean a self-electing exit from Jewishness - even if – as, apparently, in this case – you are still passionately involved in Jewish learning, Jewish thought and Jewish observance?? Some mainstream Jewish denominations have already made the decision that it doesn't. The Orthodox community – to which the school in question was affiliated – still maintains a strong view that it does. How does the school balance its loyalty and responsibility to its Alumni *as individuals*[137], and to its institutional consensus values?

These issues will multiply, with infinite variants as time progresses. It is difficult to set out policy that will cover all eventualities. The following may help frame some discussions[138]:

- Jewish life is changing, and public expectations are changing. The issue of how we, as schools, relate to our alumni – or students, or parents - who see the world in a different way than perhaps the school would like will not go away.

- The school may formulate a policy regarding alumni who veer from the school's "preferred path". If it is to the effect that such alumni are not going to be recognized by the school, then it must be expressed in as dignified a manner as possible:

  The school magazine will be pleased to celebrate and announce important events in the lives of our Alumni which themselves may be seen as celebrations of school values.

---

[137] .... should the school or alumni magazine list news of a marriage between an Alumnus and a non-Jewish partner? If it was a civil marriage? If it was an 'interfaith' ceremony? If it took place in a church? Or mosque? Or Buddhist temple? If it was a marriage between same-sex partners? Would the school invite an Alumnus in any of the above categories back to speak at a Career Day?

[138] The NYT article, by Noah Feldman, may be found at **http://tinyurl.com/l4265j** . Via Google, many comments and reactions to the article may be found, including the threads on the 'Lookjed' online forum of Bar Ilan University's Lookstein Institute (Google: 'Noah Feldman Lookjed'). My own comments (published on Lookjed, and in part incorporated in my text above) may be found in APPENDIX C at the end of this book.

Alumni invited back to the school in any capacity will be chosen as exemplars of school values.

- The same applies to the many other areas of potential content in the school magazine. There has to be a 'mission statement' for the publication, and an editorial policy, both of which have to be reasonable, published and transparent

In Noah Feldman's case, "someone" at the school apparently perceived the reunion photo as embarrassing. The question of how to handle it should have then become a matter of school management and decision-making process. It is not clear where the 'airbrush them out' decision was made (if it was made). But a school should have a culture where everyone recognizes problems when they arise. Instead of making an individual decision, such problems should be referred to a wider decision-making body who can work out a strategy for resolving them – preferably, in sensitive cases, one that preserves the dignity of all concerned. Making arbitrary decisions to airbrush a grad out of the reunion photo – or doing anything that might give the impression of having done so - was guaranteed to cause deep hurt and offense. That should have been foreseen.

Similar considerations apply to other controversial articles, photos or announcements submitted for publication[139].

8.3 Classroom and curriculum issues

8.3.1 Teachers disagree

Even in the most liberal of Jewish schools - let alone the more Orthodox - there will occasionally be tensions between honorable and earnest members of staff who will feel that it is imperative to "correct" the "misinformation" given in another classroom, and "save" the students from (on the one hand) "*apikorsus* - heresy", and on the other "obscurantism". A lesson may include material whose message does not conform to school or community values, or which is far more explicit than the school would normally sanction. Such situations are common in literature, art and drama. Students may be uncomfortable; parents or other teachers may object.

The best way to deal with these (sometimes ugly) situations is to avoid them:

- Ensure that the school 'Statement of Philosophy and Purpose", forms an integral part of the employment contract of all members of staff. Reference to the 'Statement of Philosophy',

---

[139] The magazine presumably carries a standard disclaimer ("Views expressed.." etc.) If the school decided to publish a really controversial article, it would presumably carry a few words of introduction ("We are publishing this even though…")

and the school's contractual expectation that it will be respected, may resolve the situation in a practical sense, although it will not resolve the underlying issues.

- At staff meetings initiate proactive discussion about the need for mutual respect between colleagues. The beginning of the year is a good opportunity. Point out that the school is a private school with a Jewish set of values; that the school philosophy has been set down by the Board of Directors; and that while every member of staff is entitled to their own points of view, they are expected to respect the school's identity.

- Stress that you expect mutual respect between all colleagues, and that if they do give a view or teach material in a class that they think may contradict or verge on contradicting another colleague's teaching, they must be circumspect and respectful. It is a clear breach of professionalism to encourage students to disregard or delegitimize another colleague.

- If a teacher knows that a sensitive issue is to be dealt with in the classroom, encourage them to discuss the lesson beforehand with Administration. A responsible and mature teacher should recognize which material will be controversial. That does not mean that it should not be taught. There must be an understanding that a balanced view will be given, that the treatment of the subject will be fair, and that the school's concerns will be respected. Occasionally, however, you will simply say "No"[140].

- Make it clear that this is not to become a cause célèbre. Teachers must preserve respect for all members of staff and for other points of view at all times, and respect for those with whom they disagree. The dialogue must be mutually respectful.

  Even though I disagree with my colleague, Mr. H., I respect his views. Let me also give you my point of view.

---

[140] An interesting case was a Phys Ed and Health Studies teacher who wanted to take a class to see an exhibition of plasticized (real) human bodies, displayed as an art exhibit in a Science museum. The exhibition has since toured the world, including Israel. The teacher felt that it would help the students understand basic human anatomy. The school felt that the very principle of the exhibit was contrary to Jewish ethics – including and perhaps especially the fact that it was an art, and not a scientific exhibit, and we did not allow the trip. The teacher then asked if she could tell the students that she would 'be around' the exhibition at a certain time, if any them wanted to visit with her. The answer was 'No'. To her credit, she was completely respectful of the school's point of view.

As Principal, you have to balance your educational duty to your students with your duty to your sponsoring body. Your students deserve respectful, open and frank discussions of issues, and should not be satisfied with formulaic answers. Yet dealing with controversial issues is a test of education. Unless the school can handle different views, and unless it can deal with real and controversial topics, it will not command the respect of its students (especially when, later, they view their experience in retrospect) and is not serving its students well.

8.3.2 Debate within the school

One good method of averting tension within the school is to make dialogue between diverse or different viewpoints a regular part of your school culture[141]. These can be presentations in class; they can be lunchtime events; or they can be part of a program at a retreat or Shabbaton. Some examples of the possibilities of offering different perspectives on any curriculum material include:

- a Talmud teacher and a law teacher

- a general history teacher and a Jewish history teacher

- English literature and Jewish Studies (including a literary perspective on biblical and rabbinic texts, as well as a Jewish reading of creative literature and media)

- Science and rabbinics/Tanakh teachers on Jewish dimensions of scientific issues (e.g. moral issues in science) and on scientific issues in Jewish Studies.

As a result, respectful dialogue on more contentious issues will be less controversial, certainly less confrontational – but of greater educational value. Your school program will be livelier as well…

- A related question applies to your school library. As discussed above, a library represents freedom of knowledge. Don't censor it.

---

[141] The most fascinating such occasion I ever saw involved two visitors to TanenbaumCHAT – the local Rav of the Agudah in Toronto and the City Coroner. After a much-publicized tragedy in which an elderly member of the Orthodox community was killed by a car, an enterprising teacher arranged a dialogue between the two on the question of autopsies. It was fascinating – and instructive – for students to see the very high regard in which these two very different personalities held each other, and to hear from them the way in which they worked together in cases where religious and legal obligations clashed.

8.3.3 Traditional problems: Science

Science vs. Jewish Studies[142] is an 'evergreen issue'. It will not go away until and unless the Messiah comes. It is clearly more of a problem in some schools than others, but even community-type schools may have teachers who hold contrasting (and irreconcilable) views and beliefs. In some jurisdictions, the issue of teaching theories of the origin of the world may also be an issue of public and political controversy.

Every school has to develop its own policy. My personal view[143] is that all teachers should teach the subject as they feel is honest and accurate, while observing all the guidelines for allowing a plurality of views and a respectful atmosphere. If the atmosphere heats up (and I am not here referring to Global Warming – another controversial subject!) arrange a lunchtime debate or some visiting speakers. Let the school know all of the viewpoints, let them ask all the questions and challenge all the theories - *and let the students make up their own minds.*

Have the school librarian arrange a display of books on the subject. Use it as an opportunity to expand the students' thinking into other related areas of scientific thought – the nature of mind, the relation of spirituality to scientific thought, the field of medical ethics, the sense of awe in scientific research… Stretch the minds of teachers and students – visibly! Hold an essay competition. The students will relish the debate.

- Just don't let one point of view be presented in school to the deliberate exclusion of all others. That is very boring!

8.3.4 Traditional problems: Literature

A school that teaches serious literature will always teach novels, poems, plays, and films that challenge the students' conventional morality, or that includes sexually explicit or other controversial themes. In most cases, teachers are sensible, and students can easily 'compartmentalize' the literature that they are studying into its own box, which is different from the Friday-night-family-dinner box. This is in

---

[142] During 2005-6, a major controversy on the issue of "Science and Torah' erupted around the writings of the "Zoo Rabbi" - Rabbi Natan Slifkin, a young Torah scholar who had developed a long-time fascination (and considerable expertise) with the animal kingdom. Rabbi Slifkin, originally from the UK, but living in Israel, published a series of books discussing various aspects of animals as they appear in Jewish tradition – everything from the identity of animals named in the bible and rabbinic literature to the practicalities of halachic issues involving animals. In 2006, he published an excellent book – 'The Challenge of Creation' – a survey of the treatment of science, creation, cosmogony and evolution in Jewish tradition. In it, he highlighted Orthodox thinkers and authorities who had reconciled their Orthodox beliefs with scientific theory. Somewhat lively in his approach, for his pains he attracted a veritable storm of criticism from prominent Orthodox rabbis in Israel, the USA and Canada. Details of his books and a very brave and dignified documentation of the controversy may be found on his own website www.zootorah.com. Recommended.

[143] As the reader may have discerned, on most topics, not just this one….

essence no different than their parents, who will go to see films or read books dealing with lifestyles and issues far away from their own experience. (Usually, no domestic havoc results.) The study of literature does not need defending here.

Nevertheless, there can be the occasional unsuitable choice, and some schools will always exercise close supervision over material studied in the classroom. Should questions arise – from whichever quarter – there are several basic rules:

- The first – and essential rule – is that whoever is objecting (parent, teacher, rabbi) must have read the controversial text in its entirety, or seen the film, or whatever. Complaints based on second- or third-hand 'impressions' are not acceptable. The second essential rule is that as soon as controversy arises, the Principal and other Administrators must also read the book (the poem, see the film) themselves, and acquaint themselves with the rest of the author/producer's work, and the critical consensus surrounding it. They must speak from a credible standpoint.

- The Principal should have a quiet discussion with the teacher or department concerned, and understand why the book/poem/film was chosen, and how they intend to teach it. The Principal may have some suggestions for supplementary material, or suggest some perspectives that s/he may feel would contribute to the understanding of the book in the sociological/values context of the school. There could be an opportunity for a teacher from another discipline, including Jewish Studies, to participate in a discussion in class. On the other hand, the Principal may be perfectly satisfied that the department or the teacher will handle the material responsibly, and needs no advice.

- If the Principal is fully confident in the teacher - err on the side of permissiveness. Literature does raise important questions. If the Principal feels the material is, in fact, unsuitable, discuss that with the teacher, and collaborate on finding a substitute text. Make sure that the substitute material is decided on, prepared and ready before letting it be known that the original has been changed, so that there is no space for further discussion ("We want to be part of the process... the new book has to be approved by Y and Z". Choice of material is a strictly professional prerogative)

- The Principal's decision is final. Any student or parent who really objects should be allowed to sit out the class and be given an alternative assignment.

- Do not get into a public discussion, and do not get into written or – worse – email exchanges on the detailed merits of the literature in question. They will be copied and endlessly dissected. All that needs to be put in writing is:

Dear Mr. and Mrs. P: Thank you for bringing to my attention the material suggested for study in Grade 11 Literature. I have read the book, discussed it with the teacher concerned, and am completely satisfied that it will be taught in a way that is responsible and educational. While it deals with complex issues, I don't think that there is cause for concern.

Dear Mr. and Mrs. P: Thank you for bringing to my attention the material suggested for study in Grade 11 Literature. I have read the book, and discussed it with the teacher concerned. On reflection she has decided to substitute another novel. I am very grateful to her for her professional approach and willingness to reconsider her original choice. Thanks again for expressing your concern.

8.3.5 Traditional problems: Creative arts

Problems here can be around the art room, the drama studio, the school play or the music room,

In a fairly mainstream school, students should be allowed to study reproductions of nude figures, or of Christian iconography, as part of art history or appreciation. A Jewish school should not run a course in 'The Nude in Art', or a course in 'The Portrayal of the Holy Family'. No school should have life drawing or painting classes. Some topics need sensitive handling – 'Holocaust Art' would be an example. The Art teacher should be aware of sensitivities regarding visits to art exhibitions, and should consult where necessary. On general, the school should not organize visits to art exhibitions where exhibits are degrading to other human beings (or even to animals), or may otherwise be outside the 'values' set of the school. Again, the Principal is the 'keeper'.

Parallel situations may occur in music and drama. They are not necessarily direct clashes of theology, or belief, but may be clashes with the religious, social, political or cultural conventions of the community. In music there may be objections to some modish musical sub-culture deemed to be undermining of school values, or problems relating to female voices, or relating to the performance of music in certain periods of the Jewish calendar; in drama there can be problems relating to costume, to dramatic content, or to a dozen other issues. As in art, there can be problems around proposed trips to plays, films or even concerts.

These are again difficult issues, which can spiral out of control.

- **Whatever happens, prevent these issues turning into confrontation.**

It is essential to work in cooperation with the teacher. If the incident has been caused by the teacher (e.g., in an Orthodox boys' school an inappropriate exercise has been set; or in a community school the teacher has set a politically-offensive project) then you have to clearly but firmly review the teacher's obligations to the school. They take precedence over cultural arguments. The teacher has to go back to the class and explain: "*On second thoughts... this might be a valid exercise, but I want to respect the school and its values ... here is an alternative assignment*".

8.4 Calendar and other *halachic* problems

Suggested school activities may contravene the school's level of religious observance.

Music during the '*sefirah*'[144], and limits on the public appearance and performance by girls are obvious. Others are borderline – should a debating team participate in a competition on a minor fast day? What is the school's policy about scheduling tests or exams on the day after a Festival[145] that encourages students to study on the Festival and perhaps cross a boundary? What food can be brought in to the school, or brought to school events? Each school must develop its own policies, calibrated according to its local religious 'temperature'. Occasionally, an individual student or teacher may be excused participation in an event if they feel it is contravening their personal standards. Tolerance and pluralism are two-way processes.

In fairness to the teachers, however, the permissible parameters have to be clearly explained well before the school year begins, in order to give them time to plan accordingly. It is no use telling a new music teacher on the day after Pesach that it is now the '*Sefirah*' and that your school will not allow students to perform live music, or perhaps even listen to any music, for the next six[146] weeks.

8.5 Freedom of expression / freedom of thought

8.5.1 What are the limits of student expression?

Art, music and drama – and sometimes other subjects – have incidental 'safety-valve' functions in a school. Not everything that has been created needs to be exhibited in the art room; not everything exhibited in the art room needs to be included in the annual 'Open Day' art exhibition. Without claiming the right to 'Freedom of Expression' (see following), student expression can occasionally cross boundaries. Occasionally there will be presentations that cannot be displayed under any circumstances:

---

[144] The period between Pesach and Shavuot, when semi-mourning customs are observed. Customs vary.
[145] Shavuot, normally occurring during end of the year exam time, is always a problem.
[146] If it is the day after Pesach, there are only six weeks remaining.....

We respect your right to express yourself, but we would also ask you to respect the values of our school community. Can we agree that this will stay in the Art department as your project, and will not be displayed in the school?

The use of non-prescription drugs is illegal, and, as you know, is clearly forbidden in the school or in any school-organized event. I respect your view that the law should be changed, but we cannot display artwork that advocates drug use by exploring and celebrating the drug 'experience'.

We are very upset that your music presentation to the school contained obscenities in the lyrics. Whatever the artistic / musical merits of the piece, you must have known that that sort of language is not acceptable in the school. I think an apology to the staff and other students involved would be appropriate, and I would like your promise that this won't happen again. If you want to check out the lyrics before you perform next time - my door is always open.

As you know, your short story is very explicit. I understand the point you want to make about teenage sexuality, but the language and the imagery you used are way beyond the 'vocabulary' of high school. It is a very powerful piece, but I am afraid it cannot be included in the Grade 12 'Creative Writing Anthology'. You may not wish to do this, but if you want to work together with the teacher on selecting some extracts of the total work for inclusion – that would be fine.

The school is prepared to allow expression of a range of political views, as long as they are respectfully expressed. We understand that art can also be a vehicle for political expression. You are entitled to your views, but public displays in the school cannot be in direct opposition to the school's agreed philosophy. There are also many students and members of staff who have relatives and close friends in Israel, including some who have been victims of terrorist incidents, and many who have served in the Israeli army. Some were personally very upset by your artwork. You may believe that Israel has no right to exist, but if you want to publicly campaign for that belief, you may want to consider whether this is the right school for you for next year."

If the student is crossing boundaries, understand that s/he is feeling a strong need to make a statement. It is counter-productive to penalize a student because they have something to say, assuming that their expression is genuine; is not personally offensive to others; and has not been publicized by the student in clearly mischievous ways[147].

An understanding policy, where possible, will avoid hopeless arguments, and will earn the school the respect of the students and teachers involved. There is rarely an advantage in treating these incidents as disciplinary[148], and to do so will frequently backfire. Hasty or punitive action will create martyrs and may attract publicity and press attention (*"Jewish school expels student for questioning Israeli policies"*). Basic

---

[147] An example of this would be if the student sent a copy of the project to a local newspaper before submitting it to the teacher for assessment.

[148] The only exceptions involve deliberate and malicious offense.

strategy should be to respect the integrity of the student(s) involved, while making it clear that the disputed item/action has to stay within discreet boundaries. As mentioned above, the safety valve is a useful device in every complex system. Don't close it off.

- Where the disputed material / presentation is part of a student's coursework, it should be marked on its merits, without regard to its 'controversial' content. In some circumstances, it may be advisable to have the work assessed by more than one staff member, to ensure that the mark is fair, and is seen to be fair.

8.5.2 The limits of freedom of expression

A related, but different issue is where the student claims an unfettered right to freedom of expression for the expression of opinion – not necessarily as part of an assignment. No one has an unlimited right to free expression in a school.

This may involve verbal, written or digital platforms; or issues such as decorating a locker or wearing a badge or slogan. The school is entitled to deem public presentations of certain opinions as being outside its tolerable parameters as outlined in the school 'Statement of Philosophy and Purpose'. The more respectful the expression, the easier it is to find a way to accommodate the student's desire to express themselves. Extreme expressions of opinion are rarely well received by the student body, who will distance themselves from the speaker – unless the school over-reacts, in which case they will close ranks behind their fellow student. It is better to negotiate a carefully respectful expression of opinion than to get into a confrontation where many students (and possibly a few teachers) will make a martyr out of the student, on the grounds that his or her "rights" are being "violated". In the first case, the incident will come and go. In the latter, you risk a furore.

David – the display that you want to put up on the notice board is outside the range of views held in our community. If you want to make a dignified statement – that's fine, but in school you may not present any material that encourages violence or hatred against any group or individual. Apart from anything else, it is probably against the law. I am prepared to allow you to have it on display for the rest of this week only if you take out all references – direct and indirect – to violence, and remove any text that may be understood as racist. If you want to come back to me with a revised plan – I'll be happy to look at it.

Naomi – in principle, I respect your right and your wish to make this presentation in your class about the plight of the Palestinians. I don't agree with your point of view, but I respect the fact that these are your beliefs. However, this is a school community of shared values, and the school's values are clearly stated in our 'Statement of Philosophy and Purpose'. We are also a school that tries to teach our students to be sensitive to the feelings of others. As you know, in the school and even in your class there are students and teachers who have relatives in Israel, several whose family have served in the Israeli army, and several who have had relatives affected by terrorist acts in Israel. Some of what you want to say will be deeply hurtful and offensive to them. Can we work together on the text of your presentation, so that it can be presented in a way that is sensitive and does not hurt feelings? If you are prepared to do that, I can allow you to make your presentation.

Jenny – the video presentation you made on the situation of gays in our school is very good. You understand that it is controversial. There are three or four sequences that I think are unfair to our teachers, and I'd like you to take them out, for the following reasons …. If you do that, I have no problem with showing the video.

Mark – the stickers you have on the inside of your locker are highly offensive to some students and teachers. I have to remind you that the School Handbook points out that the lockers are school property at all times, and that material displayed – whether inside or outside – must be 'tasteful and appropriate'. Please take the stickers down today.

Stuart – I understand that 'mock elections' are about democracy. But these are nevertheless 'mock elections', in a school community, not real elections outside. Can we discuss whether it is really appropriate for you to participate on such a deliberately outrageous platform?

But if Naomi refuses to change her talk, and it is outside the comfort zone; or if a student wishes to publish an article in the school newspaper that is offensive or one way or another, and no compromise is possible – then the school has to say … 'No'. Make sure this a collective decision – involve the Administrative team, and teachers who may be directly involved. Advise the President of what is happening, and prepare a short report for the Board. It is important that this is perceived as a widely shared and widely supported school decision – and not the Principal's alone. A statement that states clearly and simply the reasons for the school's decision should be communicated to staff and students.

And if there are disciplinary dimensions – make sure that the issues are separated, and it is clear that students are not being disciplined for their beliefs. If David puts up the display despite the Principal's instruction – he is disciplined because, and only because, he disobeyed a direct instruction from Administration. In that context, the content of his display is irrelevant.

8.5.3 "I don't believe in that" – argument

A student may proclaim his/her philosophical or theological disagreement with religion, Judaism, the world or society, while comfortably conforming to every school rule. A student has the right to their personal beliefs, and the wise Principal will understand that doubts and struggles should be met with engagement and even respect.

Nothing will further increase a student's antagonism more towards his/her Jewish identity than to be told that they "don't understand", or that they are "stupid", let alone "wicked" because they are asking difficult questions, or have reached difficult conclusions[149]. Telling a student to "stop asking questions" is certainly not supplying them with any answers.

As long as the student is respectful and appropriate, they should not be breaking any school rules, and should be given the same respect as any other member of the student body. Assignments they write, or presentations that they give, should be assessed on the integrity and soundness of the work, not on the views expressed.

> *Linda – although, as I am sure you expect, I profoundly disagree with your arguments, this is an excellently researched and well-argued essay, and I am happy to give you a '90' – Rabbi M.*

This comment, validating the student's sincerity, leaves an opening for dialogue, and leaves a far more respectful and positive impression on the student than:

> *Linda – I am very upset by your essay, which is very disrespectful to Chazal, to your parents, and to the school. I cannot give it a mark. Please come and discuss your views with me. – Rabbi M.*

Linda will never discuss her views with 'Rabbi M', and will remember the comment for decades.

8.5.4 "I don't believe in that" – behavior

Although only indirectly a disciplinary issue, the school can legitimately require students to observe certain practices that are necessary to preserve the community standards of the school, and enable all students and staff to participate in school events without embarrassment or discomfort.

- It cannot be a school rule that a student must believe in God[150]. You cannot force a student to pray, but you can make it a school rule that all students must come to services (and if necessary, provide prayer/non-prayer alternatives).

- The school may require that on school premises or on a school-sponsored activity a student must observe Shabbat and kashrut. A student who observes kashrut will be embarrassed and uncomfortable if on a school trip the other students with whom s/he is sharing a room order in non-kosher Chinese takeaway. The students who do so are actually being exclusionary, and are being disrespectful to school ethos. That is the disciplinary offense.

---

[149] See SECTION 7.3.3, 'The Lament of the disillusioned student', and also the telling material in "Off the Derech:Why observant Jews leave Judaism"/ Faranak Margolese / Devorah Publishing /2005.

[150] According to most views, the Ten Commandments seem to get away with it. A school has less authority!

- The non-kosher fast-food outlet near the school may be ruled 'out of bounds'. A student who eats there is breaking the bounds rule; what s/he eats is irrelevant.

- A student who does not believe in, or no longer believes in observing Shabbat as a religious experience is still bound by the school rules of behavior applying to Shabbatonim or retreats.

- A boy who claims that he no longer wishes to cover his head because he 'doesn't believe in it' as a religious practice must still do so as part of school dress code.

You may legitimately discuss with a student who persistently, or defiantly, 'acts out' in this area whether or not your school is the right place for him/her. Someone who radically dissents from the school's shared values, and chooses not to conform to the school's minimum requirements should elect to withdraw.

Some schools will be stricter, and make it clear that they expect all students (and parents) to subscribe to and conform to specified religious standards both in and out of school as a condition of registration.

8.6 Gender issues

SEE ALSO SECTION 11.3

Every High School Principal – wherever their school is on the religious spectrum – currently has to consider issues generated by gay and lesbian students. It is essential that the Jewish Studies department of every school pro-actively develop a policy for the teaching, presentation and discussion of these and related issues. Material should be available as teaching resource. Consideration should be given to incorporating a teaching unit on the subject. Every teacher must be involved. It should be honest, but it needs to be carefully thought through. If appropriate, and if the issue is one on which the school Administration wishes to have a stated policy for all staff, guidelines should be given in the Staff Handbook.

The difficulties of dealing with the issues are threefold:

- Feelings on gay rights and associated issues are deeply and emotionally held, and are politicized both within and without the Jewish community. As a result, there is a desire to make demonstrative and symbolic 'statements' that may go beyond any real situations.

- Affirmation of gay/lesbian identity (sexual and cultural) is now widely accepted in general society and even more so in youth culture.

- The Jewish community has no consensus on this issue. The Orthodox community has united agreement on the halachah, but considerable private dissent on policy towards individuals; the Conservative community is publicly divided on the issue; the Reform and Reconstructionist communities completely legitimize and accept gay and lesbian lifestyles. Non-affiliated Jews tend to accord with the views of their social/political circles. In at least two major communities – Ontario, Canada and the UK – same-sex marriage (or equivalent) is legal.

Guidelines include:

- Avoid confrontation

- Separate the issues – keep the school rules separate from the gender issue; and in teaching distinguish between the individual and his/her 'identity', and the sexual behavior.

- The Administration, and only the Administration, decides when to stop lessons for a 'teach-in'.

  > *Over the last year we have turned down X requests from different groups, representing all sorts of interests and causes, to send speakers to the school. If you want to hold a session during lunchtime for anyone interested – that's fine.*

- "The school would not permit public events based on any sexual or gender-based theme, whether heterosexual or gay; or allow extensive publicity for such events". Do not allow the school to become a platform for politicized or sexual polemics, of any variety.

- Note that these issues may affect many students' families – in every type of school - and sensitivity is essential. Many students will have siblings or other close family members, in same-sex relationships. Some may have same-sex parents. The teacher never knows the complete backgrounds of students in the class.

- Make sure that the school's view and/or staff views are stated with dignity and in way that enhances the image of the school and of its values.

- Dress Code issues should be addressed in the general context of the school standards: "Students must be appropriately dressed in a way that is consonant with the school ethos and values, and appropriate for an atmosphere of learning".

    Whether a boy or a girl was wearing this jacket – I'm afraid it doesn't fit our Dress Code, and I'd like your assurance that you won't wear it after today.

Again, only impose disciplinary consequences for breaches of school rules – not for opinions, or identity, or simply for speaking up. If the student was rude – that is a breach of school rules, whatever the subject.

Often, avoiding confrontation and allowing students to have their say in a respectful manner is a good solution and defuses highly charged situations. (In such sessions, you may also learn something about the school). Be certain that the principle of respecting your students as individuals is maintained. Make sure that your teachers understand all of the above, and that what is said in the classroom is tactful, respectful, and in accordance with school policy. Protect and defend the privacy of individuals, and their right to respect and safety in the school environment.

8.7 Animal rights and food politics

This, too, are very political (linked) topics, which have particular sensitivity in a Jewish school – both because of the central Jewish teachings on the prevention of cruelty to animals, but also and obviously because of *shechitah.* Food choice and vegetarianism are also relevant to many Jewish teachings, and vegetarianism, as is well known, has a certain approval in Jewish tradition.

An interesting and rewarding discussion on vegetarianism can develop quickly into a far more problematic discussion on *shechitah,* where any enquiring student will locate graphic and disturbing material on the internet.

The same advice applies as with the previous section. Be prepared, and be coherent.

In this perhaps more specialized area – and others that may arise in the future - ask two or three bright staff members to work together on preparing a 'Teachers' Guide'.

8.8 Global issues – universalism and particularism

This, like 'Science v. Judaism' is a perennial. Idealistic teens – not to mention adults -may find difficulty in accommodating the two strands in Jewish teaching. Commentators abound on Judaism and global poverty, racism, the environment, global warning. Some are inspiring. The comments of others are unlikely to resonate with the average Diaspora teen.

While it is, again, beyond the scope of this book to suggest curriculum content, there is some management advice:

- On each of these issues, locate a staff 'champion' who will willingly arrange displays, visiting speakers, volunteer opportunities, and generally be able to act as a role model and guide for interested students

- Allow this constituency a voice and a profile within the school — a display board and a program. The humanitarian vision should be a positive part of school values.

- Hillel's dictum (Avot 1:14): *"If I am not for myself – who will be for me? And when I am only for myself - what am I?"* – remains the pithiest statement – not to say resolution - of the particularist-universalist paradox.

8.9 Israeli and Middle Eastern politics

These issues may arise in any classroom, sometimes as a reaction to current events. Although many Jewish schools assume the collective sympathies of their sponsoring bodies, the school has a responsibility to ensure that different voices may get a fair hearing. The Principal has to determine the parameters, perhaps as a policy decision approved by the Education Committee or the Board. In general, they should not go beyond, for example, the points of view represented in mainstream Israeli society – which are wider than many views usually represented in the Diaspora!

- Make sure that all views and persons are accorded respect. Epithets and abuse have no place in a school

- Note that some views that are very widely held in Israel are hardly represented in some Diaspora communities. Conversely, Diaspora views of Israel and what it represents can sound puzzling to Israelis. A school has the duty of educating about the reality of Israel as it is, not only the dream of Israel as we would like to imagine it to be

Most educators in the Jewish school system will agree that the school does not have a duty to give platforms to views opposing the right of the State of Israel to exist; to racist views; to sympathizers with terrorist groups of any description; or – in my view – anyone advocating refusal to serve in the IDF for any reason.

Encourage attention to the facts. Occasionally, teachers and students will go beyond the boundaries deemed acceptable. The Principal must deal with it.

8.10 Sex education

One of the most difficult. First, have an agreed sex education policy approved by the Education Committee (or, occasionally, their agreed external nominee, approved of by Administration). The policy should simply and briefly enunciate the aims of the curriculum, and the principles by which it should be taught.

Jewish High seeks to educate our students in all areas of interpersonal relationships, ensuring that they have the full information with which to make responsible choices. All aspects of the teaching must be accompanied by an awareness of the range of Jewish teachings and opinions.

Alternatively:

Jewish High seeks to educate our students towards an appropriate sense of tzniut, in accordance with Orthodox Jewish practice. Teaching will also include courses in health education and human biology, delivered in a context of Jewish values.

The curriculum content is then a professional issue, designed in accordance with the policy.

In some jurisdictions, there are legally required components to sex education. Do not hide the details, and do not ignore the reality of the lives that teenagers lead – whoever they are. Areas that contravene Orthodox Jewish law (e.g. the use of condoms) should be taught, with the appropriate advisory. Make sure that the teachers dealing with this are sensible and realistic.

Whether sex education is part of, or separate from, general guidance given in the school regarding interpersonal relationships is a local choice; as is the department (Jewish Studies, biology, health education, Guidance) responsible for designing and teaching the program. Most schools will design joint programs – certainly including the Jewish Studies faculty.

In some school specialist external counselors may be brought in. (This has the advantage that the students are less embarrassed and find it easier to ask questions than if the teacher is a staff member they are going to see the following day, or who may sit near them in synagogue.) There are cogent reasons to support all choices.

8.11 Sports, extra-curricular and 'out of school'

8.11.1   Competitions, practices, fixtures

Sport has its own religious fervor. The school religion, however, is Judaism, and the program has to be conducted in accordance with school standards.

- All activities must conform to school policy, without exception[151]. If the team is traveling to an away game, then kosher food must be ensured, and the event must be structured so that the team does not play at any inappropriate time. The team cannot play or train on Shabbat, or close to Shabbat, at a time when observant students and staff do not have enough time to return home. The team is not only representing the school, but also the Jewish community. If satisfactory scheduling or other arrangements cannot be made, then the school has to withdraw and signify that they cannot play. That is part of being a proud Jewish school.

Like all staff, sports staff (Jewish or non-Jewish) must 'buy in' to school ethos[152]. They may not undermine school values. They may not encourage the students (or their parents) to lobby for "exceptions" ("*This competition is really important to the kids*") in instances where competitions clash with the Jewish standards of the school. They may not, for example, arrange 'unofficial' practice sessions on Saturday mornings, at a local field/gym/rink for 'anyone who happens to be around'. These incidents may be few and far between, and they will be fewer and further apart if the guidelines are clearly articulated in the Staff Handbook, are addressed at the time of hire, and – most effective of all – are established as part of the whole-school ethos.

More complicated, for non-Orthodox or Community schools, is where a student wants to participate *as an individual* in some sporting competition on Shabbat, but needs the school's endorsement, or signature; or where a student participating in an individual competition (which may be anything from cross-country running to karate to skiing) is listed according to the school they attend. This situation is not confined to sports – see SECTION 8.11.3).

8.11.2   School trips

School trips – as with every other activity under school auspices – must conform to school standards. Period.

8.11.3   "I want to participate on Shabbat and the school is being unfair"

A student may need the school authorization or certification of enrolment in order to participate – privately – in a course or activity that has nothing to do with the school, but breaches the school's standards. An example might be a student who wishes to participate in a sports event or course (for example, a summer course) that entails travel and activity on Shabbat; or needs school permission to participate in a drama

---

[151] Remember that any exception made, whatever the circumstances, will be a precedent for all future occasions.
[152] Sports staff and coaches, who are outstanding teachers of values and leadership in a school, have a very important part to play in establishing the school ethos.

festival or a talent contest on a Friday evening. An Orthodox Principal will uncomfortable in signing any such document, and probably will decline to do so.

There are two choices: find a pragmatic solution that does not offend religious sensibilities (a non-Jewish colleague completes the paperwork), or decline. The school may risk losing the student. Some schools may prefer the latter to the former; others will take a more accommodating view.

These are delicate situations, where the Principal needs – probably in equal measures – careful judgment, tact and courage. There are situations where the school will have to say to the student (and his/her family) that the school cannot see a way to be associated with the student's participation if it conflicts with school or community policy. Such decisions should be carefully formulated, and should be checked with the school lay leadership, as the situation is likely to lead to protests from the family. On the other hand, I have known an Orthodox rabbi work out a protocol that enabled a student to stay on-site at an athletics meeting over a Shabbat and take part in a cross-country race. These are difficult calls. They need careful, **collective** consideration that balances school principles with a sympathetic and realistic respect for the student and his/her family. Best, as always, is to try and find a solution that both parties can live with (and can be accommodated or justified within the parameters of the school).

Should the student, participating in such an event in an individually appropriate capacity, win or achieve distinction – the question arises of whether or not the school should recognize that distinction. If a student is talented, and appears in, say a local television show or a local theatre on a Friday night, should the school recognize it? It depends on the school community, and the sensitivities involved. Clearly, a school whose values are committed to traditional Shabbat observance cannot, and should not, recognize the achievement. A Community school, where some constituencies are affiliated with streams of Judaism that would not have objected to the student's participation *ab initio*, faces a different dilemma. A compromise might be a brief, perhaps low-key, congratulation that did not detail when the event took place.

> *Congratulations to X, who recently won an individual Gold Medal in the County Ski Championship*

> *Congratulations to Y on a successful appearance in the City Playhouse*

Unfortunately, in many schools these will be insoluble dilemmas, with no universally recognized correct procedures.

Constituencies - Staff

9   MANAGING STAFF

10   PROBLEMATIC TEACHERS

9 MANAGING STAFF

9.1 Building and leading the team

The Principal is the team leader and team manager of the staff.

Best practice, enshrined in Governance and contract, should be that the Board employs the Principal; but the Principal employs all other staff – i.e. all other staff report to the Principal. The Principal has the duty of recruiting the staff team, and is responsible for its performance.

For a new Principal, building a team needs tenacity and application, and can take many years – often accompanied by crises and tensions, as a different management style, with different standards and different aims is implemented on a group or on individuals who are resistant to it. SEE SECTION 9.3.2

A longer-serving Principal probably enjoys the confidence and loyalty of a large portion of the staff; some are probably 'neutral'; and a few, for a variety of reasons, good and bad, harbor negative feelings.

The Principal's must aim to establish professional, fair relations with all of them. Difficult as it sometimes may be, the Principal must strive to keep relations with individual teachers free of personal feelings and animosities[153]. While the first duty of everyone in a school is to the students, the duty of the Principal to the teachers follows very closely. S/he must ensure that teachers have the facilities, conditions of service, leadership and continued motivation to be outstanding educators. There is a reciprocal relationship of responsibility.

- The success of the school rests on the quality of the staff. They are responsible for the daily, practical implementation of the school mission.

Staff are a key constituency – very different in nature from either the Board or the students. Leadership of staff in a Yeshivah High School may be exercised in a very different style than leadership of a Community School. Consistent with the theme of this book, however – the style is different, but the substance is common ......

---

[153] As discussed elsewhere, there may be a price to pay for this in keeping yourself socially distant from your staff.

9.2 Terms of employment, contracts and Unions

A school cannot demand the loyalty or professional application of its staff unless it treats them as dignified professionals. Every school should be a partner with its staff in ensuring appropriate, dignified, professional and fair conditions of service for teachers in Jewish schools. This is not a question of cost – it is a question of values.

Conditions of employment should include:

- Salaries at least equivalent to local public school rates, with recognition of qualifications and experience

- Fair working hours, with allowance for lesson preparation and other professional duties

- Security of employment

- Options for full-time employment

- Options for pensionable employment for all employees

- Where applicable, health and other appropriate benefits

- Provision for professional development

A school should have a published, agreed salary scale incorporating a grid relating to qualifications and experience, with provision for stepped incremental salary increases. This scale should apply without discrimination. Knowledge that teacher 'A' has a higher salary than teacher 'B', although their qualifications and experience are similar (or, worse, that 'A''s are inferior to 'B''s) will create deep resentment among staff. Individual deals and contracts are always self-defeating.

The Board must approve terms of employment for all employees. Where there is a Union[154] or 'Staff association', all of the above will be subject to a properly negotiated 'Collective Agreement', in conformance with local practice and legislation. If the school grants tenure to teachers, the conditions of eligibility for tenure will be part of that agreement. If there is no Union, a sub-Committee of the Board should regularly review the terms of service of its staff.

Inequality of employment and salaries is one of the deepest causes of unrest in a staff. The more open and transparent the employment process, the fairer it is, and the less friction it will cause. A school may make whatever provisions it deems appropriate in its employment contracts and salary scales – as long as they are known to applicants in advance, and then applied fairly and consistently to all teachers.

---

[154] Very few in the USA, but commonly in Canada, the UK, and other Jewish communities.

9.2.1 Validating Qualifications

When compiling the Staff List, and certainly when assessing salaries, it is prudent to establish policy regarding the listing of qualifications.

Every jurisdiction has a central agency or regulatory body that validates university degrees. Make it clear that only degrees thus recognized will be recognized by the school (for salary purposes) and listed on the school Staff List. Degrees awarded by non-accredited institutions (i.e. degree 'mills' offering degrees for sale without credible academic standards) will not be acceptable. In the case of dispute, the onus is on the faculty member to provide evidence of the bona-fide of their degree.

An associated problem is that of the formal recognition and validation of rabbinic ordination ('*semikhah*'), and associated qualifications SEE SECTION 7.4.4 . Faculty wishing to have their ordination recognized must provide a copy of a written '*semikhah*'. Clearly, a *semikhah* granted by a recognized program, seminary or yeshivah, or, for example, validated by the Israeli Chief Rabbinate, is not a problem. But there are huge grey areas. There are 'private' *semikhot* – ordinations granted by individual rabbis, for which the qualifications and standards required vary wildly. Some programs and institutions seem to grant *semikhah* after minimal study, and appear to be the Rabbinic equivalents of the online degree industry. New "ordinations" – e.g. '*Maggid*' (= '*Storyteller or Preacher*') are appearing on the horizon, as are new titles conferring status on Orthodox women, avoiding the title of 'Rabbi' itself. Note that in Israel (and perhaps elsewhere), there is a widespread practice of according a courtesy title of 'Rav' or 'Rabbi' to every (so far, male) Jewish Studies teacher in High Schools, regardless of formal qualification. The school must decide its policy. Local rabbis or rabbinical associations may be helpful here. There are no uniform standards. It is a quagmire.

9.2.2 Letters of Appointment / Contracts

All staff – Administrative, teaching and non-teaching - are entitled to know the terms of their employment (a statutory requirement in some jurisdictions). A 'Letter of Appointment' should incorporate, as a minimum:

- Title of position

- Commencing date, duration of contract, and terminating date

- Annual salary, and frequency and method of payment

- Benefits

- Sick Day entitlement

- Vacation entitlement

- Date for notice of Renewal / Termination of Contract – tenure process and eligibility, where relevant

- To whom the post reports, and any established process of performance evaluation

- Job Description, duties and hours

- Any other conditions

9.2.3 Length of contract

In larger schools, teachers will typically enter the school on a probationary basis of up to three years. A first-year teacher's term of probation will be the maximum; an experienced teacher's probation may be less. During this time, they should be periodically observed and evaluated by Administration. At the end of their probation they may be granted security of employment for a longer-term period, or granted permanent tenure. If the school does not wish to retain their services, they will be terminated. All of this must be carefully defined by contract – either individually or collectively.

Smaller schools may employ all teachers on rolling one-year contracts, typically without any benefit package. This must be considered as undesirable practice. To build a stable school, the staff has to build long-term loyalty, and develop a sense of personal and professional 'investment'. They need professional terms of employment. It is a cost of doing business as a reputable educational establishment.

Administrators, who enjoy higher salaries, are usually employed on fixed-term contracts. Initial contracts for Vice-Principals should be two years, with a 'let-out' for both parties at the end of the first year. Thereafter all VP's should be on 3-5 year contracts. They, too, need security. When approaching retirement, a 'Retirement Contract' should be agreed.

The Principal's contract is discussed in SECTION 17.1

9.2.4 The tenure decision

A school that offers tenure does so at the end of a probationary period. Such arrangements – normally in the context of a Collective agreement with a Union – provide that at the end of probation a teacher either has to be offered tenure or let go.

The process involves a formal, written evaluation of the teacher's performance by Administration (usually contractually mandated, and based on a series of observations and interviews carried out over a period of time). This is followed by a recommendation to the school's Personnel Committee.

The school normally has the right to terminate at the end of each probationary year, and it is comparatively rare for a teacher to reach the full term of probation and then be terminated. The school should have realized by then that the teacher is not a 'fit' to the school, and terminated at the end of the first or second year of probation. Most tenure recommendations are therefore comparatively straightforward, and positive – good recruitment judgment and the opportunities to correct 'mistakes' during the probation period normally mean that candidates for tenure are teachers in whom the school has great confidence, and whom it considers will be an asset to their staff.

But not always.

There are cases where the decision is borderline. These may be teachers of 'shortage' subjects, whom the school knows will be exceptionally difficult to replace, and is reluctant to dispense with their service. They may be Judaic studies teachers who have large families, and/or relocated to join the school faculty, and where termination will bring great human difficulty. They may be cases where a teacher has really made an effort in the year preceding the tenure decision, but the Administration fears that once ensconced as a tenured teacher, their performance will revert to whatever wearyingly unsatisfactory pattern generated initial concern.

These can be very difficult decisions, and often involve painful personal and professional consequences for the teacher. In a Jewish school, again, the 'community factor' comes into play.

Yet the Principal has to act in the best interests of the school.

In case of doubt or hesitation, the correct decision is almost always to terminate. The school must maintain the best standards in its faculty. If during probation the teacher is already problematic – the unfortunate likelihood is that they will continue to be so, in greater or lesser degree, in the future. If they are tenured, that future may be very long[155]; and if later their performance really becomes problematic, terminating a tenured teacher is exceptionally difficult, and usually very expensive.

- Repeatedly granting tenure to 'borderline' teachers will slowly result in a very mediocre faculty.

How can you avoid these difficult decisions? Firstly, exercise hard judgment in the recruitment stage. Secondly, exercise equally hard judgment during a teacher's probationary period. *"If it were done ..... 'twere well it were done quickly"*[156]

> - *Do not grant tenure unless you are as sure as you possibly can be that the candidate will be a wholly positive asset to your school. If in doubt – do not proceed.*

---

[155] Particularly as more and more legislatures are moving to abolish compulsory retirement ...
[156] Shakespeare, Macbeth, Act 1, Scene 7.

9.2.5 Salaries for Jewish Studies teachers

It is very difficult to establish a satisfactory salary scale for Jewish Studies teachers., especially in their early years of teaching.

This is mainly because teacher pay scales are usually linked in some way to local public school salaries, which are based on an assumed 'life-style'. The socio-economic-family profiles of Jewish Studies teachers, however, are radically different.

This table compares two typical 28-year old teachers – one, non-Jewish, teaching Eng Lit, (Teacher 'A') one, Jewish, teaching JS (Teacher 'B'):

	Teacher 'A'	Teacher 'B'
Age	28	28
Qualifications	B.A. + Cert. Ed.	B.A. + non-accredited learning; Semikhah
Years of post-High School study	4	8
Years already working	5 – 6	1 - 2
Marital status	Not yet married. Living with partner.	Married for 7 years.
Children	None	Four
Housing	Shares small house with partner in small town 10 miles away and commutes to school	Large mortgage on house near synagogue purchased with family help
Autos	One small and sporty auto	Needs MPV to carry family
Family	May be local or within a few hours' drive.	Close family lives in Israel, New York, Antwerp ... travel is by air, and expensive.

It is difficult to come up with an equitable pay scale that takes account of those differences, does not make teacher 'A' aggrieved, and encourages people to come into Jewish Studies teaching. It is also very difficult for the school to justify paying a (comparatively) large salary to an inexperienced and (frequently) untrained teacher.

In reality, this is not a school problem – it is a community problem. There are no easy solutions, but the following alternatives are possible:

- Do nothing. It is an insoluble dilemma. There are other income sources available to JS teachers. Frequently JS teachers take second, part-time posts outside the school to balance their budgets. The salary is the rate for the job.

- The community (Federation, perhaps via the local BJE) could pay an appropriately structured 'signing-on' incentive to JS teachers. In theory, the school could do this, but that creates an in-school inequity with other staff. The 'Community' solution keeps the relationship at arms'-length.

- A very forward-looking community could provide subsidized housing (either for rental or by way of mortgage assistance) for young JS teachers coming to a community. It is not uncommon for private schools located in high-income areas to have housing available for young staff.

- Other benefits to Jewish Studies teachers may include subsidized or free tuition[157] for their own children; reduced synagogue membership dues; bonus payments at Rosh Hashanah and Pesach. None of these are free from problems.

9.3 Administrators

9.3.1 VP's and Principals

The Administrative team[158] - Vice-principals or equivalents - are the individuals (or, in a small school, individual) with whom the Principal works most closely. The Principal may inherit, promote or appoint Administrators. They need the authority, the direction and the means to do their job. Administrators must have clear job descriptions, and clearly understand their duties and responsibilities. They report to the Principal, who must find the delicate balance between supervision (desirable) and interference (not desirable) SEE SECTION 9.3.5.

A Principal relies greatly on the VP's.

It is essential that the Administrative team works, in every sense of the word.

The Administrative team should be the Principal's partners, advisers, and confidantes. Very strong and very close relationships of professional and personal regard will

---

[157] Regrettably, (at the time of writing) my own community of Toronto does not give this desirable benefit to teachers.

[158] 'Administrators' are the schools senior management team, normally equivalent to Principals and Vice-Principals. An Administrator may supervise, evaluate and, if necessary discipline a teacher, and may place material in a teacher's personal file. In a unionized environment, they are not members of the Union, are outside the Collective Agreement, and are, technically, 'Management'.

develop. The relationship should be one of trust and complete confidence. The cumulative experience and wisdom of a talented team of school Administrators can be formidable. On the other hand, a dysfunctional Administrative team will very quickly affect the school, will be an impediment to school development and growth, and will soon attract the attention of the School Board.

Profiles of Administrators differ. Some will clearly have ambitions to be Principals themselves. At a certain point they will move on, or patiently wait for the Principal in place to do so. Others will feel very comfortable occupying a high level of responsibility, but will avoid the highest responsibility that comes with the Principalship ("born VP's"). Both are recognizable profiles, and both may contribute enormously to a school.

9.3.2 Old VP's – new Principal

Relations between Principals and their Administrators can be strained. A common situation is when a Principal (often younger) is appointed from outside the school, especially if his/her predecessor has been in post for many years. The Administrators (and teachers) in place will have been appointed by the previous Principal, and chosen to fit his/her style and outlook. Many will be resistant to change.

A VP may be nursing a secret grievance at not having been invited to succeed the outgoing Principal[159], or at not having been invited by the Board to be part of the selection process. The VP may have assumed (fantasized?) that the Board would grant him/her a veto over the appointment[160]. They may resent change even at a superficial level:

> *That desk was perfectly alright where it was*

> *The old Principal managed perfectly well without a Blackberry*

They may also have difficulty in grasping the facts of life – beginning with fact that the "new Principal" is, in fact … in charge.

The dynamic of a new Principal may upset them. They may feel that their influence in the school has been downgraded:

> *The old Principal would never have spoken to Mr. T. without consulting me first*

> *S/he sent out a letter without me seeing it*

These situations are sometimes unavoidable, reflecting a resentful or immature personality (they often go together); or reflecting the cloistered culture of a small

---

[159] As a cynical rule of thumb, the louder the protestations that "I'm not interested in the job", the greater the ambition ….

[160] This surprisingly common phenomenon is sometimes encouraged by Board members, who should know better, trying to calm anxiety – "Don't worry, Morry, we'll never appoint anyone you don't approve of".

institution. They are sometimes a result of the new Principal not having been comprehensively briefed by an outgoing predecessor[161] about the routines of the Administration, and, in blissful ignorance, causing offense.

A very problematic – and difficult - situation is where a veteran VP sees him/herself as the 'Guardian of the Authentic School Values', defending them or protecting them against the new Principal. This can be a self-appointed post, or they can be encouraged in this by other teachers, parents, alumni or even Board members.

- Where the person concerned sees him/herself as 'untouchable', their influence in the school can be toxic

- Whatever their feelings, they cannot be allowed, under any circumstances, to undermine the Principal

The Principal has a duty to trust the Administrators and respect them, and to allow them to do their jobs. Administrators have a duty to respect the Principal's appointment, authority and leadership. If relationships are not cordial on a personal level, they must be proper on a professional level[162]. In time, whether through changes, retirements or promotions, the new Principal's team will be in place.

One of the key factors in the relationship is that of information, and it is sometimes used as a weapon. In the hierarchy of confidentiality within the school, the Principal is at the top of the pyramid. An Administrator cannot have secrets about the school, the staff, the students or anything else that are kept from the Principal. An Administrator cannot accept information from a teacher, parent or student "on condition that it is kept from the Principal".

> *I'm sorry – we are a professional team, and the Principal is the head of the school. I cannot accept information given me on condition that it cannot be shared with the Principal. You have to choose whether you want to share with me or not.*

---

[161] This applies to others in the system as well. If your predecessor was in the habit of phoning the founding President of the school every Friday morning to update him/her on 'what happened this week', they should tell you – because that personality will be waiting for your call, and resent the fact that it doesn't come ….

[162] If a Principal finds that a VP – or anyone else - is actively undermining, the situation should be discussed confidentially with the school President. If the Principal then senses that the President sympathizes with, or supports, the dissident personality – there is a serious problem. SEE SECTIONS 3.1 and 17.7 . The Board appointed the Principal to lead the school, and s/he has a right to their support. If the VP was a contender for the Principalship, the successful candidate should certainly have been told at an early stage – probably before final signing of contract. Equally, the Board should have appropriately informed the existing Administration (and staff) of the new appointment, and made it clear that they expect all staff to support the new Principal. If they knew that a VP (or another Administrator) would refuse to accept the new Principal, they should have squarely dealt with that situation before the new Principal arrived to take up post.

Nor can Administrators share information about the school with others before they share it with the Principal. Equally, the Principal must ensure that Administrators are well briefed in all matters concerning the school that they need to know in order to carry out their tasks. Sometimes this may include highly confidential material. They have to be able to keep confidences.

In private schools, Administrators who have been in place for years may have 'inside tracks' to Board members, which they use improperly. In best practice of School Governance, the Principal is the channel of communication to the Board. Bypassing that structure is a breach of professional etiquette – as much by the Board member who receives the information as by the Administrator. You have to call your colleague on it.

> *Jack – I was extremely surprised at last night's Board meeting when Joan started that discussion about the incident that happened the other day. It included information that was known only to you and I. She admitted to me that her information came 'from an Administrator'. There is a trust between us. I work hard to ensure that the firewall between the Board and the affairs of the school is carefully preserved, and that Board members do not interfere with the running of the school. I need your unbreakable assurance that you will respect the confidentiality of school operations.*

9.3.3 Administrators – recruitment and appointment

An Administrator is leaving (or a new post is being created) and there is a vacancy to fill. There may be an obvious candidate, but unless there are really compelling reasons to do so, resist the temptation to make an automatic appointment. Administrators are crucial to the success of the school. Mistakes (not always avoidable) are expensive, embarrassing and demoralizing. A successful appointment can thoroughly invigorate the school.

First, deal with the departing Administrator. We assume that s/he is departing amicably. Make sure that his/her departure/retirement is dignified; that (if appropriate) an agreed statement is made to the school community; and that opportunities are created, at the correct scale, to allow colleagues, students and parents to wish him/her well. It is a time to be generous. Putting up a "Thanks to Mrs. X" website, with some arrangement for past and present students to post messages (via a moderator...) can be a lot of fun, and also provide a nice opportunity for people out of town to keep contact with the school. At the retirement/departure gathering, present the Administrator with a printout of the site. Leave it up for a month or two.

If the departure is not amicable, be very careful to preserve the dignity of the departing individual.

At the same time, the Principal should consult with lay leaders about the recruitment process. It is a healthy thing for all vacancies to be internally and externally advertised. Although schools may end up appointing from within for Vice-Principals (Jewish or General Studies), you do not necessarily know who is around and may be interested. The field is better–known in Jewish Studies, for obvious reasons. Draw up a Job Description and an advertisement.

The Principal should convene a Search Committee (chaired by the Principal[163]), which may comprise representatives of the Board (who are also parents), other Administrators, and staff representatives. The Staff representatives should sit on the Committee by invitation.

Make sure that the members of the search committee are sensible, have balanced judgment, and are credible to the school 'constituencies'.

The parameters of the Search Committee should also be clear – it is essentially advisory[164]. If the consensus at the end of the process includes the Principal – that is excellent. Yet the Search Committee is exactly that – a 'Search' Committee, and not an 'Appointment' Committee'. The Principal must reserve the right to make the final decision. The School cannot appoint a candidate with whom the Principal is not comfortable. (On the other hand, the Principal should pay careful attention to the qualities that the Committee are apparently most anxious to bring to the Campus...)

Ensure that everyone is aware of the essential confidentiality of the process, and post ads in the Staff Room and the local (or national) newspaper(s). Book the interviews, and carefully plan with the committee the questions that are to be asked. While anyone can add questions, there are some important questions that should be asked of every candidate. Add some 'unseen' scenarios. It is good practice to ask every candidate some similar questions, which gives a clearer base for comparison.

In all of this, what is the school looking for in an Administrator? A good Principal will try and assess this carefully and strategically. The easiest thing to do is to look for someone in his/her own image. A more nuanced view is to seek a colleague with complementary skills and even personality to those of the existing team (or the Principal him/herself). Essential factors include, but are not limited to:

- Organizational ability – the Administrators have to be efficient and good at running a school

- Professional knowledge and expertise – whether the prospective Administrator is Jewish or General Studies, they must be masters of their craft, able to design and implement systems of curriculum, assessment and evaluation, scheduling, staff evaluation and any of the other range of tasks which they may be called on to fulfill

- Sympathy with students and staff – will they deal kindly, firmly and sensibly with the school constituencies?

---

[163] "The Board employs the Principal, and the Principal employs all other staff"
[164] Ensure that this is very clear to Search Committee at the beginning of the first meeting.

- Sound judgment – without good judgment, they will make mistakes with staff, students and parents

- Temperament and personality - how does your candidate react under pressure? Does s/he have a temper? Are they diplomatic? Do they seem approachable? How will they present to parents and community?

- Appropriate 'affect' – how does the candidate present in appearance, dress, and comportment? Is this someone who will immediately command the respect of the different school constituencies?

The list may be added to. However, there is one question that the Principal has to answer:

> *When you are out of the school for any reason, can you leave this candidate in charge and be completely confident that they can handle any situation that arises?*

9.3.4 Induction process

When a new Administrator arrives in a school, make sure that they are properly briefed, introduced and inducted to all constituencies.

9.3.5 Managing and evaluating Administrators

For a Principal, managing Administrators is extremely difficult. They are closest colleagues, trusted advisers and confidantes. Yet again, the Principal must keep a delicate and difficult balance between collegiality and distance. It is the Principal's job to supervise, guide and direct Administrators, and there will be times when their performance has to be evaluated and some of their actions queried. When necessary, the Principal must be objective and straightforward. It should be a characteristic of the qualities that qualified the Administrator for senior responsibility that they are able to accept constructive direction and criticism without taking it personally – just as you should be able to take feedback from your senior lay leadership in the same spirit. That is often easier said than done.

The easiest way to establish that framework is to make it explicit at the earliest possible point of the relationship. If the Administrator is new – part of the Job Description and the preparatory conversations of the appointment will include explicit provisions for periodic written evaluation. Add a verbal understanding:

> *Although I am looking forward to a very close and collegial relationship, we both understand that from time to time I will be evaluating your performance and giving you both positive and negative feedback.*

If the Principal is new, and is coming to an existing team of Administrators (who may never have been evaluated), then the same principle applies - make intended policies clear at the very beginning, not six months after arrival.

There will be different levels of evaluation. One will be ongoing, informal and unobtrusive feedback, the result of observation or of comments or reactions received from others. There should be very little negative feedback concerning senior Administrators; if there is a lot, the school has a problem. Sometimes, individual Administrators need to be steered away from areas where they do not perform at their best, ensuring that they concentrate on tasks they do excellently. Administrators are human beings like everyone else, and need to be consciously complimented when they do things well.

Formal, written performance evaluations should be given every two years or so, especially in the year before renewal of contract. There are different styles both of process and format[165]. A good model is to ask the Administrator to submit a self-evaluation, normally under a series of headings. This may be followed by a conversation that reviews the self-evaluation, and then the Principal will respond with a formal document that constitutes the review – typically three or four pages long. The Administrator should have the right to submit a response to the document, which is then filed with the review.

Areas of review may include:

- Evaluation of performance against the Job Description

- Relationships with different constituencies (other Administrators, teachers, students, parents)

- PD undertaken in the review period

- Areas needing further attention or concentration

- Areas of particular achievement

- Goals for the upcoming period

- A brief summary and appreciation.

Administrators carry a lot of responsibility. They should rise to that expectation, and behave accordingly, being prepared to be on call at any time, and if necessary work beyond hours.

The Principal may face a situation where an Administrator is not performing satisfactorily, and should be removed from post. These can be very complicated

---

[165] I personally favour anecdotal written reports, and intensely dislike checklists, 'scales' and the like. But it is a matter of personal preference.

situations. Before making any move, strategically consult with the President, the Chair of Personnel Committee and with the school's labor lawyer. Work out a strategy that allows the school to do what it has to do, but makes the process effective, non-confrontational and discreet.

9.4 Teachers

9.4.1 The school's core business

At the beginning of this book SEE SECTION 1.1, the 'lead characteristic' of 'Excellent Schools' and 'Truly Great Schools' was defined as:

- An inspirational faculty, carefully chosen and carefully nurtured.

Building an inspirational faculty is a two-way process – it means encouraging the best, but weeding out the teachers who are not reaching the school's standards. The school's ability to do this will vary greatly according to local conditions.

Your school is as good as its staff team. Nothing that it can do to recruit and retain the very best teachers is too much. Equally, the school must be fair but firm in dealing with teachers whose professional performance does not meet school standards.

Private schools, traditionally, may have greater opportunity to allow unusual (or idiosyncratic) teachers to flourish.

- A single wonderful teacher can alter a student's life forever.

Inspirational teachers come in different shapes and sizes, and often have a dash of amiable eccentricity – a valuable and memorable asset, but one that the wise Principal will monitor closely. Ultimately, however, **the core business of your school is teaching** – the imparting of knowledge and skills, and the encouragement of learning. The school may have faculty who are scholars, who are wonderful personalities, who are saintly characters, who are brilliant, whom the students love – but unless they are **teachers**, with all that that implies, the school is in trouble.

9.4.2 The Principal and the teacher – basic relationship

In a school where a young Principal had succeeded an older and more experienced person, a veteran teacher took me for a walk. "The difference between this Principal and the old one is simple. When the old one walked around the hallways during lessons, you knew he was there to back you up. When this one walks around during lessons, you know he's there to catch you out." Whether that was true or not, the differing impressions that the two Principals had made was telling.

The demands that the school makes on teachers take up a significant amount of this book. Yet their motivation and hence performance may depend how the Principal fulfills *their* demands -- often intangible and therefore more difficult to identify.

Among the expectations that the teaching body may have of their Principal are:

- Professional competence in leading, organizing and running the school

- Support in the classroom, and respect for teachers' professional status

- Protection, when necessary, from parents and from the Board

- Educational and school vision

- Fairness

- Ability to carry responsibility, take decisions and solve problems

- Support for worthwhile teacher initiatives

- Enabling opportunities for Professional development

- Ensuring that they have the physical and material resources to do their jobs properly

- A sympathetic ear, when necessary

If the Principal is not naturally a 'Teacher's Principal' SEE SECTION 2.3, one of the Administrative team has to have that complementary skill. Teachers need and deserve constant attention.

9.5 Teacher Recruitment

For the particular challenges of recruiting Jewish Studies teachers – SEE SECTION 7.4.3 *and for a discussion regarding the recruitment of Shlichim -* SEE SECTION 7.5

9.5.1 The best teachers

Every minute or dollar spent in locating excellent staff is worth it. A Principal in a large school may delegate some staff recruitment to other Administrators, but if so, the criteria for selection must be clear. The school wants the best teachers.

Recruiting teachers is about the individual teacher – but equally about the team.

At the individual level, the best professional teachers:

- Genuinely like, are interested in, and have sympathy for young people[166]

- Love the classroom, and are skilled pedagogues

- 'Teach the students, not the subject'[167]

- Whatever their age, are mature and stable

- Are themselves knowledgeable and passionate about their subject, and keep up with developments in their field

- Are well organized and methodical, and have excellent classroom presence

- Are collegial, team players, willing to share in every way with their colleagues and their students

- Always open to new ideas and new opportunities

- Have intellectually curious minds

- Are willing to go beyond the call of duty when necessary for the students and for the school

It is essential that all teachers support the philosophy and ethos of the school. That provision should be an explicit condition of employment.

For teachers who are not Jewish, it means that they have to understand and respect the ideology of the school, while respectfully preserving their own beliefs. Teachers who are fervently committed members of another faith must respect the integrity of the Jewish school, and recognize that any undermining of the Jewishness of the school is a serious breach of principle[168].

However, every Jewish school Principal will testify that some of the most loyal and valuable teachers (and Administrators) a Jewish school can have are not Jewish[169].

Jewish teachers -- whether of Jewish or General Studies -- must also uphold the school's philosophy, values and operational principles. This is self-evident regarding Jewish Studies teachers; but equally true of Jewish teachers of General Studies.

---

[166] Without this and the following quality, they will never make good teachers. The rest can, within limits, be learned.

[167] A formulation I owe to my colleague Sam Kapustin.

[168] The most extreme form of this is evangelism to students or staff. Very occasionally, individuals may seek employment in Jewish schools with this agenda in mind. They cannot continue at the school.

[169] 'The non-Jewish teacher in the Jewish school' is a subject that deserves further study.

Occasionally, complex emotions come into play with Jewish teachers, whose view of Judaism does not coincide with the school's values, and for whom finding themselves in an intensely Jewish environment can be an emotional experience. They must respect the school's ethos, and balance their personal beliefs and professional responsibilities.

In terms of recruitment for the team – a healthy mix is always best. A balanced staff will contain a range of teachers who will appeal to different 'constituencies' among the students, and who will bring a range of talents and skills that can be used for the benefit of the school. A good teacher does not have to be an extrovert, or charismatic; s/he just has to be a good teacher. There will always be students who warm to the intellectually rigorous, demanding teacher; others will be highly relieved to have a teacher who is quiet, sympathetic and gentle. Some students thrive on the fast-moving, no-nonsense, almost brutal teachers who do not want to hear any excuses from students about anything; others will find them traumatic. The school also needs sportsmen, musicians, 'ruach' movers, and scholars. A few characters and eccentrics will enliven the school; but never, ever, underestimate the value of the solid, professional teacher, on whom you can always rely, without fail, to get the work done.

Finally, it is a fortunate school that has the opportunity to employ its own graduates.[170]

9.5.2 Teachers – young, old, retirees

Private schools who seek part-time staff often employ retirees from the local public school system. Retirees, in turn, often welcome the opportunity – they may not be able to teach in the system from which they have retired without compromising their pension entitlements, and they often find the relatively sheltered environment of the Jewish school system very amenable. Both parties benefit, especially when the retiree is bringing huge professional competence to the school. Retirees, however, by their nature, are veteran members of staff. A careful Administration will ensure that the teaching team remains balanced between the young teachers who will bring freshness, youth, and lots of spare time; the mid-professionals who are bringing depth and quality to the faculty; and the veteran teachers who may have a slightly more laid-back attitude to life.

Every school should be prepared to give first-year teachers their first step onto the career ladder. It would be a mistake to have a staff composed of a relatively large number of new teachers, but it is a professional responsibility to give them opportunity. Most of the time, and especially in their first year, they will need a great deal of mentoring, support and encouragement. All first-year teachers are allowed to cry. We were all there once.

---

[170] At the time of writing, exactly 10% of the faculty of CHAT are own graduates – 17 out of a total faculty of 170.

9.5.3 Advertising

Other than in exceptional cases, it is good practice to advertise all teaching vacancies – internally and externally. An Administrator may know, or a colleague may know, of 'someone' who is available. Unless you advertise, you will never know whether someone better is also out there, unknown to the school. The other advantages of advertising are that it gets the name of the school known in the local professional community, and avoids a 'closed shop' image. If your ad does not bring in any suitable replies, the team may then have to start networking among friends and colleagues to 'see who is around'.

Internal advertising (a notice in the staff room or in the staff bulletin) allows present teachers to 'spread the word'. Your current faculty are usually good judges of who would be good teachers for your school. External advertising is usually in the local Jewish newspaper and the city newspaper – in most places, there is one paper that by convention carries the educational vacancies. The internet is an increasingly important medium for advertising teaching posts.

Ads need not be elaborate, but they should state the necessary information, including the qualifications necessary, the exact person to whom replies should be addressed, and a deadline for applications. As a professional 'shop window' for the school, they should be attractive. You should be aware of relevant legislation in your jurisdiction regarding advertising job vacancies.

Nowadays, most applications are submitted by email, and teachers who cannot submit an application by email would probably rule themselves out by that fact alone.

9.5.4 Applications

An application should of course include a covering letter, a resume ("c.v.") and should indicate two or three references whom you can contact. If the teacher is applying from a competing school, or if they don't want their current employer to know that they are considering a move, s/he may use the 'References available on request' formula. Normally, in these circumstances, they will ask that you only seek references if you are seriously considering their appointment.

Every application – solicited or unsolicited - deserves the courtesy of an acknowledgement, however brief. If the applicant is unsuitable or unqualified, politely point this out:

> *Thanks for your interest. Our school policy is only to consider candidates with experience or training in High School teaching. Good luck in your search for a suitable post.*

Suitable applicants should receive a packet of information about the school (or at least directions of where the information can be found online), and a Job Description.

- Deal with the applications speedily.
- Make sure that you notify the unsuccessful applicants as well:

Thank you for your application and for your interest in our school. I am writing to let you know that we have now made an appointment to the advertised post, and would like to thank you again for the time and trouble you took to submit your application. We wish you every success in your search for a new post.

If appropriate, add:

However, we are keeping your resume on file, and will contact you in the future if a suitable vacancy arises.

9.5.5 Reading a resume

Reading a resume is a skill, and most Principals develop the skill instinctively. Among the long list of things to look for in an application are:

- Is the spelling on the cover letter and resume correct?

- Is the information presented in a clear manner? If it isn't, how will this person clearly present information to students?

- Has the applicant got the required qualifications / experience?

- How often has the applicant changed jobs?

- Are there any inconsistencies / unexplained gaps in the employment record?

- Are the schools listed High Schools, and what level courses has the applicant taught?

- Is the promotion /responsibility record of the candidate what you might expect from a candidate of similar qualifications and experience?

- What do you know of the schools at which the applicant has worked?

- Has the teacher been involved in other professional activities or forums?

- What else, apart from teaching, is listed – extra-curricular activities, PD, personal hobbies/sports /interests?

- Does the resume seem to honestly describe the applicant's achievements without exaggerating? What personality comes through the document?

- Who has the candidate given as references? Are they senior professionals? Are they only personal, non-professional? Are they only professional peers?

On the answers to these will depend on whether or not the applicant gets an interview. If some details are not clear, call the references (unless there is some reason not to), or call the candidate and ask for clarification.

Seasoned professionals know how to give references. Listen carefully for what is said, and, equally, what is not said.

In calling references, ascertain exactly what the relationship was / is between the candidate and the reference. Do they know the candidate in their professional capacity, and are they able to give a serious objective assessment of strengths and weaknesses? Standard questions include:

- What are X's weak points and strong points?

- How was his/her classroom control?

- How were his/her relationships with other teachers / students / parents?

- Was X good at accepting supervision?

- Was he/she reliable / good at deadlines / paperwork ?

- Was he/she willing to help in extra-curricular activities?

- "Do you have an idea of why X wants to move at this point – he/she seems to have a very responsible post at their present school?"

- "What are the things that X might need to work on a little more?"

- "Is there anything else about X that as a prospective employer I should know?"

- "If X applied / reapplied to you for a post, would you happily employ/re-employ him/her?"

Probe tactfully, but firmly. Remember that teachers may be very unsuccessful in one school, and stunning in another – and vice-versa. Look for some life, some interest – and make very sure that the person has a stable background.

- If the reference evades a question, or gives any sort of deliberately non-committal answer – tread very carefully.

A negative reference from a source nominated by the applicant is a serious issue, and may show a remarkable lack of self-knowledge by the teacher.

Once again, JS teachers need an additional list of things to check. They very often come from varied backgrounds, and are typically well traveled – certainly geographically, and often spiritually. The Principal must decode their learning and training. A well-connected Principal (or Director of Jewish Studies) may be able to make discreet enquiries among contacts, professional colleagues, or old friends. The Jewish educational world is very small, and few schools or other institutions are more than two or three calls away. With JS teachers the question is often not what sort of teacher the candidate is, but what sort of teacher they *could be* with the right guidance and support.

9.5.6 Applicants from other community schools or other local private schools

Etiquette in these cases may vary from locality to locality. Some communities where there are several Jewish schools have a mutual 'no poaching' policy (this may apply to private schools in the same area as well). A 'no poaching' policy provides that a school may not initiate contact with a teacher currently employed by another school. Where the school receives a teacher-initiated application, and wishes to interview the candidate, good practice is as follows:

- Tell the candidate that you cannot interview them until they have indicated to the Administrator to whom they are responsible that they are considering changing posts. They do not have to disclose that they are applying to your school..

- If you are intending to hire, you must be able to speak to the persons nominated as references. In such cases, they are frequently not the candidate's Administrators, but peer teaching colleagues who are probably also good friends. That can be problematic, and you have to be careful that there is no ulterior reason for this. If the community is small, you may well have an idea of the teacher's reputation and abilities from the 'grapevine'.

- Finally – before you make the teacher an offer of employment, as a courtesy you must call your counterpart at the other school, and let him or her know that you are intending offering employment to one of their staff.

    Rabbi X / Ms. Y: It's the Principal of Jewish High calling. I need to let you know that a member of your staff, Mrs. A, has applied for a post at our school, and as a courtesy I'd like to let you know that we intend offering her the post.

9.5.7 Offers are binding – on both sides

As with all offers of employment, the school must assume that the teacher is free to give notice, and has not contracted for the coming year. If they have – the school cannot employ them, and if you have already issued a letter of appointment, it must be withdrawn. If you don't, you will quickly find yourself 'persona non grata' with your professional peers in other local schools.

> *I understand from the Principal of X Academy that when you accepted the offer of employment at our school you had already signed a contract to teach for X Academy in the coming school year. Under those circumstances, you were not free to seek employment with us, and your acceptance of a post constitutes a breach of professional standards. I very much regret that I must therefore withdraw our letter of appointment dated [date].*
>
> *cc: Principal of X Academy*

Conversely, a teacher who has accepted a post with you is not free to accept a post elsewhere. Should a teacher call you to say that they have now accepted a post at another school, after agreeing to teach for you, you are entitled to call the other school, and ask if they were aware that this teacher had accepted a post with you. If the answer is "No", you are entitled to ask the other school to withdraw their offer to that teacher. In practice, you will rarely do that, because you no longer wish to have that teacher on your staff. If the other school did know that the teacher was committed to you, they are guilty of a major breach of professional etiquette.

9.5.8 Interviewing

Interviewing is an art. Administration should have dealt with all of the technical issues via the resume and the references, although if there are issues arising from the resume, they should be cleared up at the beginning of the interview. The interview should be the chance to reach the person behind the paper. To do that, the Principal has to make sure that for most of the time, the candidate is talking, and the Principal is listening.

An interview is always a somewhat personal experience. The Principal is trying to discover whether the applicant will be a 'fit' with the team and with the school vision and values. It is difficult to give generic guidelines. It is always useful to begin by asking candidates to describe themselves, and why they are seeking to teach at your school. A good follow-up is: "What do you know about our school?" It is a bad sign if they have done no homework.

Common questions include:

- "Every teacher has some lesson or program of which they are especially proud. Can you tell me about a lesson or a course that you think was particularly successful?"

- "What was your best moment so far as a teacher?"

- "..... And your worst?"

- "...... How did you deal with it?"

- "Who do you regard as your educational / religious / Jewish / philosophical / literary / academic / personal 'gurus'?"

I also often give teachers two or three short *'What would you do if ...?"* questions – how would you deal with particular questions from students, or disciplinary scenarios. They may not know the answers (in some cases, they cannot without knowing the school) – but the way that they answer is always revealing.

Do not forget to conclude the interview:

- By asking if they have any questions for you

- By giving them some indication of time-frame before you can give them a decision

In most cases, short-listed candidates will have another interview with a V-P, and a chance to meet with a Head of Department. However, the ultimate choice must be the Principal's.

It is very easy when conducting a series of interviews for the candidates to quickly merge into each other in your memory. Take a digital photo of each candidate, and make sure that you write up clear notes for further reference *as soon as the interview is finished.*

- Who gets the job? The candidate who in the judgment of the interviewing team will be the best classroom teacher, and who will bring an inspirational, educational presence to the school, enrich the faculty and enhance the students' educational experience.

9.5.9 References (reading and writing)

One result of our litigious world is the reluctance of some institutions to write anything but the most perfunctory references. It is nevertheless the case that the one-line reference ("*X was a member of staff at this school from (date) to (date), teaching Geography, Math and Civics."*) is a real danger sign. To receive – or write – one of these is a clear indication that this person is not to be employed again as a teacher.

There are a series of codes commonly used in writing references, and a Principal will learn (and probably use) them. Examples include:

- "Lively" – in a classroom context, means 'out of control'

- "highly individual approach" – did not follow the curriculum

- "very popular with students" – did not get on at all with other teachers

- "a strong voice in the staff room" – caused problems for Administration

- "valued education above bureaucracy" – always late with marks, report cards etc

- "gained the allegiance of many students" – dangerously charismatic

- "unfortunate absences interrupted his teaching" – may indicate chronic absenteeism

- "negotiated a steep learning curve" – started off disastrously, but improved

- "always followed school procedures meticulously" – totally inflexible

Much more encouraging words and phrases include:

- "highly professional teacher"

- "sorry to see him/her leave"

- "would not hesitate to offer him her a post again"

- "definitely an asset to any school"

- 'highly respected by colleagues, students and Administration alike"

- "extremely sound judgment"

A reference may also give fulsome praise in one aspect of the teacher's talents, but be conspicuously silent (deliberately, and for good reason) in others. A reference that highlight's the teacher's role as producer of the school play, or leader of Shabbatonim, but is completely silent on his/her classroom performance, or relationships with fellow-teachers, is giving a hidden message.

Calling the writer of the reference (and every reference should include a 'Please don't hesitate to call me for further information" line) – gives opportunity to explore both the 'hidden' and the 'revealed'. Occasionally I have asked a very blunt question –

- *"Does this person have their head firmly screwed on?"*

Remember that the candidate will be in charge of young people.

In writing references, all of the above applies, but in reverse. Relying on your reference (written or verbal) an individual may be put in charge of young people somewhere else. References should give credit where it is due, with real praise where justified; but the writer is under no obligation to tell lies, and may exercise a prerogative of silence. If a teacher has been seriously problematic in the classroom – you must find a tactful way of saying it:

> *Ms. X did not find teaching at our school easy, and I supported her feeling that perhaps she should explore other careers where her talents could be more beneficially applied.*

> *Mr. X would benefit from a position where he could work by himself, without the stress of facing a class. We wish him well in his future endeavors.*

9.5.10   References for staff who wish to move on

A teacher may come to you and ask for a reference, because he/she wishes to move on.

Occasionally, this may be good news for you, in which case you write a fair reference and wish them well.

However, it is often the best teachers who reach the conclusion that to fulfill their ambition, it is time to seek another, often more senior post.

In those circumstances, you have only two options:

- Is there anything you can do to keep the teacher at your school. If the request is not outrageous, consider whether you wish to try and satisfy it.

By the time the teacher has come to talk to you, he/she is probably already 'psyched up' in anticipation of a move, or may already have had an offer. It is not always a good idea to try and keep the teacher at your school, since there may always be a "What if …" feeling, and the teacher may move on anyway a year or so later.

- Be gracious, and while making it clear that you don't want to lose the teacher, promise genuine support for the teacher's ambitions. Never hold back people who want professional advancement[171].

Doing this should earn you goodwill. If your school is training teachers who go on to senior posts elsewhere, you are creating an invaluable network of contacts and professional friends who should eventually return your graciousness by recommending you teachers and being helpful and supportive in other ways.

- The reference that you write should be fair. Samples of references are included in APPENDIX B .

---

[171] The same applies to promotions. It is very unfair to block a promotion because "We can't afford to lose W as a chemistry teacher". 'W' is likely to leave, in which case you have lost 'W' altogether.

9.6 Promotions and responsibility

Developing leadership, allocating responsibility, and giving fair opportunity for advancement are important ways of building school quality. Process should be open, and available positions for promotion should be advertised internally, and where appropriate, externally.

The formality of the process will depend on the seniority of the position. For some posts, a small selection committee is appropriate, chaired by the Principal or a senior Vice-principal. Heads of Department may be appointed by consensus of the Administration. However, for all appointments:

- Applications should be invited

- A clear Job Description and terms of employment/payable allowances should be provided

- Process, however informal, should be clear

    Interviews will be held in the next three weeks and it is hoped that an appointment will be announced by the end of May

- If the duration of the appointment is fixed, that, too, should be public knowledge ("Heads of Department are appointed for three years, after which the post will be re-advertised.") Making appointments of fixed duration is a good way of ensuring fresh faces in the team, and giving a wider pool of staff opportunity to exercise leadership. A staff member who has been carrying a title for years, but has long since ceased to be a leader is a deadly and demoralizing influence in the school.

This formality makes it clear that process in the school is fair and open, and that teachers can aspire to leadership within the school. Always promote the best and the brightest, even though others may feel that they have a claim to a particular post by longevity of service, inertia, status or some other quality. Not all good teachers make good leaders or organizers, and 'high profile' teachers are not necessarily the best candidates for responsibility. Different areas of school activity may require different leadership qualities at different times – at a certain point, a particular department may need imaginative leadership who will lead curriculum change; at another time, it may need organizational strength. Determining those needs correctly is an Administrative task. Do not compromise on quality; do not make an appointment "because we had no alternative", and make it clear to all staff that there is an expectation that they will work collegially and professionally with the new appointee.

Appoint the best; occasionally take risks; let them do their job; and publicly support them all the way.

9.6.1 Youth and experience

Because of the severe personnel shortage in the Jewish school system, it occasionally happens that totally inexperienced staff[172] are given senior appointments, usually in smaller and geographically isolated schools.

Occasionally, especially in very small schools, with very bright young candidates, such appointments can work. Yet without several years of classroom experience it is exceptionally difficult to have credibility with other staff and exercise good supervisory judgment.

A variation on this is when a charismatic informal educator is given school responsibility – again, without school experience – on the basis of successful work with young people in the community, either as a youth leader or, in Orthodox settings, as a successful *'kiruv'* (religious programming) worker.

The seasoned craft of the classroom is the indispensable professional basis of every school.

9.7 Staff evaluation and performance appraisal

Orderly staff evaluation and performance appraisal is an essential part of a good school. While evaluation is not necessarily common in the Jewish school system, resistance should dissipate when it is understood *and demonstrated* that the aim of evaluation is constructive, not critical. There is a great deal of literature on diverse methods of evaluation. Administration and staff should work together to devise an agreed assessment schedule, which should include:

- frequency of formal evaluations (in normal circumstances, probably once every two or three years)

- how the process is to be conducted

- format and content of the evaluation instrument

- how feedback is to be given

However, it remains the Administration's prerogative to decide who is to be evaluated, and when. In addition to routine evaluations, a school will often determine that a teacher whose performance seems to be problematic should be fully evaluated; in such cases, the evaluation has a diagnostic purpose.

---

[172] Sometimes holding Masters' degrees in 'Educational Administration', even though they have minimal or even no classroom experience.

The best evaluations look at the teacher's total functioning in the school. The core must always be the classroom, but every dimension of a teacher's activity may be legitimately examined. There is no teacher – however veteran – who cannot profit from an objective, constructive look at their performance. The best teachers will welcome it, and the cumulative effect should improve the accountability and professionalism of the staff. The teacher may see a largely positive evaluation as professional and personal validation. On the other hand, an evaluation that raises questions regarding a teacher's performance should also provide the teacher with a clear, documented account of areas that need improvement – with suggestions of how to achieve them. There may be suggested goals, including a time-line. However uncomfortable such a process may be for the teacher, it is fair and specific, and is better than the undefined, often unspoken air of dissatisfaction and unhappiness that is the alternative. From the school's point of view, it provides a paper trail that can be referred to on future occasions.

> *Two years ago, in November 2...., Ms. K was given a comprehensive professional evaluation. Administrators visited her class on three occasions, and conducted a series of interviews with her to discuss her classroom performance. Ms. K had several opportunities to comment on the process. The final report – to which Ms. K was given the opportunity to respond in writing – specified four areas in which the school wished to see improvement – class control, lesson preparation, implementation of orderly disciplinary procedures, and a more collegial working relationship with other teachers. We suggested two books and a series of videos which Ms. K could refer to, and we asked Mrs.L to be available as a confidential mentor to Ms. K. Unfortunately, no improvement has taken place...*

Non-teaching staff and support staff should also be evaluated from time to time.

A full evaluation is different from the ongoing classroom visits of Administration. Administrators may visit a classroom with no notice or short notice. After a short visit, a 'feedback' note should be sent to the teacher. Positive aspects of the observed lesson should be recorded, and areas needing attention carefully and clearly noted. A copy of the note (and any teacher response) should be placed in the teacher's personal file. Traditionally, a teacher's classroom was his/her 'castle'. Today, the non-aggressive and reasonable management vision of a school provides for greater accountability. Evaluation is not there to impose conformity or mediocrity on the staff (the first accusation made by teachers unhappy with the prospect of performance appraisal). There should still be room for the appropriately eccentric and individualistic teacher.

Systematic classroom visits and evaluations also provide the opportunity to develop a 'best practice' information bank for the school, and allow cross-fertilization of ideas and techniques.

9.8 The Staff Room

Teachers must have a staff room, which 'belongs' to them. It their place to 'hang out', and, by convention, Administrators, who should visit every so often, do not unduly intrude. The staff room should be comfortable and well equipped with a range of amenities – fridge, coffee maker and microwave; and where the staff room is also used for working[173], computers with on-line access, a photocopier and telephones. Every teacher should have a locker and, if possible, their own work 'carrel'.

In Jewish schools, kashrut in the staff room is occasionally an issue. Not every school will ask non-Jewish (or Jewish) staff to conform to strict kashrut for their personal supplies, although most will ask teachers not to bring non-kosher meat products to school. Some faculty will only be able to use equipment (microwaves or fridges) where kosher products only are stored or heated. Under these circumstances, avoid the argument, and provide two of everything – one clearly labeled 'For kosher use only'.

More delicate matters may arise:

- A staff member may be "stirring up" the staff room - see below, SECTION 10.2.5

- Arguments between staff may make the staff room an uncomfortable place for others. In such a case, the Principal must be as quietly firm with teachers as s/he would be with students. Personal issues cannot intrude in to professional space, and it is the responsibility of every teacher to act in an appropriate, collegial manner.

9.9 Protecting teachers

The function of the Principal includes the duty to protect teachers from parents, Board members or even students. Teachers are vulnerable to vendettas and occasionally false accusations. Vendettas are ugly and toxic, and without regard to whether the teacher's performance is satisfactory or not -- the responsibility of supervising, managing and if necessary disciplining teachers is that of the Administration, not that of a disgruntled Grade 10 parent. Parents may not be rude or inappropriate to teachers; they may not intrude on the teacher's professional or personal space, and they may not 'badmouth' them in the community.

---

[173] Where the staff room is not used for working, preparing lessons etc., a separate, appropriately-equipped teachers' workroom should be available.

The Principal, and if necessary the School President, must deal with such cases swiftly, making it clear to the offending parent that the school is a professional institution, that it does not deal with problems in that way, and that inappropriate behavior is unacceptable within the school community. There is also precedent for taking legal action to stop the public harassment of teachers. The Principal, the President and the school as an institution must do what is necessary to prevent its teachers being publicly pilloried, and should take legal advice if necessary.

A similar situation pertains to false allegations against teachers – usually, but not always, of a sexual nature - made by students or, rarely, by other members of staff or even parents. While every allegation has to be thoroughly investigated, if the school quickly reaches the conclusion that the complaint is malicious, then expert legal advice is needed – immediately and urgently. The costs may be covered by the teacher's, or the school's insurance, but the school itself must be prepared to defend a teacher against false accusations that could ruin their career and their life. Do not assume under any circumstances that the problem can be resolved within the school, without legal involvement. As is now well known, once such accusations are made, they may set in motion statutory processes that are difficult, if not impossible, to stop.

- All school staff, at every level, have a reciprocal duty to conduct themselves in deed and in speech in a wholly professional and responsible manner which does not lend itself to misinterpretation.

9.10 Professional Development

Every school – whatever its size – must provide opportunities for professional development ('PD') for all staff. An environment of learning for staff as well as students will immensely enrich the school, and will engender an expectation of continual professional improvement. An established guideline (very rarely, if ever, met) is that a school should allocate 1.5% of its gross budget to PD. PD, while usually collective, can be departmental or in special cases even individual. The school may decide to train a particular staff member for a particular purpose, and develop a personal PD program.

PD may be designed for different purposes, at different times:

- To enrich professional expertise or knowledge of the staff

- To address specific problems within the school

- To prepare staff as a group for upcoming changes in curriculum or procedure

A comprehensive PD program could include, although certainly may not be limited to, the following:

- In-school PD on a scheduled basis

- Opportunity and funding for staff to attend external courses and conferences

- Mentoring programs

- Availability of professional books, journals, videos

- Subscriptions to online PD sites

PD should be a joint enterprise between staff and Administration. Much of the most productive PD is staff-generated. However, 'PD consciousness' has to come from the top of the school. The Principal or a designated Vice-Principal should have the specific responsibility for arranging and implementing PD. Where the size of the school permits it, PD for Jewish Studies staff may be a separate, parallel responsibility.

In smaller schools, many staff are part-time. It has to be mandatory for all staff, including all part-time staff, to attend PD sessions (and staff meetings). Whether a teacher is teaching one or six courses, they are part of the faculty, and need to be participants in the collective training and teamwork of the school.

9.11 When staff leave or retire

Ceremony plays an important part in the life and dynamic of every group. It is important that the contributions of staff who are leaving or retiring are appropriately acknowledged at or close to the end of their last year.

It is important to be consistent in recognition, which should be proportionate to length of service. It is not difficult to work out a protocol of gift value (book gift vouchers are always appropriate). Keep the ceremonies short and sincere, and gently, but firmly convey the message that the school, as an institution, will continue to move forward. Unless you mean it, do not make promises of post-retirement part-time work.

9.12 Support staff

Support staff include all non-teaching staff – office staff, accounting staff, lab assistants and, very importantly, your custodial/maintenance staff. Look for the very best, and do not try and save money by paying less than the market rate. The office staff will be the primary interface with the school for most parents and others. An efficient, polite office will make a huge difference to the quality of service delivered by the school, internally and externally alike. The physical/environmental impression made by your building is in the hands of the custodians. Efficient custodians can make a huge difference to the school, and save Administration many headaches. All of them are important to you, and important to the school. Get to know them.

9.12.1 Support Staff — recruitment, appointment and management

Like all appointments, Support Staff vacancies should be advertised, and appointments made after interview and process. It avoids many arguments and petty rivalries to have a standard salary grid for support staff, with each post clearly identified and classified according to qualifications/skills, experience and level of responsibility. If the size of the school permits it, clearly indicate possibilities for promotion or improvement of salary scale following the acquisition of new skills or the assumption of new responsibilities.

Like all school employees, support staff should have written letters of appointment, job descriptions, and clear terms of employment. The CFO/Executive Director is responsible for supervising the non-academic staff. Non-academic staff should also be reviewed periodically, and written performance reviews given. They, too, should have opportunities to improve their skills and attend courses (wholly or partly at the school's expense) from time to time.

9.12.2 The Principal's secretary

The Principal's secretary occupies a crucial post. A good secretary is worth more than her weight in gold (let alone rubies!), to you and to the school, and needs executive-level skills. She (or very rarely, he) should work only for you. Do not compromise on this appointment.[174]

---

[174] This is an appropriate place to recognize the essential contributions to my own functioning rendered, in different times and different places, by Camilla, Arlene and now for a number of years, the indispensable and truly outstanding Harriet!

10 PROBLEMATIC TEACHERS

The overwhelming majority of teachers are wonderful, dedicated – even inspirational - individuals, whose careers are totally positive, and who probably do not get thanked enough or often enough. The Principal must also deal with the exceptions, who will take up much more of his/her time. Every case discussed here is an exception. A fortunate Principal may never meet any of them.

10.1 The incompetent teacher: the problem is ongoing

There tend to be four types of teacher whose classrooms are a disaster:

- New teachers, whose appointment was a mistake. (This category does not necessarily include first-year teachers, whose classes should always be carefully watched, and who frequently have a very tough first year in the profession)

- Teachers who have been around for much longer, but have somehow been 'under the radar' – usually because successive Administrations have avoided taking action. A new Administrator may decide to 'grasp the nettle'.

- Occasionally, deteriorating performance in an otherwise good teacher will signal an emotional, family or medical problem. In those cases, the Principal must take appropriate and sympathetic action.

- Teachers who are simply 'burnt out'

Incompetent teachers are not (usually) abusive, inappropriate, or in any similar category – they are simply bad teachers. Bad teaching can manifest itself in several ways:

- The teacher cannot control the class.

- The teacher cannot communicate with, or relate to, the students (or parents); or is relating to them in an unacceptable manner (e.g. sarcasm)

- Students cannot understand the teacher; do not understand what the teacher is asking them to learn; the teacher does not, or cannot, answer reasonable questions

- The teaching is very boring, failing to command the attention of the students

- Occasionally, it becomes clear that the teacher's own understanding of the subject is lacking

- The curriculum is not being delivered in a satisfactory manner – material is not being covered thoroughly, at the right pace, or at all; the teacher may be deviating (too far) from the curriculum

- The teacher does not prepare or organize his/her lessons; does not set or mark students' work, or return it in a timely manner; and does not submit marks or report cards on time

- Similar to the last point – the 'burnt-out' teacher is relying on old lesson plans (if any), or worse, on memory, having taught the same material for so many years; and has lost interest in the subject and the students

- The teacher is continually and chronically late for lessons

- The teacher is not collegial

Whatever the symptom, the results are the same – the students are not learning!

It is often possible to improve the performance of a bad, or incompetent teacher, with careful mentoring and consistent support. Some problems are more amenable to improvement than others. Improving the classroom performance of any teacher is a highly worthwhile, highly rewarding activity, and is a prime duty of school professional leadership. Both from the perspective of the school and that of the teacher, professional improvement is a much better, more constructive (first) approach than termination or threat – and is a lot more cost effective in both financial and emotional currencies.

At this stage there is no disciplinary content to the process. Strategies that can be effective include some or all of the following:

- Written classroom observations by Administration, clearly highlighting problems, followed by practical suggestions for strategies and techniques that will address the problematic issues. Follow up the discussion with suggestions in writing, and/or with helpful books or videos.

- Asking another teacher to 'mentor' the teacher, including sitting in on his/her classroom. Using another teacher rather than an Administrator makes it non-threatening. That is valuable, because teachers will immediately feel threatened when their classroom performance comes under criticism. It should be clear to both teachers that the 'Mentor' will not report to Administration, and what passes between the two teachers is confidential. However, the first teacher must be told that Administration will revisit his/her class after a defined period of time.

- Getting the problematic teacher to observe a number of other teachers' classrooms. Seeing another teacher conduct successful lessons with the class that the problematic teacher defines as 'impossible' can be a sobering experience. Sometimes the 'mentor' can sit in with the teacher, and point out carefully the techniques being used by the observed teacher that are successfully dealing with problems faced by the problematic teacher in his/her own classes.

- Asking the teacher to attend relevant Professional Development courses that may be available in your locality.

- Within reason, rectifying any circumstances that the teacher identifies as obstructing or interfering with his/her classroom performance. These may be real or excuses[175], major or minor. If they are real – deal with them immediately. Real or not, agreeing to deal with one or two may be helpful in reassuring the teacher that the school is willing to listen to their point of view, and may also be useful for tactical reasons – "If the school agrees to remedy x and y, will you in return promise that you will immediately implement a and b?"

Sometimes, a new teacher is problematic from the very first day. Most labor laws allow for employment of new employees to be terminated without cause within a given time from the date of commencement of employment (usually 45 working days). If the Principal is able to, and if you have to – do not hesitate to invoke that procedure. Your school's reputation depends on the quality of the teachers, and the Principal's reputation depends on the ability to be a leader and take decisions. The process is painful, but *if the situation is irretrievable*, and is only going to cause continual trouble, that is what has to be done. (Why the hiring mistake was made is something on which to reflect carefully, although every Principal makes occasional – occasional - mistakes).

The longer-serving teacher is a different problem, and how that is dealt with is, again, governed by local labor legislation. Very often these problems are 'inherited' by a new Principal. Dealing with them can take years.

---

[175] A flickering light, a room that is "noisy", or "freezing" or "stuffy", a desk that wobbles....

10.1.1   The 'support/warning' cycle for ongoing problems

If none of the above works, or if the teacher is resistant to help (usually in a passive-aggressive manner), then the Administration must initiate a more disciplinary approach.

The classic process is the 'support-warning' cycle. This can be applied over weeks, months or years, but follows a standard pattern – clear expressions specifying areas of concern, combined with offers of support. This should be understood as a positive and constructive exercise. If that is effective – the problem has been solved. If it is clearly ineffective, at a certain point the direction of the process changes; it no longer has the element of support, and becomes a straightforward warning of increasing seriousness, as simply represented by this diagram:

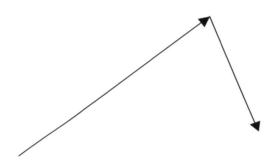

- Step one is to get the teacher to acknowledge that there is a problem, and that you are determined to do something about it. Students, who can be simultaneously kind and cruel, often have pity on poor teachers, and many such teachers will be able to produce letters of thanks and appreciation from students and parents. Do not be swayed; be straightforward, non-judgmental, and make it clear that the school sees problems. The Principal must enter the meeting with the teacher with credible documentation – complaints from students and parents, previous correspondence from the school, previous performance evaluations.

- Step two is to offer, and provide, support and help:

  As you know, both last year and the year before that the school raised with you the issue of your tendency not to return students' work, properly marked, within a reasonable time. We also raised with you, on different occasions, incidents where you let students off lessons for no apparent reason, and told them not to tell any Administrator. We do not feel that there has been any improvement in these situations, and in the last few days we understand that examples of both of these patterns of behavior reoccurred with your Grade 11 class. The school has received four calls from parents complaining that their children 'are not being taught' in your class. When we asked parents if they had spoken to you about the alleged problems, they claim that they have left messages for you that you have ignored. The school wants to support you in your classroom and ensure that there are no further opportunities for misunderstandings by parents or students. We may have some suggestions, but what do you feel the school could do to help you overcome these problematic issues?

- Step three is to make your expectations of improvement clear in writing, with a timetable.

  Following our discussion, we raised with you issues of classroom management and professional procedure that were previously raised last year and the year before. The school has suggested that you view and pay close attention to the video 'Getting yourself organized in the classroom'. We would like to see an immediate improvement in these areas before the end of this school year, and expect that none of these problems will recur in the next school year, when we will be reviewing your performance in these areas. The school Administration will be happy to suggest further material, or provide any further help or support you may request. Our aim is to ensure that you continue to be a valuable member of our faculty, and that your classroom teaching will be effective, free of problems, and personally and professionally fulfilling for you.

- Step four – monitor the situation. If there is an improvement, acknowledge that at the end of the year. If there is not, that, too has to be documented.

  I am extremely concerned that despite the school's expectation that the issues addressed in our meeting of [date] would improve by the end of this school year, there were in fact two further occasions ([date] and [date] when you cancelled classes without authorization. The school has offered you several different options of improving your organizational/preparation skills, which you claim are the cause of the problem. We would be happy to give you any necessary support. I would like to repeat the expectation that there will be no such reoccurrence of these problematic patterns of behavior next year. The school would reserve the right in those circumstances to take further appropriate action.

- Step five – clear warning

  Following complaints received, the Administration is satisfied that the assignment (essay on Hamlet) collected from your Grade 12 class three months ago has not been returned to students. We believe that this constitutes another example of an established pattern of

> *unacceptable behavior that you have been unable to rectify. The school cannot give further warnings regarding this or similar failings of reasonable professional performance, and I have to advise you that the school will take further action should these patterns of behavior persist, up to and including possible termination of your employment.*

Note that the procedure outlined above stretched over four years[176]....

10.1.2   The serious classroom incident

Depending on where your school is situated, there is almost certainly a 'School Law Newsletter' or 'Education Law Newsletter' available on subscription. These publications normally report on cases involving schools and teachers that have reached the courts in local jurisdictions. The investment is well worth it. The updates give a solid and realistic sense of legal trends in a wide range of school-related cases. Most will involve teachers. Some of these publications offer a consultancy service.

Occasionally, issues arise that need immediate and decisive attention. These are not the ongoing classroom problems of the bad teacher; they are clear breaches of professional behavior, of varying degrees of seriousness.

Common such incidents include, but are by no means limited to[177]:

- Use of grossly inappropriate language in the classroom

- Introduction of inappropriate material

- Inappropriate behavior

- Possession of, or appearing to be under the influence of, alcohol or drugs

- Displays of threatening temper

- Victimization of a student

- Rudeness to a student, colleague, Administrator or parent

- Refusal to carry out a reasonable instruction by an Administrator ('insubordination')

- Breach of safety regulations

- Unauthorized absence

---

[176] During which time the Principal has been trying to pacify parents..... The purpose is to ensure that the school has a watertight case when the process reaches its conclusion.
[177] See following 'Teachers: some problematic profiles'

- Dishonesty

- Failure to carry out professional duty in an appropriate or conscientious manner; failure to adequately supervise students

- Major breach of school ethos

Even where the incident is 'the latest' in a series, it is serious enough, or extreme enough, to constitute a dramatic 'precipitating incident'. It is impossible to predict every conceivable situation, and the Principal has to carefully judge the appropriate response.

Some general guidelines may be suggested.

Faced with an unfamiliar or unprecedented situation, the Principal may seek advice on what would be a proportionate response (or consequence) from a labor lawyer, from other local Principals, or perhaps from one of the external consultancy services (see above) available through membership in a professional consortium or association, or via subscription to an educational law publication.

- Initiating these more serious disciplinary processes may well end in legal challenge. It is therefore essential that at every stage, fair process must be followed.

There is a hierarchy of procedures, and the Principal must use judgment which to apply. However, resist the tendency 'to keep things unofficial', 'off the record', 'informal' or 'just between us' unless it is the very first, and very minor, issue. For anything else – the Principal has a duty of care to the school, and failure to protect the interests of the school is a breach of the Principal's own responsibility.

The Administration must first ensure that it has reasonable information. This depends on the situation. The 'incident' may have come to the attention of the school by a telephone call or a conversation; there may be written statements either voluntarily submitted or requested by the school. Record, in writing, initialed and dated, all conversations and phone calls.

- The first stage is an interview. If the incident is serious, the teacher should be advised that the purpose of the interview is to clarify an incident of concern, and that s/he may wish to bring an adviser to the interview. Another Administrator, who should take notes, should accompany the Principal. The Principal may wish to consult with the school's labor lawyer regarding process.

Issues of concern that have prompted the meeting should be clearly articulated. The teacher must be given a full opportunity to explain and clarify the incident. There are then a number of further possible outcomes – which will of course vary according to local conditions and conventions:

- The Principal may conclude that there is no cause for concern, either because the teacher has given a satisfactory explanation, or because there are not sufficient grounds for action. In that case, the meeting should be politely closed, and the teacher told that as far as the school is concerned the matter is closed, and that no record is being placed on file. Sometimes, the teacher will demand "an apology"[178]. The Principal should not apologize if there were reasonable grounds to request an interview. It is the school's job to investigate matters of concern. Apologies will undermine the Principal's position and authority.

- A verbal reprimand may be issued to the teacher. It may be stated that 'a note of this meeting is being placed in your file'. The record will state: "At the conclusion of the meeting, a verbal reprimand was given, and the teacher told that a record of the meeting would be placed in his/her file". The teacher should be sent a copy.

- The teacher is told that a written reprimand is to be issued. Follow up immediately with a letter recording the interview, the details of the problematic incident, and confirming the reprimand / warning. Such letters should always express the school's view that the behavior must not be repeated, and offer to be available to discuss any problems with the teacher. If the teacher has brought a lawyer or Union representative to the interview, expect the letter to be challenged, and attempts made to negotiate its phraseology.

- The teacher may be told that the matter is being further investigated, and s/he is suspended from school pending further process. In this case, the teacher may not discuss the incident with anyone else except professional (and/or spiritual) advisers. By this stage your school lawyer is heavily involved. The outcome depends on the result of the investigation.

- In serious cases, the teacher may be suspended from work (with or without pay). This must be confirmed in writing, and a suspension should carry a warning regarding consequences of further instances of the problematic behavior.

- If termination is contemplated, suspend the teacher immediately, and consult the school's lawyer – see below..

---

[178] This can happen with students as well. The same rule applies.

For everything other than a single, first, minor infraction, it is absolutely essential that the school keep a 'paper trail' of letters, aides-memoir, email printouts etc.. If you are moving to a consequence that may affect the teacher's livelihood, the teacher (and/or their legal representative) will – with complete justification – demand to know on what you are basing your action. An important point of many labor hearings is whether or not the behavior complained of constitutes an 'established pattern of behavior". The file ('paper trail') is essential.

10.2 Teachers: six problematic profiles

During the course of an Administrative career, a Principal may meet some of the following archetypal problematic teacher profiles – some certainly needing disciplinary action, some needing diplomacy, and some needing common sense.

10.2.1　　"I'll only teach this class if ...."

I once taught in a school where the entire school timetable was built around "the promise". The Founder of the school had made this some thirty years earlier to Mrs. T, around whom the Math Department revolved, and it stated that "You will never have to teach after 2:30 in the afternoon." Her husband, Vice-Principal T, was in charge of scheduling. At the time "the promise" was given, the school had thirty or forty students, and as a new start-up private school of uncertain future, the Founder was probably stretched to find teachers. (At that time, Mrs. T. had very young children. By the late 1970's, they were grown, married and parents themselves). Eventually, the school had over four hundred students, and the timetable creaked to a halt. It was impossible to accommodate Mrs.T and the other teachers who claimed similar 'promises' – albeit of lesser consequence -- from the distinguished founder-Rabbi who was tragically no longer there to confirm or deny.

Teachers have family commitments; they have preferences. A teacher will often come and say "I'll only teach this class if..." . Unless there is a compelling reason (which there sometimes is), **do not bend your timetable to individual requests.** "We will do our best, but we cannot promise", is the line.

If you do [have to] agree to a 'concession' ("I don't want to teach first lesson because I have to car-pool my own children"), put it in writing and put a time limit on the school's promise.

- Please note that this arrangement can only be promised for the current school year, and the school gives no undertaking that it can be given in the future.

The needs of the school must take precedence.

Whatever precedents you give will come back to haunt you – there are no secrets in the staff room. Another teacher, sometime in the future, will say to you *"But you changed Mr. X's timetable so that he could take his son to basketball practice – why can't you do the same for me?"*

Best, therefore, is to say 'No' to everyone, except where there is a clearly compassionate reason involving family circumstance or medical accommodations. In a private school, especially if you are reliant on part-time teachers of scarce subjects, you may not have that luxury. Do your best!

There is, however, one category of teacher 'demand' that the school should never, ever agree to – and that is the teacher who demands the 'top class', 'only Grade 12's', or 'only the best students'. A professional teacher must be prepared to give of their very best to every student in the school, without distinction. Period. If they are not, a) they are probably not very good teachers and b) you probably do not want them on your team. Over time, the school also has an equitable duty to give a teacher a range of classes, in whatever way that is possible.

10.2.2 'The student's friend' / the 'cool' teacher

A common mistake of new or inexperienced teachers is to see themselves as 'the students' friend'. A variation on this is the teacher – new or veteran - who sets out to be 'cool'. This is a route to crisis.

A teacher can be many things. They can be friend*ly* to students; but they cannot be the student's friend, because that puts them in the same emotional circle as the students.

The moment the teacher is in the same emotional circle as the students, s/he is at the mercy of the group; and the emotional characteristic of the teenage group is its fickleness and its immaturity. It cannot matter whether or not the most popular student in the class smiles at the teacher; and it cannot be of interest to the teacher whether student 'A' is talking to student 'B', or not, and why, and who phoned whom at the weekend.

Equally, the details of the teacher's personal life are nothing at all to do with the students and if – when – disclosed in an attempt to be closer to the class, will quickly be retailed all round the school.

Common results of a teacher getting too close to students are:

- *Indiscretions of many types – the teacher will both receive and give inappropriate information about other staff, and about the school. The would-be 'cool' teacher will let the class know that s/he is against 'the Establishment'. Enticing the teacher into these conversations is usually the students' first 'initiation test'.*

- *The teacher's desire to be 'accepted' (or stay 'accepted') by the students will eventually overcome his/her professional judgment.*

- *Inappropriate discussions will take place during class.*

- *The class will split into those 'in' with the teacher, and the others.*

- *The moment a 'special' student gets a bad mark, the student will feel betrayed.*

- *The students will take advantage of their 'friendship' with the teacher to transgress boundaries in some way; the teacher will try and discipline them, find it impossible, and suddenly realize that he/she has lost the respect of the students. At that point, the teacher will feel betrayed.*

- *In the worst scenario, the (usually young) teacher will agree to meet the students outside school and/or invite them over for 'cool' evenings at his/her apartment. The possibilities for disaster here are endless.*

In these situations, firm action is needed. If the situation is spotted early on, then the teacher must be counseled, including very specific techniques of refusing to discuss matters that the students have already learned that he/she is too ready to discuss.

> *At this time, we are learning chemistry, and we are going to confine our conversation to that subject.*
>
> *Yes, I did talk about that last week, but I want to stay on focus now.*
>
> *I'm afraid that topic is now off limits.*

The advice/instructions should be put in writing to the teacher. In particular, it must be made very clear that the teacher's behavior must change immediately – not "*Well, I'll gradually stop talking about things*" or "*I promised I'd discuss something with them next lesson.*".

The students, who are enjoying every minute of this, and telling their friends about it in great detail, know very well that what is happening is out of order, and that it is only a matter of time before Administration steps in.

It may be advisable for an Administrator or another senior teacher to sit in that teacher's classes for a week or so. If it is a senior class, and students may have been clearly leading the teacher on, they may be spoken to, although it would be difficult (and wrong) to impose sanctions on the class for a teacher's lack of professionalism.

If the teacher has already drastically gone over the boundaries, it may be very difficult for him/her to regain authority over the class, and s/he may be in for a very tough year until their classes are changed in the following year ... if, that is, the teacher is retained by the school.

If the behavior is really due to 'first-year teacher' syndrome, a series of sessions with the teacher should correct things. In cases where it can be shown that unprofessional behavior has been consistent over a long period (where was Administration?), you may suggest resignation to the teacher.

10.2.3   The 'Pied Piper[179]'

The 'Pied-Piper' is one of the most difficult situations for a Principal to deal with.

Many excellent and highly professional teachers have elements of charisma in their personalities. In the 'Pied Piper' situation a powerfully charismatic teacher[180] has exceeded appropriate boundaries. *The teacher's personality has become the centre of the classroom rather than the course content.* A 'Pied Piper' will deeply affect and influence some students – but will almost always leave a trail of emotional wreckage in his/her wake[181].

'Pied Pipers' - charismatic teachers who misuse their charisma - are often themselves deeply immature, but their immaturity is emotional, not intellectual, and it is not always obvious. They can be brilliant in inspiring students to go beyond their wildest expectations, and are often regarded (by their following of students, by parents, and by the Board or the community) as the 'most important' or 'best' members of staff. There is always, however, a price to be paid[182].

One of the effects of charisma is to convince the recipient that he or she is the centre of the charismatic personality's concern. A teenage student (or a particular class) may feel as though he, she or they is/are the protégé(s) of the charismatic teacher. The moment they realize that they are not (sometimes when the teacher 'moves on

---

[179] The character of the 'Pied Piper' remains a seductive and sinister figure in folklore. According to legend, in 1284 130 children mysteriously disappeared from the medieval German city of Hamelin (Hameln). A man dressed in colourful ("pied") clothing, and playing a pipe promised to rid the town of a plague of rats. By playing his pipe, he lured the rats to their deaths by drowning in the local river. The town council then refused to pay him for his services. In an act of revenge, he worked his magic on the city's children, mesmerizing them with his music.. Bewitched, and entirely under his control, they blindly followed him out of the city to an unknown destination, and were never seen again. The poet Robert Browning (1812-1889) immortalized the story in verse ('The Pied Piper of Hamelin').

[180] This section discusses situations when matters go drastically wrong. I am grateful to Bob Collins, Jory Vernon and Chaim Klein for useful suggestions of how to frame this passage.

[181] The film 'The Dead Poets Society', starring Robin Williams, deals with the impact of a charismatic teacher at a boys' school. It ends in tragedy.

[182] With great diffidence, I have to add that as time goes on, I see the complexities of the charismatic teacher / 'Pied Piper' as more and more problematic. The personality type may have unseen dimensions. Be very, very careful; and very, very strict. See the text box in the next section.

to the next'), deep emotions come into play. Many charismatic teachers will lavish attention on a student or group of students – as long as the student(s) do things the teacher's way, or accept every piece of advice or "philosophy" or Torah uncritically. The moment the student shows independence or objectivity – they are dropped. As soon as they are dropped, they are written out of the teacher's story. Deep disillusion sets in. The student(s) are devastated. Often such students, very hurt, leave the school. Whatever brand of identity and loyalty the 'Pied Piper' has inculcated – religion, sport, poetry, art, politics – may be abandoned overnight. The next set of 'favorites' takes their place.

Tears are a feature of meetings between the abandoned students, their parents, and the Administration. Mild characteristics of cult leaders may be observed.

Other parents, however, will rave about how their son/daughter "adores" Mr./Ms/ or Rabbi X, and is "learning so much from them". Events linked to that teacher will be showcase events, and in the Principal (or Head of Department) will come to be dependent on the teacher. "We need something special for the prize-giving...or the ground-breaking … or the community event... can you put something together?"

The teacher will protest that the time is short, and it's impossible, but will, of course, accept and do a fabulous job.

The problem is that at core, these are not educational relationships.

The emotional dependency and entanglement between teacher and student leads to boundaries being crossed. The teacher throws open his/her house to the students. Teens idolize the teacher, and dangerous fantasies begin to develop. Boundaries are crossed; the usual rules don't apply to the Pied Piper, or, sometimes, his/her students. The 'Pied Piper' will solve the teen's *angst* and will sympathize with their intimate family problems.

The teacher becomes party to knowledge about students and their families that reinforces the 'Pied Piper's" view that s/he is the only teacher who is "really" reaching the students. (Disdain for other teachers is another common symptom.)

The teacher, however, is neither a trained counselor nor a social worker. That knowledge becomes power. A 'Pied Piper' can end up running a 'school within a school'.

In the classroom, the teacher will often employ techniques (and texts) which take students to the extremes of emotion or logic, and will then triumphantly show them how they, the teacher, are holding the key to resolution:

> *At this moment, you have agreed that life has no meaning -- but here is the answer*

Part of the reason of why these teachers are difficult to deal with is that they are often blissfully unaware (perhaps deliberately unaware) of their own emotional power, and see their activities in the school as huge self-sacrifice:

Look at how many extra hours I put in!

Faced with this situation, the Principal is in a quandary. Parents are telling the Board that this teacher should be promoted. Local rabbis are letting it be known that "X" is *"doing wonderful work with the kids"* – and in fact may even be *"the only teacher in the school who's really worth anything"*. And the truth is that 'X" is contributing a huge amount of positive things to the school.

The other teachers, in the main, cordially dislike 'X', for both good and bad reasons. The more emotionally stable teachers see an adult playing 'mind games' with the students, and feel – probably with some justification - that the influence is 'unhealthy'. They are also angry at Administration for allowing this situation to develop. Other teachers are simply jealous of 'X''s influence over the students, which they cannot even dream of. Those that choose to drink coffee with 'X' in the staff room (although, in my experience, charismatic teachers often avoid the staff room) are also 'groupies' – themselves frequently the less mature teachers.

Although under pressure to turn a blind eye to what is going on – "X is doing so much good!"[183] - the Principal must act to bring these situations under control.

Make sure you have some facts to use as examples – inappropriate meetings, student distress, parental concerns, students asking to join his/her class (or drop it) – and invite the teacher to a meeting, with another Administrator present.

> *I need to talk to you about your relationships in the school, which is causing increasing concern. I have asked my colleague, Mr/Ms/Rabbi G to sit in on this meeting. Being a teacher can be very difficult, and part of the difficulty is drawing boundaries between intense, but professional and appropriate relationships, and relationships which go over those boundaries. I am very apprehensive that you are crossing some red lines, and for your own protection, and for the welfare of the school, we need to have a serious talk. Let me go over some examples of what I mean……*

Curb any excesses that are taking place (some of which may emerge during the meeting, as the teacher, protesting, goes to great lengths to show how much he/she cares for the students and how close he/she is to them). Lay down guidelines for future conduct; and try and save for the school the best of what the teacher has to offer. The meeting will probably have to deal with:

- The teacher's professional duties as a member of school staff

- The teacher's relationship to students

- The teacher's relationship to other teachers

---

[183] If the 'Pied Piper' is a religious figure, some elements in the community will be happy to completely ignore worrying reports as long as *'kiruv'* – religious influence - is taking place. The classic case of this is the tragedy/scandal that rocked a major North American Jewish youth movement in the 1990's.

The exact list will obviously vary according to circumstances, but may well include required undertakings from the teacher that:

- S/he will strive to act professionally and objectively, delivering the classroom curriculum with equal attention to all students, and maintaining proper professional relationships with colleagues

- Inappropriate discussions and/or introduction of inappropriate material in the classroom will cease

- Contacts with students outside the classroom on matters not connected with the curriculum, direct or indirect, will cease

- No meetings will take place with students off school premises or in any non-professional context without prior consultation and the permission of the Administration

- Students approaching the teacher for counseling or advice on personal matters will be directed to a school Guidance Counselor or other qualified professional. The teacher will not be concerned with the emotional issues of students

- The teacher will immediately disclose to the Principal any event or incident concerning a student that may be construed as being outside their professional responsibility or outside professional boundaries

A letter summarizing the meeting should be sent to the teacher, with a copy in their personal file. The charismatic teacher's behavior may lead to situations that expose the school to legal and other action. It is the Principal's duty to safeguard the educational and professional integrity of the school.

10.2.4 The inappropriate teacher – sexual / abusive

Literally as this book goes to press, I am left wondering if my warnings in either the preceding section ('The Pied Piper'), or in this section are strong enough. Both were originally written before I had to confront an alleged case of a real sexual predator in my own school, whose activities became known only years after he had left. It is sobering to understand how charm, charisma and talent can mask an altogether more sinister agenda. It is even more sobering to face the reality of how far people of all ages can be deceived by skilful confidence tricksters, sociopaths and predators – *to the extent of maintaining faith in them even after their evil has been exposed.*

The school can never be too suspicious, or too careful. The Principal must be prepared to question, even when everyone else has ceased (or have never started) to do so.

Sexual inappropriateness: The Talmud states 'There is no guardian over immorality' – meaning that no individual is immune from sexual temptation.   High schools can be stressful places for adults, with populations of students who are physically adult but still emotionally adolescent, and whose hormones are raging. This is true for both male and female teachers. At a follow-up discussion (in a mixed High School) with a number of teachers about a certain case that I had had to deal with, I talked about the pressures on male teachers who are teaching teenage girls. I was stunned when a middle-aged, highly stable and responsible female teacher turned to me and remarked: "Don't you think it's also a problem for women?".   It showed my naïveté, but of cases that reach the media, many – possibly most - involve female teachers and male students.

There cannot be any tolerance whatsoever for a teacher who is sexually or otherwise abusive or inappropriate in any way, with a student, with another teacher, or anyone else associated with the school.   The nature of such inappropriate behavior by teachers can be:

- Sexual – in conversation, communication, or action.

- Sexual – in relationship. Sexual relationships between teachers and students are illegal in every jurisdiction, and against every professional standard. If proven, termination (and possible legal action) is mandatory. Teachers – of either sex – who enter into relationships with students generally fall into standard categories[184]. Many are 'needy teachers finding needy students' - undergoing some time of crisis in their own lives, and finding solace in emotionally demanding students.   Some are simply naïve. Some are predators. Although anything is possible, the most vulnerable category of teachers are those involved in emotionally-intensive, extra-curricular activities, including sports coaching.   In a Jewish school, the combination of earnest, inexperienced religious studies teachers and the roller-coaster of teenage emotion can be a fatal combination.

- Abusive – showing anger or other threatening, inequitable or discriminatory behavior.

A Principal must always be alert to hints that unacceptable behavior is taking place. S/he has to develop antennae, and may never, ever totally disbelieve or disregard such information (*"Mrs. Y – impossible!"*) without thorough, if discrete, investigation, or without at least filing away fragments of information in memory. A casual remark may give a clue. There is often a bond of silence among students regarding incidents

---

[184] A straightforward book, describing a range of cases of illicit teacher-student relationships, with some suggestions for preventative guidelines, is: William L. Fibkins, "Innocence denied: A guide to preventing sexual misconduct by teachers and coaches"/Rowman and Littlefield Educational, 2006.

in the classroom, and it may be a school graduate who says something like "Old X's classes were always really embarrassing!". It may be a parent who, casually but deliberately, will mention that they "... saw Mr. X downtown the other day with one of the students". The Principal may receive an anonymous letter or telephone call (which demand a much more cautious approach). Another teacher may bring something to the attention of Administration.

- **If even at that stage, there is a reasonable suspicion that something clearly illegal has taken place, the Principal must take immediate legal advice, and act accordingly. In many jurisdictions, there may be a legal duty to report to a Child Protection agency.**

If the behavior is unprofessional and inappropriate, but not illegal, it is a matter of professional discipline. The Principal must deal with it swiftly and formally, acting in consultation with other Administrators and, if appropriate, the school President, Chair of Personnel committee, or the school lawyer.

From the beginning of the process, every conversation and communication relating to the incident must be properly recorded.

- The teacher must be invited to a meeting, at which another Administrator is present and taking notes

- The teacher may be advised beforehand that the conversation may be disciplinary, and they should be given the opportunity to bring a colleague (if the school is unionized – a Union representative)

- At the meeting, open 'for the record' and say that you recognize that this meeting will be uncomfortable for all of the participants. It is the beginning of an investigation regarding alleged matters of which the school has become aware; the teacher has been informed that the meeting may have disciplinary and possibly legal consequences, and has been advised to bring a colleague or other adviser to the meeting

In clear, accurate and non-judgmental language, describe the simple facts that have come to your attention, without necessarily disclosing how, and ask the teacher for an explanation.

> *Mr. X: It has been alleged to the school that in your class sometime in the last two or three weeks you made a wholly inappropriate comment to a young female student. You are alleged to have told her that her t-shirt "showed her curves very nicely". The person who brought this to our attention claims that you have made many similar comments to students in the past. Can you shed any light on these allegations?*

> *Mr. X: The parents of **** ***** have expressed concern to the school that their son is spending a great deal of time at your home over weekends and after school, sometimes when no other students or members of your family are present. This*

would seem to be inappropriate for a professional teacher, and I wonder if you could explain the circumstances of these occurrences?

Ms. X: Information has reached the school that you were seen last Saturday night in town with a senior male student. It is alleged that there was physical contact between you and the student, and that you were seen arm in arm. Teachers, as you know, are bound by a code of professional behavior, and I would like full disclosure of your alleged relationship with this young man. The school reserves the right to investigate this matter further. You should be aware that there could be legal consequences to this conversation, and you may wish to reconvene this meeting with a legal representative present.

*Rabbi X: We appreciate your dedication to increasing the learning of the students. Yet we are concerned with the amount of time you are devoting to ****** *******. We understand that you are encouraging him to spend the whole of every Shabbat with you, and not with his parents. Can you describe your relationship with this young man?*

A personal relationship with a student that goes over professional boundaries is *ipso facto* a culpable abuse and exploitation of that authority.

Clearly, the information that emerges will dictate what happens next. The school must consult a lawyer, and, if advised to do so, report to the police. The teacher may be suspended from duty pending further investigations[185], which may involve students, parents and teachers. Such interviews and investigations must be very carefully conducted, and the Principal should be aware of relevant local legislation regarding the school's rights and duties, and the proper conduct of such interviews.

Principals should understand that these interviews might not be clear at all. As rumors spread in the school community that the teacher is in trouble, and that students and parents are being interviewed, some students, parents and teachers will come forward to declare that the teacher is 'the best teacher ever' (sharing some characteristics of the 'Pied Piper'), and resentfully accuse the school of 'exaggerating' an issue.

Some students will reveal deep emotions. The school must try and arrive at a reasonable account of the truth.

It is rare (but certainly possible) that allegations of this type surrounding a teacher are totally without any foundation. The allegation may have been totally fabricated[186] – in which case the originator of the allegation will be accountable. Alternatively, some students may have misunderstood a teacher's naïveté, idiosyncrasy,

---

[185] If a police report has been made, the police may take over the investigation from the school.

[186] Many years ago, a female student accused a colleague of mine of deliberately peering down her shirt as he walked around the classroom. He came to within an inch of losing his job (and much more). Two years later, at Graduation, she apologized to him and admitted she had made up the entire story, for reasons unconnected with the school.

eccentricity, ill-advised 'humor', or well-intentioned but misjudged conduct. In such a case, the teacher is not entirely blameless -- teachers must conduct themselves in a way that is not open to misinterpretation, and which does not make any student embarrassed or uncomfortable in their presence. Their relationships with students must be totally professional, and they must be aware that a teacher is regarded as being in a position of authority over his/her students, and is responsible for exercising that authority responsibly.

However, if sexual inappropriateness has been proven to the school's satisfaction – or reasonable suspicion - consequences for the teacher may involve any or some of the following:

- If this was a single, exceptional incident, inappropriate but not outrageous, a disciplinary letter should be placed on file, recording the allegation, the teacher's response, the school's process, clear expectations of future conduct, and a warning of consequences should the behavior, or anything similar, reoccur

Be very, very cautious. The incident of which you are now aware – whatever its nature or degree of seriousness – may only be the tip of the iceberg. The investigation must query whether this incident is in fact the indicator of a much more serious pattern of behaviour, possibly far more extensive.

- A requirement that the teacher attend counseling

- Change of the teacher's duties

- Disciplinary suspension of the teacher

- Voluntary resignation

- Termination of employment

- A report to the police – either by the school or by the student or his/her parents

If the teacher leaves the school, voluntarily or otherwise, both the school and the teacher may enter into a (legally drafted) non-disclosure agreement, or other terms of separation. In these circumstances, include in the agreement:

- An agreed statement that will be the only public communication issued by the school

- An agreed written reference, which will be supplied, to the teacher. This should be short, formal and 'cold'. If indeed there has been an active sexual relationship, the school should not provide any reference

If the incident has been serious and traumatic, you must develop a plan with your Guidance counselor(s), Rabbis and others, including if necessary outside resources, to deal with the students affected, and with other students in the school.

The Principal may have to deal with parents, staff, students, community and even local media – SEE SECTION 15.5.5.

- Prepare to be astonished (and exasperated) by those who will go to great lengths to defend or excuse the teacher; and the ease with which the offender may be offered employment elsewhere[187].

Abusive inappropriateness: Teachers may display a range of abusive behavior to students, fellow staff or parents. Anger in the classroom may once have been tolerated behavior, but no longer is. A teacher may not demean, humiliate, pick on or constantly put down students; conversely, a teacher may not have 'favorites'.

All behavior where a teacher uses their authority and position to the detriment of others need to be addressed. Teachers who act in certain ways in the classroom will frequently repeat the behavior in the staff room, bullying younger teachers or being deliberately uncooperative to colleagues[188].

An investigation has to take place, in which other students, staff or parents involved must be interviewed. The process is clear, and is similar to the management of other problematic behaviors:

- A formal interview, at which the staff member is asked to give his or her own account of problematic incidents

- It may be necessary to switch the teacher's classes, or move particular students to other classes. The measures that the school has had to take should be noted in the record of the interview

- Consequences may be similar to those for the sexually abusive teacher (see above), and may also include offers of help to correct the unacceptable behavior, and suggestions of outside counseling

- A warning letter is issued. This should summarize the content of the interview. Suggest targets for improvement, and give fair warning of consequences should there be further incidents.

Further incidents are likely to trigger the application of progressive discipline.

---

[187] Probably using references supplied by one or more sympathizers / supporters.
[188] But often obsequious to Administration.

10.2.5   The staff room agitator

The Principal learns that the "staff room is in uproar", because a certain member of staff has been holding forth on some issue and is recruiting sympathizers. A variation on this is the leaked information, usually to a Board member, that *"Morale in the Staff room is at an all-time low".*

Teachers are entitled to their opinions about how the school is run, but they have a moral and professional obligation to make their views known via appropriate channels, and to be 'employees in good faith'. They may, of course, give their views on relevant topics, but they have to do so in appropriate fashion, preserving balance and without denigrating others. The Principal's door should always be open to staff. If a teacher has a problem they should first address it to the Principal, or have it addressed at a staff meeting or other appropriate forum where there is a framework for questions to be asked and alternative viewpoints expressed. In the Principal's office, accusations and allegations must be substantiated or withdrawn.

An employee has a fiduciary duty to be a loyal, fair, cooperative and constructive colleague. Freedom of speech has limits. In labor law, there is a concept of 'poisoning the workplace'.

If you hear that a teacher is making comments or allegations that have not been brought to you, and are causing dissent, then you should simply face them with it. Call the teacher to a meeting, with another Administrator present, and challenge them:

> *Mr. D – echoes reach me that you have been making allegations to other staff that I intend to terminate six teachers at the end of this year and 'get rid of all the opposition'. No such decisions have been made, although the school, as you know, is facing severe financial difficulties, and it is possible that there will be some staff reductions. If that is necessary, a strictly equitable process will be implemented, overseen by the Board's Personnel Committee and the school's labor lawyers. Perhaps you could share with me the grounds on which you are making these allegations, and in particular the personal implication concerning my professional integrity?*

> *Mrs. P – I understand that you have been expressing your unhappiness in public concerning the way that the school is run. At the Staff Meeting last week there was ample opportunity for teachers to express concerns and ask questions about the new timetable. I regret that you didn't raise any questions then. The minutes of the Staff Consultation group that helped suggest the changes have been displayed on the staff bulletin board for the last three weeks. Perhaps you would like to explain your concerns now?*

> *Rabbi T – Everyone appreciates your very devoted and distinguished service to the school. However, I was upset to learn that you have been publicly criticizing the new Vice-Principal. Mrs. H has a very difficult job to do, and she has the full support of the Administration and of the Board. Every organization changes, adapts and improves. In our case, the introduction of the 'Computers in the Classroom' program is long overdue, and our school has suffered because we are way behind in our use of*

computers. You may consider computers a 'waste of time', but this is now official school policy, and I do not expect you to undermine it. Telling other teachers to "ignore the whole idea" is unacceptable and insubordinate, and criticizing Mrs. H, who has undertaken to implement the program, is frankly obstructive. I would prefer you to be a constructive, even if critical, member of the faculty team, and I would like your assurance that the unpleasantness in the staff room will stop. An apology to Mrs. H would also be appropriate.

10.2.6   The infatuated teacher

This very dangerous problem manifests itself when a teacher or Guidance Counselor becomes obsessed with a student[189], and seeks to 'protect' the student at all costs. On the surface, there is no sexual involvement; under the surface, emotions beyond the competence of the school are in play. The staff member sets out to "save" the student, and protects the student against discipline, consequences for missing school, and failing marks in courses. Sometimes the motive is to save a star of a sports team, or another school activity ("We have to give this student special treatment"); sometimes it is emotional ("The school must save this student"). Symptoms may include:

- Long and furious arguments with other members of staff

- Over-involvement in the student's private life – the student may be invited to the staff member's house for meals, or at weekends, or may even be invited to spend part of the vacation with the teacher

- The teacher may pay for some of the student's expenses out of their own pocket, or try and persuade the school or the community to do so

- The teacher 'champions' the student to Administration, and issues dire predictions of what will happen to the school, or to the student, or both, if the normal rules are applied to this young person. There are always reasons why "Y" should be exempt

The student, in most cases, enjoys the attention, and will shamelessly manipulate the situation. They will exploit their 'protected' status, and will always be ready to appear winsome and tragic. Other staff and students will deeply resent the privileges

---

[189] I once witnessed a Guidance Counselor who insisted that a student's home life was so dire that she (the student) could not be expected to come to school properly dressed. The Counselor, it was rumoured, paid for the girl to go to a hairdresser, and on one occasion took her on vacation to Florida. Every Guidance meeting was dominated by discussion of the girl's latest 'crisis'. The student, revelling in the attention, came to school on and off for a year or so in pyjama pants, which I always suspected she changed into on her way to school. After she graduated, and still living at home, she visited the school beautifully groomed, and in stunning, expensive and smart dress. The pathology was with the adults.

extended to this student, but will not be able to voice concern or protest, as they will be accused of being 'heartless' or worse by the student's protector.

These are pathological situations, and something is seriously wrong. The Principal, working with colleagues in Administration and other appropriate staff, should reassign the student and his/her problems to someone else, with strict instructions that normal process and rules must apply. Problems should be referred directly to you. The original teacher / Counselor must be told, in writing, that while the school appreciates the depth of their concern with this student, and their apparent willingness to devote a great deal of time and effort to helping them:

- There are concerns regarding the teacher's / counselor's judgment in the exercise of supervision over this student

- There are concerns that appropriate professional boundaries may have been crossed, and that the degree of involvement between teacher and student may be unduly personal

- for the protection of both the teacher and the student, the student will now be supervised by Mr./Mrs./Rabbi K. The teacher must disclose to the second teacher any information they may possess relevant to the welfare of the student. They may not again discuss the student's problems with the student, and if approached must refer the student to the other staff member, or to an Administrator

The Principal must be very clear to the teacher that their behavior has made them vulnerable to serious misunderstanding. If they are in possession of information that leads them to think that the student is in danger, they have a duty to report to the police or to another appropriate agency.

Keep a very careful eye on this teacher afterwards.

A variant of this is the situation where the star of the basketball team (or the debating team, or the school play) has committed some major disciplinary offense. A teacher pleads that the student not be barred from participation in the upcoming match, (or other event) because "it will wreck the school's chances, and destroy everything that the rest of the team has worked for". If the offense is really serious – there is no alternative but to implement the consequence. The Principal may have to speak to the team. If there is room for discretion – allow the star to participate in the crucial match, but there must – *must* – be a consequence of credible seriousness afterwards. Make it clear that the school's concern is for the other members of the team, not for the offender.

10.3 "I have a wedding in Israel"

A completely different teacher problem – but a problem nevertheless - is where family celebrations clash with school time. It can also be a variety of 'Jewish – General' tension.

Staff have many happy[190] occasions to celebrate. In today's world, a teacher may have children in Israel, Europe, South America or the other side of the continent. When a teacher requests school-time leave to attend a *simchah ("Happy occasion")*, it is a clash between the teacher's professional (and contractual) obligations and community culture – made more acute because that very culture (or elements thereof) is what the school is meant to be teaching!

The teacher's absence interrupts the students' learning and will involve the school in expense in covering the missed lessons. The school has to define permissible absences:

- If the staff member has control over the timing of the simchah, it should be made clear that it is expected that s'machot will be timed for school vacations

- Absence may only be taken for first-degree relatives (parents, children, siblings, grandchildren), and only for major[191] life occasions

- Such leave is exceptional, cannot be regarded as a 'right', and cannot be taken with any regularity

- Teachers may not make private arrangements with colleagues to cover classes, and then claim that there is 'no problem'

  I'm going to be away for a few days, but there's no need to worry because I've already arranged for Mrs. D to cover my classes

- There are few places in the world where a maximum of five school days' absence (which can be parlayed into several more by careful timing around weekends) will not allow a traveler to reach his/her destination, celebrate[192], and return home

- Local celebrations may involve one (Monday after a bar-mitzvah), two, or at the very most three days' (normally the mother of the bride) leave

---

[190] There is no argument over absence for unhappy occasions.
[191] For example, a teacher cannot take days off school to travel to a grandchild's birthday party, or the bar/bat-mitzvah of a niece or nephew.
[192] It is unreasonable to expect to attend a full week of *Sheva brachot* in school time.

- The school Personnel Committee has to decide how much of such leave of absence is paid, and how much is unpaid

It is best if this is formalized and known. Whatever the circumstances, the Principal must know that every such request, and every such permission (as with all permissions for leave, for whatever purpose), will be immediately become part of staff room lore. They will be quoted for years afterwards.

> But when Mrs. K's daughter got married four years ago, you allowed her to take six days off school, and you are only giving me four. And her daughter was in London, and mine is in Israel.

These are decisions that are uncomfortable to administer. Yet the school has to be firm.

10.3.1 "We want to go to Israel for *Yomtov*, and I'll miss the last[193] days of school"

Don't allow it.

Next year the teacher and his/her family should book further in advance, so that they can leave after the end of school, and before Yomtov. If that is impossible – they can't go. They have a duty to fulfill their professional obligations. It is very difficult for the school to deal with angry parents who call to complain that their children are attending school right up to the end of the semester / session – but hardly any lessons are taking place because although the students are in school, the teachers have already left for vacation.

10.4 Terminating staff

Because of the legal sensitivity of the termination process, and its local variants, we have not suggested 'scripts' for these conversations. Your legal adviser will help you construct any meetings and correspondence, and suggest the terminology you should use.

10.4.1 The decision and its implementation

The decision has been made to terminate a teacher's employment. This can be 'for cause' (professional incompetence or misconduct) or 'not for cause' (because their jobs have disappeared due to falling school numbers, changes in curriculum, budget cuts or similar reasons).

---

[193] Variation: "the first days of school...."

Most Principals (as most employers and managers of all descriptions) will agree that this is one of the most difficult tasks that they have to undertake. It may be tragic for the employee, and it is always very stressful for the employer. If the circumstances warrant termination, it has to be done. Other than in exceptional circumstances involving gross misconduct, it would be unusual for a termination not be preceded by extensive consultations with the Administrative team and with senior Board members (the President and the Chair of Personnel).

In every case, termination must be implemented within the framework of local labor laws, and the Principal must seek appropriate legal advice before initiating process.

In a unionized school, the Collective Agreement will specify grounds for termination, and the Union will definitely be involved. 'Non-renewal' of contracts is, of course, a different process and unless subject to local legislation, easier.

There is no easy way to implement a termination. Correct and fair process will minimize the pain for both the employee and the Principal. Other than in exceptional cases of gross misconduct, where you may have no discretion, be sensitive to the personal and family circumstances of the employee when timing your 'termination interview'. Do not hand the employee notice of termination on Erev Shabbat, before Yom Tov (or the equivalents for non-Jewish staff), in the week(s) before they celebrate a family occasion, or at other unnecessarily wounding times. Give some thought to what happens immediately after the meeting. Offer an opportunity for the employee to return when school is not in session to remove personal effects from the premises. Quietly arrange for access to the school's computers to be disabled immediately[194].

Whatever the circumstances, termination of employment is deeply embarrassing for the employee. You must do everything possible to preserve the dignity of the individual involved.

10.4.2   Termination for cause

Finally, the school and a problematic teacher have reached the end of a long process: "relationships between the teacher and the school have irrevocably broken down".

Alternatively, an individual has committed an act so serious ("gross misconduct") that they cannot continue to teach at the school.

Termination 'for cause' may be with warning or without warning.

If with warning, the termination will have been preceded by disciplinary process. A credible 'paper trail' will exist. The mechanism of termination should be as discreet as possible, and carefully planned – where and when it will take place, and who will

---

[194] If the employee has personal files on the computer – which they probably shouldn't have, but probably do – arrange for the computer technician to copy them or delete them for the employee. Do not allow a terminated employee access to the school network after termination.

be present. A statement of decision should be given, accompanied by a letter. If there are accompanying conditions (see following, 'Terms of termination'), then the employee will have a time to consider an offer, take appropriate professional advice, and return a signed copy of an agreement (or not). The school's labor lawyer should brief the Principal. Be warned that in some jurisdictions it is extremely difficult to terminate a teacher 'for cause'.

At the termination interview, do not allow yourself to be drawn into negotiation, or explanation, other than what has been laid out in the letter. You may point out that the relationship between the school and the teacher has "irrevocably and irretrievably broken down". The decision is final, and at this point there cannot be 'another chance'.

If the termination is without warning, it will have followed some extremely serious 'precipitating incident', which makes it impossible for the teacher to continue employment at the school. Again, you must take legal advice, and ensure that fair process is followed. You must allow the teacher ample and fair opportunity to give his/her account of the incident. Circumstances may require that you conduct an investigation, in which case it its likely that the teacher will initially be suspended from duty, with or without pay, pending further process.

10.4.3   Resignation instead of termination

If the teacher does not dispute the apparent facts, and the circumstances are such that the school would be satisfied simply for the teacher to leave (e.g. if there are no further legal or other consequences[195]), you may invite the teacher to resign, effective immediately. This allows the teacher to retain a degree of self-respect, and allows you to truthfully say that the teacher resigned. This mechanism is often used where the teacher has had an otherwise blameless record, and the precipitating incident may fairly be considered an aberration. The resignation may or may not be accompanied by terms.

10.4.4   Termination –'not for cause'

These are circumstances where school no longer has appropriate employment for the teacher, as suggested above. In these circumstances, again, labor legislation or Union contract may specify the order in which employees must be let go. In many cases, staff will have foreseen that their post is vulnerable, because the trends will be visible.

---

[195] A teacher, in an inexplicable impulse, steals a credit card from another teacher's purse. On discovery, he/she returns it immediately, and reimburses the owner of the credit card for the small amount of the only (illegal) purchase made. The first teacher is overcome with shame and remorse. The second does not want to press charges or inform the police or the credit card company. Most institutions, in such (usually sad) circumstances, would quietly accept a resignation, accompanied by a modest financial settlement.

You can only be clear regarding the reasons, and sympathetic. Proper notice (or compensation in lieu) must be given[196].

10.4.5   Termination – conditions

Depending on the circumstances, terminations or 'invited resignations' may be accompanied by conditions. No school (or other employer) wants a prolonged legal battle with an ex-employee, and most employees also wish to conclude matters quickly, and not affect their future employment prospects. A common 'trade-off' is for the employer to offer a reasonable financial consideration in return for resignation, and/or the employee waiving any further claim against the school or its representatives (or possibly other specified individuals, depending on the circumstances), coupled with a 'non-disclosure' agreement binding on all parties. There may be an agreed text of a short statement to be released by the school. In such cases, the Principal will at every stage be working very closely with senior Board members and a lawyer.

10.4.6   Termination - Confidentiality and communication

It is never in anyone's interest that staff matters – especially terminations / resignations – become the subject of public discussion.

In Jewish schools, confidentiality is doubly important. The fewer people who are privy to details of what transpires between the school and its employees, the lesser the chance that confidential information will leak to the community or to the student body. The circumstances of the termination may also involve the privacy of other students or staff.

For this reason, such matters should not be discussed or disclosed in detail to the full Board. Personnel matters of great sensitivity should be handled by the Principal, the President (or his/her invited substitute), the school lawyer and the Chair of Personnel Committee. The Board must accept the assurance of their fellow Board members and the Principal that 'the issue was dealt with appropriately and fairly'. Only in the most extreme of cases – where the school's integrity or reputation is at stake – might there be fuller disclosure, and then only in special, closed (and therefore non-minuted) Board session. This process also prevents employees from calling or lobbying Board members, who may truthfully say that they are both unaware of the details, and not involved in any way in the process.

When a staff member leaves the school under unusual circumstances, the Principal should issue a short, factual statement to the staff.

---

[196] Do not try and use 'Termination – not for cause' as a means of dispensing with the services of a member of staff whom you would like to see leave the school, and then hire someone else to do the same (or a very similar) job. It is neither ethical nor legal, and you will trigger a lawsuit.

I have to inform staff that effective [date], X is no longer a member of the school faculty. We wish him/her well in his/her future endeavors. Please refer any enquiries to me. Colleagues are asked to preserve discretion, and not allow discussions or speculation in class.

If the circumstances warrant it, a sentence or two of appreciation may be appropriate. Display it in the staff room for 48 hours, and then take it down. Staff will understand.

10.4.7   Non-renewal of Contract

Administrators, and in some cases teachers, may be employed under time-defined contracts. The Principal may decide not to renew a contract when it concludes. No misconduct may have taken place; the employee is either underperforming, or is not meeting expectations or requirements, and probably never will. You may have given warnings and performance targets that have not been met. A fair contract will contain a 'notice of non-renewal' provision, which specifies that, for example, in a contract that ends on June 30th of a particular year, either party will give three months prior notice to the other of 'intention not to renew'.

I am afraid that we are not going to be able to reach agreement on the renewal of this contract, and I have to tell you that when the contract expires, the school will not be renewing it. I am sorry that our relationship will have to end....

You – and the employee – must make a judgment whether the employee is to work out their notice or take (paid) leave until the contract ends.

Again, consultation with lay leadership and legal advisers - and the reasons surrounding the decision not to renew - will determine whether the non-renewal of contract will be accompanied by any financial settlement.

10.4.8   Terminating non-teaching staff

If you have to terminate employment of non-teaching staff, there will normally be a local standard of compensation linked to length of service. If it is 'for cause' – adhere to that standard. If it is for any other reason – be rather more generous. Your institution should earn a reputation in town as a good, fair, place to work.

10.4.9   Challenge, arbitration and mediation

An employee in conflict with the school (usually over termination) may press through their lawyers for the case to be taken to arbitration or mediation. While both of these processes have merits, they can be very long, and very expensive. Most parties will try and resolve their issues before reaching such proceedings.

Constituencies – Students and Parents

11 MANAGING STUDENTS

12 DISCIPLINE, RULES, ETC.

13 MANAGING PARENTS

11 MANAGING STUDENTS

The students – collectively and individually - are the school's first responsibility, and the first responsibility of everyone associated with the school. They are the reason why the school exists, and they are the group for whose benefit the school is run.

In an obvious sense, this entire book is about the 'student' constituency. Over and above the legal and the educational duties, structures and processes, there is a larger, less tangible issue of 'school culture' manifested in the fundamental attitudes of the school towards its students.

11.1 How does the school relate to its students?

Decades after they have graduated, when all else about their school days has been forgotten, students will recall their High School within a generalized, emotional framework, probably simply expressed as:

> "I loved it" or "I hated it"

That basic memory will color their feelings towards every message the school ever tried to convey.

How can a school ensure that it commands the affection and respect of its students?

There are a few principles:

- Care for every student without distinction

A private school has the option to decline to admit a student. But once a student is in the school, be prepared to 'pull out all of the stops' to help and support every single one. All organizations, of every kind, tend to place people in a conscious or unconscious hierarchy. A Principal has the duty to give equal treatment to all students; ensuring that the weakest, most peripheral students get every possible support, and also preventing favored treatment to the children of parents who for whatever reason (wealth, importance, influence, 'standing') claim special status. There is nothing wrong in being very kind and understanding to parents who have done a great deal for your school, in whatever capacity. That cannot be at the expense of other students.

> *Mr. and Mrs. X: I think that you know that our school treats every student fairly and alike. We will do whatever we can to help Barry – as we would do for every student. I am sure that you would not want special treatment. Please have confidence in our school.*

- Treat every student with dignity and respect

'The school' – exemplified by Administration and teachers - might like a student or students, it might dislike them; it may approve of their behavior, it may disapprove of their behavior; it might see them as exemplary students, it may think that they are a disgrace to the school **– but it must treat them as individuals, and treat them with respect.** Never humiliate a student, and never belittle them or their views. They are adolescents, and their dignity is important – sometimes supremely so. There are ways to deliver messages and rebukes that will get your message across effectively, and will preserve the students' feelings that they are being heard

- Treat them (and speak to them) as adults, and make it clear that in return they are expected to behave like adults

- Make your expectations of students clear, and set them high. They will, most of the time, rise to the level of the school's[197] expectations. Schools who infantilize their students get infantile behavior in return.

- Go 'the extra mile' for students in trouble, or students who need help. Not only is it the right thing to do – educationally and morally – but the student will remember it for years and years to come

- In times of tension, treat them fairly

- When implementing discipline or other decisions with consequences for the student, check that the student understands the offense, understands the process, and has had a chance to put their point of view and to voice any mitigating circumstances. Put the outcome of disciplinary process in writing. Don't act arbitrarily

- Teenagers have a strong sense of fairness, and they are looking to the Principal as a role model. The Principal – and the school as an institution - represent an ideal. Don't let them down

- Give the students responsibility, and allow them initiative and leadership

- Trust them.

---

[197] And, it should be noted, the teacher's as well. The higher the teacher's expectations in the classroom, the easier and the better are the lessons.

11.2 Student Recruitment and admissions

11.2.1   Strategizing basic recruitment

Student recruitment and the admissions process are critical to the health of your school - they are 'oxygen functions'. Masterminding recruitment of new students is a crucial responsibility, and the Principal should carry it[198]. In a larger school, assisting the Principal should be a support-staff post of 'Admissions Coordinator' or 'Admissions Secretary', who is the central address, email address and telephone number for all enquiries, and who is responsible for receiving and processing all applications. A new school, a large school, or a school which has no 'feeder' of its own (and therefore has to competitively recruit in an 'open' market) may also have a 'Recruitment Coordinator', who will implement the logistics of the recruitment campaign, under the Principal's direction.

Before even planning your recruitment strategy, bear in mind the following:

- Recruitment and admissions constitute the first experience of the school for parents and students. The quality and tone of the process will determine much of their attitude towards the school for the remainder of their school career.

- Tuition fees over four years of High School probably represent a family's second largest expenditure after their house.

- Over four years, tuition fees may nowadays represent close to $100,000 of income to the school. How much is it worth to the school in advertising, printing and other costs to secure each student - $5? $10? $25? $100? More?

- Recruitment is essentially sales. Remember three cardinal rules:

- Unless the product is good, the best campaign won't work[199]

- **Sell the benefit, not the product** ("Your child will graduate from here as a scientist" is better than "We have three science labs");

- With regard to Tuition fees, talk value not price

---

[198] In this, I disagree with several school consulting and resource organisations that recommend appointing a separate 'Director of Admissions'.
[199] One of the classic stories of marketing is the convention of pet-food salesmen. The product was not selling. Speaker after speaker gave reasons – the campaign slogan was wrong, the packaging was wrong, the shelf-placing in supermarkets was wrong. When all explanations had been furiously debated, a lone saleman sitting at the back raised his hand. "The problem is that the cats just don't like the taste of the food."

- Even parents who are determined to send their child to the school wish to be reassured about their choice.

The most credible spokespersons for your school are past and present parents (especially if from the same school as the prospective student); Board members; past and present students; outside visitors (University professors, Rabbis), and of course school Faculty. The influence of the Principal is great. Parents identify the school with its Principal. They must feel that the school is competently led. A good presentation by a Principal at prospective parents' 'Open Evening' can be decisive in attracting parents to the school.

11.2.2   Feeder Schools

Relationships with feeder schools are central to recruitment. Feeders may be Jewish Day schools; they may be local non-Jewish schools, public or private; or if your own school is a K-12, your feeder may be your own Junior High (Grade 7 – Grade 8). Whatever the circumstances, relationships with professional peers, with parents and with potential students, should never be taken for granted.

These relationships will be affected by local circumstances (and local politics). A Principal should encourage the Grade 8 students, their parents and their teachers to see 'Jewish High' as their natural, much-desired, and *exciting* high school destination.

Some basics include:

- Get to know the Heads of School. This may sound obvious, but, especially in larger communities, it is sometimes easy to lose track of changes in Administration at other schools. A new High School Principal should call up the Elementary Head(s) and make him/herself known, or take the initiative to offer some welcome and words of encouragement if a new appointment is made at a feeder. Invite them over, or go and visit their school (a good Head always enjoys showing his or her school to professional colleagues, and is always flattered by a 'request to visit').

- Put Elementary Heads and other key Administrators on the mailing list for your school newsletter.

- Encourage peer meetings with Heads of Department and other staff – for example, exchanging information about Elementary and High School curricula.

- The Principal should attend feeder school Graduations and other selected events. In a large community, you may have to rotate attendance. If Elementary colleagues reciprocate, make sure their presence is publicly acknowledged.

- Senior High School students should visit the feeders and run programs, talk to students about High School, and generally be the elementary school students' "window" on to High School life

- At key times – e.g. the beginning and end of the school year, before Rosh Hashanah – the Principal should call colleagues just to 'touch base' and wish them well.

Every reader will be able to add to this list. The network of contacts is invaluable in every way – building confidence and knowledge, and, of course, establishing lines of communication that are obviously useful when information is needed about students or parents.

Once intake is confirmed for the following year, have Guidance Counselors or VP's visit each feeder school before year-end to get briefings from the Elementary school on incoming students[200].

11.2.3   Planning a recruitment campaign

In planning the recruitment campaign, the Principal should consult with colleagues, with Principals of feeder schools, and with parents. In many cases, the Principal may work with a 'Recruitment' or 'PR/Public relations/Marketing' committee of the Board.

Strategize your campaign.

- What are the concerns and questions that prospective parents to your school need answered? What are the barriers that are preventing parents from choosing your school? What are the negatives that need to be neutralized?

- What are the qualities of your school that you should be stressing in your literature? What are the benefits – real and perceived - of attending Jewish High?

- How can you articulate the dreams and ambitions that your prospective parents have for their children in your literature – and suggest that the school is the incomparable path to realizing them?

- When do prospective students and their parents begin to seriously think about High School? In September of Grade 8? In May of Grade 7? Or in Grade 6?

- Who or what influences their choices?

---

[200] It is probably necessary for parents to sign a legal waiver permitting this exchange of information.

- Perhaps most elusive – how can you reach the prospective parents and children?

There are guides available of how to strategize your campaign and the recruitment/admissions process in detail, including material specially designed for Jewish schools[201]. Your thinking should include:

- Identification of your target constituencies

- Planning, printing and circulation of an 'Information Pack' (see below)

- Planning of school tours for G8 students

- A Parents' Evening for prospective parents.

- Advertising in local Jewish and possibly non-Jewish media

- Arranging entrance exams

- Scheduling of interviews, and briefing of interviewers

- Determining a timetable for receipt of applications; processing them; interviewing; informing parents of your decision.

Your 'Information Pack" is an important part of the process. However expensive it is – it is money well spent[202]. It represents the school. Make sure that it is attractive, glossy and professionally designed. Choose your graphic designer carefully. Look at similar literature from other private schools in your city to see the standard that you have to match, or exceed[203]. The 'Information Pack' should contain, as a minimum:

- A comprehensive booklet about the school, with plenty of photographs. This should include details of the Admissions Process, and should clearly state the criteria for admission.

- The school's 'Statement of Philosophy and Purpose'

- The School Handbook

- A Staff List for the current year, showing your staff, their qualifications, and what they teach

---

[201] At the time of writing, good material is available from PEJE and from the AviChai Foundation.
[202] Smaller schools might consider sourcing a grant or donation specifically for this purpose.
[203] Many of these brochures – however glossy – are formulaic and very similar. Try and make yours stand out.

- A clear name, telephone number, email and address for whoever is handling parent enquiries at the school

- The school Application Form, with an addressed return envelope, and clear instructions of what has to be sent with the completed application.

As part of the recruitment literature, many schools produce CD-roms /DVD's, and/or have video of the school available on their websites. Whatever shows the students at the school active and happy is good. Your prospective parents want to imagine their children *there....* which is why pictures of the G12 Graduation Ceremony are always powerful parts of a recruitment presentation.

At the 'Prospective Parents evening', show a video or other visual display of the school. Have a senior student (or students) speaking, and a recent graduate. Perhaps show pictures of graduates in their post-High School setting. Be upbeat. Remember that every parent present is thinking about *their child's future* – not about the glorious history of the school, or what community positions the school President has held.... Allow plenty of time for questions. Offer a tour of the school. The whole program should not last more than an hour or so.

Part of the recruitment process is the 'Grade 8 visit', when potential students come to visit the school. Remember that they are still elementary (or Middle) school students, that they may not appreciate what High School is about, and that they can find the physical experience of High school overwhelming. School faculty will greet them. Senior students should show them around. Carefully plan the program[204] well in advance, and do not, ever, rely on ad-hoc improvisation ("What shall we do with them now?"). Be inventive – give them some fun (and pizza) as well as a brief experience of lessons and classes. Warn your staff and students that humor can easily be misunderstood – negative comments about the school, even in jest *("That's the torture room where they lock you away for not doing homework")* will frighten some immature students, and cost you enrolment. If the grade 8 visit is a disaster, you have a serious problem.

Occasionally, a student who really does not want to come to your school will return home with a totally, or largely, made-up story about the Grade 8 visit that bears no relation to what happened, resulting in a horrified phone call from a parent.

11.2.4   Application and Admission

The actual Admissions process will again depend on the size of the school. Admitting one class of twenty or thirty students is a far different process than dealing with a hundred, two hundred or even more.

---

[204] Hand over the planning to two of your youngest, brightest, teachers.

Whatever the size of the school, the process should be carefully thought through and carefully planned. A minimum 'communication plan' might include the following:

Date	Item	
September / October previous to entry	Information / application pack	*Your 'shop window'. This pack should be irresistible!*
On Application	Acknowledgement of Application received	*Can be email*
Late Fall	Notification of Entrance Test and Interview	*Can be email (possible to book interview time online)*
Spring	Result of Application /'Offer of a Place'	*For signature and return*
June / before summer vacation	Book list and other items needed to be purchased for September	
[According to determined school process]	Tuition Assistance process advice and application	*Local practice will determine at what stage of Application the Tuition Assistance process is activated.*
[Throughout this period]	School magazines, notices of school successes, other 'feel-good' material	*Can be print or email. Keep in touch, and ensure that applicants and parents feel that they are already part of the 'family'.*

The process should be clearly explained, with a timeline, in your recruitment literature. Every parent (and student) should fill out an Application Form, which should be quite comprehensive, and include submission of recent report cards and other documents. If a student has had a psych-ed assessment, that has to be submitted as well. An essential part of the application form is medical disclosure.

Ask the student to write a few lines – in their own handwriting – explaining why they want to come to the school, what their interests are, and, perhaps, what they can contribute to the school. The answers, including the answers clearly written by the parents, are usually informative.

It is a good idea to put a list of 'permissions and waivers' above the parent / student signatures on the Application Form – a sample formulation might read:

> *"Application to the school signifies:*
>
> *Acceptance of the school 'Statement of Philosophy and Purpose', the provisions of the School Handbook, and other instructions issued by Administration from time to time*
>
> *Recognition of the right of the Administration to determine class placement, and to amend the list of courses offered according to the needs of the school*
>
> *Permission to use images of students for school publicity and other purposes approved by School Administration"*

Collecting these signatures at the time of application may save a lot of time and trouble later.

- In all of this, the role of the Admissions Coordinator is crucial. S/he must receive all applications; chase up missing pieces of information; schedule interviews; route concerns to appropriate members of the team; issue 'Offers of a Place' and monitor returns; liaise calmly and professionally with parents – and altogether act as an effective, single 'clearing house' for all Admissions issues and information.

Application, followed by an entrance test (if that is your practice), is then followed by a student interview. Both parents should also attend the interview. If more than one person is involved in interviewing, then have a meeting early in the year and agree common process. The interview is not only a chance to discreetly check that the information supplied 'fits' the student and parents sitting in the room, but is an invaluable opportunity to pick up on important issues that are not apparent from the application.

- What are the relationships displayed between the student and parents?

- Is there something that Guidance or teachers should know about? Is the student quiet, or forthcoming?

- Is puzzling behavior displayed (by parents or student)?

It is a good idea to ask on the Application Form whether there are issues that the parents would like to discuss "in confidence" at the interview. If the box is checked, at the end of the interview ask the student to step out, and listen to the parents. Equally, an experienced interviewer will occasionally ask the parents to step out to give an opportunity to speak to the student alone.

A deposit and/or an Application Fee are usually required with an Application. Indicate that if there is financial difficulty in meeting these expenses, the school will discreetly accommodate. If there is a deadline for Applications, impose – and collect – a 'Late Application Fee'. It will take a year or so, but you will find that the applications will come in on time, saving the school the trouble of dealing with a flood of applications in August[205].

After the interview, the interviewer should write up his/her notes, in space allocated on the interview form (or on the student's new electronic file). If the application is straightforward – it may be passed back to the Admissions Coordinator for processing. If it has to be referred for further consideration – it should be marked accordingly.

To keep the admissions process under control, ensure that:

- No interviews are granted before an Application Form has been filled out and submitted, with the due fees and deposit. There may be exceptional circumstances where the Principal may decide to do so – for example, to discuss the possibility of admitting a student who may have physical disabilities — but be strict about this. Otherwise, parents will come on 'fishing trips' when they are not serious about applying, and use the meeting to try and negotiate conditions. They have to commit with a formal application.

- **Only** the 'authorized' interviewers meet with parents, and only at scheduled times. Be strict with this as well. Parents will call a teacher or a Guidance counselor whom they know, "just for an informal chat", and then when they arrive at the official interview claim "We already had an interview. Mr. Q. told us there would be no problem with Rosie attending the school". Mr. Q. did not have the full facts about Rosie, has been manipulated by the parents, and should not have met with them.

- Issue a written 'Offer of Place' for signature and return. If there are conditions of acceptance (for example, acceptance is on condition that the child has math tutoring over the summer; or acceptance is on probation) – detail them clearly in the 'Offer of Place' document. Let the parents know in good time about all

---

[205] Experience suggests that the later the application, the more problematic the student. That can be because the family is dysfunctional, and cannot get the application organized on time; or because the child is problematic, the family does not know to which school to apply, and panics in August. 'Good' late applications sometimes include students who have not thought of applying to your school, but have been influenced over the summer by a camp counselor who is one of your students, and who has suggested to them that they apply to the school.

of the arrangements for the beginning of the school year, and what they need to do in preparation.

- Make sure that your Tuition Assistance program SEE SECTION 15.1.3 - however it works – is clear, confidential and equitable.

If the school declines to accept a child, refund all deposits.

Finally, draw up a schedule of 'Penalties for Withdrawal of Application'. The school has to engage staff and offer contracts based on the number of registered students. The 'Application Fee', if charged, is non-refundable except in unusual circumstances. Once a family has accepted a place, there should be a progressively more onerous penalty (i.e. non-return of deposit) the closer the withdrawal is to the beginning of the school year. A student who does not 'show' in the first two days of school should only be admitted after interview; a student who does not show for the first three days of school is deemed to have withdrawn, and forfeits a month's tuition. This prevents students from registering at more than one school, and going to "try it out to see which one I like better". The school cannot be a pushover or an easy option – there is a benefit to asserting your own dignity.

11.2.5   Who do you admit to the school?

Admissions criteria are important statements of policy. They should be clearly articulated, approved by the Board, and part of the 'Statement of Philosophy and Purpose'. It is of the essence of a private school that it may control entry. In fairness to prospective students, you should be 'up front' in your Admissions policy, and it should be clearly stated in your recruitment literature.

In formulating Admissions Criteria, bear in mind the following:

- The school is admitting the students, not the parents

- The school must be able to offer courses to students whom it admits; and they must be courses at which those students have a reasonable chance of success.

Difficult as it is to refuse entry, it is not doing students a favor by admitting them to the school when they cannot possibly succeed – either because a rigorous program is beyond their ability, or because they have gaps in their education and do not have prerequisite knowledge. Often parents (desperate to get their children into a Jewish environment) will try and pressurize you into 'giving Y a chance'. Be careful. A student must not be brought into the school where you know that you are setting the student up for failure and frustration – adding another negative school experience to what is probably already a long list. Encourage the parents to place the student in a realistic educational environment that will meet his/her needs. Tragically, the Jewish educational range offered in many Jewish communities is relatively narrow, and a number of Jewish children will fall outside the opportunities available.

Thus, a school may offer places to students:

- Who are motivated to attend the school

- For whom the school can offer a realistic academic program at which the student has a chance of success

- Whose application is submitted in a timely fashion

- Who meet other criteria specified by the school

- and for whom there is space in their appropriate grade.

Each school will determine entry criteria relating to the Jewish status of the child (or related criteria relating to family commitment to the school's religious ethos) according to their philosophy and outlook. However, these criteria must also be clear 'up front' to prospective applicants. In some jurisdictions, the phrasing of such provisions may need legal advice.

Assessing students for entry needs a long-term perspective, a measure of flexibility, ideology and, occasionally, *'rachmanut'* (in this context: sympathy over and above the standard). The question should not be – "Is this student capable now of tackling the school program?" – but, rather, "If we do all we possibly can for this student – does s/he have an eventual chance of success?". The answer to that second question may occasionally be 'No", but it is "Yes" more often than some schools may think …. .

In rejecting a student's admission, the school has to be aware that the family may experience this as a trauma. Be sympathetic and caring. The Principal (or your Guidance Counselor) may be able to help the family with an alternative school placement.

11.2.6 "Which is the best elementary school?"

If the school has several feeders – especially several Jewish feeders – the Principal and his/her colleagues, including teachers, will often be asked by parents which elementary school they would "recommend" for little Dovid or Leah or Tyler or Samantha – at that stage usually still in their buggy.

There is only one possible answer:

> *Whichever school you think will fit your needs best*

If pressed:

> *All the feeder schools have their own strengths* [note: do not use the word 'weaknesses']. *Our experience is that students from all schools quickly adapt, and within a few months of arrival, it is impossible to tell from which school they came.*

Do not express preferences for one school over another.

One of the negative variants on this is the comment by a High School teacher to a parent, perhaps at a social occasion, or perhaps 'explaining' a low mark –

> *We always have trouble with the students coming from Jewish Elementary – they are not as well prepared as students from the other schools*

Administrators, teachers and support staff alike must be warned that any comment they make about a feeder school will spread like wildfire through the community

> *At Jewish High they say that students coming from Jewish Elementary can't cope with math as well as students from Torah Junior*

It will result in an angry call to the High School Principal from his/her Elementary counterpart (or to the High School President from the Elementary School President). No comment at all should **ever** be made about another school, except broadly positive ones. Especially problematic are direct comparisons.

It sometimes happens that staff do notice that students from a particular school are not properly prepared in say, math or Ivrit skills. In some cases, this may be the result of circumstances in the feeder – the Grade 8 Ivrit teacher may have been out of school for many lessons, or may have been on leave and a less satisfactory substitute may have been teaching the class. No matter. The proper, discreet channel is for the teacher (or Administrator) to voice their concern quietly to the Principal, who should equally discreetly place a call to the Elementary Principal.

A good way of avoiding this – or at least mitigating it – is for the High School to issue guidelines for the G8 teachers, setting out the 'knowledge assumed' standards for the main G9 subjects.

> *In G9 Science, we will assume that incoming students have a basic knowledge and understanding of the following: [.......]. If for any reason the class has not been able to cover all of these topics in G8, a call to our Head of Science, Mrs. K (extension 123) would be helpful, as we will try and take that into consideration when designing the G9 course*

If an incident does happen … the school must do whatever damage control is necessary. An offer by the Principal to meet with concerned Elementary parents at the school concerned is a good idea.

The school should not be persuaded to release 'statistics' (*"How did our students perform in the Grade 9 exams compared to others?"*). They will not necessarily be convincing, and will set off a round of further problems with other schools (including demands for similar statistics, covering every subject, from other parents).

11.2.7   New arrivals - the Israeli community

Recent years have seen sharply increased populations of Israeli families who have settled in Diaspora Jewish communities. The 'Israeli community' is now a significant proportion of the total Diaspora Jewish population. Many day schools and supplementary schools draw on the pool of local Israelis for teaching staff.

However, Israelis have been reluctant[206] to enroll their children in the Jewish educational system. The reasons are complex and sensitive, but include:

- Radically different perceptions of the challenges of maintaining identity: many Israelis, used to living in a society where Jewishness is the majority culture, do not understand at all the need to 'invest' in maintaining values and identity when living as a minority. They underestimate – or do not appreciate - the assimilatory influences to which their children will be subject when living outside Israel. A mantra which I have heard on many occasions has been *"Anachnu m'dabrim Ivrit babayit, madlikim nerot b'layl shishi, um'vakrim etzel saba ve savta baaretz kol kayitz – v'zeh maspik!* - We speak Ivrit at home, light candles on Friday night, and visit the grandparents in Israel every summer – and that's enough!" Within a couple of years, they find it isn't enough at all, but then it is too late.

- Expectation that education – including Jewish education – should be free. Sometimes the expectation is that "the Jewish community" should pay for Jewish education[207]. There is no accompanying sense that they are (now) part of the Jewish community.

- Perceptions that 'Jewish' education is 'religious', and will be characterized by all the problems of secular – religious tension in Israeli society; and that a 'Jewish' (= in their expectation, by definition intensively Orthodox) school will not teach a general curriculum, and will enforce rigorous religious practice.

- Feelings of alienation from local Jewish communities, often including the observation (less and less true) that local Jews look on Israelis living in the Diaspora as 'traitors' for leaving Israel.

---

[206] The exceptions are the more orthodox ('*dati*') Israelis, who have an instant common language with the traditional community.

[207] Some former Israelis are puzzled by the fact that a Diaspora community donated their local school back in Israel, but they are expected to pay for schooling in their new community. Some wish to transfer their status as recipients of Diaspora funding to their new location – "*Anachnu Yisraelim – anachnu lo meshalmim* – We're Israelis – we don't pay".

- In some cases, total lack of identification with Jewish life as they see it in their new community – "We are Israelis, not Jews".

- I discussed this difficult topic in an article[208] in *HaYidion* – the RAVSAK magazine, and added an additional factor: the very poor, and often inaccurate and misleading picture of Jewish life in the Diaspora portrayed in the Israeli media. Many Israelis arriving in Diaspora communities have no idea of organized Jewish community life and values outside Israel.

To get the 'Israeli' students into the school system needs careful, sustained – and difficult – outreach. While, again, this is something that deserves lengthy treatment on its own, wider than the scope of this book, some or all of the following strategies merit careful consideration:

- Involve partners – your local Federation or BJE, or other schools – in a common 'generic' marketing campaign

- Establish personal contacts and dialogue with local 'networks' of Israelis

- Invite individuals and groups to the school, and get existing Israeli/Ivrit speaking parents to speak to them

- Reach out to local Ivrit newspapers, websites and local radio

- Advertise in Ivrit, and make recruitment material about the school available in Ivrit

- Host events for the local Ivrit-speaking community at the school

A more radical move might be to offer elective courses that 'meet the group where they are' - especially in Tanakh and Ivrit. (The latter is a particular and specialized problem. Often, children of Israeli parents have an aural Ivrit – they have picked up a spoken language, but cannot read or write.)

Bringing the children of former Israelis into the Jewish school system has no more or no less moral, religious or ideological importance than bringing any other Jewish child into our system; but it is a distinct sub-set of the recruitment issue, involving a large (and growing) sector of the Jewish community.

The normal recruitment strategies will not reach this group. However, it is difficult to make the often-lobbied case that they deserve preferential (financial) treatment. All immigrants, from wherever, should enjoy a subsidy on their tuition fees in their first year(s) in their new country. After that it is impossible to justify giving [immigrant]

---

[208] See http://tinyurl.com/l3w4wd

family 'Q' different treatment than [locally born] family 'P', where the financial circumstances of both are comparable.

11.2.8   New arrivals - the Russian community

Many similar considerations apply to families from the former Soviet Union (FSU). They may be families who have migrated twice – once to Israel and then again to North America (or other Diaspora destinations).

In some communities, outreach to the FSU community is more established and 'acceptable' (although not necessarily any more successful) than to the Israelis. The common perception (perhaps a stereotype?) is that the FSU community sees academic success (especially in math and science) as a supreme value.

Again, their relationship to established Jewish communities is, for other but equally understandable reasons, distant and suspicious. I have no suggestions other than adapting rather similar strategies to marketing to Israeli families, and ensuring that every student gets a warm, understanding and caring reception in the school.

11.3 Special families

The Jewish family is rapidly changing, and as the Jewish school system is growing, it is widening its appeal to families who (for many different reasons) did not previously consider Jewish schools. That is a welcome phenomenon, and speaks to the success of our programs. However, schools now have to deal with many families and situations outside their previous, perhaps rather conventional, experience. The list includes, but is certainly not limited to:

- Single parents; including (in the religious community) the new phenomenon of single women who choose to have children

- Same-sex parents

- Families who live with unemployment, illness, addiction or trauma

- Families who are new to Jewish life

- Families who may be victims of crime (or where a parent or family member may be a convicted criminal)

- 'Blended families' -- or any of a lengthening list of family units who do not fit the traditional Jewish middle-class suburban model of 'Mom, Pop, 2.4+ children'.

The school's concern is with the children. Beginning at the recruitment stage, it is essential that the school provides a welcoming, safe environment for all of these families and their children, and that the implicit and explicit messages that the school transmits are positive, supportive to the children, and non-judgmental.

- It is particularly important that classroom teachers are sensitive to the circumstances of their students, and that they never, ever make any comments or remarks that hurt, embarrass or humiliate students. It is always a fair assumption that a class includes students who are keeping family secrets.

This can be an issue in any subject. A teacher should not hide accurate information about what the *halachah* or the law says about, for example, same-sex marriage. But in framing their remarks, they must be conscious that their class may include a child of same-sex parents; or that in any school or yeshivah, it is increasingly likely that the class will include a child with a sibling, cousin, uncle or aunt who is in a same-sex relationship. There is also a very high probability that some students in the class may be dealing with personal questions of sexual identity. The same applies to every other example. Where the curriculum includes potentially sensitive subjects, staff meetings or PD sessions may include discussions on how teachers should present them. Gratuitous remarks are totally out of place, and may cause deep and lasting hurt, remembered long afterwards, and coloring the student's entire school experience.

The same applies to all interactions between the school and the family – whether by Administration, teachers, the financial office or by Board representatives, or material contained in school publications. Every individual, and every family, deserves to be treated with dignity, respect and understanding. For many families, sending students to a Jewish school can be a huge effort in many different ways – including, but by no means limited to, the financial strain. Some parents will be uncomfortable attending school functions. Undifferentiated messages of welcome need to be in place.

From time to time regrettable incidents will occur, whether in the classroom or in the school. Apologies should be offered, and whatever appropriate discussions held. But it must be made clear to staff that the school seeks to respect every member of the school community.

11.4 Retention and attrition

As students move through the school, there will be attrition, typically 5%-10% per year[209]. Of every ten students who enter private schools in Grade 9, only seven or

---

[209] The average retention for all North American private schools is about 89 - 90% per year. I do not know of any reliable figures for Jewish High schools. At TanenbaumCHAT our average has been about 93% for a number of years.

eight will graduate at the end of Grade 12. Retention of existing students is an important operational function. Significant attrition is a destabilizing and even demoralizing factor that can gain a life of its own and be difficult to reverse. Some Jewish schools face established local 'conventional wisdom' that is difficult to shake off – *"Go to Jewish High for the first three grades, but do your final year somewhere else".*

Students leave for valid and invalid reasons – some reasonable, and some simply imaginary. They include:

- Academic difficulties: the student cannot achieve success because the program is too difficult or too full. In some cases, the school may advise a student that they should consider a different program ('Counseling out').

- "They'll get better marks elsewhere" – maybe they will (a lighter load) – maybe they won't. The family has signaled its priorities.

- "You have a better chance of getting to a good University from a non-Jewish school" – demonstrably the least accurate reason!

- A social difficulty – the student is unhappy, has no friends, or is being bullied or victimized. These cases deserve careful attention. Has the school been at fault? Can you retrieve the situation? The question of whether a change of school will actually help also has to be asked

- "I don't want the Judaic subjects" – an unwilling student should not be persuaded to stay in the school. The last thing the school needs is a student who doesn't want to be there

- Difficulties with teachers – again, check these cases out carefully. Is this the student's difficulty? Can s/he be counseled back in to the school? If there really is a teacher who is causing students to leave the school, rapid and decisive action is necessary.

- "The Judaic studies are too stifling" – See SECTION 7 – 'The Jewish Program' for a philosophy that may help avoid these confrontational situations. Check whether a particular teacher or teachers have caused this reaction....

- Student is seeking courses not available in the school – this can be general ("Not enough sciences") or particular ("I want to go to art college and I need a school with a strong arts program"). The student and parents have made their choice and set their priorities.

- Another commitment (serious sport, dance) demands hours of training each week, and the student/family seek a school with shorter hours and a less demanding program to accommodate the extra-curricular interest

- Financial difficulties – despite every effort by your Tuition committee, the school has been unable to reach amicable agreement with the family about Tuition fees. If this is genuine it is, again, traumatic. Neither the parents nor the students wish to leave. They will feel this as rejection by the Jewish community, and – again - will remember the experience for years to come. However, occasionally this reason will be given because the family doesn't want to admit to the real reason, or because they have chosen other priorities over Jewish school tuition fees

It is worth tracking students who leave. The Tuition Office (normally the address for parents who are withdrawing students) should have a system of notifying the Administration of each child who is leaving. If known, the information sheet should include a "Reason for Leaving:" box. A Principal, or VP, or Guidance Counselor, may be assigned the task of following up. Frequently, the school will know in advance that a student is not returning (and, in fact, may have 'counseled-out'). The patterns are important, and sometimes will identify problems of which the school is unaware. (*"After what happened with Jodie and those students this year .. why do you think she's leaving?"*). But some decisions will be enigmatic.

A major problem in dealing with 'exit interview' programs is that you can never be sure that you are being told the truth. A parent may say "We can't afford the tuition any more, and don't want to ask for a subsidy", when what they really mean is "We've decided to spend the money on a new kitchen, because in any case Jodie was fed up with all the Hebrew". They may say the opposite: "Jodie wanted to go to a school where she could spend more time on practicing her dance", when they really mean: "Although outwardly we are living a middle-class Jewish life, my husband's practice has been hit with huge financial problems – we don't want anyone to know about it, so we won't ask for a subsidy. But it breaks our heart to have to take Jodie out of the school"[210].

---

[210] Similar problems occur in other areas of school life. A teacher asking for leave of absence may confide to the Principal that the teacher, or their spouse, needs some medical procedures or treatment, or has some other highly confidential need to be away from school (e.g. involvement in a court case). The Principal of course is understanding, and gives the leave requested. The teacher, not wishing to share personal information with other teachers, goes back into the Staff Room and announces, "S/he gave me a week off to go to a friend's simchah." A parent, not wishing to divulge that business is in fact excellent (and profitable!), and the family are paying full tuition without a problem, tells friends and business associates that "I went to the Tuition Committee and they gave me a special deal." Or the opposite: "I'm a big supporter of the school – we're sponsoring one of the teams" – while in fact their reality is

11.5 Graduation and graduates

After four years (or more) at your school, it is time for students to graduate.

Like all transitions, the graduation process should be carefully planned. The thinking begins at the end of Grade 10, with course selections for G11 affecting prerequisites for later College / University applications. While process and preparation will vary according to jurisdiction (and to a degree according to the priorities and goals of the school community), some of the mechanisms that need to be in place include the following:

- 'Information evenings' for parents and students, outlining process and strategy for choosing and applying to college /university.

- Availability of Career and college counseling interviews

- Information guidance about different colleges and universities

- PSAT and SAT preparation

- Advice regarding available funding and scholarships

- Information and advice about post-High School Israel programs and other choices for 'year out' programs

- Help and guidance in writing applications, and preparation for interviews.

College entrance is extremely competitive, and choice is too often governed by social or other non-academic considerations. The school's responsibility is to give the advice that is best for the student. That may be to apply to an Ivy League college[211] – it may be that he student's best interest is to apply to a community college, or to go straight into the workforce. However, one of the most delicate transitions involved is to firmly, but tactfully make it clear that the process, the responsibility and the decisions are ultimately those of the student and his/her parents. The school's responsibilities are to:

- Honestly assess what it believes to be the opportunities best suited to the student

- Wherever the student decides to aim for, give positive, supportive encouragement and, where necessary,

---

very different. The Principal cannot divulge reality in any of these cases, but may well have to deal with the consequences.

[211] Or equivalent elsewhere. While this section is phrased in terms applicable in the USA, the principles are universal.

documentation. Be honest, in a kind way, but be supportive – "David – I think your chances of getting into this program are slim, and I don't want you to be disappointed if you don't make it – but if you really want to try, we'll do everything possible to help you!" – is a lot better than "You'll never get in here. Don't even bother. It's for really smart kids – a lot smarter than you." Students frequently surprise

- Offer comprehensive, up-to-date and accurate information and advice at all stages of the process

- Be efficient and prompt in preparing and submitting documentation

'Jewish life on Campus' is a natural and particular concern of Jewish schools and their graduates. Many graduates will choose campuses where there is a well-established Jewish student community. Others will do the opposite, and will consciously take the opportunity to experience their student years away from Jewish life. There can be surprises. A significant proportion of students who go to isolated campuses with very small (or inactive) Jewish student populations find themselves as leaders and organizers of Jewish life, and the experience becomes formative and positive. Equally, other students can go to vibrant centers of Jewish student life -- and never go near their Hillel or any other Jewish activity. What matters, ultimately, is what is going on inside the student's head.

The 'Israel Dimension' of campus life is far more problematic. While there are many pressures on High Schools to "prepare" their students for the political situation on campus, their ability to do so, for many good reasons, is extremely limited – as discussed in SECTION 7.6.6. A wise Principal will not give undertakings that cannot be fulfilled. However, under present circumstances a school that allows its students to graduate without a reasonable grounding in Jewish history, including the Jewish political history of the twentieth century, is seriously failing its students and its community.

11.5.1   Failure to graduate High School

Most students will graduate without problems. Some – probably very few – will graduate with difficulty, or will fail to graduate High School altogether.

It is extremely important that students who are in danger of failing graduation are given warning of that, in writing, several months before the end of the year. A copy of the letter, and a confirmatory phone call, must also be made to parents. If there is a chance for students to improve and reach the necessary standard, spell out clearly, in writing, the steps that the student needs to take. In such cases, where recriminations will follow, it is essential to avoid surprises. Whatever the outcome, supply counseling, advice and help.

Students who fail should nevertheless be allowed to take part in the Graduation ceremony. Don't humiliate them further.

11.5.2 The Graduation ceremony

The Graduation ceremony should be memorable, dignified and 'classy'. It is a major 'shop window' for the school. Students, staff, parents, extended families, and local community representatives should be given a chance to celebrate the students' conclusion of High School. There are many models of ceremony available. Keep the speeches few, and short. Whatever the length of the ceremony (and no ceremony should much exceed two hours[212], whatever the number of graduates), the pace is more important than the length. A smooth, fast-moving ceremony will keep everyone's attention. One that falters, or is punctuated by pauses, runs the risk of losing the attention of the audience. Remember that the majority of the audience are waiting patiently for the moment when their son/daughter/grandchild/niece/nephew walks across the podium to collect their certificate.

Other suggestions include:

- Take an ad in the local Jewish or general community paper listing and congratulating your graduates

- If the venue is large, hire a large-screen projection system so that all speakers, and every graduate, is clearly visible to the crowd

- Normally, the School president is the chair of Graduation. Write him/her a detailed script for every step of the ceremony.

- If there are prizes and awards that are only announced at Graduation, issue a separate Graduation memento that lists all[213] of the graduating students, the prize and award winners, and post it on

- Graduation is also a time when students feel a need to act out. Disciplinary issues around Graduation are discussed in SECTION 12.5.4

---

[212] TanenbaumCHAT, Southern Campus, with some 200 graduating students, many presentations and prizes, two musical interludes and a number of speeches, has now got Graduation down to less than two-and-a-quarter hours.
[213] Listing only the prize and award winners will cause unnecessary hurt. The school is proud of all of its graduates.

11.6 Keeping the school 'calm, successful and happy'

Whether or not this very desirable aim is achieved is usually a reflection of the all-encompassing management style of the Administration and faculty. The school will resonate with the 'vibrations' of the leadership team. There are mechanisms and programs that will help. In addition to those discussed below, the effect of a good Guidance Department SEE SECTION 6.2.3 in defusing tension in the school should never be underestimated.

11.6.1 Essential services and facilities

As every educator (and parent) will know, High School years are a roller-coaster of energies, emotions and hormones. There are a number of safety valves and a number of services that the school can offer which will give students legitimate opportunities to express themselves, and opportunities to 'talk things through' if pressure is building.

- A healthy school must provide a Phys Ed/Sports program, and creative opportunities for expression through drama, art and music

- A strong Guidance and Counseling Department SEE SECTION 6.2.3 is essential

- A varied extra-curricular program

- A sympathetic and tolerant Administration and staff, ready to listen, and respectful of the individual student

Occasionally, Yeshivah High Schools / Seminaries do not provide such programs; or make them voluntary; or provide minimal programs or facilities. It is a mistake, whose consequences will often surface in other ways in the school.

11.6.2 Student council and student responsibility

High School should be a time of leadership opportunity and training. A well-supervised Student Council is part of the High school experience, and is again, a 'safety-valve' of sorts. A Student Council can be something of a risk; the skill is to structure it in such a way that the most common problems are avoided in advance.

The quicksand areas of Student Council include, but are not limited to:

- Supervision -- The key to a successful Student Council is skilled and sympathetic supervision by a teacher. Try and identify a staff member who has the personality, maturity, judgment and interest to be the Student Council Advisor. Avoid teachers who will be intimidated by the students; who want to be part of the student 'experience'; who want to be 'cool' etc. Whether male or female, they should probably be married. Most of all – they have to have their heads screwed firmly on. By training, experience or intuition, they should be skilled in youth leadership – to be able to guide, to advise, where necessary to warn. They should be able to assess the practical viability of Student Council ideas – to contribute constructive advice; but also to say "No" when necessary, without 'squashing' the students. They must also keep an appropriately distant, but constant eye on the Student Council. If the Advisor neglects their duty – the potential for trouble increases exponentially.

- Constitution -- There must be a written Student Council Constitution. The Constitution should provide for open, democratic elections at defined times, and carefully define the 'rules of order' for committees, the role and responsibilities of office holders, and the defined Terms of Reference / scope of responsibilities of the Student Council itself. The Constitution should be very clear regarding all financial matters, including the power of the Student Council to decide how to allocate charity funds raised[214], and the process to arrive at those decisions. Carefully draft how and under what circumstances the Constitution may be amended. The Constitution including all amendments, must ALWAYS be subject to the approval of the school Administration.

- Finances -- One of the commonest problem areas, if not carefully set up. Students are inexperienced in handling money, whether it is the Student Council bank account (or, worse, credit card) or cash receipts at a Student Council function. Suddenly, irregularities surface. The potential for problems is infinite. Despite the temptations, make it mandatory that there is no separate Student Council Bank account. Even though the money is theirs, and not the school's, ALL Student Council accounts have to be administered through the school accounts office. The school, against requisitions co-signed by a responsible teacher, must make all payments. All cash (and other) receipts are paid into the school office, and banked by them. No student may hold a credit card on behalf of the student council (or any other school account); and the Treasurer (in some schools a teacher, not a student) must keep accounts that are under constant inspection.

- Wild schemes -- Occasionally, a group of well-meaning but immature students will decide on a scheme (usually to raise

---

[214] Some student funds raised should, by agreement, go to the school.

money for tzedakah) that is just wild – kidnapping the local Rabbi and holding him/her for ransom, or something equally outlandish and, unfortunately, usually dangerous. At such times your Student Council Advisor, and if necessary the Administration, needs to assert authority.

But having said all of the above, a healthy Student Council, with good student leadership, can make a huge contribution to school life. The experience of student council leadership can be memorable, and formative, for students. It should be a lot of fun. Student Council should also have a representative on the School Board of Governors, with observer[215] status, who should give a 'Student Council Report' on a regular basis.

In addition to Student Council, many other responsibilities can be given to students. They will rise to your expectations. Their creativity and powers of organization will astonish you.

11.7   Our students are "Millennials'

More mature readers of this book will probably fall into the generational category often referred to as 'Baby Boomers'. The parents of many of our students are 'Generation X'ers'. Students, however, will come from the group already identified as 'Millennials' – children of the closing decade of the 20th century[216] and the opening decade of the 21st.

Our times have their unique defining character. Global culture and global digital technology leave their irrevocable imprint on popular culture and on the educational world. Intangible currents flow around our institutions. Some are positive and admirable; others may cause teachers (and others) to shake their heads in part-sorrow, part-disappointment and part-frustration. They affect the expectations, the attitudes and the behavior of our students. Without comment, I offer this list of the characteristics of the 'Millennial' generation:

"Millennials are:

- Special – they are special individuals, with special needs, who will go to a special University, where they will prepare to play a special role in life. ("25% of entrants to USA Universities have hired advisers to help them in planning their applications")

---

[215] As observers, they generally do not attend when confidential matters or budget are being discussed. A sensible Board Chair will schedule the Student Council Report for early in the meeting, and then let the rep know that after their report they 'don't have to stay if they need to be somewhere else'.

[216] "Le'minyanam". But most of our students are culturally children of the wider world.

- Sheltered – Millennial parents ("Helicopter parents", who hover over their children constantly) have sought to keep their children safe from early childhood.

- Confident – motivated by possibility, opportunity and positive reinforcement.

- Team-oriented – love group work, cooperative activities like volunteer service, and participation in something larger than the individual. Conformity is a motivator.

- Conventional – no revolutionaries among the Millennials! They love their parents, embrace parental values, respect them, share their views "and even like their music".

- Pressured – The 'arms race' is to build your resume and get into College (where it becomes: Get a place in Grad school and then get a job...)

- Achievers – The most all-round achievement –oriented teenage generation ever. The SAC scores [increase each year].

- Hypercommunicators – and multi-taskers, constantly in touch via cell-phone, email, messaging – while watching television and surfing the web.

- They have multiple identities – that are distributed like a set of 'Windows' on a computer screen."

All involved with young people will recognize some of those patterns. To the list may be added that they appear to see themselves as:

- Deserving or entitled– they 'deserve' or are 'entitled to' marks, rather than need to earn them.

11.8   The 'Founding Grade' in a new school

When a new school is founded, the 'Founding Grade' is always special, and always needs special management.

Students and parents begin as pioneers, often with very high expectations. New schools, able to market their high intentions untrammeled and untainted by the realities of actually running a school, often attract parents and students who have been unhappy at other schools. It is characteristic of 'founding grades' that there is a dropout after the first year, sometimes of the initially most enthusiastic families (whose super-idealistic expectations of the new school cannot be met). Despite that, the first group in any school is always distinctive.

They are in the unusual situation of being the school leadership for four years. The class that followed them are in the equally unusual situation of always being dominated by the first grade. The founding grade develops exceptional leadership skills, has wonderful opportunities to excel and star at every school activity, bond exceptionally strongly and, certainly in the first two years, have the almost undivided personal attention of the staff.

The flip side of that is that they often develop an inappropriate and exaggerated (even if understandable) sense of ownership of the school. They will be reluctant to share leadership with either students or, it must be said, staff. It can manifest itself in occasionally unpleasant ways. That seems to be inevitable, and may be a source of tension between students and Administration.

In the first, pioneering year, when the school will have some elements of a year-long summer camp, the activities of the school – educational and otherwise – will come under an unremitting spotlight by parents and, occasionally, community. Just as the 'founding students' feel ownership, so do the 'founding parents', who may be as reluctant as their children to pass school leadership over to their 'next generation'.

Ultimately, time does its work. The school grows and achieves a more normal profile. The core group of students (and teachers) will always be nostalgic about the early days. But the school has been created.

11.9   The Principal's relationship with students

The relationship of the Principal to students is unavoidably linked to the size of the school. A Principal in a school of up to 400 students or so should know the names of almost all, if not all of the students. A Principal in a high school of 800 or more cannot know all of the students, and a Principal in a school[217] of over 1,000 or so will spend most of his or her time quite distant from the everyday life of the student body, and will know only a few of them.

Deciding how to allocate time is a very difficult decision to make, and particularly so when it comes to deciding how much time the Principal wants to devote to students – because every School Principal, at heart, must value working with students above almost all other professional preferences.

Administrators, if possible, should teach a course. It helps them keep a finger on the pulse of the school in a number of ways, and teachers will often appreciate the fact that Administrators are teaching. If the Principal is not teaching, s/he can nevertheless stay in touch with students by, for example:

---

[217] This may be even truer in a private school, where the Principal has many responsibilities that in a public system are the responsibility of a local School Board.

- Subbing the occasional class for absent teachers

- Attending Shabbatonim, retreats or school trips

- Inviting groups of students for occasional lunches to hear what's on their mind (free falafel or pizza is part of this deal!)

- Giving a regular shiur or discussion group at lunch break or after school.

It is unavoidable that in larger schools, the Principal may become a distant figure to many students – especially, as I can testify[218], when major school projects or issues demand the Principal's attention on an ongoing basis.

12 DISCIPLINE, RULES, ETC

Students respect structure, and respond well to it. They dislike rules that they see as "stupid", and they are quicker than adults to spot inconsistency. Some students see it as a matter of trust and honor to obey (most) school rules; others are happy to disregard school rules if they can get away with it (just as some of us did when we were their age).

School ethos will determine the behavior of students in the school, and the school must transmit a high expectation of conduct to its student body – reaching the situation where students, parents and staff know that "in this school, everyone expects you to behave properly". It is a very good school indeed where the *students* feel that it is their duty to uphold school standards and behavior.

For Administration, discipline is an art, not a science, and should be firm – but applied with wisdom and common sense (two concepts usefully combined in the single Hebrew/Yiddish word "s*echel'*).

In this as in other areas, **the School must assert its dignity**, and not be afraid to uphold principles and rules when necessary. As the adage goes, better to be respected than popular. A great deal depends on the content and style of the School Handbook – especially the 'Safety and Behavior Code'. If the School Handbook – SEE SECTION 4.6.3 circulated at the beginning of the year to every student and every family – has been reasonably drafted, it is very difficult for students or parents to argue with the school.

---

[218] Ediitng this very passage on an El Al flight from Ben Gurion to Toronto, I found myself seated next a very charming TanenbaumCHAT Class of '04 graduate, returning from a summer in Israel, where she had been volunteering as a nurse working with African refugees. I looked familiar, but she could not quite place me.....

Commonly exasperating attitudes regarding school discipline include:

- Parents who are strong supporters of school discipline and school rules, except when their own children are involved

- Teachers who do not hesitate to make known their views that the Administration are hopelessly lax about enforcing discipline and standards in the school, but are often strangely reluctant to report breaches of discipline to the Administration, especially when they occur in the teacher's own classroom

- The school Board which expects discipline to be enforced whatever the circumstances

- The school's neighbors who are "disgusted" with the behavior of the students (and frequently with car-pooling, and hence car-parking, parents), but whose way of dealing with it often does not help resolve the issues

- Local Rabbis who cannot understand why the school does not enforce standards of behavior and religious observance on its students

Increasingly, parents are threatening and occasionally resorting to legal action in challenging disciplinary action taken by schools. As noted elsewhere, the Principal must be aware of applicable Education Law, and must have access to a lawyer specializing in the field SEE SECTION 4.9.4. Good administration of school discipline should leave students and parents feeling that they have been dealt with fairly, and hence avoid further unpleasantness, including legal action.

The school must formulate disciplinary policy. This can be a task of the Administration, or of the Administration jointly with the Board, staff, parents and students. While the latter model has its obvious appeal, at least the first draft must be done by Administration. As those responsible for making disciplinary policy work, Administration must retain control of the process, and must be free to make alterations from time to time according to its judgment.

There are guiding principles:

- Without reasonable school rules, clearly published, the school will be chaotic. That does not mean that there has to be a draconian regime. It means that there have to be reasonable boundaries, reasonably – but consistently – enforced.

- Wherever possible, good practice is to try and frame school rules as expectations ("do's") rather than prohibitions ("don't's").

- In all dealings with students - and parents, and staff - there must be meticulous adherence to fair process.

12.1 Who administers discipline?

For discipline to be credible, fair and impartial, it has to be managed properly. It has to be followed up and enforced.   Direction has to be clear regarding who is authorized to impose consequences.   Classroom teachers may have authority to impose consequences of a certain level, but if so the guidelines have to be clear, and the consequence has to be reported and logged with Administration.   (The school needs to know whether there are patterns, which will be revealing.)   Administrators in a larger school will have authority to impose one- or two-day suspensions, or their equivalent.   The Principal should be involved – either directly or as part of the consultative process – on anything more serious than that, or on anything that may have legal consequences.   On complex issues, (and discipline is frequently complex), Administration should work as a team.

Often, Administration will have one VP (or equivalent) who is the discipline 'address'.   Since the essence of discipline at High school level is not to punish, but to try and teach the student values and responsibility, the VP handling discipline should be someone with great wisdom, natural authority and the ability to form trusting relationships with teenagers. Avoid putting an insensitive colleague in this post.

In a large school, this can be a full-time post. The advantage of this is that there is consistency and accumulated wisdom in the office.

If detentions after school hours are part of your system of consequences, they have to be properly supervised. Reasonable notice (normally at least 24 hours) has to be given to parents that students will be required to stay in school after hours.

Finally, discipline is a professional matter.   No lay person should be involved in disciplinary process, except where a Principal may advise the President of the school that an expulsion is contemplated.   Board members, if called by parents on disciplinary matters, must say that that they trust and support the Administration, and that for reasons of privacy they cannot be involved in disciplinary issues.   A Board member may not 'lobby' the Principal (let alone any other member of staff) regarding someone else's child. The Principal cannot divulge details of conversations or disciplinary process to any uninvolved party.   In schools where – entirely inappropriately – Board interference is the norm, it may take years to change the culture.

- **The reputation for fairness and impartiality in the administration of discipline is one of the most important – and desirable - assets a school can have.**

12.2 Fair process in school discipline

A school should have a locally-devised protocol available for School Administration to use in disciplinary processes, which may include standard report forms and other templates.

'Fair process' in these circumstances should include, but may not be limited to, the following elements.   Clearly, the circumstances may vary somewhat in every individual case:

- Reasonable awareness of expectations / definition of the infraction

    Students cannot be held accountable for offenses of which they cannot reasonably have been aware. If the school has an ad-hoc rule or instruction that it wants to enact – post it in writing on the school notice board, and make sure it is announced clearly to all students. However, every School Handbook will have some 'catch-all' provisions capable of dealing with the unexpected.

- Thorough investigation

    A school must carry out a methodical and thorough investigation of alleged disciplinary infractions, obviously proportional to the seriousness of the offense. Circumstances vary, and often it is in the nature of incidents that they create a maelstrom of events. The school must not be panicked by pressure. The ability to keep a cool head is a major attribute of good leadership.

- The investigation may take the following sequence:

    First, secure the safety and privacy of the school and the students involved. Then, as soon as possible, get written, dated and signed219 accounts from everyone involved – the victim (if any), the alleged perpetrator, the teacher(s), and any other students with knowledge of the event. Take whatever steps are necessary to advise parents who need to know of what is happening.   Call the school lawyer if

---

[219] It is very important to do this as quickly as possible, and to have those statements written in isolation from each other. Nowadays, the first step is to require all involved to deposit cell phones and any other text-messaging enabled instruments with Administration. Those telling the truth will be happy to write and sign a statement; those who were exaggerating when verbally asked ("*I saw...*") may suddenly become more circumspect ("*Although I didn't see the teacher do it myself, Johnny told me that....*") when asked to put their report in a signed document.

necessary. While the investigation is under way, the alleged perpetrator(s) may be suspended from school, and may not communicate with other students regarding the issue.

Secondly, interview those involved, with the sole purpose of establishing facts – not opinions, not rumors not 'common knowledge', but facts. Take careful notes. If the incident is serious, make sure that two adults are present at every interview, including at least one of the same sex as the student.

Thirdly, when you have assembled and assessed the data, make your determination of what the consequences should be. A short Administration meeting at this point is highly recommended. In most jurisdictions, a school does not have to "prove beyond reasonable doubt", but may make decisions on "balance of probabilities".

Lastly – advise parents and students of what is going to happen. Record your decision in a letter to the parents and student(s) affected that sets out the provisions of the School Handbook, how the student contravened them, what the consequence is going to be, and for how long this offense is going to stay on the student record. Advise them in the letter of the appeal process, if applicable. Then express hope that the student will now put this incident in the past, etc.

- Opportunity for all parties to state their case

You must make sure that at every stage everyone involved has a fair and complete opportunity to give their version of events. Do not give leading or pressurized questions. "Can you explain exactly what happened on Tuesday afternoon?" is better than "You should be ashamed of what you did, and I want a full confession". In really serious cases, and if it is possible, you may want to delay interviewing a student until parents are present.

- Proper and reasonable advice to parents of processes in which their children are involved.

Ensure that parents are advised as soon as possible of incidents involving their children. The urgency of this is directly proportional to the seriousness of the incident, and in minor infractions the parents may not need to be advised altogether. But if the incident is serious – especially if it may result in suspension, expulsion, or legal consequences of any description – you must advise the parents immediately. They should be advised of the alleged incident, and the steps that the school is taking to deal with it. Be firm but sympathetic with parents. Try and give them a timetable of process. Parents will be anxious to give their views on other students involved:

"Mr. X, just as I would not discuss your child with other parents, I am sure that you appreciate that I cannot discuss any other student with you. Please be assured that the school that the school is relating to this incident with great seriousness, and we are taking every

precaution to ensure that all parties involved are being treated with fairness and respect."

At the school's discretion, parents may be present[220] when their child is interviewed. They must be given reasonable notice of meetings.

- Timely process

All disciplinary processes must be dealt with quickly and swiftly. Do not delay, and do not allow the process to drag on unreasonably. This is a reciprocal obligation – parents cannot tell you "It isn't convenient to meet with you this week". Your response is:

"Mr. X – an incident has occurred which the school regards as serious. Your daughter is involved. We have a duty to investigate this, and part of the fair and thorough investigation entails advising you and your wife of the circumstances. We cannot delay this, and therefore I would like to know whether you and your wife could attend a meeting in the next 24 hours? "

- Reasonable decisions

Decisions must be reasonable in the light of the information at the school's disposal. The school cannot impose a consequence – especially a serious consequence such as expulsion - based on unsubstantiated accusations, or less than compelling evidence. If it is impossible to establish the circumstances, and the Administration feels that in conscience it cannot punish a suspected student, the Staff, the Board, and occasionally other parents may challenge the Principal's decision. The response has to be:

"If this was your child, you would – justifiably – demand to know the evidence on which the school was basing its action. In this case, although I had clear suspicions, I did not have actual proof that Noah made that telephone call."

- Documentation of process and decisions

The process should be documented from its very beginnings. Good practice is to keep all relevant notes and documents in an 'Incident File'. The Administrator responsible should collect written accounts from others, and keep his/her own notes, making sure that they are dated and initialed. It is most important to keep a log of telephone conversations. Download emails (and be careful about the content of emails originated by the school).

---

[220] This must be weighed carefully. Check the local school law. Usually, the school has the right to interview students without parents being present, as part of the school's right and duty to maintain order in the school, and as part of its prerogative of being 'in loco parentis'. If the school feels, for any reason, that the parents' presence will impede the willingness of the student to speak freely, they should not be present. In other cases, parental presence may be very helpful. A first step is to ask the student which they prefer.

- Right of appeal

  In serious cases, especially involving extended suspension or expulsion, a student is entitled to a right of appeal. The right of appeal can be conducted at different levels of formality. If the Principal has not been involved in the case in question (for example, a Vice-Principal may have dealt with the incident), then the Principal may serve as a first recourse. The Principal may ask a Board member or an external third party to join him / her - perhaps another school Principal, or retired Principal, or a local Rabbi. In complex cases, the school and parents involved may refer the matter to an independently constituted tribunal.   By this stage, lawyers will be involved and the Principal will be outside the decision-making process.

-

12.3 The basic areas of discipline

12.3.1   THE ESSENTIAL LIST OF POSITIVES

A positive, 'catch-all' list similar to the following will help you enormously. Whatever is not covered specifically in your School handbook may be subsumed under Paragraph (a).

"How you should behave ….

Students at [Jewish High] are expected to:

(a)   act safely, sensibly, responsibly, courteously and with honesty and integrity at all times, and implement the provisions of the School Handbook;

(b)   strive to enhance the community spirit of our school 'family';

(c)   be in school promptly and attend lessons on time with the correct books and equipment;

(d)   be conscientious regarding school work; complete assignments on time; implement teachers' instructions; be appropriate in speech; and never disturb the learning of others;

(e)   respect teachers, peers and all school staff;

(f)   respect school property and the property of others using the school;

(g)   respect our neighbors and other members of the local community, and keep off their property;

(h)   respect road safety provisions, whether as pedestrian, driver or passenger;

(i)   observe the Dress Code, and dress neatly, sensibly and appropriately for school and all school occasions; and

(j)   seek staff assistance, if necessary, to resolve conflicts peacefully, and not get into fights."

12.3.2   Attendance

A student's first duty is to be in school, in class, on time, for all scheduled lessons and activities, properly equipped and ready to be "assiduous in pursuit of their studies". A parent's first duty is to ensure that their child is in proper attendance at school. The school cannot educate a student who is not in class.

Exceptions are for medical reasons, certified if necessary with a note from a medical practitioner; and other reasons provided by law, or as authorized by the school, in advance.

Sanctions must ultimately include refusal to re-register a student whose attendance record has been consistently unsatisfactory. The School handbook must have a clear Attendance policy, including a policy for absences for tests and exams, and it must be enforced. Where a student does not arrive at school, and the school has not been notified of the reason for absence, a call must be made to a parent. Some School Administration computer programs will call parents automatically with a prerecorded message once an absence has been recorded.

12.3.3   Safety and security

A student who puts him/herself or other students or staff in danger by disregarding any security or safety provision may expect expulsion, as does a student who deliberately causes a false security alarm.

12.3.4   Honesty and integrity

It is a basic expectation of all students that they conduct themselves with honesty and integrity at all times, and in a way that enhances the reputation of the school.

12.3.5   Classroom behavior; respect for the school and staff

No instance of impoliteness to any member of staff (whether the Principal or the custodian) should be allowed to go without consequence. This starts at the basic level – not pushing in front of a staff member (or other adult) in the hallways. Failure to observe a direct instruction by a staff member is a very serious offense. Every student is expected to contribute towards maintaining a positive learning atmosphere in the classroom (and in the school generally). Anything that disturbs the learning of others is a major issue.

12.3.6   Drugs

Drug use, possession, possession of drug-associated paraphernalia, trafficking in school, in the vicinity of the school, or during any school-sponsored activity should be reason to cause the student to leave the school[221]. The students cannot be left in any doubt about school policy.

Drugs are, unfortunately, endemic in our society. There is no school in the world – whatever its level, affiliation or character - that is free of drugs, or where the students do not have access to drugs if they wish. A principal who claims otherwise is either deliberately not telling the truth, or is unaware of reality. All the school can do is make it very, very clear that if students are caught with drugs or drug-related equipment or materials in school they will be required to leave. If you are consistent, the message will get through.

The School Handbook should also make it clear that the school will involve the local police if necessary. This has to be considered very carefully, but if you find hard drugs in school, or evidence of trafficking, you should carefully check the legal as well as the moral duty. From time to time, the Principal should speak to local police and other local professionals (social workers, pediatricians, youth Counselors, rabbis, youth workers) and ask them what they are hearing about the school. Private schools, with the perception that that there are lots of 'rich kids' to be found, will inevitably attract attention from traffickers. If drug dealing is tolerated in or in the vicinity of the school, criminal elements will very soon establish their presence.

The school cannot control what happens out of school, at home, over weekends or during vacations. Those are areas of parental responsibility.

The Principal will hear accusations about students. Whether these come from parents or from other students, they must be substantiated or ignored. A parent who tells you that "everyone knows" that a particular student deals drugs is retailing hearsay. Does the parent know any student who has bought drugs from this student? Is there a substantiated incident where someone has actually witnessed a drug transaction taking place? A careful and responsible investigation must take place.

It is also necessary to make sure that staff are given guidance on how to recognize symptoms of drug use among students. Parents should be advised on how to recognize danger signs that may indicate that their child is involved with drugs – the information is easily available. It is a good idea to write to parents once a year to remind them of this and other information about the common dangers to adolescents. The month of May, before Graduation and before the summer, with its attendant opportunities and temptations, is a good time …

---

[221] I have only once acted differently. A new, naïve Grade 9 student, in the first weeks of the school year, was persuaded by an older student to buy a 'joint', on the grounds that if he refused, he would be regarded as a 'wimp'. The transaction was noticed by a teacher, who properly reported it. I could not bring myself to expel the young student two weeks after he started High school, and who had clearly been terrified by the incident. I was totally unsympathetic to the G11 trafficker, who left the school immediately. An anonymous website then appeared, threatening the G9 student by name with violence and death.

Finally, the alert Principal will also want to ensure that school staff are neither involved in drugs in any way, nor are they covering up knowledge about drugs in the school or in the school community. The same applies to parents. At the time of writing, many parents of high-school age students are themselves children of the drug age, and either have a tolerance of drug use – especially 'soft' drugs – or are themselves recreational users. As in other areas, parents who discover that their children are involved in hard drugs may be reluctant to tell the school. A Board member of a certain school once told me that a child of his (at that time already a few years out of school) had been treated for cocaine addiction while a student at school. The school did not ever know. The student's supplies had been obtained at school. The consequences of the Board member leaving the school in ignorance of a cocaine trafficker within the school are unknown.

12.3.7   Alcohol

Alcohol is a growing problem in the Jewish community. Some synagogues are sources of alcohol access for young people, especially at Purim and Simchat Torah. Synagogues that have so-called 'Kiddush Clubs' are modeling exactly the wrong behavior for young people – both in regard to alcohol, and in their attitude to the synagogue.

Similar stringencies apply to alcohol as apply to drugs; and similar complexities of parental behavior may be observed. In a variety of ways, alcohol can be life-threatening to the drinker and to others.

- It has to be absolutely clear to teachers who invite students to their homes on Shabbat and *chagim* that they must not serve alcohol in any form, or in any quantity. For Kiddush, grape juice should be used.

12.3.8   Sex

The religious orientation of the school will very largely determine the policy regarding personal and inter-personal behavior. In general, every school will wish to impart a sense of appropriate behavior that is respectful of others, treats inter-personal relationships with seriousness and responsibility, and which seeks to relate decision-making in these areas to Jewish tradition. The rules will follow from the philosophy.

Anyone who manages to stop sexual chemistry between teenage boys and girls will earn their place in history. There is a different dimension of problem in a co-ed school. It is best to phrase your rules in terms of expectations:

> *Students are expected to conduct themselves at all times in a manner appropriate to the ethos of the school, and the relevant Jewish traditions regarding interpersonal relationships. Physical contact between students is not permitted in school or in the vicinity of the school, or on any school-sponsored activity.*

Again, the school cannot control or take responsibility for the behavior of students outside school. Inside school, firmness and discretion are good qualities in this area where the first observed offense is fleeting and not offensive to any non-consensual third party. However, physical contact cannot be permitted. No offensive behavior of any sort can be tolerated, and sometimes consequences may include counseling at different levels.

Whether in single-sex or co-ed schools, when dealing with teenagers who are not always in control of their emotions and occasionally tormented by them, great caution is needed in dealing with behavior that has sexual overtones or undertones. Never underestimate the depth or the power of those emotions, especially when they are veering out of control. Anything is possible.

A different issue is the possession (or digital accessing) of offensive material, which should be treated with seriousness. The universal possession of cell-phone cameras and other digital media devices increase the need to be careful (SEE SECTION 12.3.12). Sexual problems that involve harassment or bullying also have to be dealt with firmly. The students cannot be left in any doubt about the school's policy. Every student has a right to attend school without being teased or harassed in any way because of sexual or gender issues.

- Sexual contact or relationships of any sort between students and staff are absolutely forbidden, constitute grave breaches of professional conduct, and are illegal. They can involve the teacher in criminal charges, and in some circumstances may make the school vulnerable to legal action. SEE SECTION 10.2.4.

- See also SECTION 8.6 Gay and gender issues

12.3.9   Bullying and harassment – verbal and electronic

Cannot be tolerated under any circumstances. Period.

12.3.10   Media

Students are expected to maintain the good name of the school and not communicate or publish anything, in any print or electronic media that brings the name of its students or staff into disrepute; is offensive; or is an invasion of privacy[222]. A student may not use the name or logo of the school in any publication or communication without permission of Administration.

12.3.11   Computer abuse and harassment

Every school must ensure that it has clear disciplinary guidelines regarding computer use, and the use of digital devices. They should be part of the 'School Handbook'. Policies are widely available, and should include policies regarding:

---

[222] If a student publishes something on a website about the kid who lives next door, but who does not attend your school, it is not normally a school disciplinary offense (but the school should definitely address the issue). If they publish something about another school student, or teacher, or the person who owns the store opposite the school – it is.

- Material to be accessed at school

- Intellectual property

- Appropriate use of school computers and networks (may only be used for school purposes)

- Respectful uses of digital communications with other members of the school community – in or out of school

- Digital use of the school name or logo

- Privacy issues of all sorts, including the publication of names, email addresses, and images

- Pseudonymous or anonymous messages or online publications

- Any type of 'cyber-bullying' or harassment

- Use of 'social networking' sites and similar programs. The school Code should include a provision that requires the student to give the school Administration access to any of their personal websites (or equivalents) if required.

The school should make it clear that there are no rights of privacy regarding work stored on school computers or school networks, and the software should be set up accordingly.

12.3.12   Cell phones, cameras, PDA's, Blackberries, iPhones, MP3's and similar

From the TanenbaumCHAT School Handbook (2009-10):

"The imaging, recording and transmission capabilities of digital equipment is constantly changing and developing.

For this reason cell phones, iPods, Blackberries, PDAs, cameras or similar equipment may not be used in or near school changing rooms, washrooms, exercise rooms, gyms, or any other location or situation where students or staff have a reasonable expectation of privacy. Students may not make any recordings – visual or audio – in class without the knowledge and permission of the teacher.

Laptops and other devices must always be used appropriately in class and in the school environment.

No digital device of any description is allowed into an examination room – they must be left outside. Possession of such a device in an exam room may jeopardize the exam mark. For routine classroom tests, phones etc. must be switched off and be securely out of sight – and preferably should not be in the room at all. The use of calculators must follow instructions.

In addition to the applicable provisions of this School Handbook, students are warned that there may be entirely separate legal consequences for inappropriate recording or transmission of digital images or other information.

Use of digital or other media to harass others connected with the school, including but not limited to any of the actions described above will be regarded as a very serious breach of discipline.

• Cell phones and similar devices may not be used in any way that interferes with lessons or other school activity.

Cell phones must be switched off and out of sight during class and other school events (assemblies etc). If they are used in a lesson – in any function, including text messaging – they may be confiscated.

A student out of class during a lesson who is using a cell phone (or similar device) may expect disciplinary consequences."

12.4 Can the school impose discipline for events that happen out of school hours?

A school has to think about the areas of student life over which it wishes to claim authority – and hence responsibility. Generally, a school will legitimately claim spatial and temporal responsibility over students:

- On school premises at any time

- During the school day, or any other time that a student is bound to attend school

- In the immediate vicinity of the school

- At any event organized or otherwise under the auspices of the school

- At any time that a student is representing the school, or is identified as a member of the school

In the Handbook the school may put students on notice that it has expectations regarding their good conduct in other settings as well (a local Shopping Mall, local synagogues, or other places where they are seen as part of the school 'community').

Schools where there is a uniform may specify that a student is regarded as representing the school at any time that they are wearing school uniform. The further afield you claim authority[223], the further afield you have responsibility.

The school has authority in any incident that arises between students and other members of the school community – students, teachers or parents, where the common connection is obviously the school. Common sense needs to be applied. It is clearly the school's concern if a student places a harassing or abusive phone call to another teacher or student at the school. If, in the middle of summer, on vacation at some remote location, a student gets into an argument with another student (or parent) who happens to be in the same place – the school should not get involved.

More difficult is where a group of students from the school get into trouble on a weekend. Their parents (or even the police) punish them. The community knows that they are all students at your school, and wants to know what "the school" is going to do. In these cases, meeting with the students as a group or individually with the students and their parents and discussing what happened, expressing the school's disappointment and hoping that they will understand that the school expects excellent behavior from them from now on is probably the fairest thing to do. If the nature of the incident – e.g. alcohol consumption – shows a widespread problem within a particular grade, the school might arrange some Guidance sessions.

The school cannot be responsible for what happens when students are out of your jurisdiction, and where what happened has nothing to do with the school or its activities. You should not inflict double punishments. The only exceptions to this might be where violence has occurred and two students cannot remain in the same school. You should take appropriate advice, but in many jurisdictions a school may act on 'reasonable grounds', especially where student safety is concerned, and you may ask parents to withdraw the aggressive child without waiting for conviction or trial.

Different again might be case where a student is arrested for drug-dealing, say during school vacations and away from the school. (If it is in school, or within the jurisdiction of the school, then there is no question of the school's right to impose consequences.) Take advice; but the school may well reach the conclusion that it has no grounds for action. Again, a talk with the student is probably appropriate.

- Whatever the circumstances, the clearer the delineation of boundaries in your School Handbook, the easier it will be to handle problems when they arise.

---

[223] School authority over student conduct outside school may be locally legislated. The Ontario 'Bill 212' is an example.

12.4.1   Parties

A frequent 'out of school issue' is weekend parties that go out of control. The school cannot control parties in private homes, nor can it take responsibility for them. The publicity surrounding horrendous stories of parties that 'go wrong' (let alone the instances that escape publicity...) is now so established that only foolish parents would allow their son/daughter to have an unsupervised party. There is an ongoing supply of foolish (alternatively, naïve) parents.

The school has to be clear that the responsibility for all that happens in private homes (or bar/bat mitzvah parties, or private Grad trips or parties) is squarely on the shoulders of parents. From time to time (in the same annual letter than warns about safety, drugs and alcohol), the school should remind parents of sensible advice:

> ***Never allow your sons or daughters to have an unsupervised party.*** *If a party is going on, the adult supervision should be present in or near the "action", and not absent in some other part of the house. Make clear to your children the standards of behavior that you expect. Call the police immediately if 'uninvited guests' suddenly appear.*
>
> *If your children are invited to a party or event at someone else's house – at any time during the year -* ***call the host parents beforehand*** *and satisfy yourself about the supervision and safety. Ask if adults will be present, and ask whether alcohol will be served. If you are not satisfied with the answers – don't allow your child to attend. (You may be unpopular with your child, but you will have a better sense of their safety, and you also will have sent a message to the community.)*
>
> *If you are going out-of-town, do not leave teenagers at home by themselves. Another fully responsible adult must be in the house. If your children are staying elsewhere while you are out-of-town, and they have access to your house, make it clear to them that they cannot and must not invite others into the house in your absence.*

If a group of your students are involved at an 'incident' at a party, Administration should think carefully about the school's response, and the limits of the school's involvement. A good plan is to ask some of the parents involved to a closed meeting to discuss with Administration and Guidance whether the school should react, and how it should react. Make it clear that the school's function here can only be educational and counseling – not disciplinary.

12.5 Well-known issues of contention

SEE ALSO - SECTION 8 – MANAGING TENSIONS BETWEEN 'GENERAL' AND 'JEWISH' for an extensive discussion of contentious issues in that sphere, including SECTION 8.5.4

The following issues are not all disciplinary. Some are; others are borderline, and may occasionally become disciplinary. They are all, however, "areas of contention".

In all of the following issues – especially 'Dress Code' and 'Hair' – make it clear in the School Handbook that the Administration reserves the right, at its complete discretion, to decide what may be deemed appropriate and what not. Do not allow the school to be drawn into arguments over a required or superfluous inch of any description, or what is an acceptable or unacceptable shade of green. Reserve the right of decision. Period.

Whatever the policies – make sure they are evenly and consistently applied. If the students sense or see that the school is unwilling or incapable of enforcing the School Code – they will disregard it.

12.5.1 Uniform / dress code

There is no greater ongoing source of contention in schools than uniform/dress code, and nothing harder to enforce.

There are excellent arguments for and against uniforms. You will develop local policy. Parents may love uniforms, but students (usually) dislike them. Having taught (and been an Administrator and Principal) in schools that have, variously, had ultra-strict uniform rules and, at the other extreme, almost meaningless 'dress codes', my conclusions (at the time of writing!) may be summarized as follows:

- It makes little difference to the quality of the school whether there is uniform or not. The genuine quality of the school depends on other things entirely.

- Dress should be neat, clean and tidy, and appropriate for a school environment. The school has every right to set reasonable limits.

- 'Traditional' school uniforms, on the British model, are now inappropriate for today's teenagers. They were designed for teenagers of a different age, and, more importantly, teenagers of a different size and shape, before modern nutrition and when the age of puberty was perhaps fourteen or fifteen (at which time most children left school).

- If the school 'community' insists on uniform, the best compromise would probably be a 'smart casual' uniform of modern comfortable clothing, incorporating plenty of choice.

Good luck!

12.5.2　Hair

One veteran Principal for whom I once worked, actually a very conservative individual, advised me "Don't make a fuss about hair". It was sound advice. If that is the way that a teenager wants to express rebellion or individuality – on the scale of possibilities it is relatively harmless.

Having said that – hair must be clean, and it must be neat. There may be situations (Phys Ed, Science, Art) where for safety reasons you require boys and girls (the rules should be the same for both) to tie or restrain their hair. Length should be reasonable in the context of contemporary fashion. If it is fashionable for boys to wear hair at shoulder length – that may be allowed, if you decide to do so. To wear it at waist-length – or nearly so – may be more problematic, but the student will have few imitators, and it is not clear who he is harming. Girls who wish to wear 'freaky' hair are in the same category. The question of the "image of the school" is a red herring – you are running the school for the benefit of the students. The student has some deep reason why s/he wants to make this demonstration. Leave him in peace.

Hair coloring – male or female – is an equally contentious issue. Boys and girls in the school may be allowed to color their hair, but most schools will insist that the color be reasonably subdued[224]. The school sets out a code of appearance.

> *You are welcome to color your hair however you like during vacations, but in school it has to be appropriate – just as we ask students to wear particular types of clothing. When do you think you can arrange for your hair color to be muted somewhat?*

One of the best Talmud students I have seen in recent years was a girl with (soft) blue streaks in her hair, who confounded a visiting Israeli Haredi Member of Knesset by asking a question on Tosefot in fluent Ivrit in the class he was observing. I once asked a student who turned up after the Summer vacation with brilliant aquamarine hair to grow it out. He was furious – not because I asked him to grow it out, but because he had hoped for a confrontation. "Why won't you expel me?" he protested. In the event it took a few weeks to grow it out, and he found other ways to make his mark. Some schools, however, will carefully restrict hair style.

---

[224] As I write this, I am not sure why it is a *'klal* – a universal rule'. Clearly, in some schools the school ethos will be much more prescriptive, and all aspects of appearance will be closely regulated. But in every school?

12.5.3   Piercings, tattoos etc

- Begin by scheduling a unit in your Rabbinics / Traditions syllabus that looks at piercings and tattoos in the light of Jewish tradition.

It should be noted that, according to most understandings, in Biblical times, men and women wore nose rings. Schools will formulate their own policy regarding piercings, which will range across the entire spectrum from completely forbidding piercings of any type to (probably limited) tolerance.

In schools there are good reasons to strictly control piercings on safety grounds alone. Schools are crowded environments; school bags are swung around; students play in the Phys Ed / sports program, and are physically active in drama – all of which are potentially dangerous to students with facial or other piercings. Other piercings (tongue, lip etc) are medically problematic as well, and there are certainly sources in Jewish tradition that can be brought to any discussion of the subject.

On safety grounds, I would not allow any facial piercings except limited ear piercings (simple earrings or 'sleepers') and – perhaps – the very tiny nostril piercings ('nose studs') that are less prominent and less noticeable. In a large school, they are also easy to overlook, and it is always a problem when you discipline a student who then tells you that she has been wearing nose studs for a year, and no teacher has noticed or objected.

Tattoos are directly contrary to Jewish tradition. If they are 'fake' tattoos, they can be washed off, and if the student wants to reapply them over the weekends – that is their business. Real tattoos are a much greater problem – by the time you discover them they are almost impossible to eradicate, except by medical/surgical means. It is reasonable to insist that they are covered entirely in school. If that is impossible (they are on hands or wrists etc) – you may wish to call in parents and ask for an assurance that the tattoos will be removed at some time in the future. You can try and insist that a student wears gloves, or uses a band-aid to cover the tattoo in school.

12.5.4   Grade 12 and Graduation – behavior

- For a discussion of the ceremony: See SECTION 11.5.2

Grade 12 can be difficult. Mentally, students are already halfway out of school and on to their next stage of life. If students misbehave towards the end of the year, it is difficult to give disciplinary consequences. Sanctions available include putting students on probation for participation in the Grad trip; withdrawing permission for a student to participate in the Grad banquet (if you have one – but what do you do if they turn up?), and, for really serious offenses, barring them from the Graduation ceremony itself. Students who are suspended or commit other serious disciplinary infractions in Grade 12 may be deemed ineligible for prizes and special awards at the end of the year. If you want to have such policies, make sure they are in your School handbook.

However, be warned that these are all highly contentious actions, not to be lightly imposed. Parents and students sometimes feel that Grade 12 students have a 'right' to do whatever they want at Graduation, and a 'right' to attend all of the ceremonies and celebrations.

A Graduation class sometimes feels the need to make a statement and leave their mark on the collective school memory. These can positive and even impressive – they can decide to mount some special fundraising or social service project; they can be amusing/annoying (student pranks); sometimes they can be ill-advised and dangerous.

First principle is avoidance:

- Plan the Graduation year and its events well in advance with staff, parents and student council

- In the plans, allow for a variety of events to celebrate, to have some fun, and to allow students and parents to mark the students' Graduation appropriately and with dignity. Try and cover a range of emotional and formal/informal bases. Make sure that all Grad events are well supervised, with a responsible and strong staff presence.

- Publicize the schedule of events well in advance; the feeling that the students have to fill a vacuum is a fertile ground for trouble

The actual Graduation Ceremony is an important 'feel-good' occasion for your school community. Make sure that it is impressive, well-organized, well-presented, and that the students themselves feel proud to take part

Speak to your student leaders and make it clear that the school recognizes that every Graduating class wants, and deserves, some fun as part of the graduation 'process'. That does not absolve them of responsibility. The odd prank (dancing through the halls etc) is understandable. ANYTHING that is dangerous[225], even risky, or irresponsible in any way is not, and the school will take whatever action it needs to ensure the safety of all students (and others), and to protect property. If the 'prank' involves cars and driving, the school's attitude should be clear – the police will be called if there is dangerous driving.

In addition to advice about drugs SECTION 12.3.6 and parties SECTION 12.4.1 the annual pre-summer letter to parents should address Graduation issues, and suggest that parents should be proactive in ensuring that they know about their childrens' plans

---

[225] At a previous school, I once expelled four students on the last day of the year (their last day at the school) for organizing and leading a dangerous, violent, illegal and malicious Graduation "prank".

for the evening of the Grad Banquet/Prom. In particular, they should carefully control the use of cars, and be very careful about accessibility and use of alcohol.

> *The only year-end events under school supervision are the Grad Banquet/Dance, at the announced times and venues for each campus. The school has neither control, supervision nor responsibility for events before the Banquet, at private houses or elsewhere, nor for further events and celebrations after the "official" Banquet and Dance is finished, nor for any events involving other grades.*

> *Parents hosting 'pre-Banquet' parties are strongly advised and requested by the school not to serve any alcoholic drinks. Students who arrive at the Grad Banquet under the influence of alcohol or other substances will be refused admittance, and their parents will be called.*

> *Every parent must inform themselves of their son's / daughter's plans for that evening, and satisfy themselves that he/she is doing nothing that will endanger his/her personal safety, or the safety of others, and that he/she will be acting in a responsible manner.*

Decide your policy well in advance regarding who can attend the Grad Banquet and dance following. Can your students bring guests? Do they have to be approved[226] in advance? May guests be non-Jewish? *('Students may invite guests from the local Jewish community')* May they be same-sex?

12.5.5 Cars

The School Handbook should give rules and guidelines about the student use of cars. If the school provides student parking, annually issue numbered school identity window stickers, and keep records of which cars are being brought to school. Students should show proof of valid insurance. A note that details local law regarding insurance and liability for passengers should be included in the School Handbook. Ascertain liability for a student who transports other students (or even staff) to and from school or school events, and make sure that arrangements conform to the law. Establish rules regarding students driving themselves (and others) to and from field trips and other grade or class events. In general, don't allow it –

> *The bus will leave from, and return to, school, and all students travel on it under staff supervision.*

Make it clear that the school will inform police without hesitation of dangerous driving observed in the vicinity of the school, and do not hesitate to inform parents if students are seen speeding, driving dangerously or overloading their cars. Students should not be allowed to 'hang out' in cars during the school day.

---

[226] I once refused a student permission to have as her guest a former student at the school who had been involved in drug dealing, including evidence that he had been selling drugs in the vicinity of the school after he left.

12.5.6   Right of search / right of privacy / lockers, bags etc.

In certain circumstances, normally during investigation of serious disciplinary offenses, school Administration may want to search the lockers, school bags, other property and in exceptional cases even the person of students.

There are several considerations:

- Balancing the 'duty of the school to maintain order' and the civil rights of the student

- Establishing "that there are reasonable grounds for suspecting that the search will turn up evidence that the student has violated or is violating either the law or the rules of school."

- Taking care that any search must be 'reasonable in scope' related to the suspicion.

- However - rights of search and rights of privacy are highly sensitive areas of law. A school should NEVER undertake a search of ANY description except in consultation with the school's legal adviser, or unless the Principal is fully satisfied that s/he knows the applicable law in the relevant jurisdiction -- not 'thinks' that they know it, but really knows it.

In most places, public school boards have formulated reasonably well-established procedures for conducting searches, and it is likely that the instructions given by the school's lawyer will echo them. Instructions given must be followed meticulously, and if for any reason it is not possible to carry out the exact instructions – don't carry out the search. Mistakes may lead to serious legal complications, including possible charges of assault against the adults implementing the search.

A school should give appropriately drafted notice in the School Handbook that under all circumstances it retains ownership and complete rights of access to school lockers and desks, and other fixtures and fittings on school property. Easily accessible texts on the internet will give formulations that extend the reserved right of search to school bags and other student possessions. This may vary from jurisdiction to jurisdiction, and should be carefully vetted by your school lawyer. There may be differences between the law applying to public schools, and the law applying to private schools, where the relationship between students, parents and the school is contractual. Staff must be made aware that that all searches may only be done under the supervision of Administration.

Similar considerations apply to the expectation (or otherwise) of privacy. The school should take advice on how to protect its right of access to student digital files that may be held on school computers (or other equipment), or to images or recordings of the school and its personnel.

12.6 Consequences

Consequences should be:

- Clear

- Consistent

- Swiftly administered

- Reasonable

- Fair

- Supervised

- Documented

A school should never give consequences that:

- Mandate the student to undertake religious practices or ritual of any sort (making Jewish practice part of your disciplinary process is a disastrous route)

- Are by their nature unreasonable, impractical or impossible

- Vary greatly between comparable incidents

- Are capricious and personal

The consequences for disciplinary infractions consist of a fairly well established list. For most offenses, the school may impose some or a combination of processes, including but not limited to:

- Detentions

- Loss of privilege (a student may not participate in general or particular activities for a set period of time)

- Tasks (the student must undertake some task that, preferably, relates to the offense)

- Parental interview

- Ongoing duty to report to an Administrator as a 'Weekly report', 'Daily report' or 'Lesson report' – the student has a sheet which has to be 'signed off' by every teacher at the end of each week, day or lesson, checking behavior, attitude etc., and brought to an Administrator at appropriate intervals.

- Probation

Serious offenses may involve suspension or expulsion.

12.7 Suspension and expulsion

12.7.1   Suspension

On occasion every school will have to exclude students from school for varying periods of time.   On rare occasions, the school will reach the conclusion that a student's behavior has been such that they should be required to leave the school. The behavior that will cause those consequences will be described in the School handbook.

Suspension from school usually varies from one day[227] (a relatively serious punishment, accompanied by a letter in the school file that stays there for twelve months) to a week.   Some public school districts provide for suspensions of up to twenty school days (i.e. one calendar month).   In Jewish schools, which are highly academic and have heavy workloads, suspension for longer than a week (five school days) may cause the student problems in catching up work missed, and may be counter-productive.

A student suspended for a week would be returning on strict probation, and a further breach of school rules might "cause his/her status in the school to come under review" – meaning, probably, that the school would not re-register that student for the next school year.   In extreme cases, the student might return on probation, with a signed undertaking from the parents that they accept the right of the school to require them to withdraw the student at any time if there are further breaches of discipline.   A student on suspension may not be in the vicinity of the school, may not take part in any school activity, on or off the premises, and may not discuss his/her offense with other students.

Where the suspension is for two or more days, arrangements should be made for work to be set for the student to complete at home.   Assignments may be set in addition to class work.

Students returning from suspension – even for a day – should come with their parents for a reentry interview before returning to the classroom.

12.7.2   Expulsion

Far more serious is the contemplation of expulsion.   This can be traumatic for the student and for the family – especially where there is no other Jewish school for the

---

[227] A one-day suspension can even be an 'in-school suspension' – working under supervision in a school office. This is useful when parents claim that if given a day's suspension the student will treat it as a vacation.

student to attend. It may have life-changing long-term consequences. Where it seems possible that an investigation will result in expulsion, the Principal has to be meticulous regarding fair process – as described above. It used to be the case that a private school could expel a student on the spot, almost at the whim of the Principal. Now, expulsions from private schools are attracting attention from the courts in different jurisdictions. A number of factors seem to be figuring in the legal discussions:

- Increasing regulation of public schools' disciplinary process is, inevitably, 'spilling over' to the courts' interest in private schools

- The contractual relationship between parents/students and private schools is increasingly being seen in the light of broad 'consumer rights' precedents applying to any citizen purchasing goods or services

- Expulsion/exclusion from any institution is seen as a civil rights issue

- Higher standards are being demanded of institutional/corporate behavior in all contexts

It would be a mistake to imagine that private schools are immune or exempt from these concerns. A school may no longer rely on the defense that it is a 'religious institution' and therefore has freedom to conduct its affairs according to its self-understanding of its cultural or religious standards.

Perhaps more important than this, however, are the moral and religious principles of *yosher* – ethical behavior. An educational institution, especially a Jewish school, must behave and be seen to behave with scrupulous fairness to its students, parents and staff. That does not mean that a school cannot apply discipline, and, regrettably, there will be occasions when a school has to expel students. But it must be done with fair process and with *mentschlichkeit*. Every Principal who has to expel a student should lose some sleep over the decision.

The process leading to possible expulsion should be determined by school policy, drawn up in consultation with local lawyers, approved by the School Board, and should be transparent and understandable to parents[228]. It is highly desirable that it be formalized as a school policy document available to parents on request. While it may not be necessary to incorporate the entire document in the School handbook, the Handbook should certainly include a statement that:

---

[228] The Toronto Jewish School system, through its 'Association of Principals of Jewish Schools', devised a voluntary policy of common process for dealing with suspension and expulsion. It was published in 2001, and although subsequently overtaken by new legislation ('Bill 212'), as far as I know, this was the first and only similar common policy subscribed to by a majority of Jewish schools in one city.

> *In the administration of suspensions and expulsions, [School] will follow the guidelines laid down in "Procedures for Suspension and Expulsion from [School]" – a policy document approved by our Board in ..... Copies of these procedures are available from the School Office.*

The document will clearly point out that the process may vary according to specific circumstances.

In outline, such a policy may specify:

- A guarantee that the school will directly inform parents of any serious disciplinary incident

- Assurances regarding fair process

- Information regarding which Administrators are empowered to administer suspensions or expulsions

- Specification of a parent's right to voluntarily withdraw a child from the school

- Information regarding right of appeal, and, where applicable, the makeup of an Appeal Tribunal

- Advice as to how the suspension/expulsion will be communicated to parents

- Procedure for readmitting a student to school at the end of a suspension.

- Policy regarding possible subsequent readmittance to the school of a student who has been expelled.

However, the reality is that in most cases real expulsion will not take place. Where a student faces expulsion, it is normally only in cases involving a most serious offense, and the culpability of the student has been established beyond reasonable doubt. In those circumstances, the parents may opt to withdraw their child from the school, effective immediately. This prevents an expulsion appearing on the student's school record. The school may point this out to parents.

> *Mr. and Mrs. X – following the incident at the end of last week, the school has carried out a thorough investigation. I am afraid that the facts of the case cannot be in reasonable doubt, and David has admitted, in writing, that he was in possession of an illegal substance in school. In addition, when Administration searched his locker, we found three cell phones, two of which had been reported as stolen by other students. David could not account for their presence in his locker. The school Handbook states clearly that a student found in possession of illegal substances in school will be required to leave. I have to advise you that the school will now be instituting process that may result in David's formal expulsion from the school. While these are under*

way, David will be suspended from school, pending resolution. This sheet explains to you the process that may now be initiated, including your right of appeal. You may wish to take legal advice.

If David is expelled from the school, that fact would be on his school record, and the school may be obliged to disclose it if asked at any time in the future by a University, College, Israel program or even by a future employer.

However, you may wish to consider voluntarily withdrawing David from [school], effective immediately. If you do so, no further action can be taken, and the school will not pass on reference to this incident to any third party. Would you like a few minutes to consider that?

Should the parents decide to take that route (which happens in most cases), prepare a short letter of withdrawal for their signature. The only announcement that the school makes to staff is that "David X is no longer a student at the school, effective [date]".

This would be separate entirely from any possible police involvement, which would again depend on the circumstances of the case. Other parents may have independently made reports to the police over which you have no control. If the circumstances are such that the school has to inform the police (or any other statutory body) of the incident, you must clearly tell the parents that you are doing so.

Whatever the circumstances – even if they are extreme – discreetly arrange for the student to have some limited advice and help from Guidance or Administration in arranging an alternative school to attend.

12.7.3 "Zero tolerance"

By declaring 'Zero tolerance' to any phenomenon or behavior, the school is setting itself an extremely high and inflexible standard. Be extremely cautious in your use of this phrase, and consider deleting it from your vocabulary altogether.

13 MANAGING PARENTS

13.1 Parents as partners

Parents are a crucial constituency. Unless they are true 'partners', both with the school and with their children, the joint educational enterprise will be more difficult, and occasionally impossible.

In most cases they are the decision-makers about whether or not to register (or re-register) a student at the school. Parent perception of how they are related to by the school can be a decisive factor in recruitment and retention.

Apart from this somewhat base calculation, the parents are …. well, they are the parents of the students! The Principal's office can be the scene of extremely tense and deep parent-child interactions. We discuss below how the Principal may deal with some of the more common Principal-Parent issues; and a little further on, in SECTION 13.5 offer some guidelines about how to deal with emotionally fraught parent-child conversations.

The school will be a much more effective institution if it has the parents 'on side'. If students come to school knowing that their parents are proud of the school and strongly support the professionalism and judgment of the faculty, the student's attitude in the class is going to be very different than if the student arrives having heard a car-pool parent dismiss the school and its teachers as

> *'not knowing how to run a school'* … *'they couldn't run my business for a day' or 'I'll sort them out'* …….

Equally, your teachers will feel very differently if teaching at the school is perceived by parents and in the community as a high-status professional position.

Whichever way – the parent body are partners, not adversaries, and, like all partnerships, deserve an investment of time to make the relationship work.

Dealing with parents needs a range of flexible skills, and is often unpredictable[229]. The one thing to always remember when dealing with parents is that the common purpose between the school and the parents is the interest and welfare of their child:

> *Mr. and Mrs. X, the purpose of this meeting is so that the school may work with you as partners to reach the best possible arrangement for your child. Could we agree to concentrate on that and leave aside other issues?*

Parents are advocates for their children, and so they should be. There is something wrong when a parent does not want the very best for their child. Most parents are reasonable and rational (and for that reason 'most parents' do not get the space they deserve in this book!). A minority of parents are difficult to deal with; a very small percentage of parents may appear to be consistently irrational in their dealings with the school.

The first necessities of building a relationship with the parent body (for the Principal and Administrators as individuals, and for the school as an institution) are *communication* and *accessibility*.

Many, many problems are avoidable or are soluble by effective communication. Whatever your communications strategy SEE SECTION 4.8, communicate clearly and

---

[229] Dealing with students is often unpredictable as well, but, after all, they are teenagers and unpredictability is part of the package. Parents are adults, and unpredictability therefore can surprise….

often with your parents. If the Principal cannot write clearly or communicate effectively, get letters and circulars written or revised by someone who can.

The same applies to accessibility. The school must be reasonably accessible to parents. That does not mean that parents have the right to instant attention on every matter, large or small. It certainly does not mean that parents have the right to infringe on the any faculty member's right to privacy. At home, in the supermarket or synagogue, the line is:

> *I'd be very happy to discuss that with you. Please could you call me at school? I'll be in the office at 8:30 tomorrow / Monday morning.*

But there must be clear, user-friendly channels for parents to reach the right person in the school. It begins with the person who answers the phone (or the clarity of the school's answering system), continues with how long it takes for phone messages to be returned, and includes how parents are received when they have meetings or conversations with staff.

The belief that if there is a problem, a question or an issue, a parent can find a quick, friendly, sympathetic and effective answer at the school is an immensely calming influence on the parent body.

If getting an answer to every question is a struggle, every approach to the school will find the parent gearing up for a fight.

Give parents the facts, and engage them as responsible partners in the education of their children. The more information the parents have, the more they should understand the school, including the school's limitations and the school's expectations of parents. Parents have a right to expect information from the school[230]; but the school has a legitimate expectation that parents will support the authority of the teachers and Administration, and the reasonable actions of the school, including disciplinary actions.

- The first duty of a parent is to make sure that their children attend school punctually and regularly. If the child is not in school – the school cannot even begin to fulfil its duty of education.

---

[230] Not, however, an absolute right – students also have rights to privacy, and the school has a right to conduct its professional affairs in private. A parent does not have a right to know the content of conversations or process between the school and its staff.

13.2 Parents and the Board of Directors

Parents who are on the Board of Directors of the school[231] must clearly separate their rights and responsibilities as parents from their responsibilities as members of the Board. They may not 'pull rank' with teachers or Administration on any matter connected with their own child. A Board member who starts a conversation with a teacher by saying *"I'm a member of the Board..."* should receive a tactful, courteous phone call from the Principal pointing out that in their dealings with staff regarding their own children, they are parents, and not Board members. Similar protocols apply to Board members who try and use staff to ferret out information about the school (*"Morry, so what happened at the staff meeting last week?"*)

If any individual persists, then the Principal may eventually ask the Board Chair/School President to intervene and remind the individual concerned of Governance protocol, hopefully as explained at the first meeting of the Board in every school year.

Some parents with 'issues' will call members of the Board, hoping that the intervention of a Board member will immediately get their problem solved. The names of Board members who are always ready to receive such calls[232] become well known.

A Board member receiving a call of concern from a parent should neither accept nor reject the parent's version of events, but, without getting involved or expressing an opinion, should refer them directly to school Administration, so that they may be dealt with in a properly professional manner. That should be followed up by a discreet call to the Principal to *"expect a call from Mr. X..."*. Just as a Principal must support the teachers, regardless of what may be said behind closed doors, the Board must support Administration. Legitimate concern for what may have happened to a student or parent must be tempered with confidence in the Administration to investigate and deal with problems, and with a respect for process.

A Board member may not - under any circumstances - call a teacher directly to take up a parental complaint or concern. Teachers receiving such calls should politely refer them to the Principal. It is the Administration's job to supervise teachers.

---

[231] It is a feature of the Jewish (and other faith-based) school systems that usually the Board is predominantly composed of current or very recent school parents. In other private schools – especially those that are older foundations – the Board, which concerns itself mainly with financial and similar matters, is completely 'arms length', with perhaps one or two parent representatives.

[232] Occasionally, Board members with an "agenda" will receive these calls, keep records of them, and bring them forward much later – usually around the time when the Principal's contract is up for renewal. The Principal's response has to be – "If you were aware of parental concerns, it was your responsibility as a Board member to refer them to me at the time, or if you felt there was a real problem, to advise me directly or advise me through the School President."

- If the school culture is appropriate, these issues will only rarely arise, as parents (and Board members) will know that the Board does not interfere with the day-to-day running of the school.

13.3 Parents and teachers

Many problems between Principals and parents start between parents and teachers. A mutual relationship of respect should pertain between teachers and parents, but from time to time the relationship will break down. Whether the teacher or the parent brings the problem to the Principal, the first question must always be "Have you discussed this directly?".

After their duty to the student, the Principal's first duty is to professionally support and advise the teacher.

Even if the teacher is at fault, the Principal must be discreet and professional in dealing with parents, and not undermine the teacher. Teachers must feel confident in approaching Principals with 'parent problems'. Some parents are irrational, and mount 'campaigns' against individual teachers. These are both unpleasant and dangerous. There may be a point where a teacher has to be instructed to refer all contact from a particular parent to the Administration. Legal steps may be necessary. The school must have a careful and complete record of interactions to date, and must protect its teachers.

> But Mr. K, on March 21st the teacher wrote to you pointing out that your son had not handed in a series of assignments, and that his end-of-year mark was at risk. I have a copy of the letter here. What did you do when you received it?

Teachers should be able to employ a range of techniques in dealing with parents. The school may provide workshops, especially for younger teachers.

Occasionally teachers will 'lose it' with parents, and make very inappropriate comments. In such circumstances, the Principal must simultaneously try and retrieve the situation with the parents, and deal with the teacher. Problems with parents are often indications that all is not well in the classroom. A parent who calls a teacher because their child claims that they have not had assignments returned, may be met with a defensive and evasive response, which in turn will trigger an aggressive attitude from the parent. In the ensuing fracas, the Principal must not forget to check whether, in fact, the teacher is overwhelmed and is unacceptably behind with marking.

Common points of friction between parents and teachers include:

Student performance – in explaining bad marks, the student is telling the parent that the teacher is either 'not teaching' or has 'got it in for me'. The teacher's response is that the student is not paying attention, is making no effort, and is failing to do any work. If the teacher has been keeping proper records, there should be documentation to support the teacher's view. If the student has special needs, the school must check that the teacher understands them and is properly accommodating them. Solutions here must look forward, and should be carefully structured. A VP or Guidance Counselor may be asked to oversee the process.

Inappropriate classroom comments – these are much more difficult situations, and often arise from the Jewish Studies classroom. (A parent will rarely take exception to a teacher's views on Hamlet, climate change or physics.) Typically, a teacher faced with questioning by the class will offer an answer that the student will report at home. The teacher may be quoted out of context, be misunderstood, may have phrased an answer in a clumsy fashion - or may actually have said what was reported. The comment may have been ill advised, with an implication which parents find offensive. The comment may also have reflected accurate information, but suggested an idea that the parent finds unpalatable.

Every teacher (and every Principal, Rabbi and politician) will occasionally have a slip of the tongue, where a comment comes out in a way that is subsequently regretted. If this has been the case, then a simple, straightforward and swift apology should be the end of the matter.

If the comment is accurate, reflecting responsible teaching, but the parent takes exception (*"Judaism permits the death penalty under certain circumstances"*), then the parent should be invited to discuss the comment with the teacher, who should prepare short but relevant material, and explain how the issue was presented. The parent may have suggestions about how the topic can be presented in the future in a way that prevents misunderstanding.

Much more difficult are comments which impinge on family pride, status, tradition or belief. Teachers have to be extremely sensitive to these issues, and understand that they cannot know the family background and circumstances of all students sitting in the classroom. Any comment that the teacher makes which may carry such implications has to be very, very carefully phrased – if it is made at all. A teacher who is persistently making such comments (*"Your parents are not really Jewish"*; *"The Holocaust was caused by ...."*) should be clearly warned, and disciplinary process leading to termination should be considered. The teacher is entitled to hold his or her views; they are not entitled to irresponsibly embarrass or offend students in their classes.

Whatever the teacher is teaching, they have a duty to respect their students and to behave appropriately. Personal comments about students are inadmissible under any circumstances. If a teacher has concerns about a student's appearance, personal hygiene or any other personal circumstance – s/he should refer the issue to a Guidance Counselor for their tactful and discrete attention.

13.4 Meetings with parents

The nature and tone of many of the Principal's interactions with parents – in individual meetings, in larger meetings with groups of parents, or even in telephone conversations – will be determined before any meeting begins.

The parent(s) will come with an expectation of how they will be received which has been formed on the basis of the Principal's known reputation.

The way that the Principal (or any senior Administrator) behaves at meetings has already been endlessly dissected in the school parking lot and over countless phone conversations, in discussions in synagogue on Shabbat morning, and among parents who find themselves sitting together at weddings, bar/bat mitzvah celebrations or charity dinners. If the parent enters with the words of their best friend still ringing in their ears – *"He/she won't even listen to you"* (whether that is true or not), their approach will be very different than if the same friend has told them *"He/she is always very fair"* (whether that is true or not!). Ideally, parents should leave meetings feeling that they have been listened to, and feeling that they have been treated fairly, reasonably and honestly, even if their request has not been met, or their problem not solved.

If it is anticipated that the meeting will be difficult, or if the meeting concerns a potentially serious issue, at least two Administrators must be present in the meeting. One should be taking notes.

The first rule of meeting with angry parents (or any parents, or any member of staff, or angry neighbours, or anyone) is …. allow them to vent!

Let them say what they have come to say, fully and without interruption.

The meeting will make no progress until the aggrieved parties have had their say, and they feel that they have been listened to. There are many books on negotiation techniques. They repay careful reading, because every meeting is about – or should be about – negotiation.

Occasionally, the 'angle' that the parent brings to the meeting may be different from that expected. New information or evidence may be presented. The Principal may reach the conclusion that the parents' complaint, in part or in whole, is justified.

There are several stages to a successful meeting, and the basic rules apply most of the time, whatever the subject:

- Listen

- Find out what the parents want as a successful outcome to the meeting

- Shift the meeting to negotiation stage as soon as possible, and at all costs avoid confrontation – always pointless

- Try and reach an agreed outcome that gives both parties something of what they need

- Conclude the meeting, and articulate the outcome. That may involve an agreement to meet again, especially if some action or investigation is called for because of what has been heard at the meeting. If a follow-up phone call is agreed, it is a good technique to ask the parents to call back, which puts the onus on them to make the follow-up contact.

13.4.1   Common agendas

It is difficult to anticipate every type of meeting between parents and Principals. There are some common themes, defined by tone and emotional 'temperature' as much as by subject and/or content. They include:

- Academic issues – failure to meet expectations. The parents sometimes see this as the fault of the child; sometimes as the fault of the school

- Disciplinary or behavioral issues – the meeting is usually at the school's request

- Complaints about a particular teacher or course

- Complaints about the (falling) standards of the school – academic, religious, or behavioral

- Grievances about perceived 'unfair' treatment of a child -- usually about the student not being chosen for a team, or a prize, or to represent the school at some occasion or event

Where the parent has complained about a staff member, the Principal must protect his/her colleague. Staff will not forgive a Principal who does not defend them. A complaint about a teacher cannot be accepted – explicitly or implicitly - until and unless the teacher's account of the incident(s) has been fairly heard. (The first question is, of course, "Have you discussed this directly with the teacher?") If the parent is insistent that the version of events they are giving you is correct, a possible response is:

> Mr. X, you will understand that the correct professional procedure is for me to investigate this matter, which means that first I must speak to the teacher. If I do find that the events happened as you described them, then that would be a matter of serious concern for the school Administration. However, I am sure that you also understand that I cannot share with you any professional conversations that I may have with a member of staff.

Other useful phrases are:

> *Mr. X, neither you nor I were actually present when these alleged incidents took place [when these alleged remarks were made]. I have to investigate this before the school can determine its appropriate course of action.*

After the meeting, there should be a written confirmation of what took place, including the agreed 'next step'.

Although the overwhelming majority of parents are sensible and supportive, occasionally parents can make the Principal's life a misery. A very common feature of problems with parents is differing accounts of what actually happened in the interaction (personal or written) with them. In such cases – and this may be years later – both the presence of a second Administrator and a 'paper trail' may give the Principal some credibility.

Battles with parents are wearying, usually fruitless, and rarely serve the interests of the child. A skilful Principal will learn or develop techniques to avoid them. If a conflict does develop, then the Principal's relationship with the Board becomes critical, as the first thing that an aggrieved parent will do is lobby the Board. Good practice is for the Principal to advise the President, in confidence, of parental issues that seem to be particularly problematic. To respect the privacy of the parents (and students), this can be done without identifying the parties.

> *Joe / Ruth – you may get a call from a G10 parent about an alleged incident with a Math teacher. I don't know at this stage whether or not the complaint is justified – we are meeting the teacher tomorrow. The father is really angry. There is some background here. I'll update you.*

It is a great help if your President can stand up and say, "The Principal advised me of this developing situation, and I support the Principal's decisions."

The other key technique is employing techniques[233] to defuse the situation, de-personalize it and move to negotiation. This shifts the meeting towards practical resolution. While, again, every Principal will build their own list, some useful formulae that I have employed include:

> *Mr. and Mrs. X – I understand what you are asking. You will understand that I can only work within the limits available to me and to the school. Let me tell you what I think I can do to help you, and, unfortunately, what I don't think I am able to do ……*

> *If you were sitting in my chair, what would you say?*

> *Acknowledging both the interests of you as parents, and the interests of the school, what do you think would be a fair outcome here?*

---

[233] As mentioned elsewhere, Principals can learn a lot from books on negotiation which can be found in the Business>Management section of actual or online booksellers (together with books on many other useful and relevant skills).

Mr. and Mrs. X – just as I would never dream of discussing you / your child with other parents, I cannot under any circumstances discuss another parent / another student with you.

Let's take this away from the immediate issue for a moment. What are the principles we should be applying in this case?

In a somewhat similar case the school had some time ago, we were able to resolve it in the following manner … Could that be an example for how we can reach agreement here?

What would you like me to do?

13.4.2   Preparing for difficult meetings

The Principal can prepare for an anticipated 'difficult' meeting:

- Ascertain the agenda beforehand. The Principal's secretary can do this. "We would like to make sure that the Principal is the correct person to help you". If a parent refuses to disclose the subject, that is their right. The school may say to them that in that case, it will do its best, but without knowing the subject of the meeting, cannot promise that it can be of help. Sometimes a pre-emptive phone call will obviate the need for a meeting.

  Mrs. H, my secretary tells me that the reason for tomorrow's meeting is …….. I think that's actually a relatively simple matter. I'd be happy to meet with you, but I think we can resolve it over the phone. Is that OK with you?

- Do your homework. If the meeting is about the student, ask all the student's teachers for a quick written report of what is happening with the student over the recent weeks (academic / behavioral / social / attendance). It is a lot easier talking to parents if you have some facts:

  Naomi seems to be upset about something for at least two weeks – five of her teachers report that she has been late with assignments, and two report that she seems to have come to class red-eyed. Apart from this latest incident, is there something happening that might help us understand her unhappiness?

- Consult with senior colleagues – "Mr. and Mrs. X have insisted on a meeting with me, but don't want to say what it's about. Can you think of any reason why they want to meet with me?"

A senior colleague should join you at the meeting, and should take notes, while you concentrate on the meeting.

Ask the parents if the student should also attend. It is a lot more difficult for parents to make unsupported or outlandish remarks if the student is present –

> *Is that true, Johnny? Can you think of a reason for the teacher's comment?*

Pay attention to the physical setting of the meeting – which room it is in[234], how the seating is arranged, whether you offer some refreshment. Make sure that the other parties to the meeting are properly seated and comfortable.

13.4.3   The unexpected

It sometimes happens that the Principal is deliberately led into a trap, which can happen in several ways:

<u>One parent calls to arrange a meeting and a whole group turns up.</u>

Their intention is to intimidate. **The Principal must stay in control of the proceedings.** In this case, alternatives include:

> *I'm sorry, Mr. And Mrs. X, but I thought this was to be a private meeting. I'm very happy to meet with you, but please would you all wait for a few minutes, as I will ask some of my colleagues to join me. ["I'm afraid that none of my colleagues are free for at least half an hour. Perhaps we could re-schedule, and at the same time it would be useful if you could give me a clear indication of what is under discussion, so that we can properly prepare for the meeting."]*

> *I'm very happy to meet with this group, although I didn't expect it. However, I need to make it clear that to preserve confidentiality I cannot discuss individual students with other parents.*

> *Without knowing the facts of this situation, all I can do today is listen to you.*

<u>A parent turns up with a lawyer</u>

The Principal should decide whether s/he wishes to meet with the parents' lawyer present, or reschedule for a time when the school's legal representative can also be present.

If you feel confident, go ahead with the meeting, but you **must** have another colleague present who will take notes. By agreement, these notes may be typed up afterwards and circulated to the other parties. They may also end up in court, UNLESS you specify, and it is clearly recorded in the notes, that this is to be a meeting on a 'Without Prejudice' basis. [Even this may have different status in different jurisdictions.] Under these circumstances, **do not concede any issues of**

---

[234] I often find it useful to hold difficult meetings in a convenient 'meeting room', with a simple table and chairs, a coffee pot etc. Removing the meeting from the Principal's office, and removing yourself from behind a desk, can immediately lower the confrontational temperature.

fact or principle unless you are absolutely certain of your ground, and do not allow yourself to be interrogated or bullied by the lawyer. Remember that you may elect to conclude the meeting. Some helpful lines might include:

> *Mr. X, I am happy to discuss in good faith issues related to the welfare and interests of your child within the normal parameters of school process. If you believe that this is a legal matter, then I would like to close this meeting, and we can reconvene with the school's own lawyer present.*

> *Mr. Y – this is not a court of law, and I am not under interrogation. Your attitude is not helpful in furthering the interests of your client's child.*

> *Mr. X, these are clearly legal questions. It is not appropriate for me to address them in this meeting. I would invite you to submit them to me in writing, and I will refer them to the school's lawyer for attention.*

> *Mr. X, I'm sorry, but I have to repeat: It is not appropriate for me to address these questions in this meeting. Please submit these questions in writing, and I will refer them to the school's lawyer for attention.*

> *Mr. X - I am afraid that this meeting is now concluded.*

> *Mr. X, I cannot comment on unsubstantiated allegations.*

> *I understand and note that that is your [your child's] understanding of those events, but the school has not had a chance to carry out its own investigation, and at this stage I cannot make any assumptions.*

Lawyers come in different shapes and sizes.

> The relative: In a noticeable percentage of such meetings, they turn out to be a brother-in-law or other relative of the parent, brought along to intimidate rather than because the parent is contemplating spending significant sums on legal fees. If so, they will generally be reasonable, and be willing to be your partner in lowering the temperature of the issue (they are themselves probably uncomfortable at being dragged into this). They may not know anything at all about the legal status of schools, students or process. A variation on this is the 'older sibling - lawyer', who either comes with the parent(s) or only with the student. In the nature of things, they are young. They make up for lack of experience (and knowledge) with often-unreasonable aggression.

> The school-law lawyer: Lawyers specializing in school law are relatively few, and if a parent turns up with one of these, you should be very cautious, and it is best to refuse to allow the meeting to proceed. Reschedule with the school lawyer present. There are only very rare cases where issues involving students are in fact legal issues; and when they are, in all probability you will share the parent's concern. Yet we live in increasingly litigious

times, and where an aggressive lawyer has been hired, they will frequently see 'Jewish private schools' as potentially lucrative and vulnerable targets. (The reality, of course, is that the resources of the school are typically far less than those of the public system). In all of these incidents, the more familiar you are with the law relevant to your school, the more secure and professional you will appear.

The family-law lawyer: The family-law lawyer will normally appear where there is marital conflict, and will be there representing one of the parents only. The lawyer will be guided in behavior and attitude by his/her client's interest, not the interest of the student. This can go either way: if the lawyer feels that his/her client's interests are best served by a compromise and reasonable resolution, that is what they will go for. If they believe that this is a good opportunity to show that the other parent is clearly unable to care for or control the child, or that the choice of school, which their client "opposed from the beginning", can now be shown to be disastrous for the student, the meeting will be adversarial. Call the school lawyer.

The child-protection lawyer: In rare cases, a lawyer representing a child-protection agency may appear, if the student is in care, or has left home. Again, the meeting is unpredictable.

The corporate lawyer: High-powered parents, who are used to their lawyers handling all of their family affairs, may send or arrive with a 'downtown' lawyer. They will either try and bully the school (because their client has instructed them to achieve a certain outcome) or they will regard this as a waste of their time.

The parent(s) or their representative want(s) to record the meeting

This is both a challenge and a trap. If you object, it immediately puts you in a difficult light ('What are you afraid of?'), and if you agree you run the risk of some slip of the tongue, or awkwardly phrased comment, being preserved on tape (or disk) from where it is very difficult to withdraw or amend.

The participants may or may not have the right to record the meeting – this depends on local legislation, which you must check. They may not have the right to record the conversation without your knowledge (but then you will not know this until after the meeting!). However, demanding to record a meeting in most cases is an adversarial signal of lack of trust, and it is not conducive to a constructive atmosphere. Since that signal is clear, at the very least immediately excuse yourself, and invite another Administrator to join the meeting.

Again, there are no hard or fast rules (except if there is local legislation which governs the process) and you have to think on your feet.

Your range of responses might include:

> *Mr./Mrs. X – I am very happy to meet with you to discuss this situation, and I have no problem if one of you wishes to take notes – in fact, I would encourage you to do so, as my colleague will be taking notes – but I am uncomfortable at having this meeting recorded. These are not legal proceedings – we are here for one purpose only, and that is to forward the welfare of your child. I would like our discussion to take place in a mutually respectful atmosphere, where everyone feels that they can speak freely and frankly, and I am afraid that the presence of this tape recorder is uncomfortable. Could we agree not to use it?*

> *Mr./Mrs. X – I am not comfortable with the fact that you feel that it is necessary to record this meeting, which I would like to feel is taking place on a basis of trust and respect between all of the parties. However, I respect your view that you insist on a recording. I can only proceed on the basis that you undertake to furnish the school with an unedited copy of the tape within 48 hours of the conclusion of the meeting, and perhaps you would be kind enough to sign an undertaking to that effect? In addition, I would like it clearly acknowledged for the record, on the tape, that this is a meeting held 'Without Prejudice', and that the recording is being made at the request of the family, without the agreement of the school.*

Otherwise, be cautious in what you say, and refer to the list of strategies suggested above in dealing with other 'unexpected' events in meetings. Be careful that the parent(s) are not intent on getting you to admit, on tape, things that are going to sound unreasonable or incriminating. Sharpen your negotiating skills!

If the conversation is aggressive and clearly adversarial, you may wish to conclude the meeting, and ask them to put their issues in writing, and the school will consider how to respond. Alternatively, say that in light of the manner in which the meeting is being conducted, you feel that it is more appropriate to close this meeting now, and reconvene it in the presence of a legal representative of the school. Then take the appropriate steps.

> *Mr./Mrs. X – I am not prepared to continue this meeting in what I feel is an adversarial atmosphere, and therefore we will conclude the meeting now, and reconvene in the presence of the school lawyer.*

13.5 Parents and children in the Principal's office

Few meetings are as revealing and illuminating as those in which parents and students are together in the Principal's office. While there is something to be said for the old adage that 'there are no problem students, only problem parents', occasionally such meetings will leave the Principal full of compassion for parents who are struggling with enormous issues within their own family.

The ability of the Principal to deal with many of these situations may be limited, and often the Principal will suggest (and sometimes insist) on a referral to outside professional help. Do not underestimate the ability of the child to understand the essence of the issue, the child's ability to rationally discuss parents' seemingly irrational behavior, or the child's ability to suggest practical solutions. It can be a constant source of astonishment, occasionally bordering on inspiration and sobering appreciation, to see how teenagers are quietly shouldering huge responsibilities outside school.

Common scenarios may include the following:

The parent(s) who cannot say "No" -- despite being among the most common situations, this can be one of the most difficult for the school to deal with. The student has no interest in helping to correct this situation; the problematic parent-child interaction is taking place outside the school; and the causes of the parents' inability to restrain the student are deep, may be buried in family history, and outside the school's ability to deal with them. If the student has become used to totally permissive and indulgent parents who do not set any limits – including limits (actually, *demands*) made by the student with the express purpose of checking whether the parents are still ready to fulfill any and every wish – it will be very difficult to institute change. However, the school may have a basic discussion with the parents about their responsibilities, and suggest some further reading or some outside professional help.

In some cases, the parents may feel that they are obligated to give their children "everything that the other children have", when that exceeds their financial ability to do so. Firstly, the parents should be firmly told the facts of life – that every community is composed of families of different economic profiles; that all the other families are not rich; that while some students may seem to have a great deal, many live more modest lives, and that not "every" child has the latest or most fashionable clothing or possessions. In that case, a full and frank discussion with the student by a sympathetic adult may help the student understand that they, too, have responsibilities to understand their family's financial circumstances.

The parents who cannot say "Yes" – in this case, the Principal must be very straightforward with the parents and suggest to them that they are making their own situation worse. You may refer them to outside counseling, or suggest books for them to read. They must learn to trust their child, allow them to grow up, and give them freedom, responsibility – and the chance to make and learn from their mistakes. To continually deny appropriate and responsible freedom is as irresponsible as giving a child complete freedom.

Parents who wish to realize their ambitions through their children – here the parent is typically trying to insist that the student take courses that the student either doesn't want to take, or with which the child simply cannot cope. Investigation elicits the information that the parent themselves 'always wanted to do medicine, and I want my child to do so'. A variant on this is the parent who wishes to send an unwilling child to yeshivah or Seminary "because I never had the chance to go". There are feelings of expectation and, conversely, of disappointment and even betrayal. The parents have to understand that each student is an individual, and should have the freedom to make their own way in life. Their child, too has a right to be happy and to make choices. The parents' pride and fulfillment has to be in raising happy children who are themselves fulfilled. Forcing the child into a choice that they don't want will result in bitterness and resentment that will reverberate for decades. Forcing a child to go to yeshivah or seminary when the child really does not want to go (and does not have the strength to be independent) will, of course, have exactly the opposite effect of that desired.

Parents who 'baby' their children – currently termed 'helicopter parents' because they hover over their children the whole time. These are the parents who come with their children to arrange their lockers, and want to sit in with them in the school opening orientation. Generally they (i.e. the parents) grow out of it – usually after the first time the student goes on a school trip and 'forgets' to call home. Gentle reassurance will usually work:

> *Mrs. A, your daughter will be just fine. All the students manage. So will Jennifer. Arranging her own timetable change is part of becoming a high school student.*

In many cases, a few simple questions will show that parents are arguing over issues that their children do not think are important.

Parents with blameless children – nothing is ever the child's fault. The teachers, the school, 'the wrong friends' are all to blame for the student's problems. (The parents rarely figure in the list!). "The school must put things right". Plain talking is needed, to the student as much as to the parents. A productive tactic is dealing with the student without the parents being present, and effectively excluding the parents from discussion of the problem. If this fails, the parents may 'threaten' to withdraw the child from the school. Let them.

Parents who dislike or disapprove of their children – this is a step on the path to rejection, and therefore both serious and tragic. The consequences of parental disapproval or dislike are devastating for the child. Parental love for a child must be unconditional. If the child does not feel that whatever the circumstances, a sympathetic welcome awaits them as they turn the key in the front door, they have no incentive to return home, and, in fact, every incentive to stay out and stay away. If they cannot find approval and love from their parents, they will seek it elsewhere, often from individuals or groups who will offer acceptance and 'support' – but in return for something else. Events may enter a self-fulfilling, tragic spiral. Serious professional counseling is needed.

Parents who reject their children – Very occasionally, parents simply reject their own children. Your sympathy must be with the children. Expert advice is necessary.

Parents who are victims of their children – while children are often victims of their parents, occasionally the reverse is true. Parents may be totally dominated by their children, and, in rare cases, victimized by them. This may be because the child has sociopathic or psychopathic tendencies. There may be other reasons. The child may sense a vulnerability in the parents which, consciously or unconsciously, they exploit – for example, a sense of guilt over some undisclosed or hidden component of family or personal history[235]. Again, these are circumstances way beyond the capacity of the school to deal with. The school can only insist that the student obey the rules of the school, and advise the parents that they must seek qualified, professional advice to deal with their family dynamics. The school cannot "tell" the child how to behave at home, nor can it deal with the surprisingly far-reaching – and frequently toxic - influence of secrets in families.

Single parent families – whether the parent is a mother or, more rarely, a father, the single-parent family is increasingly common, and every school now has a significant number of children who are being raised by one parent. In some cases, there is another parent in the background; in some cases the custodial parent is virtually alone in the world. Circumstances – emotional, financial, and legal - can vary greatly. For parents in pressured circumstances, the school should be compassionate, realistic and helpful. The Jewish community is not always friendly to single parents, and the school has to be very, very careful not to exacerbate already difficult situations, and make sure that the children concerned do not become disadvantaged in any way in the school program. A particular area of sensitivity here is the extra-curricular program, where the financial, practical and logistic resources of single-parent families often cannot match those of the two-parent family. A good school will keep a conscientious eye on such circumstances, and have a fund to ensure that no child is prevented from participating in any activity because of financial reasons.

Parents in conflict – quite apart from cases where conflict has reached the point of separation or divorce (or close to it), there are occasions where a Principal's office is the setting for arguments and conflicts between parents. Again, the school should not get in the middle, nor should it meddle. The school's concern (and the parents' concern) can only be the welfare of the student. If the parents are in disagreement (*"She should go on the trip"* / *"No way is she going on that trip – she's been on*

---

[235] I once dealt with a student whose parents seemed to allow him total freedom, and who could not deny him anything – involving expenditure, financial and emotional, way beyond the family's means. The son exploited this shamelessly. The father seemed unable to resist any request of the son's. After months of meetings, the father disclosed that he had been married previously, and the student had a half-sibling of whose existence the student was totally unaware. I advised the father (and his wife) to take urgent family therapy from a qualified professional, and to take professional advice on whether, when, and how to disclose the secret that had made them prisoners. I do not know what happened.

vacation twice already this year") then at a certain point the Principal should simply invite the parents to settle their disagreement outside the school, and let the Principal know the decision. If the logistics or the issue(s) are complex, you may want a note signed by both parents, to avoid later arguments. Parental /marital conflict (see below) is difficult for students to deal with, and is very often a background to students 'acting out' in school.

Parents in religious conflict - One parent is at a different religious 'place' than the other, and is trying to impose (or remove) religious practices and standards on the child. Common sense, a relatively rare commodity in many such situations, is needed. What does the child want? Is the action proposed by either parent going to achieve positive results for the child – or is it going to either increase the child's resentment or the child's confusion? Can the child understand the issues, and can the child 'navigate' between the parents? Again, the school can only determine what happens in school. A skilled Guidance Counselor or teacher may be able to help the child. A sympathetic and reasonable community rabbi may be able to help the parents, and help the school ensure the comfort of the child. Occasionally, without regard to the educational interests of the child, community rabbis will be strongly partisan where religious observance is an issue. That is never helpful.

13.6 The school and marital conflicts

While the school – through the child -- is always indirectly involved with family emotions, marital conflict may reach stages where the school is directly involved. The Jewish family is rapidly changing, and no school escapes the consequences[236]. Where relations between parents are acrimonious, issues relating to children are frequently central, and, regrettably, schools are often seen as an extension of the battleground. All of us will be familiar with the sad child who is being torn apart by parental conflict.

The ground rules for dealing with these situations as a Principal are:

- Uncompromising insistence that the welfare of the child – emotional and even physical - is your primary, and only concern. Do not be tempted to take sides between parents, unless the law demands that you do so.

  Mr. X, you will be aware that under the provisions of the court ruling I cannot allow you to visit your child at school.

- Uncompromising insistence that marital conflict be left at the school gate, and that the behavior and attitudes of parents

---

[236] You can never know what is going on inside someone else's head, and you can never know what is happening behind a closed front door.

within the school – to each other and to everyone else – are respectful and correct.

- Take legal advice[237] regarding the school's duties of providing access and information to divorced or separated parents (this differs in different jurisdictions). This may involve the school or its lawyer asking parents (or their lawyers) for copies of legal judgments and rulings. The school must ascertain whether a non-custodial parent

  o has the right to receive report cards

  o has the right to enquire at the school about a child's progress or welfare

  o has the right to attend parent evenings and meet with teachers

Brief your teachers, appropriately and without divulging any more information than either necessary or legally permitted, regarding special understanding for a child who is 'caught in the middle'; and about possible dangers of parents seeking unauthorized access via the school.

This is also important for your office / attendance staff. Parents who have no right of access will occasionally phone the school, acting innocently, and spin lines such as *"I'm going to be in town on business next week, and I'd like to take my son/daughter out of school for the afternoon"*. Another common tactic is to call teachers (often younger or less experienced teachers), ask about the child's welfare/progress, and then use those statements as weapons against the other parent[238]. Advise teachers to refer such calls to you, and if – as occasionally will happen – they realize that they have given information that could be potentially embarrassing, they should advise you immediately, and you should take legal advice on whether the matter needs further action on your part.

The school must take precautions to ensure that no one in the school (teachers, Guidance Counsellors, office staff or even other students) gets manipulated or enlisted by estranged parents to act as message-bearers (written or telephone) to children, or are otherwise recruited as 'accomplices'. This can be a particular problem in a Jewish school, where often members of staff (teaching or support) may know the parties socially, and may want to "help".

However compelling the emotions – keep the school out of it, and allow the child to feel that the school is a safe haven where the family conflict does not intrude. No

---

[237] See SECTION 4.9.4. Professional and expert legal advice is absolutely essential in matters of family law.

[238] The classic is to call the first-lesson Monday morning teacher, when the child has spent the weekend with the other spouse, and ask whether the child looks "Pale ... stressed ... tired... distressed ... upset" etc.

teacher should EVER, under any circumstances, permit reference to a child's family conflict on the classroom.

Another common scenario is where divorced parents are conflicted over choice of school. In such cases, religious divergence may have been a factor in the marital breakup. Again, you have to establish who has the legal right to make the choice of school, and respect it. Occasionally, it is possible to meet with and reassure the opposing parent that your school is, and will only be, acting in the interests of the child, and will not be acting as the 'agent' of the other parent in promoting a family or non-educational agenda.

In all of these scenarios, feelings and emotions run high, and they need exceptionally delicate handling. Human beings can find themselves in the most difficult situations. Often the children are the most rational and sensible players in the situation. If a parent persists in inappropriate presence or behavior in the school, you may end up calling the police.

Schools may find themselves dealing with even more complex situations of 'blended families', same-sex parents and, certainly, one-parent families. It is the child who attends your school, not the parents. Separate the issues, be respectful to the parents, who in some of these situations may have their own agonies, and focus on the welfare and interests of the child,

Constituencies - Community

14   MANAGING COMMUNITY

14 MANAGING COMMUNITY

14.1 Rabbis and synagogues

Many years ago, I was part of a team that started a new, co-ed Modern Orthodox high school. I invited the local Rabbis to visit the school shortly before it opened. One rather pugnacious Rabbi came, headed for the library, and proceeded to pull books off the shelves and criticize them because they were not consistent with his brand of Orthodoxy. (I think his criticism of the books included criticism of his guide, but that's another story). In the neighborhood a Hassidic shtiebl had recently opened. Was there any point in inviting the young Rebbe? I decided that a phone call was in order. He arrived in 'Rebbeishe' garb, including a coat with a fur collar, and a silver-topped cane. I took him around the school, explaining what we were trying to achieve. He didn't comment. At the end of the tour, I felt awkward, and said to him "Rabbi, I cannot promise that this school is going to be one to which you will want to send your own children." He replied: "If you make a school here to which I would send my own children, you will have failed hugely. Your job is to bring in the other 99.9% of Jewish children, and you will do whatever is necessary to achieve that. I give you a complete brachah."

Local Rabbi(s) can be wonderful partners in managing the school, in managing relationships with community, and as confidential sources who can be helpful in filling in 'background' in dealing with families or with potential or even present staff; and of course they can be important teachers.

Rabbis are on the list of partners with whom the Principal has to have a relationship of trust and confidentiality. Whatever their denominations, the school should take the initiative in cultivating positive relationships. Most schools, whatever their orientation, encompass families from different streams within the Jewish community, or different 'tendencies' within the same denomination. The Principal, when it comes to the welfare of students, must be denominationally 'blind'. Whatever the Principal's own denomination, in personal and professional relationships the other denominations, and their Rabbis, are partners, not enemies.

Keeping contact with local Rabbis can include:

- Inviting them, individually or as a group, to tour the school

- Ensuring that they are on school mailing lists to receive information about what is going on in the school

- Inviting them to selected school events (not necessarily to speak)

- Letting them know when students who are members of their synagogue excel in some school activity; or, alternatively, when a student may need their support

In some communities, where the school is very closely connected to the synagogue (and may even share premises), the Rabbi will be part of the daily life of the school.

So, in many places local Rabbis are the most enthusiastic supporters of the local day school system. It is nevertheless a curious fact that some Jewish schools have ambivalent relationships with local community Rabbis.

Rabbi-school problems may derive from some of the following factors:

- The Rabbi does not understand the difference between the function and purpose of a 'shul' and a school. The Rabbi may see the school only in its Jewish dimension, and not appreciate school's multiple educational responsibilities

- A school's responsibility to its students will often mandate a more flexible Jewish approach – including halachic approaches – than may be possible or desired in a synagogue context

- The school cannot order the students to be observant or compliant with religious demands

- Rabbis may not appreciate that in recruiting (and managing) staff, your criteria include, but are not exclusively concerned with, the religious commitment of any individual

- While 'lobbying' on behalf of students and parents, from wherever it comes, should always be listened to respectfully and appropriately - Rabbis may not appreciate that in administering discipline in the school, or in administering admissions, there are issues that may arise which the school cannot share with others (including clergy). The school can only act in the interests of its students and in the broader interests of the school

- The Rabbi may assume that he/she has an automatic 'right of entry' to the school

- Rabbis tend to be used to giving 'derashot'; high-school students like to participate, question and argue

- A successful High school will affect the synagogue's Supplementary / Hebrew school, especially the crucial 'post-Bar/bat Mitzvah' classes. These are membership 'feeders' for the synagogue, and a channel for the Rabbi to get to know the teenagers of his/her community. If numbers decline because of the local Day School, the synagogue may resent their loss.

There can be institutional tension. For twenty or thirty years, Jewish schools have been growing in importance and influence, at exactly the same time that many synagogues (especially large suburban synagogues) have been struggling with many challenges. A transformation has taken place – because for many parents who send their children to Jewish schools, **the school has replaced the synagogue as the major institution of Jewish family affiliation** (see below). There are a number of clear reasons for this, but local Rabbis can show frustration at the apparent strength of the school compared to the synagogue.

14.1.1 Has the school replaced the synagogue?

Schools and synagogues should be natural complementary partners.

The central place of synagogues in Jewish life is indisputable. Equally, every synagogue should recognize the vital role of Jewish schools in contemporary Jewish life, and in the Jewish future.

However, as indicated above, the school/synagogue relationship, which on the surface should be totally mutually supportive, can occasionally be surprisingly tricky at every level.

One common source of tension is where the school and the synagogue share premises. The possibilities of problems are endless. The patterns of usage between synagogues and schools are entirely different, and the average age group of the two groups of users is different. The spatial needs of the synagogue may be ritual/ceremonial/social; that of the school educational/practical.

A more difficult situation is where there are ideological or religious differences between the school and the synagogue. There is no way around this except by building close bridges of personal trust and understanding between the Principal and the Rabbi(s) of the synagogue(s) concerned. Historically, education has always been a central issue in Jewish religious conflicts. It is a sad fact that some Rabbis, however good the school, will feel unable to give it public legitimacy – and that is true whether they are religiously to the right or the left of the school. A certain generosity of spirit is occasionally wanting.

Part of this is surely the very close relationship that a good Jewish school will have built with its students and families – often much closer and much more engaged than the synagogue. The school and its staff see the student for perhaps forty hours or more per week; the synagogue and its Rabbi will never see the student for that much time. In a large suburban congregation, especially if the family are not regular synagogue attendees, the Rabbi may hardly know the names of the teenage children in his congregation.

And, crucially, the educational relationship enjoyed by a teacher in a classroom is usually much more wide ranging and searching than the relationship a student feels to their Rabbi or to their synagogue.

In all of this, the contemporary situation is faithful to Jewish history.

Schools (and other educational institutions) have frequently been the harbingers, if not the instigators, of radical change in every denomination.

Examples include:

- the 'Freischule' of the late eighteenth century in Germany, from where many important characteristics of the Reform movement emerged

- Camp Ramah, which drove huge change in the Conservative movement

- the Beis Yaacov school system of Sara Schenirer (1883-1935), which irretrievably changed education for women in the Orthodox community

- and, finally, the institution of the modern Yeshivah itself. The 'Rosh Yeshivah' is a clear rival to the authority of the synagogue and the local Rabbi.

So, at a time when the suburban synagogue is facing multiple challenges of identity and direction, it is no wonder that consciously or subconsciously, the huge growth of the Diaspora Day School movement makes the synagogues nervous.

A recent UK Report on Jewish Education commented[239]:

> There are many more children in Jewish schools every day than the number of parents in synagogues every week.

It is worth spending a moment, too, to explore the implications of this for the future. One small, but clear tendency is that schools are increasingly being called on to provide pastoral and ritual services that were once the province of the synagogue or Rabbi.

---

[239] Reported in the 'Jewish Chronicle', July 18 2008. The number of children in (publicly-funded) Jewish schools in the UK has skyrocketed over the last twenty years. However, the hours spent on Jewish Studies in these schools falls way, way below the North American norm. Additionally, the Jewish dimension of the school – not Government-funded – must be paid for by 'Voluntary Contributions' (of around US$2,000 per year), which by law the schools cannot enforce. Few parents pay. In 2009, a legal ruling threw the admissions policies of most Jewish schools in the UK – arcane at the best of times to most other observers - into chaos.

Examples include:

- A popular Talmud teacher answers his door late on a Saturday night. One of his students, together with her father and mother, are standing there. "Our grandmother has just died in our house in the next street. What should we do?"

- A teacher returns a call from a mother, thinking it concerns a recent test he has given her daughter. Instead, the mother launches into an account of her marital problems, and concludes by saying: "My daughter tells me you are a wonderful teacher. My husband and I have agreed to ask you to help us with our family problems."

- A parent asks to meet a school Administrator to discuss a "family issue". At the meeting, the mother wants advice about whether or not the family should attend the wedding of another family member who is marrying a non-Jewish partner in a civil ceremony.

- A father confides in a teacher (who is a Rabbi) that he is not Jewish, and asks the teacher to help him prepare for and undergo a formal religious conversion to Judaism.

It is clearly possible to interpret these incidents (all drawn from real life) in several different ways, and the teacher has to handle them appropriately. However, they all speak to 'school' being perceived as closer to the family than their local Rabbi.

Neither the school as an institution nor its teachers as individuals are equipped or trained to deal with these situations. If they become more commonplace, it will generate a need for the school to allocate resources (human and financial) to address a new role[240]. Only time will tell if the role of the Jewish school is to expand to fill a much different community–social function.

Finally, the issue of Jewish denominational affiliation is another area where some schools may be both a cause and an effect of a trend. The fastest growing sector in the Jewish school system is the 'Community School'. While the definition of 'Community School' may vary, they seem to be indicative of a post-denominational trend in the community, particularly – but not only - in the non-Orthodox community. Many families may have connections to a particular synagogue, but that apart, they do not seem to be worried too much about denominational distinctions. The issue is perceptively addressed in this quote:

---

[240] The frequent suggestions that schools should run 'Family Shabbatonim' or other family programs, which may be excellent ideas, seem to me to be coming from the same trend, and present the same issues.

....if you have learned something about Reform, Conservative, and Orthodox Judaism, let me share with you ...that all these labels and divisions are meaningless and obsolete. There are only two kinds of Jews — serious Jews and non-serious Jews. Serious Jews try to do what Jews have always done... to pattern their lives on the insights of Judaism, whether in a Reform, Conservative, or Orthodox idiom, while to the non-serious Jew, it doesn't matter what style of synagogue service he stays home from or which definition of mitzvah he ignores....

.... The question is whether you are interested in doing what Jews have always done, recapturing the feeling of standing at Sinai, bringing holiness into your life by sanctifying even its ordinary moments --- especially its ordinary moments.

-- 'To Life!' by Rabbi Harold Kushner[241], Little Brown and Company, 1993

A school characterized by 'user-friendly' traditionalism is a very attractive Jewish 'one-size-more-or-less-fits-all' program. It should be noted that currently, some Orthodox groups like Chabad and Aish haTorah aggressively promote a 'non-judgmental' image that minimizes denominational barriers. How that will affect synagogues whose raison d'être is a denominational label remains to be seen.

14.1.2 Rabbis as Board members

A different issue is the question of whether local Rabbis should be on the Board of the school.

In some communities, this will be natural, and the local Rabbi should be a valuable and supportive ally. In particular, he/she should be sympathetic and understanding of the Principal's professional position.

The responsible Rabbi — as with any member of the Board — will function in that capacity only with the interests of the school at heart. Occasionally, as with every Board member, other agendas can intrude[242].

The personality, skill and status of the local Rabbi will determine how that special relationship is exercised. It will work best where there is a strong relationship (e.g. historic, geographic, ideological) between the school and a particular synagogue.

However, where that relationship is perceived as exclusionary it may limit the appeal of the school - *"Rabbi X makes sure that members of his synagogue get preference at the school".* In those circumstances (and this is a Board / Governance issue), a

---

[241] Rabbi Harold Kushner is the well-known author of 'When Bad Things Happen To Good People'

[242] For a truly illuminating account of the psychological dynamics in religious institutions, and among leaders in religious institutions (including synagogues and Jewish schools), see (the oddly and even misleadingly entitled): " Generation to Generation: Family Process in Church and Synagogue", by Edwin H. Friedman. Edwin Friedman was a practising psychotherapist, specialising in religious organisations of all denominations, and practising congregational Rabbi, who suggests that the emotional and psychological dynamics of religious institutions resemble the issues that are often seen in family therapy.

different structure may be easier – for example, get the local Rabbi to chair a 'Rabbinic Advisory Group', composed of a number of local Rabbis, with whom the Principal (and perhaps the school President) can meet once or twice a year to exchange views, information and concerns. The school has to work at ensuring that local synagogues and Rabbis are its partners.

'Community Schools' (who do not have a denominational affiliation) may face particular problem. Local policies may preclude easy co-operation between Rabbis of different streams. In this situation, it may be best not to have a designated 'School Rabbi' (internal or external), and it may be impossible to have balanced Rabbinic representation of your Board. The function of the Principal in holding the balance in that situation is crucial, and demands extraordinary skill[243].

14.2 The Jewish Community

14.2.1   The Principal in the local Jewish community

The local Jewish community is the school Principal's primary 'non-school' constituency.

As time and opportunity permit, the Principal should see and be seen in the local community, demonstrating the school's support of the local Jewish community. A conscientious Principal will be at community events, rallies, ceremonies, and meetings. Just as the presence of community representatives at school occasions will be publicly recognized, the Principal's presence should be recognized from the platform at other occasions.

Invitations to speak at community events and organizations, large and small, should be accepted whenever possible. In all of these opportunities, public exposure is not only publicizing the school – it is also giving parents and others a source of pride and reassurance in the school leadership.

The Principal should make a more-than-minimum commitment to the local Jewish Federation and modest contributions to other appropriate charities. For the many invitations to bar/bat mitzvahs, weddings etc., from school families (and staff) with whom the Principal does not have a personal relationship beyond the school, the

---

[243] On a personal note, currently occupying a post as Head of a Community School, not being a Rabbi seems to be a noticeable advantage. I reason that this is because whatever decisions I take do not carry a Rabbinic (and therefore denominational) tag. Although Rabbis have traditionally been Heads of Schools, I see that increasingly, school Principalships are occupied by non-Rabbis (see Appendix 'A'). A similar process happened with Hillel Directors in North America, and perhaps a comparative study would shed light on developing community dynamics.

Board should make a discreet budget available to the Principal from which small gifts can be given.

In all community activity, the Principal should take care not to be politically or religiously partisan to the extent that it becomes problematic. Neither parents nor teachers nor students should feel that the Principal's own views and beliefs will compromise their comfort level in the school.

14.2.2 The local Jewish press

- For a general discussion of how to build relationships with the press and media SEE SECTION 15.7.

The Principal's personal relationship to the local Jewish press is extremely important, and can make a great deal of difference to how your school is portrayed in the community.

The Principal should get know the editor of the local Jewish paper, and the reporter who covers Jewish education. Both should be invited to the school. Make them your partners. The Principal and school faculty should be encouraged to write for the local Jewish paper. Their personalities and enthusiasm(s) should come across. The writing should be fresh, non-formulaic / non-sermonic, and readable!

14.2.3 The Federation

The local Jewish Federation is a key element in every Jewish community. Its job is fundraising. Fundraising and education are two separate worlds, and it is always tempting to stress the values that separate them, rather than the values that they have in common – chief among them, the welfare of the Jewish community.

If the existing relationship in your community is good – that is excellent. If there is tension between the school (as an institution) and the local Federation, it is very much in your interests to be a leader in closing the gap. The future of Jewish schools is very likely to be bound up with Federation funding, and the faster you engage with your Federation, the better.

Jewish school students should be front and central in participation in Federation and community events, and promoting 'Federation consciousness' to students and parents should be a regular part of school programs. As in all things, it pays to be pro-active. If the local Federation leadership (lay or professional) changes, invite the new leadership to visit the school. Make sure that Federation leaders and professionals are on the school mailing list. When student attend a community rally or event, ensure that they are wearing school t-shirts, and/or are waving a photogenic school banner.

14.2.4 National and international networks

The English metaphysical poet John Donne (1572-1631) famously observed that 'No man is an island'. Both from a personal-professional point of view, and from an institutional point of view, it is useful, interesting (and usually enjoyable) to position your school with a visible profile in wider Jewish life. It enables you to see a context of more general trends; the interactions with others should be an enriching experience; and your community and parents will be proud at the exposure of the school to a wider horizon. Keep an eye out for organizations, meetings, websites, and publications that have direct or indirect relevance to your school.

In the last few years the 'networking' opportunities for Jewish schools have increased almost beyond recognition. New North American organizations such as PEJE, the AviChai Foundation, RAVSAK, AMODS all offer innovative and valuable programs and resources for school professionals and lay leadership, joining established organizations such as JESNA, Torah Umesorah, the Solomon Schechter network and others. Educational leadership in Israel from the Hebrew University Melton Centre, the Lookstein centre in Bar Ilan University, the Pardes Institute and the Hartman Institute have all increased the range and depth of their involvement with Diaspora schools. There can be few schools whose faculty or Administration do not participate in or at least read the online 'Lookjed' forum of Bar Ilan.

14.3 Wider Community

14.3.1   Educational

Similar considerations apply to involvement with forums and associations in the wider educational community. In some cities, Jewish schools are leading members of local associations of independent schools, or of Principals' forums. Some national service consortia (ISM – Independent School Management - is perhaps the foremost example) work extensively with Jewish schools. In the USA, accreditation processes have drawn many Jewish schools into wider engagement with the educational community.

All of this can only be to the benefit of Jewish education.

The higher and more consistently professional service we are able to offer our community, the higher the regard for Jewish schools will be, and the more effective we will be in achieving our educational and community ideals.

14.3.2   Civic

There has been little or no theoretical discussion of the role of the Jewish schools in the general, non-Jewish community.

The issue is problematic at the basic level of tension between the particularistic and the universalistic components of Jewish vision. It may be observed that this is an issue for every Jewish (and other ethnic or religious) organization, not only for schools.

Many school Administrators will claim pragmatic reasoning for not facing the issue — *"We have no time to fill our Jewish community commitments, let alone commitments to the wider community"*. Others will point out the moral and religious imperatives currently widely grouped under the rubric of 'Tikkun Olam' ("Repairing the world"). A few will strongly challenge the idea that Jewish schools should be involved in any non-Jewish community projects.

The first commitment of every Jewish school will be to Jewish community causes, certainly including Israeli causes. Yet there are compelling reasons why every Jewish school — without exception — should contribute to the humanitarian wellbeing and the cultural life of the society in which we live, at both local and global scale. They can do so in many ways. These range from sustained personal voluntarism in local communities to fund-raising projects for famine or disaster relief. It would be an educational and religious failure for any student to pass through any Jewish school without being part of ongoing *tzedakah* for their fellow human beings.

Non-charitable activities are also involved. Schools may, and should, participate in inter-school competitions, drama and music festivals, and, of course, sports leagues. There are often logistic problems regarding (most commonly) Shabbat and kashrut observance SEE SECTION 8.11. In some instances, these will be irresolvable, and the school will simply choose not to take part, as a matter of religious sensibility for some schools, and community pride or honor for others. Careful, practical and tactful negotiations well beforehand will in many cases allow fixtures and competitions to be scheduled to accommodate the participation of Jewish schools. The more the school participates, and is perceived as a 'community partner', in general the easier it will be to achieve user-friendly programming.

14.3.3   Interfaith and community relations

Jewish schools are often invited to take part in interfaith or inter-community activities, encounters and 'dialogues'. While in general I am very much in favor of Jewish community involvement in such activities (and believe that the community does not do nearly enough in that respect), I am much more circumspect in involving school students.

There is definitely place for such activities, and it may be argued that the more that Jewish students are recruited into the Jewish educational system (and therefore are withdrawn from non-Jewish schools), the more they are necessary. A frequent argument heard from opponents of Jewish schools is that not only are Jewish students "segregated", without opportunities to meet others from other backgrounds and communities, but the reverse is also true — that young people in the general school system do not have opportunities to meet and get to know Jewish students. While I think that the benefits of Jewish education outweigh this and other possible 'downsides', there is an element of truth in the point being made.

However — and this is a major 'however' — there are differences between the different categories of activity. Anything that involves religious or political 'dialogue' needs very, very careful preparation, and only exceptional students may be capable of handling it. For whatever reason, the Jewish community as a whole seems to have trouble in conceptualizing and articulating its identity, let alone its beliefs. Many Jews, better-educated than the average Jewish High School student, struggle to describe Judaism in a theological framework, or in other ways that use a universal religious vocabulary, which is intelligible to others. Equally, few Jewish students are literate in basic Christian beliefs – let alone those of Islam, Hinduism, Sikhism or Buddhism[244], and may find themselves challenged to understand and respond to even well-meaning enquiries in a vocabulary to which the questioner can relate.

In addition, we live in an increasingly politicized world. The Jewish community's view of itself, and, particularly, of its link to Israel, is religious, emotional and idealistic – but it is very, very rarely political. Most others see the Middle East through political eyes. (This is a major reason why Jewish students are ill-equipped and ill prepared to deal with campus anti-Israel activity).

Finally, as anyone who has participated in such discussions (political or religious) knows, it is a sad fact that questions often arise that have clearly antisemitic roots. For better or for worse, most contemporary Jewish students, especially those growing up in large, active, socially intense Jewish communities, live in blissful ignorance of the themes of classic antisemitism.

For all the pitfalls – and anticipated objections from parents and local community leaders may be added to the difficulties discussed above – neither our community nor our schools can refuse such contact, and may even initiate it. But be careful, and be prepared.

14.3.4   Antisemitism

From time to time, the Principal will have to deal with antisemitic incidents involving the school, staff or students. It may be graffiti, neighborhood harassment or, very commonly, comments and catcalls at sports fixtures. The general policy – sports fixtures apart SEE SECTION 6.4.1 should be to call the police, and in appropriate cases consult with Jewish Community agencies.

In cases involving other schools, the first call should be to the counterpart School Principal. A tone of regret is initially appropriate. Sometimes, the Jewish school Principal will be taken aback at the dismissive reaction of his or her counterpart, perhaps because racial or prejudiced comments are fairly common at other schools, involving other minorities.

These can be traumatic incidents for students (and occasionally staff.) Act carefully, act decisively, and take advice. Keep a cool head, and keep the school's reaction and response in proportion.

---

[244] It would do no harm to teach a course in world religions in our schools.

Occasionally, a teacher (usually new), or a guest speaker, will make an offensive remark. In most cases, these are either misplaced attempts at humor or naïve remarks made out of ignorance. A quiet and reasonable talk should suffice. Anger is pointless, and will only alienate and humiliate a (probably) already embarrassed individual. If it turns out that you have a real antisemite on staff, they should be terminated.

14.4 'I'd like to visit the school'

Visitors may fall into several categories:

- Educational professionals

- Community visitors / VIP's

- Prospective donors

- Prospective parents

The relaxed Principal should always enjoy showing the school to visitors, and it is a professional and community courtesy to be welcoming. Visitors come in different categories, and, like guest speakers, should be efficiently managed. As a matter of courtesy, the Principal should greet all visitors; but the Principal does not have to personally show all visitors around.

Visitors should have the politeness to enquire in advance if it is convenient to visit the school. The occasional 'walk-in' may be accommodated if it is not disruptive to do so, and if a senior student can be pulled from the library to show the visitors around – but they cannot expect time from senior staff.

Standard routines for dealing with visitors include the following:

- Assess the importance of the visitor, using whatever appropriate criteria

- Determine exactly what the visitor wants to see (classes … the building … students… the Jewish Studies … the organization), and with whom they need to meet. Groups need more comprehensive programming.

- Decide whether the proposed time of visit is convenient for the school, and whether the features of the school that the visitor is coming to see will be easily accessible. If the visitor wants to see classes, then it is pointless visiting during exam. If it is not convenient – say so. If the visitor(s) are on a tight schedule, can only visit at a certain time, but nevertheless wish to come, explain what they will be able to see, and what, unfortunately, will not be available for then at that time.

We are very happy to have you visit the school, but please be aware that on Tuesday afternoons after 2:30PM there are no Ivrit lessons being taught.

- Work out a schedule. If possible, email it to the visitor in advance. Give them a copy on arrival. If they need to meet with staff, schedule the meetings. If they want to meet students, try and schedule a lunchtime (not class-time) encounter – 'free pizza' time again. It is the rare visitor who wants or needs to spend more than an hour or so in a school. For most visitors, five or ten minutes with the Principal, a 20-minute tour of the school, including one or two class visits (see below), and a subsequent 'wrap-up' in the Principal's office is sufficient. Give every visitor some material (your recruitment pack) to take away. It is useful to also have on file a single sheet of 'Facts about our school' – enrolment, budget, tuition fees, academic profile etc., which will save ten minutes' of factual questions.

Teachers should expect that every so often the Principal or another Administrator may bring visitors into their classes for a minute or two, unannounced. Good teachers will not mind. The wise Administrator will know which classrooms show the school to its best advantage, and which are more tactfully avoided. Before entering the class, give the visitor brief information about the grade, class, subject and teacher they are about to see. Aware visitors will also understand that walking around a high school sometimes involves encounters with the unexpected. If a visitor requests to sit in on a class, the teacher must be asked in advance. If necessary, announce the visit a few days before in your staff newsletter.

On Thursday morning, a group of visitors from Israel will be in the school, and may briefly visit classes. Your cooperation and hospitality are appreciated!

The Principal can take visitors around the school. Alternatively, after greeting them, a senior student can take visitors on tour. Give the student some guidance on where to take the visitors, and how long the tour should last. Trust them. Students normally take this as a compliment, and visitors enjoy the experience – especially prospective parents. It is good publicity for the school. Note, however, that students should not take visitors into classes. The Principal should always personally accompany visiting educational professionals – especially Principals of other schools (a function of professional etiquette). The Director of Development should plan Donor visits. On occasion, you might invite your President or a Board member to join a tour.

Do not allow visitors to speak to, or interrupt, classes in session, unless there is a good reason to, or the teacher invites the visitor to ask a question or make a comment. Do not leave a visitor alone in a class, except by prior arrangement, and having given the teacher and the visitor clear instructions:

> *Mrs. B – could you ask a student to take our visitor back to the office in fifteen minutes' time?*

Occasionally, local Rabbis, Board members, Federation executives and others may ask to bring visitors to the school (more often: *announce* that they are bringing visitors to the school....). That is fine, assuming it is convenient. However, NEVER allow persons who are not members of the school staff to show visitors around the school unaccompanied. They will not know the correct answers to questions, and will give out wrong information. Insist that a senior member of staff accompany them.

> *Mrs. H is our Vice-Principal, and I have asked her to show you round the school and answer your questions*

Finally – always be candid and honest to visitors. They do not come from perfect institutions, either!

Operations – Non-academic

15 MANAGING NON-ACADEMIC ISSUES

16 FUNDRAISING AND ALUMNI

15 MANAGING NON-ACADEMIC ISSUES

The Principal's duty to the school and its students includes important non-academic areas of responsibility. They are crucial to the functioning of the institution, and may be crucial to the welfare of students and staff.

For many Jewish School Principals, these include subjects and potential situations of which they have little or no expertise or experience. Principals' certification courses in the public sector may incorporate material that deals with them, and Principals coming into the Jewish system from the public sector will usually have had broader familiarity with school management issues. (The former public-school personnel, however, have the steep learning curve of the private / Jewish dimensions of the school with which to contend.)

A Principal must take steps to acquire the skills and knowledge necessary to exercise responsible leadership in all areas of school life, whether by individually researching the issues or by attending training courses.

15.1 Financial management

The financial affairs of the school must be administered properly, with appropriate controls and appropriate accountability.

Proper financial administration includes:

- Annual budgeting (see below)

- Appropriate financial controls and systems

- Systematic accounting of income and expenditure

- Compliance with all accounting requirements, conventions and procedures appropriate and relevant to a non-profit

- Oversight of a lay Budget and Finance Committee

- Full reporting

- Independent audit

Every school will have a lay Treasurer (normally a CPA), who, with an appropriately qualified committee, oversees school finances. In very small schools, lay volunteers (perhaps with a school bookkeeper) will do most of the school financial administration. Larger schools[245] may have fully-fledged accounts offices.

15.1.1   Control and authority

Proper controls on expenditure must be in place in the school. Any CPA will be able to suggest systems. They will include, but will not necessarily be limited to:

- A system of authorizing expenditure at Administrative level. Staff should not be able to order supplies or services, or arrange events, without authorization. School events cannot be arranged without an approved budget.

- No expenses should be reimbursed without receipts and documentation.

- Without exception, ALL income and expenditure associated with the school – whether it applies to the academic program, the sports program, school trips, the charity collections, or anything else – must come through the school accounting office.

- An ironclad rule applies to bank accounts: No member of staff or anyone associated with the school may operate a bank account that is independent of the school's accounting system.

- Cheques may only be signed by authorized signatories, and there must be two for each cheque – normally one Administrator and one lay leader.

- The school credit card must be very carefully controlled, and its use very closely restricted.

- Expenditure outside the provision of the annual budget should need special authorization –at Board or Finance Committee level for major items.

- Student Council accounts, which is money belonging to the students, should be properly structured, with checks and balances in place to ensure that the administration of the funds are open, accountable, and above suspicion. They, too, should be administered through the school Accounts office.

- All purchases of supplies or services above agreed amounts should be open to competitive tender.

---

[245] Schools can be very large operations. Currently, TanenbaumCHAT's annual operating (non-capital) budget is in the region of CAN$25m/USD$22m.

All expenditure should be scrutinized. The Principal and the CFO should have authority to authorize expenditure up to an agreed limit, in order to allow for the daily running of the school, and to allow for minor, immediate expenditure. A Principal should also have access to a small discretionary fund (properly accounted) to help students in financial need for books, outings etc.

15.1.2   Accounts and analysis

The accounting system must be accurate and up to date. The more sophisticated the financial information, the easier it is to understand — and therefore plan for — the school budget.

Tracking mechanisms should be in place regarding expenditures — quarterly or monthly reporting, set up to show unexpected divergence from budgeted figures. This will take account of the typical patterns of school expenditure — for example, salaries are paid evenly throughout the year, but the ordering of books and supplies is heavily weighted to the beginning of the year. Comparative data will show how the rate of expenditure varies through the year, each year, which should both clarify how the school is performing financially relative to the budget; give information for future budgeting and cash flow planning; and also help predict year-end figures, and enable the school to generate corrective measures, if necessary.

15.1.3   Tuition assistance

Most schools grant Tuition assistance in greater or lesser amounts to families who cannot pay full Tuition Fees. The School Principal and Administration should not be involved in the administration of Tuition Assistance programs, which are generally lay-driven.

Criteria and process will be fixed locally[246], but the following principles must apply:

- Tuition assistance must be confidential and equitable, applied without favor or distinction

- As far as possible, the process should be objective, based on agreed scales

- The process should be dignified and sympathetic, and clear to parents and prospective parents

---

[246] In larger communities, where families may have children in two or more schools, there may be centrally-administered schemes, co-operation between schools, or, alternatively, centrally agreed criteria to which schools will subscribe. This ensures a consistent level of subsidy available from all schools, with obvious advantages. In most communities, families applying for Tuition Assistance have to make detailed and comprehensive disclosures of their financial circumstances. The formulae applicable to the calculations of assistance can be complex. It should be noted that the value of the reductions granted may amount to tens of thousands of dollars over a four-year High School career. It is expected that families will allocate high priority to Tuition Fees in their family budgets.

For reasons of confidentiality and objectivity, the 'Tuition Committee' should be at arms' length from the Board, and, if possible at arms' length from the current parent body. Many schools ask former parents who are also accountants (or have other relevant expertise) to serve on the Tuition Committee.

Confidentiality extends to the academic staff. No teacher or Administrator should have knowledge of which students receive Tuition Assistance. The school Principal may, from time to time, be party to that information.

Teachers and other school staff, and, frequently, community rabbis, may get automatic reductions on Tuition Fees for their own children. While the argument for this is strong (and it is always both good principle and good optics to have teachers' own children in the school), it should be noted that parents whose incomes are less than those of the teachers may question the practice.

15.1.4 Annual accounts

Your CFO/Executive Director will prepare Annual Accounts for the Board, which will in due course be audited in compliance with local practice and legal requirements.

15.1.5 Statistical data

It is immensely helpful to be able to address issues – whether they are routine (e.g. budgeting) or exceptional (a sudden change in enrolment) from an informed perspective, and have hard statistical data to present to the Board. Is what is happening in the school a 'blip' or a 'trend'? The only way to assess this is to have data. A cumulative record of key statistics and key indicators will give a reliable picture of school performance. The aware School Principal will become adept at using Microsoft Excel, and especially its visual graphing function. Key figures that affect budget projection and financial control, and should be tracked year by year include:

- Overall enrolment

- Enrolment figures – month-by-month from the close of registration until one month after the school opening – when your students enrolled, where they are coming from, who registers early and who registers late

- The proportion of students from each of your feeder school(s) whom you successfully recruit each year

- Retention figures by Grade (and, if necessary, by class)

- The proportion of students who pay full fees each year

- Total budget, income and expenditure, broken down by line and category

- Class sizes

- Annual cost per student.

- Trends of the tuition subsidy program, including the average fees paid by students receiving Tuition assistance

- Forward projections of enrolment based on analyses of enrolments in your feeder schools

- and other analyses which your Finance Committee will undoubtedly initiate.

15.2 Budgeting process

Rigorous budgeting is the integral basis of financial control, and is an essential aspect of a properly run school. It has to be a collaborative effort between lay and professional school leaders. The CFO/Executive Director and the Chair of the Budget and Finance Committee should be taking the lead and driving the process.

The CFO/Executive Director, with the Principal and the Finance Committee, should annually prepare a detailed budget for the next year's operations, and an outline budget for several years forward. Administration and Heads of Department should list and budget for their own needs.

Typically, salaries and associated personnel costs (insurance, pension contributions etc.) account for 80% - 85% of a private school budget. Establishing the correct staffing complement of the school is relatively easy when the school is small, with only one or two sections in each grade; it is far more complicated in a larger school. It may be assumed that the Principal and Vice-principals possess these skills.

Other costs will include plant and utilities (rent/property taxes, heating/lighting, cleaning, maintenance), office costs (paper, photocopying, supplies), and, of course, program costs of running school activities. There will be an appropriate allocation for Professional Development.

Every school will have its own particular budget requirements. They should all be identified, isolated, quantified for previous years and estimated for the coming year. A fortunate school will be able to account its capital expenditure separately; many Jewish schools will find that they are financing capital expenditure on equipment and buildings largely out of current income.

A budget is an essential mechanism. It forces the Principal and the Administrative team to think ahead and plan ahead, anticipating the school needs. It also gives the Administration opportunity to build items into the budget, so that necessary funds are assured, and do not become a tug-of-war with the Board in the middle of the year. The budget, which in young or small schools may be outline (because difficult to predict), will be fine-tuned and developed as the school grows. Over time, the school can compile valuable comparative data on income and expenditure.

The draft Budget will probably go through several revisions. Once the Administration and the Finance Committee have drawn up, reviewed and agreed the budget, the Chair of the Finance Committee will present it to the Board for approval – frequently at a special 'Budget Meeting'. Together with the Board, the next task, which is an integral part of the budgeting process, is fixing the Tuition Fee for the coming year, and communicating that to the parent body.

All of this should be done in good time, usually by the end of April preceding the following school year. This allows ample time for dealing with registration and re-registration of students (including dealing with applications for Tuition Assistance); it gives parents reasonable notice of their own commitments for the coming year; and it allows the school to order supplies and engage staff in good time.

As with all budgets for all purposes, the problems come with the variables.

Student numbers are the crucial element in the school budget for both income and expenditure. They cannot be exactly predicted, and even minor variations can affect the budget. A rise in numbers just before the beginning of the school year may entail creating a new class, or splitting a class that has become too big. While this may increase tuition income, overall cost may actually rise, because one large class (= economic) has been replaced with two small ones (= less economic). The alternative is to turn away students, which brings other problems. A drop in numbers will have the opposite effect. However, it is possible to minimize the unpredictability of registration by setting – and enforcing - an early registration date[247], before the budget process begins, so that the budget begins with a realistic idea of student numbers. The only way to do this is by adding progressive, effective penalties[248] for late registration and, conversely, late withdrawal.

If your heating system breaks down in November (or your air-conditioning in May), your budget will equally be affected, unless you have contingency funding for such events. Schools also deal with human beings of all ages; and human beings are living, changing, and to a degree unpredictable.

A tough Finance Committee ultimately works to the advantage of the Principal. The Administration must be answerable for the proposed budget, and there will be Finance Committee members who will want to know why class sizes cannot be bigger, or whether the new computers are essential, or whether the school really

---

[247] Mid-January.

[248] By setting and enforcing a significant 'Late Registration' surcharge. At TanenbaumCHAT it is currently $200. Exceptions /reductions should only be made for families moving into the city, economic hardship and similar reasonable grounds. Similarly, the penalties for withdrawal of an application should be real, with a substantial penalty to be paid as the beginning of the school year approaches.

needs to expand the office staff. Assuming you can satisfy them, the budget then becomes their budget as well. At the Board, it is the Committee, not the Administration, who are answerable for the budget and for the Tuition Fee.

The budget may exceed the projected income. Cuts are required. The correct process is for the Budget Committee to give the responsibility to the Principal and Administration to implement the cuts, bring the school's projected expenditure back within the limits of the budget, and report back.

The professional staff of the school have the task – never pleasant, and never easy – of deciding priorities, and cancelling, reducing or postponing expenditure. The alternative is for the lay committee to decide, which means, in practice that the Budget Committee is making educational decisions – an undesirable practice.

15.2.1   The Tuition Fee

The 'Tuition Fee' must be realistic; must be based on the budget as a realistic and responsible statement of school needs; and must at least be a 'break-even' figure, including allowances for contingency expenses. Budgeting for a deficit is really dangerous, and may be setting the school on the path to disaster. If the projected school income (from all sources) does not meet the projected expenditure, then either or both must be adjusted. Boards are sometimes scared of setting Tuition above various round-figure 'optical' thresholds. Experience shows that this is usually unfounded. Perceived value is more important than cost.

Parents are more sensitive to unpredicted changes in the rate of increase. If the increase has been x% (more or less) for the last three or four years, parents will be concerned if in any year the cost of Tuition rises by double or triple that rate. It is prudent to budget for a small surplus so that the school has a reserve that it can draw on in years when costs sharply increase.

A more interesting idea – yet to be applied in any Jewish school, as far as I know – is the 'Guaranteed Tuition Fee' currently being adopted by some Universities and colleges. The institution predicts its budget for the next four years (the length of the High School program), and offers an option of an averaged, 'guaranteed' fixed[249] annual Tuition Fee for four years. This allows parents to know exactly, to the dollar, what their Tuition fee cost will be for their child's High School career, and plan accordingly. A variation on this is the 'Guaranteed Percentage Rise', where, for example, parents may have the option of contracting for a four-year fixed annual percentage rise determined in advance.

---

[249] Under this system, each new intake is contracting for a different fee.

15.2.2   Privacy in the budget process

There should be a hierarchy of privacy in the budget process.

This is especially the case regarding individual salaries. The accounts and draft budgets may be prepared in different formats. The copies of the Budget considered by the Budget Committee may have detailed salaries of individual employees – not identified by name, but by some other label ('English-3"). These documents should be issued under conditions of high confidentiality, and may be collected back after each meeting. Administrative salaries (which would be identifiable, as these are single positions) should be aggregated. Staff have an entitlement of privacy regarding their salaries, especially in a school that is intimately involved with a community.

The budget (or accounts) documents issued for approval at the wider forum of the Board should contain aggregate salary figures, together with the assurance of the finance Committee (and, where applicable, the auditors) that the staffing levels of the school and the salary levels of individual staff have been correctly established and paid.

Equally, most schools will not release the full, detailed budget to their Board members, but will make a copy of the full accounts 'available for inspection' in the school offices before the Board meeting that will deal with the budget. At the meeting, numbered copies of the budget will be distributed and collected at the end of the meeting. These procedures will be familiar from corporate and non-profit settings.

A budget summary will be issued in due course to parents, probably as part of the Annual Report, but the school cannot function if detailed copies of the school budget are publicly available, and become the subject of discussion and gossip.

15.3 Equipment, furniture, plant and maintenance

The school does not have to be new, or lavishly decorated or equipped. Many outstanding schools operate out of sub-standard buildings. However, the school has to be clean and safe, and, whatever its physical circumstances, well maintained. The same applies to furniture and equipment. The school has to project a message of a well-run, dignified entity that has standards for itself as well as for its students.

Expenditure on physical plant (buildings, systems, equipment and grounds maintenance and upkeep) is money well spent. It does not have to be lavish – the front of the school does not have to be landscaped as if it was a corporate HQ – but it does have to be clean, neat and tidy. There is sometimes a tendency to begrudge all money spent on plant, equipment, maintenance and repairs, and to try and make the cheapest deals possible, regardless of the consequences. A school whose maintenance is sub-standard will very soon begin to look like a slum. Similarly, a well-maintained and sparkling school sends a message of an institution that is proud of itself.

15.3.1 Computers, Projectors, 'SmartBoards' and other digital equipment

These are now necessary parts of the classroom. The school's technology policy should include a realistic assessment of equipment needs, and this in turn must be reflected in the budget. Unfortunately, the cost of purchasing (or leasing) digital equipment is huge (even though it is falling), and it has a very fast process of obsolescence. Rather than haphazardly purchase equipment ('The Science Department wants a laptop'), a school standard of equipment should be established. This may be by department ('Every department will have x equipment'), by space ('Half of all teaching spaces will be equipped with a SmartBoard within two years') or even by teacher ('Every teacher will have a laptop').

The technology is changing the whole time, and for this reason alone it is prudent not to invest in a particular technology throughout the school that will then need to be replaced in its entirety within two or three years. The budget should provide for 'rolling replacement' of a proportion of the equipment every year, which allows the school to continually introduce newer equipment.

15.3.2 Photocopiers, fax machines, and phones

Keep photocopiers under strict control, or their cost will be astronomical. The first stage is to examine very carefully the terms of the contract with the suppliers of the machine and the suppliers of paper, toner and servicing. Are you paying per copy? Per machine? Is the arrangement the most economic for the school?

Student access to photocopiers should be on a 'for payment' basis only, most conveniently with pre-paid cards. Staff access to photocopiers should be by pass-code. Track the usage carefully, and if necessary give each a department a 'budget'. Staff who make excessive amounts of copies should be spoken to. If the curriculum need is there, they must make a course reader or source-book which can be more cheaply printed and sold. It is always useful to issue reminders to staff from time to time about the number of copies that have been registered to their pass-code numbers.

Are all staff aware of, and compliant with, copyright law? If applicable, does the school hold a copying license?

The fax machine should be kept in the main school office, and personal use by staff strongly discouraged. It can be a source of embarrassment if personal documents for staff members sit around in the 'in tray'. For reasons of confidentiality, the Principal's office and the Tuition Office should have their own fax machines.

The plummeting costs of telephone calls (and the spread of cell phones) make accessibility to phones less of an issue than it once was. But phones in public places, and in offices, staffrooms and the like should still be carefully programmed to restrict the possibilities of long-distance and international calling, except where appropriate. The school should keep one or two cell phones for use by staff on school trips.

If you are a school where either the Principal or other staff regularly travel to Israel on school business, it is well worth buying an Israeli cell phone with 'pay as you go' prepaid capacity – you then have one, regular Israel contact number, and all of the school contacts can be permanently programmed into the cell phone. It will save a lot of time and trouble.

15.4 Security

- Statutory and legal safety standards – fire codes, alarms, exit signage, building standards – must be a first priority for any school, and no school should be open and operating unless they comply with all applicable requirements.

The issue of security in Jewish schools is sensitive, and difficult[250].

In most jurisdictions the legal responsibility for the safety and security of students lies with the Principal.

The degree of security at the school will be a function of local conditions. Police, local school boards and Jewish Community agencies will all have locally-devised and locally applicable protocols for school security. There are also national standards[251]. The physical location of the school and the design of the school buildings will affect the security assessment, and the security measures that the school is able to take.

The issue of security is both practical and emotional. For wholly understandable reasons, school security arouses very strong concern in parents. Schools may meet with two extreme emotional reactions to the security issue:

- Parents and others who seek maximum (and often impractical) security measures in the school.

- Parents who react very negatively to security in Jewish schools, and believe that being at a Jewish school will make their

---

[250] No advice given here will realistically protect the school from premeditated violent or armed attack, which is the greatest fear of any Jewish community.

[251] Googling 'Safe Schools' will show a comprehensive range of resources.

children 'targets'. This is heard as a reason for unwillingness to send children to Jewish schools.

As usual, the correct path is somewhere in between. At times of heightened concern special security measures may be taken. Generally, for security to be effective it has to be enforceable and acceptable, and for it to be workable it has to be realistic for a High School. That has to be a local assessment. There is no point in trying to institute measures that the students or parents cannot or will not observe, or that will be impossible to maintain within the normal routine of the school.

Ultimately, the eyes and ears of staff and students are the best security

It is often the non-teaching and support staff who are particularly important – Administration, secretaries, receptionists and (especially) custodians. A sixth sense that something or someone is not in the right place at the right time can be invaluable in alerting the school to a developing situation. Is a door that should be locked shut, open for no reason? Is a student or visitor in a part of the building or site where they have no reason to be? Is a car parked for no reason near the school?

The Administration and the Board, together with local police and Jewish community resources, should undertake a basic security assessment of the premises. This need not be a formal exercise, but there should be a consultative process. Inviting professional security companies to carry out this exercise will frequently prove expensive, and produce unworkable results – SEE SECTION 15.5.2

A security assessment should deal with the following basic issues:

- Is there reasonable control over physical access and exit to the building?

- Is there a sense of security awareness in the school community? Are staff and students trained to be alert for, and report suspicious persons, events, objects, or incidents?

- Can unauthorized visitors to the building be readily identified and reported?

- Is the building and its vicinity well-lit and safe, and can the space in and around the school be easily supervised and monitored?

- Does the intruder alarm system meet the needs of the school?

- Is there one person who receives (and can therefore collate) all security-related information?

The security assessment should then be followed by response protocol:

- What happens in the case of an emergency?

- How does the school respond?

- Does it bring the situation under control?

The Principal's performance as a leader and manager will be under close scrutiny in any emergency, and will be a formative part of the institutional memory of the Principal's performance.

15.4.1   Security Guards and CCTV

It is a local decision whether or not to have security guards at the school. The phrase 'Security Guard' has many meanings.

If guards are needed under circumstances where their presence has to be more than routine, consider hiring off-duty policemen.

Closed-circuit television (CCTV) is increasingly being used in many locations. It cannot actively prevent incidents, except by its deterrent value. Permanent monitoring is expensive and is not foolproof. However, a CCTV system will digitally record images, and retain them for 24 hours or more (as programmed). It can be invaluable in providing a record of incidents of all sorts. Further, developing technology promises several school-applicable developments – for example, intelligent software that will identify and alarm unusual patterns of movement in a given area (e.g. sudden running in a corridor, or sudden movement in a science lab), or hand-held units that will enable any Administrator to monitor any CCTV camera from anywhere in the building.

- If CCTV is installed in or around the school, appropriate notice should be given in the School Handbook to ensure compliance with privacy legislation. Use of and access to the images recorded should be similarly supervised.

15.4.2   Computer security and network design

All of the school's computer networks have to have appropriate, professional security. Teenagers can be unnervingly adept at 'hacking' and otherwise compromising computer networks. School computer facilities have to be professionally designed and installed. Do not rely on well-meaning offers of low-cost help *("My brother-in-law knows computers")*. Make sure that the advice the school is receiving is expert, and regard any cost as legitimate expense.

- Attractive as it may be, never, ever allow your computer-whiz students to set up the school computer network

- Keep careful control over the set up of the computers in the school, and have clearly-formulated policy for student use.

A school may have three distinct computer networks:

The Student network – used by students to access the internet, their own email, and for composing and sending schoolwork. This system – accessible by students from the school library, classrooms, labs and by wireless from anywhere in the school – has the lowest security. Published policy should include clear statements that the school has no responsibility for the security of this network, and it retains complete control over the network administration and content. Where school computers are in use (as opposed to students' own laptops), the network should allow the teacher or librarian to see what is on any screen at any time. There will be other restrictions on the facilities offered, including blocking categories of sites. Many schools will not allow students to save material in the school system, or if so will annually 'wipe' its storage. Students can email files to other networks, or use portable memory. Partly for legal reasons, and partly because free email accounts are so easily available, there is now no need to allocate school email boxes (and thus addresses) to students.

The Staff network – accessible to staff from the staff room, from staff work-rooms, and possibly remotely from their homes, and used to prepare and store documents, lesson plans and teaching material, send and receive emails, and record marks and teachers' records. This may be on the same network as the students, but if so must be behind a heavily protected, professionally installed firewall. Simple password protection is not sufficient. Any interface to the Administrative network where marks and other data can be uploaded must be professionally secured. Despite the higher level of security, staff should be clearly warned not to store personal or confidential information on any computer that is part of the main school network, and to independently back-up all material. The students will seek the unknown weakness in the system. They may find it.

The Administrative network – used to store official student records, the school scheduling, personnel and (possibly) financial and accounting records, and the correspondence and documents of school Administration. This must be a **physically separate** network from any computer accessible by students or staff, with different computers, a separate server, and without access from any student-accessible space. Until and unless wireless security can be guaranteed, this network should be hard-wired only. Other than the carefully controlled interface with staff computers, no link should exist between this network and any other, and access should be carefully controlled.

Network concepts and technicalities change and develop the whole time. Make sure you have ongoing, updated, expert advice for all aspects of digital security.

15.5 Emergencies and crises

Management of crisis, including assessment of risk, is a real test of the Principal's leadership and judgment. There are no universally applicable instructions. The Principal has to think quickly and take the best possible decisions.

A crisis can fundamentally affect any institution, and, of course, may have profound and possibly tragic consequences on individuals and families.

It is in the nature of a crisis that the less predictable it is, the more difficult it is to deal with. In a Jewish High School, a 'crisis' can be caused by a daunting list of possibilities, singly or in combination, including but not limited to the following list:

- Medical emergency, including accident, injury, sudden illness, death, outbreaks of infectious disease.

- Unauthorized intruders to the school, or other threat from individuals

- Actual immediate threat to the school

- Vandalism or graffiti on school buildings (especially if there is an anti-Semitic motive)

- Suspicious objects, including suspicious incoming mail.

- Threatening telephone calls (or emails), including bomb threats

- Fire or other building emergency

- Serious incidents initiated by students

- News of terrorist or other incidents in other communities, or in Israel

Other sorts of crisis, not be so sudden, may involve:

- Incidents or allegations concerning the school and/or students, staff, Board members or parents

- Unwelcome publicity

- Personnel crises – sudden resignations

- Illness or death of students or staff

In a High School, with teenagers who can get all sorts of impulses into their heads, anything is possible, at any time. The responsibility of worrying what the next moment may bring is one of the genuine and probably underappreciated stresses of the Principal's job. The Principal may not be able to control what happens; but must assert control, as quickly and as effectively as possible, in the event of emergency.

15.5.1 General guidelines

Some emergencies and crises are sudden and short-lived (e.g. a medical emergency on campus); others may be of very long duration (e.g. coping with a scandal involving a staff member). Whatever the circumstances, the Principal must:

- Calmly and authoritatively take control

- Ensure that the safety and security of students and staff takes precedence over all other considerations

- Use very best judgment, in collaboration with all other relevant and responsible agencies, to resolve the situation

- If possible under the circumstances, ensure that there is minimal disruption to school functioning

- Preserve the dignity of the school

- Communicate clearly at all times to the school constituencies and to the community

- Deal with all post-crisis issues

- Ensure that at a suitable time there is an opportunity to review the events, assess the quality of the school's response, learn any lessons and incorporate them into continuing school procedures

15.5.2 Anticipation and planning

A school should have provisions for plausible scenarios. Some may be statutory duties – the need to maintain a well-rehearsed procedure for evacuation of the school buildings in case of fire, for example. Others should include procedures for dealing with bomb threats, suspicious objects found near or at the school, intruder alarms etc.

In devising these procedures, the school must consider;

- Who is responsible for drawing up these instructions, and for assessing their practicality?

- What eventualities should be considered?

- For whom should instructions be provided? (Teachers, students, support staff)

- What is the procedure for periodic review and, if applicable, rehearsal?

The first hurdle is drawing up instructions[252]. In some institutions, outside experts may be commissioned to do so. Private security companies – large and small – are a growing industry. They vary greatly in the quality of the advice they provide, and many have a tendency to recommend totally impractical (and expensive) security plans. If the advice given ignores the reality of school routine, or school life, or the nature of teenagers, or the budgets available, it is useless. Advice may be available from the local police. In some places, short courses are commercially available to school (and college) personnel that suggest ways of dealing with Emergency Planning. In larger communities, there may be resources available from the Jewish community or its associated agencies.

Every school must decide for itself how to do emergency planning. But the team must include those who know the school and its buildings intimately – Administration, teachers, support staff – if the recommendations are to be realistic. Any report must go through a process of assessment before it is adopted as policy:

- Is it realistic?

- Will it work?

- Can it be communicated?

- Can it be implemented?

In making that assessment, the following have to be borne in mind:

- Schools have steady turnovers. A school population briefed and rehearsed on a particular procedure may be substantially changed within twelve months.

- Teenagers cannot be relied on to remember or even (in some cases) obey instructions, unless they are thoroughly and regularly rehearsed and drilled.

In many cases, an internal school committee will draw up the best plans.

15.5.3   The first twenty minutes

If an incident happens in school, the reaction in the first twenty minutes or so will determine a great deal of what happens subsequently. 'Emergency drill' includes:

---

[252] It should be noted that once security recommendations are given to the school – whatever their usefulness – in subsequent legal action the school may be legally challenged on its failure to implement them.

- Calling emergency services, and ensuring that someone is deputed to meet them and direct them to the scene of the emergency when they arrive

- Ensuring safety and security of the students (by evacuation or other emergency drill).

- If the situation is non-threatening to other students (e.g. a medical emergency), isolating the area of the building where the patient is by stationing staff (or senior students) at key points to keep others away, and keep the way clear for access by emergency services. If, for example, a patient has to be transported to hospital by ambulance, and a lesson is due to end, you do not want the corridors filling with students who may obstruct the paramedics. Announce over the PA that teachers are to keep their classes in their rooms until further notice.

- Checking the building

- Advising key people connected with the school (President, local Jewish community security, other local Jewish schools) – see below

- Dealing with telephones

- Determining when the emergency is over, and arranging or announcing a return to routine.

A further complication can be the arrival of anxious parents at the school. Students will call parents (and friends) on their cell phones, and word (and rumor) will spread very quickly about an incident or emergency at the school. Parents may come (even at High Schools) and demand to withdraw their children. This can cause chaos and even danger, but it is difficult to do anything about it. If the police are on the scene they can be helpful.

15.5.4   Authority in time of crisis

Clear authority is essential in time of crisis. The Principal will normally assume responsible control. However, it is important that there is a designated chain of authority for times when the Principal is off-campus or may be out of action. The Staff Handbook should clearly state that

> When the Principal is away from the Campus, or indisposed, the senior staff member is the [Vice Principal], Mr/s. X.

15.5.5   Communicating in time of crisis

The first, immediate duty of communication is to students and staff in the building, giving whatever practical information is necessary. As soon as the immediate situation is under control, and those in the building are safe, there will be demands for further information.

Circumstances may dictate different practice

The extent of information initially disclosed to each group (or at all) is a matter of judgment:

- First priority – staff and students on site

- Second priority –the Board and senior community members

- Third priority – parents

- Fourth priority – press and media

In any crisis, communications are vital. The quality of communications will determine how key constituencies understand what is happening, and will form their view of how the school has dealt with the crisis. The school's reputation is at stake.

The school's ability to deal with the press and media will depend largely on having already built a good relationship with them. SEE SECTION 15.7.1

Communicating with parents follows similar rules. As outlined SEE SECTION 4.8 it is essential to maintain a clear *and credible* flow of information to the parent body. If the school already has a reputation of being open, clear and truthful in its communications with parents, they will trust the school when it has to communicate with them in times of crisis. If the school has, unfortunately, acquired a reputation with its parent body of being evasive and secretive, it will have a much more difficult time.

Strategic objectives in communicating with parents are clear:

- to deal with their fears concerning their own child.

- to retain their confidence in the school

As always, circumstances will dictate the response. It is important that the school speaks with a consistent voice, and therefore an early step – preferably within hours -- must be consultation with your lay leadership.

If the crisis is really serious consider engaging a Communications Consultant – SEE SECTION 4.9.6

Whether you do or you don't, determine the school's basic statement, which should be issued as quickly as possible (within hours) and include:

- Acknowledgement of the facts

- Description of the moves already taken by the school

- What the school intends to do next

- Information regarding the ongoing operation of the school

- (Re)statement of policy

- Clear directions of where parents can direct questions and concerns, and where they can find further (developing) information.

The School President and the Principal should issue the statement. Keep it short, clear and unemotional. It is then essential that Board members and school staff be asked to reinforce the content of the statement, and not give contrary information. If they believe that the statement is wrong, or misleading, make it clear that they may make their feelings felt – but they should not publicly undermine the school's statement. They should not speak to the press, but refer all enquiries to the school's sole spokesperson – the Principal.

The media for publicizing the statement can be varied – it can be posted on a school website, emailed to parents, posted in the school, issued as a press statement, or all of the above. The important thing is that parents must feel that the school is being responsible. Issue further statements if there are developments that need to be communicated. Make sure that they are clearly timed and dated, and sequentially numbered.

Another tactic that may be used at an appropriate stage is a parent meeting, at which a briefing is given and parents have a chance to ask questions. The chair of such an event should be carefully chosen, as should the speakers. If relevant or appropriate, a local police officer or other civic representative may be invited. The event should open with full statements by the Principal and the School President, which should outline the events and try and anticipate parent concerns. It is much better if you volunteer the answers to the key issues rather than be perceived as having to disclose information in response to parent pressure.

At all times, work with a small group of lay leaders, senior colleagues and perhaps some parents to identify the concerns of your constituencies.

Communications will only be effective if they are conveying accurate news of sound actions and policies. If the school is not handling the crisis competently, no amount of communications will help.

15.5.6   Staff and students

Similar considerations apply to staff and students.

Staff communication should precede (or at least be simultaneous with) community and public statements, and should be equally frank and open. It is important that all other communications be copied directly to staff, and that they do not learn what is happening via the press or from third parties.

> *To: All staff*
>
> *For your information – the school is issuing the following statement tomorrow which will be circulated to parents and press…*

It is important that staff, who will have to deal with students, have as comprehensive a view as possible of the crisis.

Information to students should be simple, clear and straightforward, and should discourage speculation. Emphasis should be on going forward.

15.5.7   Back to school

When school resumes after an emergency – whether school has been disrupted for an hour or a week – direction must be given to staff about dealing with the emotional and possibly other consequences of the incident. Time must be given to discussing or responding to whatever happened, but it should be given a limit.

> *In third lesson, staff are asked to devote time to discussing with students the recent incident at the school. Allow them to voice any remaining concerns and anxieties, and reflect on their own feelings and reactions – individually and as a community. It is at the teacher's discretion whether to devote part or all of the lesson to this. Our colleague Mrs. X has compiled some guidelines and suggestions of possible staff response to issues that students might raise, and copies are available in the staff room. However, after third lesson, when all students will have had time to talk, school should return to normal lessons, and we would then like to try and resume normal school life.*

An appropriate school assembly can give a semi-ceremonial recognition of significant incidents, and provide a way of dealing with feelings as a school community.

15.6 Bereavement

SEE SECTION 7.2.6

In cases involving bereavement, Rabbis and Counselors may be brought in to help students (and staff) talk through their grief. A table with a memorial in or near the school entrance can be a focal point of expression. Later, articles in the school newspaper can give appropriate 'memory' to crisis. Keeping school response balanced is a very delicate issue. Sometimes students and/or parents, especially if they are meeting death for the first time, will want to memorialize the deceased in ways that are perhaps out of proportion to school life[253], impractical, inappropriate in other ways, or involve very long-term commitments that, realistically, are unlikely to be sustainable. Suggestions involving raising funds for a spouse or family have to be very carefully handled indeed, and -- *if allowed to take place at all* -- must be done in a way that preserves the dignity of the bereaved family members. In all cases, the good intentions, emotions and pain of the students who want to help must be very carefully handled.

The Principal has to steer the school through a very complex sequence of grief, mourning, perhaps trauma – and then return to school routine.

15.6.1   Suicide

A particularly difficult situation of bereavement involves suicide within the school 'community' – especially if is a student. This is a very, very tragic, but also dangerous situation.

The school should call in professional help without delay. Most 'Family Service' agencies have school bereavement teams. At the earliest possible opportunity – if necessary on an emergency basis - convene a meeting of senior staff and Guidance Counselors, local rabbis and any other individuals who can help, and invite either a school bereavement team or a local psychologist to join the meeting.

Devise a plan of action that includes (as a minimum):

- Finding a sensitive, reliable contact with the bereaved family, and check that whatever the school plans, it is agreeable to the family

- Ensuring that if they wish to, and the family agrees, students who attend the funeral are accompanied by a strong group of staff

- Making counseling available in school – a 'drop-in centre' is a good idea

- Giving staff help in dealing with students' feelings in the classroom. Staff, too, may need an opportunity to discuss their personal feelings

- In particular, keeping a discreet, close check on the feelings of close friends of the deceased student

---

[253] Other than in exceptional circumstances, there may be students and staff who did not know the deceased, their family or community circle, and are not affected or not involved in the bereavement.

- Arranging appropriate recognition in the school

- Giving students guidance with regard to shivah visits

Use judgment in returning the school to normal routine.

* * * * * * *

In all of these difficult situations, schools and young people are remarkably resilient. As discussed above -- with your colleagues, try to sense the appropriate scale of response; deal with it; but then, again, purposefully move the school back to normal routine.

15.7 Press and media

15.7.1   Make the media your partners

An incident – real or imagined – happens at the school. There are reporters outside, the telephone is ringing off the hook, and a local TV news crew is suddenly filming outside the school gate.

- At that moment, it is too late for the Principal to begin to learn how to deal with the press.

Knowing how to deal with the press, and having a sense of how to manage public relations are essential skills for a Principal. In the contemporary world, there is a presumed right of the public to know, and the presumption of a right to institutional or individual privacy is all but gone. A private school – particularly a Jewish private school – is fertile ground for news.

At all times, the Principal should be the sole designated spokesperson for the school to the press and media, and to other official entities. That must be clearly understood by staff and Board[254]. Preparing media strategy should start well before the media come looking for the school.

In dealing with the press (which may include all types of print and electronic media), remember the following:

- Reporters and writers are ordinary people doing a job. They want news. Not information, and not explanation – they want news, and they are working to deadlines.

- Supplying them with news is the best way to earn their cooperation.

---

[254] That role should be specified in the Job Description that is part of the Principal's contract.

- Refusing them news will frustrate them, and they will turn to someone else to get (a version) of the news that you are refusing to give them.

- Tell the truth. "Principal tells truth to the media" is not news. "Principal deliberately lies to the media" is big news.

The Principal needs to be aware of strategy and tactics. Strategic goals may include:

- Protecting the reputation and public face of the school and its constituents

- Satisfying media concern without exposing the school to unwelcome exposure

- Building bridges of credibility and trust with local and community media

Good tactical moves for the Principal include:

- Always agree to speak to the press, and always be cooperative

- Disclose whatever information you are able to, and offer the media help

- Give reasonable statements if asked for comment

- Be frank and fair

- From time to time, take the initiative and offer or suggest stories. Are a group of your students involved in an innovative school project? Are they helping in an unusual social service project? Has a graduate of your school obtained some distinction, or received an important appointment? Is there an issue being discussed that might benefit from a wider discussion?

- Make the school media-conscious. Have a member of staff, or a volunteer parent, send regular stories[255] and — especially — photos of school events to the local press.

- Contribute occasional articles to local Jewish and non-Jewish press. Get the name of the Principal known to the editors and staff.

Finally, perhaps the most important advice:

---

[255] The Principal should briefly OK all suggested stories.

- If you have a crisis – call the media before they call you.

> *Hi, this is the Principal of Jewish High School on Side Street calling. We have a situation that has developed in the school, and I'm sure that you are going to hear about it. I'd like to give you the accurate picture of what is happening so that if you feature this, you'll have the correct facts...*

At that point, the Principal is in control of the information, and is looking good in the eyes of the reporter. S/he will be quoted authoritatively and positively, instead of being quoted as denying what a disaffected or misinformed student, parent, teacher, Board member or neighbor has fed a reporter who is relying on them for information because the school isn't returning their calls.

Learn to be diplomatic and speak in ways that only enhance the dignity of the school. Speak positively about everyone and everything.

> *We respect Mr. X's point of view, but would like him to consider whether he is being fair*

sounds a lot better than

> *Mr. X doesn't know what he is talking about*

Avoid saying *"No comment"*. Always respect the privacy of others, and say so if that is the reason you cannot give information:

> *Our school is a caring school, and we are very sensitive to the right of all involved to privacy. For that reason I can't answer your question, and I am sure you will understand.*

If the school builds a relationship of trust and acquaintance with media, it is in a position to occasionally – but only very occasionally – ask them to 'bury' a story, or at least restrain themselves in reporting it. Unless the story is sensational, and a sensationalist news source has got hold of it, most news media are responsible and conscientious, and will listen to a sober, non-threatening request from a friendly source to treat a story in a particular manner if there are good reasons (usually compassionate) to do so.

15.7.2   How to get your material published

Remember that local media – Jewish or general, print or electronic – want **news**. They do not want to be a free service for acknowledging important people in the school. So, on the occasions when you actually want the school in the media, frame your material as news. The 'news threshold' of a local Jewish community newspaper, or a local radio or TV station may be appreciably lower than their national counterparts – but they still want news.

Isolate what is important and interesting in the report and highlight it.

A press release beginning:

> *'Local High school involved in international online project – Newtown students studying in real time with Australian and Israeli peers'*

-- is much more appealing than:

> "*At a meeting held by the teachers of the X Jewish high school (founded in 1980 by Mr. and Mrs. Y, in memory of their wonderful parents, Rifka and Sholom z"l), they decided to participate in an exciting project suggested to them by Yossi Z., the Jewish National Fund shaliach, to get involved in an internet project with other Jewish schools in different countries...*"

Every newspaper wants pictures. Make sure that you have a good school digital camera, capable of taking press-quality pictures, and someone who knows how to use it. Feed good pictures of students looking happy and doing interesting things to the local press. Avoid pictures of people shaking hands.

15.7.3   Electronic and online media

The school may want to use online media – posting news and records of school news and events on YouTube and other online forums. Use with great care.

15.8 Health and safety

A school 'Health and Safety Committee', normally lay-professional, should deal with such issues as they affect the workplace and monitor compliance with local regulations. The committee should report to the Board. In some jurisdictions, this may be a statutory requirement.

There may be health issues that are not covered by local statutory requirements. The school should have a doctor to whom it can turn for advice on health issues and health policies for both staff and students, and occasionally appropriate advice concerning individuals. There can be a variety of issues, ranging from providing 'flu shots for staff before the winter to dealing with outbreaks of infection in the school. In some schools, there may be a call for health information to be provided to students.

The committee should also ensure that the school has proper first-aid equipment on the premises, and that staff training is at the appropriate level (see below).

A different and potentially more complex area is that of emotional/behavioral difficulties. Again, the Principal should have a qualified professional with whom to consult when making judgments and decisions regarding staff and students. Care must be taken to keep such conversations on a professional level. In most cases, questions will include seeking assurances regarding the safety of others in the school, and/or the ability of a particular individual (teacher or student) to function in a school environment.

15.8.1 Compliance

As with Safety and Fire Codes, in most jurisdictions there are standards for schools specified by local health, environmental and employment legislation. It is inconceivable that any school tries to operate without full compliance.

The school premises should be subject to inspection and approval by the local Fire Service and other bodies.

Local employment law should be followed scrupulously. Apart from the moral, legal and religious dimensions of correctly treating employees, a reputation as a bad employer will cause your school great harm.

15.8.2 Staff training in First Aid and CPR

Whether required by law or not, key staff should be trained in first aid and CPR. In most places, this will be a requirement for gym and sports staff. Training should be offered to other staff as part of Professional Development.

15.8.3 Student and staff health records

Student and staff health records should be up to date, and on file. If there is no clear legal requirement for a private school, follow the standards of the local public system. Increasingly, schools are required to put staff on notice regarding students who suffer conditions making them vulnerable to anaphylactic shock, asthmatic attack or other reactions. Staff training in the use of 'Epi-pens' is now common.

- For both students and staff, 'Medic-Alert' bracelets are an exceptionally good idea[256]. A bracelet with a 24/7 telephone number and a unique registration number is worn. In an emergency, contacting the telephone number will give any medic instant access to the wearer's medical records and medications. A local office will send you registration leaflets which you can include in school mailings.

15.9 Insurance and liability

Comprehensive school insurance must be held, usually from a specialist broker. The staff, students, officers, volunteers and Board of Directors must be insured against all risks and liabilities associated with or arising from their activity under the auspices of the school, together with other usual and appropriate insurance. It is again inconceivable that any school should operate without proper insurance.

---

[256] www.medicalert.org

All categories of persons insured by the school should be appropriately notified – in, for example, the School handbook, the staff handbook, and/or in notices circulated to the Board.

Similarly, exclusions must be noted – the most common being a disclaimer of responsibility for the personal property of students and staff. Your insurance broker will advise. Some schools offer parents opportunities to take out varieties of additional personal insurance for their children covering common school situations – for example, injuries from sports or gym activity necessitating dental or other treatment.

15.9.1 Proper reporting of incidents

Every incident or accident involving injury to a student (or teacher) must be immediately reported and recorded. The school should have a standard 'Incident Report Form'. As soon as possible after the incident – whatever it is – the staff member dealing with it must record their account of what they believe happened, how the incident was responded to, the subsequent cycle of events (with approximate or exact timings), including how and when parents were notified, and all relevant details. The report must be dated and signed, and submitted to school Administration. This will be required by the school insurance company should a claim be forthcoming.

A school should operate a logbook for minor incidents not needing further medical attention.

16 FUNDRAISING AND ALUMNI

16.1 Fundraising

Fundraising is a specialist profession of its own, with its own professionals and its own literature, in general beyond the scope of this book.

These notes address some of the issues as they impact on the general management of the school.

Every school has, or certainly should have, a fund-raising operation, which may carry any one of a range of names[257]. Budget invested in Fundraising is money well spent.

The school will raise money for Capital Campaigns (to improve buildings, purchase equipment or spend on other capital assets); for its 'Annual Fund' (direct subsidy of

---

[257] Fundraising, Development, Advancement, Foundation, Friends etc.

annual operating budget items) and, ideally, for an Endowment Fund (providing annual income from an otherwise 'untouchable' capital fund). Different tax and charity legislative environments will determine the school's fundraising strategy and aims. The benchmark is that fundraising should provide 10% of a school's operating budget[258].

Fundraising is done by a variety of means – direct solicitation, fundraising events and any other effective means that can be devised. Some schools give each parent an annual fundraising obligation – 'Raise it or pay it'; and others ask for a Capital Fund commitment on entry to the school. Parents – often struggling to meet their tuition obligations – sometimes resent being solicited for additional funds. Jewish communities have a measure of 'fundraising fatigue'. However, the school has to meet its bills, invest for the future – and keep tuition down. It is a very difficult balancing act, financially and socially.

In every academic institution, there is tension between the fundraising and academic personnel – the academic faculty regard fundraising as faintly distasteful, and the fundraisers may regard the faculty (and their attitudes) as hopelessly out of touch with reality. They cannot understand why the faculty does not understand that without fundraising they would not have a school (or University).... An astute Principal will try and moderate between the need to maintain tasteful and appropriate standards associated with all school activities, and the absolute necessity of every independent school to raise funds.

Skilled and effective fundraisers are exceptionally difficult to find, and there are few more precious assets for a school than a successful fundraiser. There is a huge literature on fundraising, and many training seminars available. The Jewish community has immense expertise on fundraising; all of it points out that successful fundraising has to lead by example[259]. People give to people - the Board of Directors must both contribute to the school's fundraising, at personally appropriate levels, and must also be active in canvassing others. All fundraising needs credible lay leadership. A good fundraiser/Director of Development will be able to mobilize several different constituencies within the school – Board, Alumni, Parents' Association, 'Development Committee' – to be part of school fundraising.

The Principal has to carefully manage participation – let alone leadership – in the school's Fundraising activities. The Principal must wholeheartedly support the

---

[258] An elusive target. Few Jewish schools are fortunate enough to have the substantial endowments common to some private schools and Universities. Most operate under constant financial pressure.

[259] The basic rules are:
- People give to people; then people give to causes because of people; then people give to causes
- Donors give to satisfy their own needs; rarely those of the recipient
- The commonest reason why people don't give is that they are not asked...

school's campaigns and fundraising events, and should be continually 'feeding' the Fundraising department with information and ideas. A Principal has to be careful in direct solicitation, and cannot create a relationship – real or imagined – that will impinge on his or her integrity, or on the school's ability to deal with students, staff or parents. SEE SECTION 3.6.2 .Some Principals will elegantly avoid direct solicitation of existing or future parents. They may make presentations at meetings, or to groups – but someone else should do the 'ask'. But there is often no one better than the Principal to represent the school.

A different question is whether staff should be expected to contribute to school or Federation campaigns, or whether they should be canvassed to do so in their professional, rather than personal, capacities. There are two opposing views:

- The staff are members of the school community, and as such should take their share of commitment to the school's ideals – including a commitment to the school's fundraising efforts, in the same way that parents are expected to aid the school's fundraising over and above their responsibility for Tuition. It is relevant to note that staff who work for agencies that are recipients of United Way funding are expected (in some places: required) to be contributors in good standing to United Way. In many communities, schools are recipients of Federation funding, and similar standards should apply.

- Jewish and non-Jewish staff are recruited to schools as professionals. Their obligation to the school is contractual and professional, and to canvass them for personal contributions to school or community – let alone require it - infringes on their privacy.

16.2 Alumni

For many private schools, Alumni are the primary source of support and funding. My impression is that this is not (possibly not yet) the case in many Jewish schools. There may be several plausible reasons:

- Most Jewish schools (especially High Schools) have not been in existence long enough to build a mature body of Alumni

- The concentration of current parent involvement in many schools tends to leave little room for Alumni involvement

- Alumni of Jewish schools will have financial and volunteering demands made on them from many other, competing, Jewish community sources and organizations.

Nevertheless, they are an important constituency. How to cultivate and structure an 'Alumni Association' should be a Board decision, and, in general terms, is not really part of the focus of this book. Most of the time, 'Alumni' is a division of the Development department. From a school Principal's point of view, the Alumni can be very useful in terms of promoting the school's community profile and student recruitment. They are also an invaluable resource for events like Career Days. Hopefully, too, your Alumni eventually become parents.

It can be a frustrating task keeping track of Alumni. If you do not have an existing Alumni database, set about creating one. The best people to do it are Alumni themselves, via social networking. In theory, email makes this task a lot easier than it used to be. Once you have a viable database, update your Alumni on current events and current life at the school. When communicating to Alumni, the school has to somehow simultaneously assure them that the school is, of course, preserving the school that they "remember" (and I use the quote marks advisedly) – but on the other hand is 'cutting edge', and giving 'today's students the very best of opportunity and education.

A good Alumni Association can fulfill some or all of the following roles:

- Fund-raising and support for the school.

- Maintain a social network that allows the school to develop a relationship with its graduates, and the graduates to keep in touch with each other. Some Alumni networks function as informal professional/business networks.

- Act as 'Ambassadors' for the school in the community and with prospective parents.

- Act as a resource for the school in diverse functions – examples include: Career Day speakers; University and academic contacts; sources for school supplies.

- Alumni can occasionally be mobilized in support of the school for political or community campaigns.

Pitfalls around Alumni associations may include some or all of the following:

- The Association is monopolized or dominated by 'volunteers' who have never mentally graduated from school

- Alumni identify with staff members who were their teachers, who may have been young and inspirational at the time, but are by now your biggest staff-room problems. In some cases such teachers can manipulate the Alumni into interfering / lobbying with the Board on their behalf

- Alumni will not recognize or legitimize necessary change in the school

- Alumni wish to engage in inappropriate or unwelcome activities

Again, a healthy Board will be able to avoid these problems, or solve them if they arise. It can be – and should be -- a truly moving experience to see a reunion of former students and hear from them the impact that the school has had on their lives.

(Personal) To: The Principal ...

17   MEMO TO: THE PRINCIPAL

18   AFTERWORD

17 Memo To: The Principal

As well as learning how to manage the school, you have to learn how to manage yourself. The school will not run properly unless you are motivated, fit and equipped to head it. You have to feel comfortable with yourself and your family. You also have to feel that that the task that you are doing is possible; that you are secure and appropriately recognized in your professional status and remuneration; and that you still have a life and an existence separate from your school. This chapter is addressed directly to you!

17.1 Your contract with the school

The basis of your relationship with the school (your employer) is your contract, which is for the benefit of both parties. It lays out the professional services you are expected to provide to the school (your Job Description), and the salary and benefits that the school promises you in return. It should also set out a framework of communication between you and the school, an agreed framework for settling disagreements, procedures and a timeline for negotiating renewal of contract, and agreed conditions for the termination of the contract by either party.

If relations between you and the school are going well, your contract will barely be referred to between its commencement and the end of its term. If relations between you and the school break down, the wording of your contract will be crucial.

Conditions of employment for Jewish School Principals vary widely from place to place. There are no uniform contracts, although schools affiliated with denominational networks may have suggested guidelines.

You must not begin working (or resign your previous post) without a contract, or at the very least a binding written agreement of general terms. The essential elements of a contract specify:

- Term (commencement date and length of contract)[260]

- Job Description

---

[260] After salary, length of contract is perhaps the next most contentious point. Practice varies very greatly. A new Principal with reasonable experience may expect a three-year initial contract, subsequently renewable for four-year or five-year terms. A Principal (or other Administrator) who has given length of service should be given a contract to age 65 once they reach their late 50's.

- Reporting responsibility

- Salary, including provisions for salary review if applicable

- Pension arrangements

- Health insurance (and associated issues, including sick days allowance), life insurance and disability insurance

- Vacation entitlement

- Additional allowances where applicable (e.g. relocation. housing, tuition fees, travel, books, telephone/cell phone/internet etc)

- Provision to attend conferences, courses and meetings

- Agreed process for Annual Performance Review

- Process for resolving disputes between the parties

- Process and timetable for renegotiation of contract, or notice of non-renewal

- Agreed terms and process for termination of the Contract by either party

- Any other provisions that you or the school wish to be included in your terms of employment.

You must have professional advice regarding your contract negotiation. It can be appropriate for your representative (a lawyer, accountant or professional negotiator) to do the negotiation by him/herself. This means that you are never in the position of personally negotiating, which can be more dignified. Part of the agreement should be that the school covers your representative's professional fees. Your professional adviser should also be able to determine the correct level of remuneration for your post and advise you accordingly. Other local professionals may advise you on the local standards for contracts. It doesn't mean that you have to stay within those parameters, but you are unlikely to be able to go very far beyond them.

Your Contract is an important document, and your first contract will determine the tone and, to a degree, the content of all subsequent contracts. Think about it carefully, and quietly but firmly decide your minimum conditions and stick to them. All the rest is negotiation.

17.1.1   Your Job Description

Like all other employees of your school, you need a Job Description, which should be an integral part of your contract. This should be drawn up at the time of your engagement, and reviewed at the time of each renewal or renegotiation of your contract, or by agreement at other times.

Your Job Description defines your responsibilities and your authority. Your performance will be measured against it. You have an interest (shared, hopefully, by the Board) that it is both a fair and comprehensive document. For principles of drawing up a Job Description SEE SECTION 4.3.4 , and some samples – including a Principal's Job Description - are given in Appendix B.

The Principal's Job Description is likely to be closely tailored to the needs of the particular school – more so than the Job Descriptions of other faculty.

If you are a new Principal, or agreeing a Job Description for the first time:

- Get your lawyer to check that the Job Description agrees with the Contract …..

  There are frequently areas where the Contract and the Job Description will overlap (e.g. reporting responsibility). Sometimes, different people will have drawn up the two documents – the Board President will have had the Contract drawn up, and ensured that it ties you strongly to the Board (if not the President). S/he may well have asked someone else entirely (Chair of Education Committee, local retired School Principal) to draw up the Job Description - sometimes considered the 'non-business' document. Check that out before it becomes a problem.

Questions to ask about a Principal's Job Description include, but may not be limited to, the following:

- Does the Job Description give you the authority to do your job?

- Is it possible to do the job described in the Job Description?

- How does the proposed Job Description compare with that of the outgoing Principal? Are there areas of responsibility being added or subtracted?

- Does the Job Description include all the areas of responsibility that you expect following your discussions with the school? Are some areas missing? Are any unexpected areas of responsibility included?

  You are a Rabbi/Principal. Part of the attraction of this post was that you would also be the Rabbi of the small synagogue attached to the school. That responsibility is unaccountably missing from your Job Description. In its place is a paragraph stating that 'The Principal is responsible for supervising the kashrut of the synagogue kitchen, including when it is hired for outside functions'.

> *The Job Description states that 'The Principal is responsible for coordinating the school's Annual Campaign'. No mention has been made of fund-raising.*
>
> *You understood that you would be the Head of School. In the Job Description, it states that the 'Vice-Principal of Jewish Studies' reports to you. No mention is made of the Vice-Principal of General Studies, who has been in the school for many years, and who does not like the idea of a new, young Principal. Has a deal been struck without your knowledge, in an attempt to placate the V-P? ("Mr. Y, alright, you can report directly to the President.")*

- Is your Job Description, as Principal, clearly understood by the Administration and staff of the school?

The Board must make the roles and responsibilities of the new Principal clear to every constituency in the school – lay and community leaders, the Administration, the staff and the parents. This is particularly important where the Board is appointing a new Principal to institute changes in a school. **They have to make it clear to all concerned – *well before the Principal arrives* – that they are seeking a pro-active new appointee, and expect that both professionals and lay leadership will support a fresh approach to the school and its operations.** Boards sometimes duck this responsibility[261]. It is totally unfair to the incoming Principal, who will find very quickly that s/he is running into serious trouble. If you are going into a 'school in crisis', with the mandate of turning it around, this is particularly important.

It is essential that you are comfortable with the Job Description before you sign it. Do not under any circumstances leave problematic provisions in place, out of a desire not to make trouble, and with the belief that you will 'sort it out' later.

17.2 Reviewing your performance

Every Principal should undergo Performance Reviews – just as you should give periodic[262] Performance Reviews to your Administrators and other staff. As the most senior professional in the school, and presumably the best-paid, you are also the most accountable. 'Internal' Performance Reviews should be done annually; 'External' Reviews, much more extensive, should be done every few years, and their frequency should be agreed as part of your contract. External Reviews are 'heavy duty'. It is impossible to hide the fact that an external review is taking place, and, like a 'School review', even if routine will inevitably generate comment. It would be

---

[261] I hope to deal in a future book with the process of applying for a new post, and the process of inducting a new Principal into a school.

[262] Annually or every other year for Administrators; not less than once every three years for teachers and support staff - SEE SECTION 9.3.5

unreasonable to expect an external review of the Principal more than once every five[263] years or so, except in exceptional circumstances. Normally, an External Review is a precursor to negotiating a new contract.

Many Principals will initially find the process of Review uncomfortable. It is not yet part of the culture of the Jewish School system, especially in smaller schools. Yet a properly administered Review process is part of correct, constructive and healthy school management, of benefit to all of the parties involved.

- It affords the Principal an opportunity to hear constructive feedback on his/her performance. Complimentary feedback will give the Principal reassurance that s/he is doing a good job, and provides a formal record of positive performance. Feedback on less satisfactory performance demands thoughtful reflection on the part of the Principal. If it is justified – it gives the Principal clear guidelines on how to be better professional. If it is not – it tells the Principal that somehow s/he is transmitting a wrong impression to key school constituencies, and, conversely, failing to accurately transmit his/her good qualities. An Annual Review also affords the Principal protection against comment that s/he is operating without supervision, and 'does what s/he wants'.

- The Board has comfort that the management of the school is being correctly monitored, and that the Board is fulfilling its responsibility of oversight and accountability to the parent body.

- Parents understand that the quality of performance of the school leadership is properly evaluated and that the Board has a confidential and appropriate mechanism for discussing professional performance issues with the Principal.

- Staff respect the fact that the Principal is also evaluated, as they are.

Having said all of the above, there are two essential components of the Principal's Review:

- Correct and fair process

- Complete and reliable confidentiality

---

[263] Every six or seven years is more customary. Some schools will seek an External review of the Principal prior to renewing or renegotiating a contract of employment. The length of contract becomes a crucial part of the process. But even if the contracts are relatively short, no Principal can withstand frequent, full, external reviews. The answer must be to find a more discreet process for alternate renewals. A Board which implements an Annual Review, and which has a good working relationship with its Principal should not need external reviews more often than every six or seven years.

17.2.1   Process for Annual performance Review

The process for conducting your Annual Review should be part of your contract. In most cases, the Principal will be asked to submit a 'Self Evaluation', covering an agreed range of topics. This can be timed for submission in September, to cover the previous school year. For whatever reason, I have found it easier to review on a January–December period, perhaps because that timeframe incorporates an opportunity to look at the beginning of the school year, and also to begin looking forward to the necessary priorities and goals for the next year. This document will probably be three to six pages long, and should be very frank, about both self-perceived successes and failures. It is also an opportunity to appropriately reflect on external problems faced in the operation of the school.

Unlike an External Review, an Annual Review is submitted to the President of the Board. The President should share the document with two or three other senior lay leaders, usually the senior elected Officers of the Board, and then respond – either verbally or (preferably) in writing, or both. This provides a good opportunity for the Principal and the lay leadership to exchange views and ideas about the school, its operation, and the Principal's contribution and performance. The quality (and hence usefulness) of that exchange will reflect the quality of the relationship between the Principal and the Board.

At the end of the process, the President will make a short report to the Executive committee (not necessarily to the full Board). It is of the essence of the process that that report does not disclose the content of the self-evaluation, or details of the subsequent 'feedback'. The Principal has to be able to operate without every detail of his/her performance being known and discussed, while also being able to receive constructive feedback.

As basis for your annual Review, that formal, but relatively straightforward process should be perfectly adequate.

17.2.2   Process for External Review

Process will vary from school to school, depending on all sorts of variables, and different models are easily accessible. Most schools will constitute a 'Review Committee'. While the structure and process of the Committee is the prerogative of the board, you should have some input and the process must be acceptable to you. That avoids uncomfortable and stressful negotiations between the Board and the Principal that can only create a negative atmosphere even before the Review process begins.

Good practice commonly includes:

- Establishment of a small Review Committee (3 -6 people), which should include an independent outside consultant. In addition, the Principal should be able to nominate one (or more) members of the committee[264].

- Chairing of the Review Committee by someone not currently involved with the school – certainly not by the current School president. The Chair can be a Past president of the school, or, better, someone from outside the school framework entirely. The Review Committee may ask the outside independent consultant to suggest a process, and then carry out the Review on their behalf.

- The Review Committee will make discreet enquiries of the Board and other constituencies (lay and professional) regarding the Principal's performance. The scope of the Review, and the scope of those interviewed, may vary greatly.

- Submission of a self-assessment by the Principal, usually in an agreed format. Styles vary for these documents – they may be quantitative ("Rate your performance on a scale in the following categories") or discursive ("Describe your performance during the past year in the following areas"). Normally, they include provision for the Principal to suggest objectives for the coming year. After receipt and review by the Committee, a personal interview should take place.

- A preliminary Report by the Committee, after consideration of all data collected

- Opportunity for the Principal to comment on the Review Committee preliminary Report

- Review Committee summary report to the Board in private session

The aim of the exercise is to build a better school, and help the Principal improve performance in a constructive and supportive manner. The Principal's Review should not, and must not, be a subject for discussion in the school community. The full

---

[264] Choose your representative(s) thoughtfully, and for maximum credibility. Do not be afraid to think out of the box. Clearly, they should be individuals whom you believe are approving of your performance, and have a realistic understanding of the dynamics in place in your school. They also have to be independent, and impervious to social or other pressures that may be exerted at the Review Committee. Professors, retired professionals (including other Principals, not necessarily Jewish and not necessarily from within the Jewish school system), School principals from other cities, lawyers, respected business personalities – are all good choices. Preferably, your nominee(s) should be individuals who are objective, not close friends or associates, and people whom you will not be embarrassed to have participate in full and frank discussions about you and your performance.

details should be strictly confidential to the Review Committee, and only a summary given to the Board. Nothing will be more undermining to the Principal than to have the details of his/her performance become the subject of discussion in the community, the Staff Room, the parents' parking lot or, worst, the school playground.

Areas of evaluation will normally cover the major areas of responsibility as specified in the Principal's Job Description (e.g. Overall school leadership and advancement, Academic Supervision, Curriculum Advancement), plus areas of relationships (e.g. Administration, Staff, Parents, Students, Community). If you have had difficulties in any area during the year under review, you should be frank and open. Explain the nature of the difficulty encountered, give your perspective of your performance in the episode, and, if necessary, any lessons you may have learned for the future. Record your successes plainly but clearly. A good Review Committee will be looking for quality of judgment and quality of leadership, which can be displayed even in episodes that have no happy ending.

If, unfortunately, you receive a very negative Review, or if you feel that it has been unfair or adversarial, you should seek legal advice at a very early stage, and consider the options open to you – SEE SECTION 17.7

17.3 Personal issues

A sensible person – whatever their occupation – looks after themself. Schools can be all-consuming of time and energy, but this should not be at the expense of your own wellbeing – financial, emotional, spiritual and, of course, health. Problems in any of these areas will not help you to be a better Principal – they will either add a layer of worry and stress, or (more typically) you will put off dealing with them until they constitute unavoidable problems.

Make sure that you have a life of your own outside your job. Check that your financial affairs (including insurance and pension) are in order. Take regular exercise[265]. Have periodic medical check-ups – in other words, do all the sensible things. One complication in this conscientiousness is running into parents or Board members in areas of your private life. You may choose to visit banks, doctors, dentists, accountants, insurance agents, pharmacists and other professional advisers in neighborhoods far from your home or school, or to choose such advisers from outside the Jewish community altogether.

A definite and important dimension of this is your appearance, clothing and behavior – your 'affect'. Part of asserting your position is looking and acting the part. The

---

[265] "... there will be sections here and there where my colleagues ... will give indulgent smiles and wonder why I don't follow my own advice more closely. Family and friends may do the same. I plead inconsistency and fallibility. " – from the Foreword to this book.

messages you transmit by your appearance, body language, and the way you conduct yourself in your speech and behavior will affect the way that others relate to you, even before a word has been exchanged. The position of Principal is respected and is regarded as a responsible and authoritative position of dignity and importance. Dress smartly. Males should always wear a jacket, tie and dress shirt; females should be equally formal. Invest in clothing. You need to look smart.

The way you speak should also reflect the expectation of your constituencies that they are being addressed by a Principal.

- Humor should be used only sparingly; sarcasm never.

- Never, ever make self-deprecating or negative remarks about yourself or the school.

- Do not speak about other schools except in positive terms.

In correspondence, be grammatical, concise and gracious. Do not use extreme language. Be diplomatic. Never make statements that cannot be substantiated. Make sure you *listen*.

On formal or ceremonial occasions, be appropriate, and let the participants know that they are participating in a special occasion. Don't speak for too long — six or seven minutes should be enough for most occasions.

- Remember - no speech, letter or article is made worse by being made shorter.

Take careful note of feedback you may receive. If you are uncomfortable speaking in public — take coaching.

- Don't be late for meetings, and if you are unavoidably delayed, call ahead.

In short — be professional.

The social complexities of the Principal's position are discussed in SECTION 2.3.1 — 'Keeping distance'.

17.4 Family

Do not ignore your family. Schools can devour time that for others is family time (early mornings, evenings and Sundays). If possible, train yourself to reserve time for your family and, if you can, 'switch off' when you are at home.

- Make sure that you take the vacations to which you are entitled.

- Fiercely protect the right of your spouse and your children to live their own lives, and do not expect them to be 'the Principal's children'.

- Remember to act as 'parent' to your own children when it comes to School Parent evenings, attendance at sports, school plays etc.

- When reading your child's Report Card, be a parent and not a Principal.

These are easier said than done, as my own family will readily attest, should they be reading this passage.

17.4.1   Your children at your school?

The question of whether or not to send your own children to the school at which you are Principal is a common dilemma. Occasionally – for example, where your school is the only Jewish school in town, and attending a Jewish school is non-negotiable – there may not be a choice.

If there is a choice, the School community wants to see if you send your own children to your own school. It is often taken as your own expression of confidence (or otherwise) in the school that you lead.

Resist that pressure.

The feelings of your own children must come first. There are children who don't mind being students at the school where their parent is Principal. For others, it is highly uncomfortable. They come under pressure from peers and even teachers. If you, as Principal, discipline a student or students, your children may suffer. Whatever they do can be wrong – if they are successful, or chosen for a team, it is clearly "favoritism"; if they are in trouble, it is immediately magnified. Some teachers will favor them; some will deliberately penalize them. They may feel that they cannot make their feelings known on school issues – or alternatively, they may feel the need to express radical views in order to show that they are 'one of the gang'. It can be difficult for them to invite friends home. Hearing others talk about you can embarrass them.

So – if practical, give them the choice. Some may laugh the experience off; many will opt for the more anonymous setting. In response to questions from your Board or others – the answer is simple:

> My children would rather not to go to the school where their father/mother is Principal. I understand and respect that completely.

Don't force your children to attend your school. If they do – by choice or otherwise – be sensible in how you relate to them in day-to-day matters. All staff should relate to them exactly as they relate to every other student – fairly and respectfully.

Finally, never, ever allow your own children to be sources or conveyors of information. They must have the chance to talk about school when they are at home, just like every other child – but that is information that you cannot and must not use in your professional capacity.

- What you may know as a parent is completely different to what you may know as a Principal[266].

17.5 Professional enrichment / keeping up to date

One of the important functions of the Principal is to be the promoter of innovation and new thinking in the school. That does not mean that the school has to adopt every new theory or method that appears on the horizon; but it does mean that you should maintain a lively and intelligent interest in new developments of all sorts in fields relevant to the operation and philosophy of the school. That is one of the unique dimensions of the job, because there are few things that happen in the entire world that are *not* relevant to education!

Two areas where it is essential that you need to be very aware of developing trends are educational thinking, and Jewish Community issues. Techniques of keeping abreast are a matter of personal taste and choice (journals, books, internet). Attendance at conferences and meetings, and participation in local educational forums are essential opportunities to network and understand what others in the field are thinking and doing. Principals should ensure that adequate budgetary provision is made for their participation.

There are also opportunities in most cities to attend short courses on specialized topics related to management techniques, relevant areas of law and school administration. National and regional educational associations offer all sorts of courses helpful to the Principal – common topics include recruitment, budgeting and financial management and development. All will give some insight, some positive ideas, and will stimulate strategic thinking. Most can be of benefit to Vice-Principals and other senior staff as well, and their participation should be seen in the context of overall encouragement of the management team and the personal PD of senior colleagues.

---

[266] The only rare and very exceptional case being information indicating that a child is in danger; in which case you must act, but you must find a way to 'know' that information from another source.

17.6 Time to move on?

Even under normal circumstances, patterns of 'professional longevity' among private High School Principals vary greatly. There are schools that seem to experience changes of Principals every four[267] to eight years; in others, Principals may stay for decades. Your decision to move on will depend on several factors.

This book has dwelt at length on the difficulty and complexity of the task of Principal in the Jewish High School, and the lack of established processes and principles by which the schools should be administered[268]. Under those circumstances, it is hardly surprising that the turnover in these positions can be high, and the movement of individuals from post to post can be rapid – often involving a series of movements across the North American continent and even further afield. In public school systems throughout the western world the post of High School Principal is also regarded as increasingly stressful, and increasingly difficult to fill.

The following[269] are the most common reasons that encourage Jewish School Principals to consider exploring other opportunities:

- "A well presented and attractive offer

- Desire to move to a school where they might have a chance to implement a new or developing vision and/or challenge

- Feeling that they have reached their maximum level of achievement in their present position and wish to explore new directions

- Desire to move to a different community for personal/family reasons

- Feeling of frustration and/or 'burnout' in their present post

- Stress

- Desire to leave the Jewish school system

- Tensions and dissatisfaction between the Principal and staff, parents or the Board

- Failure of the Board to meet the agreed provisions of the Principal's contract and/or expectations.

---

[267] Some schools go through Principals with even greater regularity. Steer clear of them.
[268] ..... and to correcting which situation this book is, hopefully, a modest contribution!
[269] I am grateful to Joel Paul, President of Joel Paul Associates of NYC, for this list, generated by his considerable experience in facilitating senior appointments in the Jewish school system across North America.

- Community politics

- Introspection that s/he should not serve in such a demanding position.

- Funding challenges and problems which make the post untenable and / or even unbearable for the Principal and / or family"

It will be noted that negative reasons outnumber the positive.

For any of these reasons, and perhaps for some additional reason, you may begin to feel that you wish to move on. Often, the idea is generated by seeing an advertisement, or by a direct approach.

Moving has to be a family decision. Spouse and children have serious votes. But if you decide to move, be purposeful and serious about it.

17.7 If things go wrong ....

- None of the following applies if you are facing dismissal 'for cause', *and you acknowledge that the school has a case.* Your only resort then is to immediately take the best legal advice accessible to you, and follow it to the letter.

Few Principals go through their entire career without facing professional crisis at one time or another. 'Professional Crisis' is a situation where your future in the school is under serious threat. The reasons can be many:

- You may have made mistakes, and lost the confidence of the staff or the Board

- Changes in your personal or family life have impinged negatively on your professional life

- A new school President may make your life intolerable

- Falling school enrolment or financial crisis may provoke a crisis of confidence in school leadership

- You are asked to be party to processes which may be illegal or immoral

- A school crisis (including tragedy or accident) may provoke institutional trauma from which the you cannot recover credibility, especially if it is judged that your performance in crisis was below expectations

- There may be a feeling that the school has outgrown the Principal

- A School Review (or a Personal Review) has recommended your termination.

Occasionally, an appointment has been wrong from the beginning and your relationship with the school has broken down very quickly[270].

These are very difficult episodes to face, and you will need every ounce of emotional reserve. The results of professional crisis can reverberate through your family, and have many long-term consequences.

There are four stages to managing professional crisis:

- Prevent it

- Recognize it

- Manage it – stay or leave

- Recover from it

Prevention is obviously the first, and best, strategy. Remember – 'no surprises' is one of the key operating principles. The processes described above (especially the Principal's Annual Review – SECTION 17.2.1) are designed to ensure that you are getting feedback about your performance, and you therefore have opportunity to put right any performance-based issues. If you know that there are present or upcoming issues that will be impossible for you to cope with – think of quietly and amicably moving on. If you are maintaining close and professional relationships with your President and your Administrative team, have a reasonable degree of self-awareness, and sensitive antennae, you should be aware of wrong directions long before they reach crisis level.

If you feel that there is a certain atmosphere in the air, it does no harm to ask your President, or a trusted senior Administrator, to indicate to you the cause of tension.

---

[270] Usually because of factors that only emerge once the new Principal is in place -- but emerge very quickly. These can be anything from the characteristics or management style of the Principal, to the 'agenda' of the board, the Administration in place, the staff or the parents. Better or more careful research by the School or the Principal during recruitment might have revealed them, but they may have been suppressed in the general 'good feelings' that surround an appointment. Simple issues of personal style are often significant. A variation on this is where the Board are bringing in the new Principal to institute change, but have forgotten to share this with the school…. These exercises may be read as bringing in a Principal to carry out all that the Board and the outgoing Principal have failed to do over the preceding few years. A symptom of this is the instruction to the incoming Principal that his/her early tasks will include terminating several members of staff.

- The fact that they have not done so until you ask them must be in itself cause for reflection.

If opinions (or facts) are not being shared or voiced, there is trouble afoot.

However, if you discover disagreeable information[271]– try and pin down the source, and try and correct the problem(s). Acknowledge issues. If your colleagues feel them – the perception is as powerful as the reality. Work with your colleagues (or your President) to put things right. Check every couple of weeks or so that the new processes are working. Take advice, if necessary.

There is a difference between short-term unpopularity – an inescapable part of the job – and long-term underlying problems. Short-term unpopularity normally comes because of some difficult decision that has been made – terminating or disciplining a teacher, changing a schedule or some other unpopular move. However careful you may have been in communicating the decision, it remains unpopular – at best you may be able to minimize opposition or upset.

Nevertheless, at this stage the situation is merely uncomfortable – it is nowhere near crisis.

Recognizing crisis is part of the trauma. There can be many different signs that you are facing crisis. Some are obvious – anger, confrontation, obvious resentment. Others are more subtle – information to which you are not privy, hints of meetings to which you are not invited, colleagues who appear to be speaking to Board members behind your back, 'leaks' of overheard conversations from colleagues or even students. Whatever the signs – there will come a point where you suddenly realize that your position in the school is under review. By this time, you must accept that you are in serious trouble, and that there are probably individuals who are already anticipating the termination of your contract. It is, in a sense, irrelevant whose fault it is, and whether, in your view, it is justified or not. You may have made some mistakes; you may be the victim of circumstances. It makes little difference to your predicament.

The strategy you employ will depend on your local circumstances. There are some overall guidelines:

- Take immediate legal advice. Do not delay. If you are a member of a Union or professional association, consult them straight away. If you are not, or if the advice you need is not available, consult a lawyer who deals with contracts and employment. It is essential that the lawyer you consult is not connected with the school in any way, and is able to give you independent legal advice free of social or professional pressure.

---

[271] *"The staff seem very discontented ... Everyone feels that you are unapproachable ... Lately no-one is able to disagree with you ..."*

Consider consulting a non-Jewish lawyer, and go for the most eminent lawyer that you can find. The school has already taken legal advice, and probably has it available free. Note that part of any eventual settlement with the school should include reimbursement of legal fees you have incurred. Follow the advice of your lawyer.

- Identify allies, and speak to them. Be very, very careful. In these ugly situations even friends may distinguish between their friendship for you and their estimate of "what is best for the school", and even best for you. You cannot always count on their confidence. They will feel torn, and out of good intention may share your confidences with others. You should be able to form a picture of what is happening.

> *David – I want to speak to you in confidence regarding recent developments in the school. If you don't feel that you can have this conversation, or keep it totally confidential – please tell me now …. Over the last few weeks, I have felt a real change in the atmosphere between the school and myself. The President is hardly returning my phone calls, and when he does, the conversations are very awkward. Can you fill me in on what is happening?"*

Manage the crisis – stay or leave? Your first decision is whether you wish to try and repair this situation, or leave. If the Board has not yet reached a decision about your future - consider your options carefully. Do you really want to struggle in a difficult situation, working with people – lay or professional – with whom you have a 'toxic' relationship? Is it worth it? If you do, then the school has to engage expert professional help (Organizational Consultants, preferably with school experience) to steer you and the school through the process of resolution.

- A rare, but not unknown situation, is where your situation is the result of clearly demonstrable malicious and untrue rumors or actions. In this case, legal advice is doubly necessary.

If the school Board has already decided that at some point you and the school need to part company, there may be little that you can do, or even should do, to reverse that decision. If the relationship of trust between you and the Board has broken down, it is very difficult, and probably impossible, to repair it. Either you go, or the Board has to go[272]. As Principal, carrying the responsibility of leadership, that is the difference between you and almost any other member of staff. They can repair breakdowns in relationships. You may not be able to.

---

[272] Unless the origin of your difficulty is a totally unreasonable Board which is clearly recognised as such by parents who are willing to take concerted and far-reaching action on your behalf, you will not win.

There are only two questions left:

- Why has this happened?

- How can the situation be managed with the least damage to all parties?

Your first reaction in these stressful circumstances will be to want to discover all the details of your alleged misbehavior, and explain or justify them.

That may not be helpful to you or to others.

Focus on your immediate task, which is to extricate yourself (and your family) from this mess. You will have ample time in the coming months or even years to think over the circumstances. A priority must be to protect your own situation, especially as you will be looking for another position. Talking will provoke discussion and gossip. You have no control over that, and it is very much in your interest to simply say nothing, and act with dignity, difficult as that may be.

At this point, your legal representative should seek a meeting (with or without you) with the school. Your representative, who will have dealt with similar situations before (not necessarily in schools) should know what to do, which in most cases is negotiating an agreement to be implemented on receipt of your resignation.

This will incorporate:

- A financial settlement with you, which will involve pay in lieu of notice or in settlement of a contract, including any benefits. The school will be ready to pay a reasonable amount to ensure a quiet parting of the ways, mindful of its image and reputation. It will not pay you an excessive amount. The financial settlement should include reimbursement of your legal costs, and should offer you relocation expenses to your next post.

- A 'non-disclosure' clause, imposing silence on all parties, except for an agreed statement to parents, staff and the local Jewish press.

- A waiver of liability, acknowledging that after the agreement has been executed, neither side will have further claims on the other.

- An agreed reference for you to use in the future.

You may be wondering why this book assumes this process, rather than advising you to fight what is happening at every step[273].

The uncomfortable answer is that it is not at all in your interest. Whatever the circumstances, if matters have reached this stage, you have enemies. The last thing you want is your professional (let alone personal) life argued, debated and gossiped about in public. All sorts of material about you – true, half-true, misunderstood and plainly false – will surface and be discussed all over the community. From a professional point of view, you do not wish to be identified as controversial. It is far better for you to approach a future employer being able to say:

> I was the Principal at X. Unfortunately, we could not reach agreement about certain aspects of the school, and I tendered my resignation. I cannot discuss the circumstances, which I know you will understand, and I can certainly give you references from that community who will testify to the positive contribution I made to the school.

- than to have your prospective employer's brother-in-law fax him articles from the local Jewish newspaper which discuss in sensational terms some wildly exaggerated account of what happened at a staff meeting when you were in a bad mood, and which portray you as a *'Ba'al machlokes[274]'*.

It is also better that your previous Board President can say

> We didn't get on, but s/he behaved honorably

than to say

> S/he was a lot of trouble, and drove us crazy – cost us tens of thousands in legal fees alone!

So, you are probably leaving. Speak carefully and clearly to your family, including your children. Tell everyone not to discuss what is happening, and not to respond to gossip or to comments.

The good news, which may also be a blow to your ego, is that the world will move on, the school will survive and carry on, and people will lose interest in your affairs very quickly. Parents will be concerned about their children and the school, not, I am afraid, about you. That is – again – probably to your benefit.

---

[273] Arbitration, or asking for a *'Din Torah'* (ruling at a Beth Din) also involves lengthy hearings, great expense, and uncertain outcomes. Mediation may be a more useful avenue, but should only be resorted to in case of deadlock. Both the school and you have powerful incentives to close this matter as quickly as possible – incentives usually reflected in the terms of the settlement.

[274] One who is continually getting into disputes.

Recovery is where you have to expend most of your energy.

- First task – close the book, and move on. Resentment and anger will achieve nothing, except hamper your ability to deal with your situation and embarrass others[275]. Again, you may seek short-term counseling advice.

- Next task – start the search for an alternative position. You must decide your goal, which will be determined by many different circumstances. How mobile is the family? Where are equivalent posts available? Do you want to be a Principal again? Should you go to a smaller school? A different type of school? On the assumption that your settlement will afford you some 'breathing space', use it wisely. Consult with some of the agencies and placement bureaux to see what is available. Draft your resume, and contact old friends and contacts to let them know you are looking for a post. Don't go into details about what happened – simply say that "I had a difficult relationship at the school, and resigned / we parted company". Most people in the field know that these situations happen, that they are not always the fault of the Principal, and that a Principal who has run into difficulties in one situation may do well in another.

- Third task – reflection, introspection and learning. You need distance for this one. When you have calmed down and are able to be objective about your own situation, you must ask yourself, and/or a trusted friend who was able to observe you in your post, whether there are any reasons why you should not apply for further Principalships; and what were the mistakes that you made in your previous school.

    The answer may be "None – nothing you could have done could have prevented that. From the moment that Y became President, it was obvious that s/he wanted a different type of Principal". That is also valuable for you to know. However, there may well be styles of behavior, or strategy, or inter-personal relationships that you need to know about and be more careful about in your next appointment. They may have been unwitting mistakes, which means that you have to be more aware in the future. In short – turn your unhappy experience into a learning experience, which will make you a better-performing professional in the future.

As noted at the beginning of this section, professional crisis is unfortunately relatively common among High School Principals, and probably more common among Jewish

---

[275] "Resentment is giving someone else rent-free accommodation in your head'.

High School Principals. This probably arises from a combination of factors, certainly including the following three, which if present together are certainly fatal:

- Appointment of inexperienced and /or untrained Principals

- Relatively unstructured character of some Jewish schools

- Direct involvement of the Board of Directors in the running of the school.

The only counsel to both Principals and schools is to work very hard on increasing the level of professionalism of both individuals and institutions. The Principal emerging from crisis has to be very reflective, very determined, and very strong.

---

18 AFTERWORD

In the reading of the Torah, the Haftarot and the Megillot and in the subdivisioning of the Torah into *parshiot* and *aliyot*, it is a principle that one never closes on a negative word or expression. I couldn't end the book on such a negative dimension of the Principal's experience. Working in education, in schools and in Jewish schools is a wonderful experience. It is the possibility of positively affecting the lives of individuals and community. Good educational environments, with great colleagues and good friends, are stimulating workplaces. Schools are never boring.

But they should be run properly...

Appendices

A PROFILES OF JEWISH SCHOOL PRINCIPALS

B SAMPLE REFERENCES

C "L'AFFAIRE NOAH FELDMAN" - A RESPONSE

Appendix A: Profiles of Jewish School Principals

Jewish school Principals come from varied backgrounds. Given the huge shortage of suitable candidates, as the number of schools increases, Principals are likely to be recruited from wider and wider backgrounds, including many who have no experience in the Jewish system, and perhaps including some who come from outside education altogether. There is no uniformity in the profession, in the way that, for example, Principals in a public system in a particular area will all have very similar backgrounds and training.

In the Jewish system, the current 'profiles' include:

> **MODE 'A':** The School Principal as Jewish and General educational leader

   In this mode, the Principal is:

   - Qualified in both Jewish and General Studies, and is culturally literate in both; can clearly and credibly lead both Jewish Studies and General Studies staff
   - Has a proven track record of high-quality educational administration
   - Is an educational visionary and leader, with the ability to implement as well

Every school wants one of these; however, they are in short supply.

> **MODE 'B':** The School Principal as Jewish leader / role model

   In this mode, the Principal may be:

   - A Rabbi or non-Rabbi[276]
   - Trained and qualified in education – or qualified by experience
   - Occasionally – a Community Rabbi, perhaps with some part-time experience in running a supplementary school, or in

---

[276] Orthodox all-girls' schools often have male Rabbis as their Principals. The few exceptions tend to be outstanding female educators. Until recently, the restrictions on career opportunities for Orthodox women mean that the most talented and able women in the Orthodox community became teachers, with the result that in many communities, the Orthodox girls schools had uniformly first-class faculties. Broadening of career horizons for women, including very Orthodox women, will, I predict, lead to a lower level of professional talent in Orthodox girls' schools.

part-time High-school teaching, who wants to transfer to a full-time post in the Jewish educational system.

- In some communities – without direct experience as a High School teacher, but highly regarded because of charisma and / or Rabbinic authority, and often teamed with a 'General Studies' or 'Secular Studies' near-parallel colleague.

> **MODE 'C':**   The School Principal as General Educator / Administrator

In this mode, the Principal may be:

- Jewish or non-Jewish
- A veteran of the Jewish system, seeking leadership
- A veteran of the non-Jewish public or private sector, to whom the Jewish school system is a new world
- Teamed with a Jewish Studies near-parallel colleague

> **MODE 'D':**   The Community member who wants a new challenge

In the early drafts of this book, I wrote: "I don't know any examples of this mode - yet – but I am sure they will come." I currently know of at least one major appointment that fits this description exactly.

In this mode, the Principal may be:

- A committed Community member – perhaps one of those pushing for the establishment of the new school – who sees no other candidate, and decides to put themselves forward in anticipation of a mid-career switch
- An interim appointment, pending a search for a permanent Principal
-

Appendix B: Sample References

This is an example of a wholly positive reference:

A brief description of your school:	Jewish High is a single-sex private High School, with 280 students in G9-G12. Students follow a comprehensive Hebrew and Religious Studies curriculum in addition to the regular High School courses
How long the teacher worked for you, what they taught, and other positions of responsibility or school leadership functions held:	Mrs. G worked at Jewish High from [date] until [date]. She taught Math and Science to Grades 9, 11 and 12. In addition, she was in charge of our Basketball team from [year] to [year].
An assessment of her class performance:	She showed herself to be a highly professional, versatile and effective teacher, with a particular talent for 'connecting' with students who were weak at maths. She was also always available to help students.
A note about her relationships:	During her time at the school, she was a popular member of staff with colleagues, students and parents. On several occasions she was asked to 'mentor' new members of staff, which she did with great sympathy and expertise. Parents found her approachable and constructive.
Summary:	Mrs. G was a very valuable member of our staff, and I am sorry that a family move to another city means that she will be leaving. Should she wish to, I am very confident that she could take on a post of more responsibility. I highly recommend her to other potential employers, and would be pleased to add to this very positive recommendation – please contact me at ....

A different reference could read:

A brief description of your school:	Jewish High is a single-sex private High School, with 280 students in G9-G12. Students follow a comprehensive Hebrew and Religious Studies curriculum in addition to the regular High School courses
How long the teacher worked for you, what they taught, and other positions of responsibility or school leadership functions held:	Mrs. H. worked at Jewish High from [date] until [date]. She taught Math and Science to Grades 9, 11 and 12. In addition, she was in charge of our Basketball team from [year] to [year].
An assessment of her class performance:	She took some time to adjust to the routine of our school. Mrs. H seemed to be more comfortable with our older, more academic students, with whom she was a fair and competent teacher.
A note about her relationships:	Mrs. H took a strong interest in the procedures of the Math Department, and made many suggestions for improving the teaching modules and departmental procedures. Some of her colleagues appreciated her deep concern for the quality of instruction in the school. Parents and students sometimes found it a challenge to meet the very high standards she set; others found her a most inspiring teacher from whom they learned a great deal.
Summary:	Mrs. H is a strong personality who undoubtedly left an imprint on our school. She will be a valuable addition to a school where her many talents may be used to the full. We wish her well in her future endeavors; I will be pleased to discuss this reference, and may be contacted ....

Appendix C: 'L'affaire Noah Feldman'- a response

SEE SECTION 8.2.5

The NYT article, by Noah Feldman, was published on July 22, 2007, and may be found at **http://tinyurl.com/l4265j** .

Via Google, many comments and reactions to the article may be found, including the threads on the 'Lookjed' online forum of Bar Ilan University's Lookstein Institute (Google: 'Noah Feldman Lookjed').

I was invited by the 'Lookjed' editors to be one of several 'lead' respondents, and this is what I wrote:

> "Would you have airbrushed Noah Feldman and his girlfriend?
>
> The most perceptive commentator on Noah Feldman and his *cause célèbre* article in the NYT is neither Shmuley Boteach (Jerusalem Post, July 22), nor Harry Maryles ('Emes ve-Emunah' blog), nor Rabbi Gil Student ('Hirhurim' blog), nor any of the other bloggers, nor the many hundreds of comments they have attracted ... but – Noah Feldman himself.
>
> He describes the clearly painful experience of being 'edited out' of his class reunion photo, together with his non-Jewish then-girlfriend-now-wife, as "just one small symptom of the challenge of reconciling the vastly disparate values of tradition and modernity". The whole *parashah* is exactly that: a symptom of the 'boundary challenges' – social, theological and intellectual - Judaism faces in surviving in an open society. Intrinsically, there is nothing new in this. I suspect that Moses Mendelssohn would have what to say about Prof. Feldman and his dilemmas. It is possible that Mendelssohn's "Jerusalem" (1783), is not on the Jewish History curriculum at Maimonides school. It should be.
>
> The protests (all over the internet) that 'he shouldn't have written it ... they shouldn't have printed it' are meaningless. We live in a free society. In an age when every western nation is grappling with the consequences of the Islamic presence in their midst, only the most unperceptive Jews would think that a beautifully written piece about the particularistic/universalistic tensions between religion and modern society has no interest for the general reader.

Problem was, he wrote from the micro-experience and not from the macro-philosophical. It is one thing when your sibling writes the textbook on family relationships ("My brother just wrote an important work – I'm so proud!"); it is quite another when he illustrates his theories by describing the intimacies of your own household, not even bothering to disguise the names!

As a community of educators, and looking at the essay specifically from the point of view of School Administrators – what can we learn from it?

Initial thoughts suggest that the issues should include – but are not limited to – the following, listed in no particular order except the first:

Firstly, all of our sympathies and empathies should go out to our colleagues at Maimonides School in Boston. No school, of any description, would like to be the subject of an article in the 'New York Times', spotlighting casual remarks and everyday incidents – albeit significant to the writer then and now - long forgotten by everyone else. Whatever the issues, we should feel solidarity with the school leadership who will now have to grapple with the tsunami of publicity and comment.

The content speaks for itself. He is an obvious sense a failure of 'the system'; but he is also a notable success of the system. His enduring love for Jewish learning and the Maimonidean ideal is palpable – which may be a clue as to why his piece is entitled "The Orthodox paradox". His lament (and I read his piece as a lament, not an attack) – may be paraphrased as: 'You teach us to be independent thinkers, and then complain when we exercise that independence. You – the school, 'Modern Orthodoxy' – cannot cope with the occasional but inevitable product of your system.'

Criticism of the school and its overall philosophy is pointless. There is no such thing as 'guaranteed outcome' education in any system, certainly including the Haredi system, whose representatives are enjoying a blog-based *schadenfreude*. The school, its community, and its faculty, did their best to transmit central values. With many, presumably most, of their students they did a good job. This individual ultimately (apparently many years after leaving school) did not see the world in the same way as his teachers. It happens; it happens everywhere; it will continue to happen.

We all live in the public domain. Whether it is newspapers, or internet, or simply rumors, everything said and done in a school is potentially open to public scrutiny. There are no such things as 'throw-away comments'. A teacher or Rabbi who makes some ill-advised comment about Jewish law and non-Jews has to understand that the comment will never be forgotten by [at least] one student; and that one day his ill-expressed words may appear in the NYT. Professional Development, training, discussion of standards, of pedagogy, of classroom policy; teacher guides which give suggestions of how to approach delicate issues .. all these should build a different classroom atmosphere, *where issues that the teacher should know will be contentious* will be presented in a careful manner. Not untruthful – but careful, tactful and respectful.

Jewish life is changing, and public expectations are changing. The issue of how we, as schools, relate to our alumni who the schools consider less than exemplary products of the school will not go away.

If the school wishes to have a policy regarding its attitude to its alumni who veer from the school's preferred path, it must be upfront about its policies, and express them in as dignified a manner as possible. A statement such as*: "The school Alumni magazine will be pleased to celebrate and announce important events in the lives of our Alumni which themselves may be seen as celebrations of school values"* -- is pretty clear, and I think it is inoffensive.

The question of how to handle an embarrassing '*b'dieved*' situation – as happened at the now infamous reunion – is a matter of school management and decision-making process. It is not clear where the 'edit them out' decision was made. But a school should have a culture where everyone recognizes problems when they arise, and instead of deciding on the spot, refers them to a wider decision-making body that can work out a strategy for resolving them. Making arbitrary and deeply insulting decisions to airbrush a grad out of the reunion photo is guaranteed to cause deep hurt and offense. The action was breathtakingly insensitive, and the lasting hurt – the complete depersonalization – seems to have been the catalyst for the public action. Not to publicly humiliate your fellow is a Jewish value. Where was it in this situation? The penalty for one who is '*Malbin et pnei chavero b'rabbim*' is more severe than for one who intermarries ......

The question that transcends the school is, of course, the overall question of how the Jewish community, and in this case the 'Modern Orthodox" community, relates personally, communally and institutionally to our fellow Jews who marry non-Jewish partners, or otherwise are clearly 'crossing red lines' in their public lives. Many commentators on Prof. Feldman point out that the "community" is much more tolerant of individuals who transgress *halachah* in other ways. I can only give the following observation. I come from the UK, where the Orthodox community, even the 'mainstream'

Orthodox community, has from time immemorial maintained the most stringent boycotts and ostracism of non-Orthodox Jewish movements, to a degree undreamed of by the most rigorously Orthodox in North America, and all but the most rigorously Orthodox in Israel. This includes the 'outmarried', the heretics (real or imagined) and every other non-conformist. It hasn't worked. It hasn't deterred anyone from marrying non-Jewish partners; it hasn't inhibited the growth of non-orthodox movements (it may have stimulated them). It has resulted in schism, divisiveness and *'sinat chinam'*. On this issue, I am wholeheartedly with Rabbi Shmuley Boteach. In our age, we should reach out to every single Jew with kindness, tact, courtesy, understanding and love. Period."

Made in the USA
Charleston, SC
04 February 2010